Hand Book of Bakery Industries

(How to Manufacture Bakery & Confectionery)

With Directory of Machinery & Raw Material Suppliers

Hand Book of Bakery Industries

(How to Manufacture Bakery & Confectionery)

With Directory of Machinery & Raw Material Suppliers

A complete encyclopaedia on ***Hand Book of Bakery Industries (How to manufacture Bakery & Confectionery)*** which deals with new technologies, processing, formulaes, project profiles and directory section. The book is covering with the new recipies of the Bakery & Allied Bakery products including Bread Biscuits, Cakes, Buns etc. & Packaging of Bakery products with details of machineries & equipments for Bakery & Its various products processing industries.

Written By

EIRI Board of Consultants & Engineers

and

Compiled by

SUDHIR GUPTA

ENGINEERS INDIA RESEARCH INSTITUTE

4449, Nai Sarak, Main Road, Delhi - 110006 (India)
Ph: +91-11-23918117, 23916431, 45120361, 23947058, 64727385
*** E-Mail: eiritechnology@gmail.com & eiriprojects@gmail.com**
***Website: www.eiriindia.org & www.industrialprojects.in**

PRINTED & PUBLISHED BY

ENGINEERS INDIA RESEARCH INSTITUTE

4449, Nai Sarak, Main Road, Delhi - 110006 (India)

Ph: +91-11-23918117, 23916431, 45120361, 23947058, 64727385

* E-Mail: eiritechnology@gmail.com & eiriprojects@gmail.com

*Website: www.eiriindia.org & www.industrialprojects.in

Distributors:

EIRI PROJECT CONSULTANTS AND PUBLISHERS
4/54 Roop Nagar, Delhi-110007
and
INDUSTRIAL TECHNOLOGIES, INDIA
Nai Sarak, Delhi-110006

ISBN: 9788186732182

Printed in New Delhi (INDIA)

₹950/- or US $ 95

Printed & Published by Sudhir Gupta for "Engineers India Research Institute", 4449 Nai Sarak, Main Road, New Delhi -110006

Preface

Bakery Products are having a great demand from past three or four decades and become very popular not only in India but throughout the world so bakery products gaining a new dimension in modern times owing to their versatility in day-to-day life. Being highly demandable products, their popularity is increasing tremendously.

The book is great asset to new entrepreneurs who are interested to start their own bakeries or bakery plant, the book however provides much more valuable information such as formulations/recipes, project profiles, technologies, machineries details with their availabilities, raw materials details with their availabilities. The book also comprises for the very first time the most valuable informations with formulations of chapaties, poori, paratha, instant mix for halwa, dalia, makki di roti te sarson da sag, golgappa, mathis, gulabjuman, pinni, rice products, chiwra, kheer, expanded extruded snacks, sattu, ganne ka ras, suji halwa, jalebi, malpura, rice khichri, samosa, papad, laddo, pakora, gachak apart from the other regular bakery products including bread, biscuit, cake, confectionery, toffee etc. etc.

The use of bread, cakes, biscuits & other bakery products is increasing immensely in ordinary and posh families both in cities as well as towns, even in the country states, thus have their duw significance. The existing bakeries are unable to meet the out growing demand and eventually there exists a wide gulf between demand and supply. Keeping in view all these aspects, this book has been written comprising relevant information on the subject. This is equally good for carrying out bakery industry on cottage, small medium and large scale.

The book contains the following chapters: Bakery Raw Materials, Flour Milling, Bread Making Processes, Biscuits, Cookies & Crackers, Sponge, Cakes And Allied Products, Pies & Puff Pastries, Bakery Adjuncts, Sweet Yeast Dough Products, Formulations & The Procedures For Chemically Leavened Bakery Products, Bakery Machinery, Confectionery Manufacturing Process, Packaging For Biscuits, Cereal And Legume Based Foods-Raw Material, Preparation, Packaging, Miscellaneous Formulaes, Project Profiles, Manufacturers & Suppliers of Plant & Machineries, Manufacturers & Suppliers of Raw Materials

We thank to all those who have extended their valuable co-opertation in the completion of this book.

EIRI Board of Consultants & Engineers

PREFACE

Bakery Products are having a great demand from past three or four decades and become very popular not only in India but throughout the world so bakery products gaining a new dimension in modern times owing to their versatility in day-to-day life. Being highly demandable products, their popularity is increasing tremendously.

The book is great asset to new entrepreneurs who are interested to start their own bakeries or bakery plant, the book however provides much more valuable informations such as formulations/recipes, project profiles, technologies, machineries details with their availabiiities, raw materials details with their availabilities. The book also comprises for the very first time the most valuable informations with formulations of chapaties, poori, paratha, instant mix for halwa, dalia, makki di roti te sarson da sag, golgappa, mathis, gulabjuman, pinni, rice products, chiwra, kheer, expanded extruded snacks, sattu, ganne ka ras, suji halwa, jalebi, malpura, rice khichri, samosa, papad, laddo, pakora, gachak apart from the other regular bakery products including bread, biscuit, cake, confectionery, toffee etc. etc.

The use of bread, cakes, biscuits & other bakery products is increasing immensely in ordinary and posh families both in cities as well as towns, even in the country states, thus have their duw significance. The existing bakeries are unable to meet the out growing demand and eventually there exists a wide gulf between demand and supply. Keeping in view all these aspects, this book has been written comprising relevant information on the subject. This is equally good for carrying out bakery industry on cottage, small medium and large scale.

We thank to all those who have extended their valuable co-opertation in the completion of this book.

Director
ENGINEERS INDIA RESEARCH INSTITUTE
Nai Sarak, New Delhi.
Fax : 91-11-291 6431

CONTENTS AND SUBJECT INDEX

BREAD MAKING PROCESSES 35-90

PACKAGING FOR BISCUITS 291-296

CEREAL AND LEGUME BASED FOODS-RAW MATERIAL, PREPARATION, PACKAGING 297-322

1

BAKERY RAW MATERIAL

Bakery industry needs a variety of raw materials; the raw material requirement differ with different bakery items. Even within the same product, the input composition varies considerably, and depends on the nutritional requirements of the end product, the consumer taste, and the pricing of the product. This chapter deals with the different ingredients that go into the making of bakery products, and the role that each will play in the manufacture of these products.

Whereas the raw materials requirement for conventional bread and biscuits produced in mechanised units are well defined, a variety of raw materials in different 'mixes' are used for a number of traditional bakery items and also items such as cakes, pastries etc. depending upon quality and taste requirements and local practices.

General Ingredients

The major raw materials required for bread are (a) wheat, atta, maida, leavening agents such as bakers' yeast, bran and hops, fermented juices obtained from palm and lactic acid ferment, edible common salt and water and milk products such as condensed milk, milk powder, whey and curd; fats-hydrogenated oil or refined edible oil of a suitable type or butter ghee, margarine of their mixture; gluten, sugar and sugar products, honey, liquid glucose, malt products, edible starches such as those of potato, corn and tapioca; groundnut flour, vitamins, lecithin, glycerin, and glycerol monostearate, albumin, lime water, fungal enzymes, lysine and sorbitol etc. Items of the list (a) are essential in nature while those of list (b) are considered to be optional. In addition to these improvers such as ammonium persulphate, calcium phosphate, calcium carbonate and potassium bromate and mould inhibitors such as calcium or sodium propionate, acetic or lactic acid, vinegar, acid calcium phosphate, sodium diacetate and acid sodium pyrophosphate are also used in the bread industry.

For biscuits the choice of ingredients is from (a) cereal and cereal products including maida; whole wheat meal, wheat atta, sanilina (suzi or rava), wheat bran, edible wheat germ, barley powder, oat flour, edible besan flour, rice flour and malt flour (b) oil seed products including processed soyabean flour (full fat or solvent extract), peanuts, peanut butter, edible groundnut flour, expressed or solvent extracted, edible cottonseed flour (c) shortening such as butter and vegetable ghee (d) edible starches including tapioca flour edible potato flour, edible sweet-potato flour, edible arrowroot starch, maize starch, tapioca starch and rice starch (e) milk and milk products including casein, edible milk powder (whole and skim), butter-milk and its solids, liquid or condensed milk, cheese, whey solid, malted milkfood, (f) sugars including sugar, liquid glucose, dextrose monohydrate, jaggery and khandsari, edible molasses, lactose malt extract, invert syrup, golden syrup, honey (g) fruit and fruit products including desiccated coconut, dry fruits, edible nuts, pectin jam, and (h) spices including ginger, chilly powder, black pepper, saffron, ajowan, cardamom and cumin.

In addition to the various ingredients enumerated above others such as, coffee powder, cocoa powder, covering chocolate, edible vegetables, enzymes and gluten conditioners, proteolytic and amylases, sodium bisulphite and sodium metabisulphate are also used. Flavoring essences, improvers and fixers, coloring materials, antioxidants such as tartaric acid and citric acid, emulsifying agents such as lecithin and glycerol monostearate, leaving agents baking powder, ammonium bicarbonate, sodium bicarbonate, ammonium carbonate, active bakers' yeast and other approved aerating agents, are also used. Nutrients used in the manufacture of biscuits include vitamins, calcium phosphate, calcium diphosphate, calcium triphosphate, calcium carbonate, lysine and protein concentrates.

Thus large number of ingredients are employed in bakery industry, but of course the main constituent is wheat flour. Now we shall give the individual ingredients used in this industry.

WHEAT FLOUR

Wheat flour is the primary ingredient in all bakery products.

No other cereal flour can substitute wheat flour, as it contains a com bination of 'gluten' and 'gliadin' which in the presence of water com bine to form gluten. Gluten is necessary to form the sustaining wall o the whole structure of the bakery products. The flour is obtained by milling wheat. Many varieties of wheat are available viz. (1) Hard Sprin (2) Durum (3) Hard Red Winter, (4) Soft Red winter and, (5) Whit Wheat. Durum wheat flour is never used in the bakery products. Th Winter Wheat is grown in winter season in warm climates while th spring wheat is planted in spring season of colder climates. The term 'hard' and 'soft' refer to the consistency of the kernel and the flour.

Hard flours are used for bread and rolls special sweet yeas products requiring a stronger flour; while the soft flours are used fo more delicate products such as cakes, pastries and cookies. Hard wheat mill well and yield flour that is rich in good quality protein from whic strong, elastic dough can be made with proper development. Thes doughs show good tolerance to conditions prevailing in a bakery with respect to mixing, fermentation, temperature etc. and have excellen gas holding properties and will yield bread with good volume, grain and texture under a wide range of conditions. The hard wheat doughs have high water-absorptive capacities and generally have excellen dough handling properties when properly matured. Soft wheats are deficient in protein.

Manufacture of wheat flour.

Wheat is first washed, cleaned and tempered (moistening the wheat under controlled conditions to standard moisture content). The wheat is then cracked by passing through corrugated rollers. Bran is separated out and the midilings flour is passed through smooth rollers where additional germ portions are flaked out. This is repeated severa times to remove fatty portions and bran particles. The shorts are normally used for special foods and animal feed; the remain flour, after removal of impurities is called straight flour or 100% extraction flour. This may be further sifted to get 25 to 75% extraction which is known as patent flour. The clear flour remains after the patent flour is re moved. Finer portions of the flour obtained from sifting with fine screens contain gluten of high quality. The coarser particles generally add darker color to the flour. Clear flour contains more protein than patent, but this does not indicate that its gluten components are of a better qual ity; generally it is inferior.

The table shows the average composition of various flours from ne same wheat. The compositions will be different for different wheats ut the trends will be similar:

Average	Average Wheat	Average Patent	Cake or pastry
Moisture %	14.5	12-13	12-13
Protein %	11-14	11-13	7-9.5
Carbohydrates, %	69-72	74-76	75-77
Fat, %	2	1-1.5	1-1.5
Ash, %	1.8	0.5	0.4

Whole wheat flour has shorter storage life due to its larger percentage of fat. Gluten flour is that from which a good portion of the tarch has been removed. It contains about 47% protein and 53% carohydrate. The simple flour is known as green flour and contains higher noisture content and traces of yellowish color bodies. If left as it is for 3 to 12 weeks, it matures and colour becomes whiter due to oxidation of proteins and colour bodies. Use of chlorine etc. gives whiter product in shorter time. Bromates may be added to bread flours to help mprove the grain and texture of the end product but they have no effect on the bleaching of the carotenoid pigments present in flour.

Rye flour is milled from rye in the same manner as other flours. Pamper-nickel flour is milled from the whole rey berry after cleaning and processing.

Properties of flours

Various properties and characteristics to flour have bearing on he properties of the final bakery product. The flour should have been properly sifted to eliminate lumps. Aeration resulting from sifting insures proper moistening of the flour in the subsequent mixing. Blended flours are also made to get balanced properties. Various sheets may be nixed before milling or flours may be suitably blended. A high gluten flour may be used alone in the production of hard-type rolls.

Absorption quality of the flour is the ability of the flour to absorb and retain moisture from the mixing of the dough to the final baking of the product; this particularly depends upon the quantity and quality of the protein present in it. Absorption of moisture usually varies from 54 to 65% based on the flour weight. The flour should be stored in a light ventilated room at about 24-27°C otherwise it will absorb additional moisture resulting in a loss in absorption property; this phenomenon is known as 'sweating'. The ability of the flour to produce products of large volume and well 'piled' loaves is related to flour strength. Piling refers to an even smooth grain and fine texture; a large volume with a coarse uneven grain may indicate that the flour is not of high quality.

Flour can be identified by color, feel and smell. Patent bread flour has creamy color, dry touch and does not pack when squeezed and dusts easily while the cake flour is whiter in color, packs easily and lumps when squeezed or dusted. Rye flour is grayish in color, lumps easily and has a slight characteristic odor.

Gluten occurs in dry protein form in flour and forms the doughs, rubbery, elastic substance when flour is mixed with water or other liquids, containing water such as milk. It gives the dough strength to hold leavening gases and also good elastic and stretching structure. Diastase and protase and main enzymes present in flour, Diastase acts upon some starch and liquefies it converting it into malt sugar. This assumes importance for fermentation of lean doughs in which little or no sugar or syrup is used. Protease converts a portion of the proteins in doughs into a soluble form which improves the elasticity of the gluten by mellowing and softening it.

Flours for Cakes & Pastries

Cake flours are obtained from soft winter wheat but such wheat is of different varieties. Cake flour has a lower amount of protein and forms soft-yielding gluten when mixed into the cake mix; this avoids toughness in the product. As indicated in the chart the protein content of cake flour varies from 7 to 9% and it need be just sufficient to hold the cake structure together. In flour for angel cake only 7% protein is sufficient as the required amount of protein is supplied by egg white also; while for heavier cakes such as pound cake the flour should have 8.5 to 9.5% protein. When required the protein content of the flour can be reduced by mixing some corn starch. Usual bleaching agent for cake flours is chlorine, it reduces the pH from 5.6 to 5.3; making the flour mellower, and also starch is made more soluble.

Other Wheat Based Materials

Apart from wheat flour or atta, fine flour or maida, there is wheat suzi also. In the following table ISI specifications for wheat atta, maida and suzi have been given. It is interesting to note that some of the ISI specifications prescribed for maida differ from the specifications prescribed for bread flour which suggests that all maida even when according to ISI specifications is not suitable for bread making. Thus flours for specific purposes of making bread, biscuits, cakes or other bakery products should be purchased and kept separately to get the products of best quality.

As mentioned earlier the flour should be properly selected but toughness in baked goods is not always caused by the flour and may be due to improper mixing or lack of sifting. It has also been mentioned that in rich doughs a strong flour should be used for example 80% high gluten (HG) flour and 20% cake or pastry flour; or a short-patent bread flour alone. In puff-pastry dough high gluten flour is required to support the high percentage of fat rolled into the dough. astry flour, rather than cake flour is used for pie crusts. This flour is higher in Protein and is able to sustain the high percentage of fat without becoming too tough and overly short-the point where the baked crust crumbles easily.

Characteristies of Wheat Flour for Bakery Industry

	Characteristics	Bread Flour	Biscuit Flour Fermented	Biscuit Flour Hard Doughs	Biscuit Flour Short Doughs	Cake Flour	Test Method
A.	Protein, %	11.5-12.5	10-11	9-10	8-9	7-8.5	ISI
B.	Gluten Quality						
	(a) Resistence	450-500	650-750	550-6500	450-550	-	Henry Simon
	(b) Extensibility	18-22	18-20	18-20	20-22	-	Extensometer
C.	Total-Ash, % max.	0.44	0.44	0.44	0.33	0.33	
D.	Acid Insoluble, Ash, % max.	0.05	0.05	0.05	0.05	0.05	ISI
E.	Moisture, % max.	12.5	12.5	12.5	12.5	12.5	
F.	Water absorption, %	60-64	60-64	55-60	50-55	-	Farinograph
G.	Maltose Fidure	1.5-2.3	1.5-2.3	-	-	-	Rmsey
H.	Gassing powermls. in 4 hours, Min. 2% of flour	40		40	-	-	-
I.	Acidity , Max.	9.15	0.15	0.15	0.15	-	Copressed
J.	Particle size						
	(a) 105-55	40%	22%	20%	20%	20%	ISI
	(b) 55-35	22%	20%	25%	25%	15%	
	(c) 35-25	20%	25%	25%	25%	20%	
	(d) 25-15	18%	30%	30%	30%	45%	
K.	Rope spores	Less than 29 per 100 grammes of flour					
L.	pH	-	-	-	-	5.5-5.0	MAc Michael
M.	Viscosity	-	-	-	-	40^0-50^0	

N. Colour — White with no creaminess-bleached by chlorene or its agent to give good colour and correct pH for cake flour.

O. Baking — Must satisfy the test and produce a good product

Note : *(1)* Gluten Quality - Resistance figures for bread flour are on yeasted doughs and othwers are based on unyeasted doughs.

(2) Protein figures are based on 12.5 % moisture.

ISI Quality Standards for Wheat Atta, Maida & Suji

Wheat Product		Moisture % Max.	Total Ash % Max. (Dry basis)	Acid insoluble Ash, % Max (Dry basis)	Gluten % Max. (Dry basis) alcohol by wt. max.	Alcoholic Acidity with 90 %	Granularity	Crude Fibre
1. Wheat Atta	LG	13	2.50	0.10	7 to 9	0.10	98% should pass 600 micron IS Sieve	2.50
	HG	13	2.50	0.10	Above 9	0.10		2.50
2. Maida	LG	13	0.70	0.05	7 to 8	0.1 0	100% should pass through 8 micron sieve	
	MG	13	0.70	0.05	Above 8 to 10	0.10		
3. Suji	LG	13	1.00	0.05	Above 10	0.10		
	HG	13.50	1.00	0.05	6.00	0.10		

Storage of Flours

Flour is stored for economic considerations, to ensure regular availability and also to keep it in maturing. Proper storage is very essential to safeguard against spoilage. The flour should be piled off the flour on skids or flates. The storage areas should be well ventilated. Direct sunlight should not enter it. Too dry air and too high relative humidity are both detrimental to the flour. The temperature and humidity should be between 20° to 25°C and 55 to 65% respectively. Flour has a tendency to pick up foreign odors, hence it should be stored away from any ingredients which will impart an odor e.g. petrol, kerosene oil, spices, onions etc. It should also be ensured before hand that it is free from insect contamination. Under these conditions, bleached flour may be stored upto 5 months and unbleached flour upto eight months.

SUGARS

The principal purpose of using sugar in baked goods is to sweaten the product. By varying the grades and types of sugars, other effects are also achieved.

Uses of Sugar

Sugar serves the following purposes in the production of bakery products:

- It gives the necessary sweetness.
- Serves as food for yeast in fermentation.
- It is used in the preparation of a variety of icing for baked products.
- In assists in creaming and whipping processes of mixing.
- It provides good grain and texture to the finished product.
- It aids in the retention of moisture due to its hygroscopic nature, and prolongs freshness.
- It promotes a good crust color; sugars brown better in alkaline conditions.
- It adds nutritional value to the product.

As the sugar content increases, the biscuits become harder until a hard brittle biscuit with 'snap' is obtained. In addition to the bite, altering the texture will make the biscuit spread, the degree of which is largely dependent on the softening or tendering effect which sugar has on gluten. As gluten becomes softer, the biscuits flows easily, and the more the sugar that dissolves, the more the gluten is softened.

Types of Sugars

There are various types of sugars which can be broadly classified into (a) simple or Mono-saccharides e.g. glucose, dextrose etc. which are directly fermentable by yeast; and (b) double sugars or disaccharides, e.g. sucrose, maltose etc. which must be converted by the enzymic action of yeast into simple sugars before they can serve as food for yeast.

Sucrose or cane sugar is available in granulated or powder forms; the latter is generally sufficiently fine to meet the needs in preparing variety of icings, fillings etc. Confectionery or powdered sugar contains about 3% corn starch to retard lumping or crystallization. It is primarily used in icings and is also often a component of cake mixes in which part of the sugar is first blended with the flour and then added in the final stages of mixing. The fineness of this sugar lends itself to easier blending and is often used in this way in angel cakes. Brown or yellowish sugars contain some caramel, mineral matter and moisture, some sugars are used in products where the flavour and colour are desired; for example in the preparation of Streusel topping where it adds to the color and flavor and blends well with the cinnamon and other spices used. They are also used in dark cookies and cakes, but should be avoided in light cakes and cakes of delicate blend.

Corn Sugar or Dextrose : Dextrose or corn sugar is made from corn starch. Dextrose is about 75% as sweet as sucrose and it is used primarily for the making of yeast doughs. Since dextrose is directly fermentable by yeast, using it increases the rate of fermentation. Liquid glucose or corn syrup is a clear, thick viscous liquid about half as sweet as sucrose. Glucose cramalises readily during baking, giving good color to the face of the biscuit. It also acts as a moisture retainer in baked goods.

Invert Sugar or Syrup : This is a syrup produced by the action of an acid on the sucrose solution, yielding equal parts of glucose and fructose. Because of its fructose content it is used on baked goods to retain moisture. It is also used for good color development in baked products.

Golden Syrup : it is made from low grade sugars and uncrystallised syrup. It is a mixture of sucrose and invert sugar in solution, with a small proportion of gum, acids and mineral salts.

Malt syrup : While malt extract is produced from malted barley, malt syrup is produced from barley and maize starch, and is thus sweeter. It is used for flavor and as yeast food, particularly in hard bread and rolls.

Treacle or Molasses : It is a dark colored uncrystallised syrup, which remains after the production of raw sugar. It consists of a solution of sucrose, invert sugar and various impurities which impart colour and flavour.

Jaggery : This is prepared from sugarcane juice by open pan evaporation to 25% moisture and on cooling solidifies to golden brown blocks. Jaggery or Gur gives a characteristic flavor and taste to the product.

Honey : It consists mainly of invert sugar and small quantity of sucrose in solution. The distinctive flavor of honey depends on the essential oils present in the pollen of flowers, from which the nectar is gathered by bees. It imparts characteristic flavor to the baked product.

Incorporation of Sugar in the mix

Usually fine grain sugar is used in bakery products, but when coarse material is to be used it creates problems and results in spots on the crust of baked products, coarse grain and poor volume. Coarse sugar does not lend itself to proper creaming due to the difficulty in dissolution. This problem is particularly acute with sponge or angel-cake mixes where the eggs and sugar are not heated above 40°C. During heating in the oven crystals start dissolving and those present on the surface start caramelizing creating spots. In the mix, the coarse crystals dissolve forming droplets of concentrated syrup. They also act as abrasives in the mixing kettle causing detaining, and gray discoloration of the product. Coarse grain sugar is particularly useful for making sugar sprinkled cookies. Coarse sugar may be used in cooking fillings and preparing syrups for icings or wash also.

In the preparation of rich doughs, such as coffee cake, sweet yeast doughs the sugar is either creamed with the fat or is dissolved in the milk or water and then added to the sponge. Complete mixing and dissolution of sugar in the mix should be ensured to avoid dark spots on the crusts or the formation of holes in baked products. Method of mixing the sugar with other ingredients is dictated by the sugar:flour ratio. If the amount of sugar is 100% or less based on flour, the sugar is creamed with the fat or whipped entirely with eggs; this is done in most creamed mixes. If the amount of sugar is more than 100% (e.g. in the case of high ratio cakes), a special method is required to blend the sugar with emulsified shortening. In the case of whipped mixes, such as sponge or angel cake, the sugar excess over 100% is dissolved in the milk or water and then added alternately with the flour; this insures complete solution of the sugar. Confectioner's sugar is usually difficult to dissolve due to tendency to lump, hence it should be mixed and sifted with the flour rather than to dissolve in the liquid.

While using sugars in bakery products, their relative sweetness should be kept in mind. Following gives the relative sweetness of various sugars based on sucrose as 100%.

Sugar	Comparative Sweetness
Invert Syrup (78% solids)	80-90
Dextrose (8% water crystal)	65
Malt extract	30
Corn Syrup	30
Honey	65-70
Lactose (milk sugar)	16

Lactose is not used separately in bakery products but being present in milk, it imparts additional flavor and sweetness to the product. It may be emphasized again that addition of sugar makes the latter less fluid, and absorbs moisture thus reduces the rate of scaling of the product. Sugars in the form of syrups further add moisture and sweetness to the mix.

SHORTENINGS

Shortening means fat or oil used to tender the baked products. This is one of the major nutritive ingredients used in the bakery industry and may constitute upto 40% of the product weight. The type and amount of fat used has direct bearing on the following vital characteristics of the baked products:

1. **Bread & Cookies**

A. Increases loaf volume.
B. Improves crumb grain
C. Strengthens dough structure by its high melting compounds.

2. **Biscuits & Cookies**

A. Improves the dough for machining and sheeting.
B. Controls the flow of biscuits.
C. Gives shorter bite to the goods.
D. Enhances their flavor.

Shortening agent contributes to the plasticity of the dough, acts as a lubricant between the films of gluten, and thereby slackens the bread flow. In biscuits dough, it prevents excessive development of gluten by not allowing water to come in too close a contact with the gluten during mixing. In the oven, gluten-fat interfaces and acts as gas promoting nuclei. The entrapped air in the fat contributes to a leavening action out, of proportion to its normal thermal expansion in the oven.

Types of Fats & Oils

Various types of fats and oils are used in the bakery industry; they may be broadly classified as solids and liquids or those derived from animal sources and those derived from vegetable sources. Solid fats have melting points/ranging from 33°C to 45°C. Butter and lard come under the category of animal fats while oils, vegetable glue and cocoa butter come under vegetable fats. Margarine and puff paste may be made from vegetable or animal raw materials. Some of the important shortenings are given below :-

Vegetable Oils : They are usually extracted from seeds. When refined they are free from odor, color and fibrous material. Groundnut and cottonseed oils are practically of neutral color, while corn and soyabean oils may have light-yellow color. Soyabean oils contains mild flavor but it has no effect on the product flavor when used in small quantities. Vegetables oils are used mainly in doughs, particularly for rolls, bread and hard products. Melted hard fats are also sometimes used in place of the oil.

Hydrogenated Vegetable Fat : Hydrogenated vegetable fat or Ghee is made by hydrogenation of vegetable oil; it has solid consistency at room temperature. It is well suited for creaming and can be used for most purposes. Emulsified shortening for high-ratio shortening, contain some mono-and di-glycerides, for greated absorption and retention of moisture; they do not cream well but retain a higher percentage of sugar and liquid. Simple shortening should not be used for a high ratio type. Cake mix while emulsified shortening should not be used for a creamed type cake mix.

Butter : Butter is obtained from milk and has yellowish color, sweet and pleasant odor, solid consistency and 80% fat content. Usually sweet butter is used but if salted butter is used its salt content should be kept in mind; as excess salt retards the fermentation in yeast-raised products. If desired, salt may be dissolved out from the butter by kneading it in cold water. If butter is to be substituted by fat in a recipe then shortening weight should be decreased by about 15% and moisture be increased by 10%.

Lard : Lard is derived from hogs; it is a solid white fat having mild odor. Its fat content is 98%; it is used to impart pleasing flavor to the products e.g. in pie crust.

Margarine : Margarine is made by churning animal or vegetable fat with milk or cream. It has a solid consistency, white to yellow color, neutral to milk butter flavor and 80-85% fat content. Cake type or baker's margarine is relatively soft, contains emulsifiers for superior creaming properties. Roll-in type margarine is firmer with waxy consistency; puff paste type margarine is even firmer. All these margarines have higher melting points then butter and usual margarine.

Cocoa butter : It is mainly used in confectionery work. In chocolates it gives finer shine or lusture and increases the tenderness.

Characteristics of Shortenings

To achieve the best performance, fat should confirm to the predeterminated physical and chemical characteristics. The melting point, plasticity, and uniform smooth texture is directly related to the degree of dispersion in the dough, whereas chemical characteristics like iodine value and period valuē, control the shelf life and fat bloom of the product. An ideal fat for baking should have the following properties :

- Short plastic range.
- Resistance to oxidation.
- Consistency which makes its ready incorporation into dough.
- Melting point lower than human body temperature.
- It should aerate with inert gas.

Use of Shortenings

Correct amounts of shortenings should be used to get best results. With incorrect amounts dense, grease, lean, tough or poor keeping quality cakes will be obtained. Correct amount of fat might have been used but the blending may not be proper. Instead of using only butter, a blend of equal parts of butter and hydrogenated fat may be used resulting in butter creaming properties, with less chance of curdling in the creaming process. Butter contains about 15% moisture, which tends to separate from the fatty solids, especially upon the addition and creaming of the eggs or egg whites. 50% blend is cheaper and also has a adequate flavor of the butter.

As distinguished from sugar, eggs and milk etc. which lose their identity in the mix due to dissolution and absorption, fat does not do so. Fat does not dissolve in water hence on mixing it only gets dispersed throughout the mix, either as water-in-fat emulsion or air-in-fat foam, when the mix is well creamed. Fat should be well mixed to get tenderness in the baked product particularly in cake mixes. When two types of shortenings are to be mixed in, the harder one should be first worked into the mix until it becomes plastic and of the same consistency as the other fat which is also then mixed in. In a rich, sweet dough hard butter and vegetable shortening are often melted before being added. In the case of leaner doughs, the fat or vegetable shortening acts as a lubricant in developing the gluten, e.g. in pan bread, where 5% or less fat is used, the fat is added after the flour and dough development takes place. The fat helps prevent the breakdown or tearing of the gluten during mixing. In richer doughs, such as bun dough, the fat is blended and creamed with the sugar.

Storage of Fats

Shortenings are affected by light, heat and oxygen (air) resulting in rancidity. Flavor and color of the fats of oils changes on becoming rancid, and their use in the process will affect the baked products. Shortenings should not be stored near odorous materials as they pick up foreign odors very rapidly. Shortening containers should be kept closed and thus exposure to light, oxygen and also to high temperatures should be avoided. Butter, being perishable, should be stored under refrigeration.

MILK

Except for breads and rolls, milk is the basic means of supplying liquid to the dough or cake mix. Fresh milk when left standing for a few hours a cream line on the surface as the fat particles are lighter than water; and if left for longer period it gets sour due to lactic acid fermentation resulting in change of pH to 4.6 from 6.6 . The functions of milk in baking are as follows :-

1. Improves nutritive value because of its protein minerals and vitamin content.
2. Increases absorption of flour in the dough.
3. Improvers crest color by combining lactose with protein during baking.
4. Increases volume and improves texture.
5. Increases mixing tolerance i.e. reduces the tendency of doughs to slacken on over-mixing.
6. Increases fermentation tolerance i.e. yields a satisfactory loaf of bread even when the dough is underfermented or overfermented.
7. Supplies liquid to the dough or cake mix.
8. Improves keeping qualities of the product.

Types of Milk

Various types of milk are available which are used in bakery industry. Broadly, milk can be classified viz., (a) Fresh products-liquid whole milk, non-fat milk, butter milk, etc. (b) Concentrated products-condensed whole milk, condensed skim milk, butter, sweetened condensed whole milk and, (c) Dry products whole milk powder, skim milk powder, butter milk powder and whey powder.

Whole milk contains about 88% water, 3.5% butter fat, 3.25% protein when it is forced through fine openings under high pressure, it is known as homogenised milk. Fat particle size is reduced in this way, this cream preparation does not take place in this milk when left standing for a few hours. Pasteurization, means the quick heating and cooling of the milk to destroy the bacteria, thus increasing the keeping quality of the milk. Evaporated whole milk is obtained by evaporating off some moisture followed by homogenization; it contains 72% water, 8% butter fat, 7.2% protein. Skim milk is the one from which fat has been removed by centrifuging. It contains 91% water and 3-1/2% protein. Evaporated skim milk contains 72% water and 11% protein. Dried milk is a powder obtain by spray drying or roller drying the evaporated whole or skim milk. Dried whole milk contains 1.5% water, 27.5% butter fat, 27% protein while the dried skim milk contains 2.5% water, 1.5% butter fat, and 36% protein. Sweetened condensed milk is an evaporated milk to which 40 to 55% sugar is also added to act as a preservative. All these milks contain minerals and milk sugar or lactose in varying quantities.

Whey is the product that remains after removing most of the casein and butterfat from milk. When cream is churned, the fat in water emulsion changes to water-in-fat emulsion i.e. butter, and the liquid which remains is known as buttermilk.

Use of Milk

While using milk products, two factors have to be considered viz. (1) water, (2) Total solid content in milk. Milk solids have a blinding effect on flour proteins and create a toughening effect. Lactose helps in regulating the crust color and milk solids improves the flavor. When milk powder is to be used in place of whole milk, 120 gms. of whole milk powder and 900 cc. water should be used in place of 1 litre milk. In place of 1 litre of skim milk, 90 gms. of skim milk powder and 925 cc. of water should be used. For every litre of skim milk used to replace whole milk about 25-30 gms. of fat should be added to the mix. When a recipe mentions one type of milk can be substituted by alternating other ingredients keeping in mind the composition of various milks given above. As an example if sweetened condensed milk is to be added in place of whole milk, suagr should be accordingly reduced, and water should be increased.

In lean doughs the milk powder may be added with the flour

and the dough then developed; for rich doughs and cake mixes dried milk powder may be creamed in with the sugar and shortening. Thus for these products milk powder need not to be dissolved in water. But in the case of custards and fillings milk powder should be dissolved, in cold water with stirring, otherwise later on heating hard lumps will form. Due to the same reason hot water should not be used. Addition of sour milk or butter milk in yeast-raised doughs, increases their acidity, reducing the fermentation and make-up period. When used in cake mixes, particularly those containing cocoa and chocolate, excessive acidity should be neutralised with sodium bicarbonate. For every liter of butter milk about 15 gms. of bicarbonate is added and about 30 gms. of baking powder is reduced.

Storage of milk

Milk and milk products should be properly stored to prevent spoilage. Evaporated milk is packed in sealed cans. Fresh whole or skim milk should be kept under refrigeration. Condensed milk has a life of about a few weeks. When exposed, milk powder tends to absorb moisture from air, hence container lid should be securely closed. Skim milk powder is free from fat hence it keep better than whole milk powder (fat is liable to turn rancid). Milk powder which has lumped should be ground and sifted and soaked in cold water before using.

YEAST

Yeast is a one-cell microorganism of the fungus type. The function of yeast in the bakery mix or dough is to lighten it and impart to its characteristic flavor and aroma. While yeast is important primarily to bring about fermentation, it is also a nutritious food, being a rich source of of some important vitamins and enzymes. Thus yeast is of great importance to the baker.

The fresh yeast generally has grey to light yellow brown color, is springly to the touch, breaks easily and sharply and has a yeasty odor, usually fresh yeast consists of about 14% protein, 10% carbohydrates, 0.5% fat, 2.3% mineral matter, 68 to 73% moisture and some enzymes and vitamins.

Fermentation by yeast transforms the sugars into carbon dioxide and alcohol, yeast derives fermentable sugars from four sources viz. (1) yeast cell (2) wheat flour (3) hydrolysis of starch (4) added sugar.

The evolution of carbon dioxide gas gives rise to a network of bubbles which raise the dough. The small quantities of alcohols etc. produced during fermentation contributes to aroma and flavor. Yeast grows best at temperatures between 20° and 35°C and dough ferments best between 25° and 27°C. At temperatures below that range, the fermentation will be slow and at higher temperatures, the fermentation may outpace the rate at which dough is conditioned.

Yeast ferments and grows best in an acidic environment, tolerating as low as pH 2.0. A pH of 5.5 at the start of fermentation is suitable for good yeast growth. During normal fermentation the acidity increases slightly so that at the end of fermentation the pH is about 4.5. Yeast requires food like any living plant or animal; sugar is necessary for yeast to obtain its energy, while minerals and nitrogen compounds are also needed.

Types of Yeast

There are two types of yeast viz., compressed and active dry yeast. Compressed is obtained by somewhat concentrating the dilute yeast suspension, from the fermentation vat, by cream-type centrifugal separators, followed by filtration in a cloth-lined filter press. The compressed yeast should be stored in a refrigerator at 0°C and should not be exposed to extreme heat or cold for even a short time. It will keep well for 14 days in a refrigerator provided it should not get wet. Active dry yeast is made the same way as regular fresh yeast followed by one major step. After the filtration step the yeast is passed through a drier at a carefully controlled temperature of 35° to 40°C, and a regulated drying speed to avoid destruction of the yeast cells and the moisture is reduced to about 8%. Drying makes the yeast passively inactive, but does not destroy activity; it may be rehydrated in lukewarm water for about 10 minutes before using.

Compressed yeast should be broken up and suspended in about one and a half times its weight of warm water. The temperature of water should be about 25°-27°C and the yeast should remain in this water for 5 to 10 minutes before it is added to the dough. Hot water should not be used for this purpose; and the yeast is killed at 50°C. Active dry yeast is twice as effective as compressed yeast hence only half as much as compressed yeast is used. Dry yeast does not require refrigeration for storage but still be stored in a dry and cool place. It keeps well for many months when properly stored. It is suspended in

4 times its weight of water at 40°C for 5 to 10 minutes before use. Colder water results in slower fermentation while much warm water may harm the yeast.

Uses of Yeast

Method of making yeast suspension has already been given. Salt reduces rate of fermentation hence it should not be added to yeast slurry. Yeast suspension should be added, together with flour, to the dough. In mixing a sponge dough, the yeast suspension is added with part of flour and water and the sponge is set. Due to the lack of salt in sponge dough, fermentation is rapid. In sweet doughs for rapid fermentation more yeast has to be added but it will add to the cost, also flavor will be affected. In warm moist weather yeast activity increases. In hot weather cold water should be used. Richness or leanness of the dough also affects the amount of yeast required. More yeast is required in rich coffee cake dough than in bun dough, as sugar retards the action of yeast. Bun dough contains less sugars; and in bread doughs even smaller amounts of yeast (3 to 2.5% of compressed yeast based on the wheat flour) is required to raise the dough.

Specifications for Bakers Yeast

Characteristics	Requirements for	
	Baker's Yeast (Compressed)	Baker's Yeast (Dried)
(1) Moisture, % by wt., max.	75	8
(2) Dispersibility in water	To satisfy	To satisfy
(3) Fermenting Power, min.	80	160
(4) Yeast cell count, millions per gram (Dru basis), Min.	5000	10,000
(5) Dough raising capacity	To satisfy test	To satisfy test
(6) Microflora, other than yeast,million per gram (on dry basis) max.	3.0	8.0

Only the best quality yeast should be used as the amount used in smaller as compared to other ingredients, otherwise the cheaper grade (poorer quality yeast) may prove to be even costlier practically.

In India GUL is also used as leavening agent in large number of small scale bakeries.

SALT

Salt is one of the important ingredients of a dough. It's use in proper amount is important for the production of good product. Usually common salt or table salt is used and it should have the following characteristics :-

- It should be completely soluble in water.
- It should give a clear solution. Cloudy solution will indicate presence of certain impurities.
- It should be free from lumps.
- It should be as pure as possible.
- It should be free from a bitter or biting taste.

Use of salt

The functions of salt used in baking are as follows:

- It brings out the taste of other ingredients particularly sugar, and helps to improve the flavor of the product.
- It toughens the gluten thereby improving the grain and texture of loaf.
- It stabilizes fermentation. Doughs containing salt ferment more slowly than those with out salt.
- It prevents the growth of wild yeast.
- It acts as flavor retainer and as preservative.

Salt should be used carefully; particularly it should not be added to yeast suspension. Otherwise yeast activity will be reduced. Salt should be whipped or creamed with fat or sugar when adding to cake mixes. In yeast raised doughs 25-30 gms. of salt should be used per liter of water or milk used in the dough. Sponge cake mixes lack fat, hence in them less salt is required than in creamed-type cake even when quantity of sugar used is same. Only dry powder salt should be used.

EGG & EGG PRODUCTS

Eggs are highly nutritious and therefore enrich any recipe in which they are included, whole egg consists of yolk and the white, they have following average composition :

Content	Whole Egg	Yolk	White
Moisture%	73	50	86
Protein%	14	17	12
Fat,%	12	31	0.2
Sugar (Glucose),%	traces	0.2	0.4
Ash,%	1	1.5	1

Thus yolk contains most of the fatty material of the egg in finely emulsified state. It improves creaming and volume of the mix. Only good quality fresh eggs should be used; stale eggs ruin the products. Dried egg powder is also sometimes used in bakery products; it is produced by spray drying.

Use of Eggs

Apart from increasing the nutrition value, eggs, because of their albumen, assist in structure formation both in dough form, and when baked. They also improve crispness, texture and eating qualities of biscuit. They also enhance the biscuit color and flavor. Yolk gives desirable yellow color to the cake. When whipped or beaten eggs produce foam due to entrapment of air bubbles, this gives some leavening effect to the mix.

Whole dried egg powder should be soaked with three times its weight of water for 1 hour before use. In the case of dried yolks 2.5 times water should be used for soaking 1 hour before use, while with dried whites 8 times water should be used, 3 hours before use.

When eggs are reduced in a mix, allowance must be made for reduction in liquid and leavening supplied by eggs. Keeping in view the egg composition given above when 1 kg. of eggs is reduced in a mix, 750 cc. of water must be added and also to compensate for the reduction in leavening about 40 gms. of extra baking powder will have to be added. Of course, even then, quality, shortness and richness of the mix will be affected.

CHEMICAL LEAVENING/AERATING AGENTS

Dough or mix is aerated or leavened to improve the texture, bite and appearance of baked products. This may be achieved by whipping, fermentation by yeasts or by using chemical agents. The last method is very important, in which chemicals are used to produce gas and do not leave an unpleasant flavor or harmful effects. Baking powders are mixtures of chemicals which react in the presence of moisture and heat to release a gas. Single action baking powders release gas when they come into contact with moisture, slow acting release very little gas at low temperature and require heat for the release of gas, and multiple acting which release a small amount of gas at low temperature and require oven temperature for full reaction. The last is the most popular type of baking powder.

Single acting powders contain tartaric acid or cream of tartar and sodium bicarbonate. The unpopular slow acting powders contain phosphates (e.g. mono-calcium phosphate) which are not soluble at low temperatures, and sodium bicarbonate. Double action powders contain sodium aluminium sulphate (SAS) or sodium acid, pyrophosphate and the mono-calcium phosphates, with sodium bicarbonate. About 20-30% starch is also present as a filler and stabilizer against moisture.

During baking, sodium bicarbonate releases carbon dioxide and water, leaving sodium carbonate as a residue which has an unpleasant flavor and can react with the fats causing a soapy taste. But the presence of acid ingredient counteracts this problem. After mixing mixes or doughs should be quickly baked to avoid loss of volume. Ammonium bicarbonate also reacts very rapidly in the presence of moisture and heat to give carbon dioxide, ammonia gas and water. It should also be handled without delay and baked quickly. It is also used in special products such as cookies, eclairs etc. Used in excess, it can completely break the structure of the biscuit. It is important that the ammonia gas is eventually released from the biscuit, lest it should impart it a pungent flavor.

Use of Leavening Agents

Chemical leavening agents do the job, but leavening produced by mixing and whipping when eggs are present, is also important. Thus in wonder cake mix (containing eggs) less leavening agent is required, compared to that in a high-ratio mix. Baking powder is used also with yeast doughs, e.g. for getting cake like doughnut. Baking powder should be used carefully, excess should be avoided. Otherwise open grain, crumbly texture product will be obtained. At the same time if too small leavening agent is used then product will have small volume, dense structure and will shrink.

Mixing should be proper ; too much mixing will result in loss of gas and too little mixing will result in holes, and non uniform, dense structure. Baking powder container should be kept tightly closed and lid should be replaced immediately after use ; of course starch is present but it cannot take up unlimited moisture. Ammonium and sodium bi-carbonates should also be kept sealed to avoid loss of gassing power.

COCOA & CHOCOLATE

Cocoa and chocolate are used to impart characteristic color, flavor and body to the cakes, pies, pastries and cookies. Cocoa and chocolate are produced from Cocoa beans. Chocolate paste by hydraulic pressing gives cocoa butter and cocoa. 8 kgs. of chocolate paste gives 3 kgs. of cocoa butter and 5 kgs. of cocoa containing 4 kgs. of solids and 1 kg. cocoa butter. For replacing 48 parts chocolate liquor 30 parts cocoa and 9 parts shortening should be added. In the same way to replace 30 parts of cocoa 48 parts of chocolate liquor should be added and shortening should be reduced by 9 parts.

Mixing

For each 100 parts of cocoa added about 37 parts of flour should be reduced to eliminate binding and toughness. For making yellow cake chocolate, melted chocolate should be used as it reduces toughness ; and for each 100 parts of melted chocolate added 20 parts of milk and 1.5 parts of soda should also be added. Chocolate flavor is characteristic hence other flavors should be added after proper selection. Vanilla, almond and sun flavors may be used to add to the flavor of chocolate and give variety to it.

Cocoa should be dissolved in milk with some additional sugar and melted fat before adding to the mix. While adding cocoa to cake mixes, it should be creamed or blended with sugar and shortening when making creamed or blended cake mixer. For chocolate sponge or angel cake cocoa may be sifted with flour and then folded into the mix at the last stage. In the case of custards and other cooked fillings, cocoa may be dissolved in part of the milk or water with some starch (thickener) before adding to the boiling milk or water. When chocolate is to be used it should be wetted and then added to the creaming sugar and shortening or to the first stage of a blended mix.

Chocolate should be melted carefully as at too high temperature it gets scorched and becomes hard, its color also becomes grey. To soften the hardened chocolate some oil or melted fat may be added to it : addition of milk should be avoided for this purpose as it further hardens it.

FLAVORS

Addition of flavors makes the product more acceptable to the customer. Some flavors are extracted from natural sources; such flavors are known as natural flavors and are alcoholic extracts of essential oils from fruits, beans and rinds etc. such as of lemon and orange Imitation flavors are made synthetically. Mixtures of these two types of flavors are usually employed. Only the best quality flavor should be used. Vanillin powder may be blended with twice its weight of confectioner's sugar to this starch (half of vanillin powder) is added. One part of this preparation is mixed with 2 parts of vanilla. The flavor is now ready for use.

Flavors are also available as emulsions, which are more concentrated than extracts. Only half of the amount of emulsion is necessary as compared to that of extract for the same effect. In foam type mixes e.g. in sponge or angel cake, emulsion should be added or folded in lightly just before the flour is added. When butter is present in a formulation lesser amount of flavor is needed. When cooking custards and fillings add flavor after the custard or filling has been cooked. To avoid loss of flavor, it should be added to fruit fillings after cooking and cooling. In cakes and icings blend of flavors should be used, e.g. in orange cakes a little lemon flavor also, improves the orange flavor. Addition of little vanilla improves flavor of chocolate cakes.

Flavors should be stored carefully in amber bottles, lid securely closed, to prevent loss of flavor strength and prevent its deterioration by oxidation etc.

SPICES

Spices are vegetable products which may be in the form of

ground bark, fruit or root etc. or may be in the form of whole seeds. Thus cinnamon, maca, nutmeg, caraway, anise, coriander, ginger, cloves and funnel etc. are used in bakery products. They enhance taste and flavor of the product. Ground spices should be stored carefully, stopper should be kept closed and they should be stored away from heat. Moisture and air exert bad influence on spices. Their aroma is very volatile, therefore apart from storing in closed containers the ground spices should not be kept in storage for a long time; as far as possible freshly ground spice should be used. Amount of spice added should be carefully controlled, if added too much, it may ruin the product by making it pungent and distasteful.

EMULSIFIERS

Emulsifiers are used in baked foods to improve palatability, texture and seals appeal. They inhibit the firming of the crumb associated with staling, by retarding the rate at which starch crystallizes. Glycerol monostearate (GMS) is an important emulsifier. Its main function is to increase the volume of cakes. Apart from other effects mentioned above it improves the ability of protein film to entrap air in the latter, during creaming or mixing.

LECITHIN

Lecithin is a phosphotide containing phosphorus and nitrogen, and is obtained from soyabean and ground nut during fat extraction and refining process. It is an effective emulsifier used in biscuit filling creams at about 0.5% on fat to improve their fluidity. It may be used in biscuits also, to improve distribution and emulsification of ingredients.

BREAD IMPROVERS

Addition of bread improvers to dough improves the bread quality. The essential constituent of the bread improver is a chemical that acts as an oxidizing agent in maturing the dough. The common oxidizing agents are potassium bromate and potassium iodate. Potassium bromate releases oxygen to the dough and becomes potassium bromide which is a harmless material. Bread improvers are used in very small quantity (about 15 ppm). Potassium bromate is first mixed with some flour (0.3% to 99.7% of flour). Then 1/2 kg. of this mix is added to 100 kgs. of flour. Ammonium chloride is also a mild bread improver as it acts as yeast food. In that case potassim bromate (0.3%), ammonium chloride (9.7%) and flour (90%) are mixed together and 1/2 kg of this mix is added to 100 kgs. of flour to get 15 ppm. of potassium bromate in the dough. Among the non-chemical bread improvers, malted barley flour and soyabean flour help in the diastatic and enzymatic activities during the processing of baked foods.

The function of bread improver is to soften the gluten, help in gas retention and add to the volume of the loaf. Whenever bread improver is used, additional water to the extent of 3 to 5% should be added to the dough.

ENRICHING AGENTS

When white, fine flour is obtained from wheat the natural vitamins and minerals which are more concentrated in the darker portion of the wheat get separated from it. Thus to add to the nutrition value of the product artificial vitamins and minerals like thiamin, riboflavin, niacin and iron etc. are incorporated, in the flour at the flour mill or, in the dough by the baker, in the form of a tablet. This is known as fortification or enrichment of the product. Wheat protein is low in amino acid lysine. When lysine is added to bread the protein is upgraded biologically and becomes equivalent to animal protein. Thus lysine is added to the bread or flour, in some countries, to increase the protein efficiency. At least 0.2% lysine based on the flour must be added for reasonable effect. Taste and other characteristics of the bread are not affected by the addition of these enrichment agents.

WATER

Water is also an important raw material particularly of bread. Its use is necessary to form gluten from the flour protein, which gives dough elasticity and gas retaining properties. It determines the consistency of the dough, and helps in controlling its temperature. It dissolves salts and water thereby ensures their uniform distribution throughout the dough. Water makes possible for the enzymes to act on flour and for the yeast to cause fermentation. If sufficient water is allowed to remain in the finished loaf, the bread remains palatable for longer period.

For bread production water used should neither be too hard nor too soft; it should be medium hard. Soft water is low in minerals, it results in lack of gas production during the fermentation of dough and also the gas retention will be poor, resulting in sticky dough. Addition of 0.25% to 0.5% of dough conditioner or mineral yeast food shall eliminate the harmful effects of using soft water; sometimes amount of salt in the dough is also slightly increased.

MISCELLANEOUS INGREDIENTS

Some antioxidants are added to fat containing foods to retard the development of certain off-flavors during storage. Some natural antioxidants are found in non-purified fats e.g. in cocoa butter, and sometimes some chemicals antioxidants are to be added. Antioxidants are not important for high moisture products e.g. bread and cakes but are needed in crackers and cookies etc. which are usually stored for many months. They are usually added to the fats. Addition of some citric acid or phosphoric acids improves the effectiveness of these antioxidants. Butylated hydroxyanisole (BHA) butylated hydroxy toluene (BHT) and propyl gallate are the only antioxidants sometimes used in bakery products.

Fruits and nuts are used in bakery products particularly in pies, bread and buns etc. Candied apple and pumpkin (petha) are most important. Dried fruits used are raisins and dates. Groundnut and cashewnuts are also used in paste and finely cut form. Coconut in the form of fine powder is suitable for cookies. Macaroon coconut passes (95%) through 40 mesh screen. According to particle size coconut is known as medium, coarse, rice, short shred, bancy shred and flake coconut. In some cases walnut is also used.

Certified food colours are used in the decoration of cakes etc. in icings and fillings etc.

2

FLOUR MILLING

The oldest method of milling, which was most widely practised, was stone milling. The earliest records, dating back to about 4000 B.C., show that hand-stones or querns were used. Next came the period (about 2000 B.C.) of slave- or cattle-driven mill stones. until by 450 B.C. the greeks nad introduced single water wheel mill stones. Later the Romans used geared water-wheels with several stones, and subsequently windmills. These came into use from A.D. 600 until 1784, when steam power was introduced with consequent widespread changes in milling processes. With a new motive power at hand a revolution took place in the method of milling itself, stone milling being superseded by the introduction of roller milling.

The last phase in the history of milling, from the introduction of steam upto the present day, has been marked by improvements in roller milling, development of grain handling, storage, cleaning, conditioning, reduction, bleaching, and treating of the flour.

Stone milling. In the stone mill two circular stones are employed, the bottom one being stationery whilst the top stone revolves. The shearing movement of the revolving top stone is the important factor. The stones are frequently made up of four segments fastened together by an iron band and the surfaces are corrugated radially, so that when the top stone is running a shearing effect is produced on the wheat. The top stone is balanced on an iron spindle, so that it can be adjusted by raising or lowering the stone to an extend depending on the nature of the meal to be produced.

The wheat to be ground enters through a hopper at the centre and is carried outwards by the revolving stone, leaving the mill by an aperture round the outside of the bedstone as meal.

The important point is that the wheat is ground to a meal in one operation so that a product is obtained containing all the constituents of the wheat mixed together. Further, the grinding operation always produces heat and so warms up the meal.

In such a process some of the bran is ground very fine, with the result that some of it passes through the finest silks. This results in the flour being of a darker color than that now produced by roller milling. the particles of the bran which are so mixed contain amongst them portion of the germ and the aleurone layer, and as a result the gluten is modified, being rendered less stable. Owing to the presence of the ground germ such flours will not keep for a great length of time, since the enzymes present become active, and what is termed 'mustiness' tends to develop.

Stone-milled flour should be kept two weeks before being used, since the baking quality improves until a loaf of quite good volume can be obtained from a dough which has stood a fairly long fermentation. With this improvement in stability, however, there is an impoverishment in flavour.

The flavour characteristic of stone-milled flour is no doubt due to the presence of the germ, and it has been suggested that the heating which takes place during grinding assists the distribution of the volatile flavouring constituents, for flour is a substance readily susceptible to violate flavors as well as foreign odours.

Roller milling. This consists of a very gradual process of reduction or breaking down of the wheat grain. First of all the wheat is thoroughly cleaned, every precaution being taken so as to render the flour as pure as white and possible. A process known as 'conditioning' is carried out, which is virtually the treatment of the grain with moisture and heat in order to give all the wheats a more uniform moisture content so that they grind efficiently on the mill.

The grinding is carried out in two main processes. First the wheat goes to the break rolls, which are fluted, where it is split open on the first break roll. The flour produced is sifted out and the residue goes to the second break roll where it is ground so as to remove as much of the endosperm as possible. The residue, after the flour has been removed, goes to the third break roll where further grinding takes place, and the residue this time goes to the fourth break roll whose function should be to clean off any remaining endosperm from the bran. Since the introduction of long-extraction flours a fifth break roll is generally used to ensure a full rate of extraction. The granular product, which is called 'semolina', obtained from these different pairs of rolls is now graded according to size of particle, and (after purification from branny particles by air currents in machines known as purifiers) is conveyed to the final rollers, called 'reduction rolls', where flour is made, each pair of rolls being adjusted to a pressure suitable for the size of semolina. All the flour from the various reduction rolls is sifted through specially woven silks in machines known as centrifugals.

The flour obtained is now mixed, and the different grades can be produced according to the extraction of flour required from wheat. Before the war this was 70 per cent. of its total weight, today it is 80 per cent. Roller-milled flour today is all mixed together and sold as one grade, known as National flour.

The better grades of flour were termed 'Patents', and a 'First Patent' usually consisted of 30-40 per cent. of the total weight of wheat, whilst a second patent would contain between 50 and 60 per cent. Many grades were sold by trade names, and consequently many varieties could be produced containing different percentages.

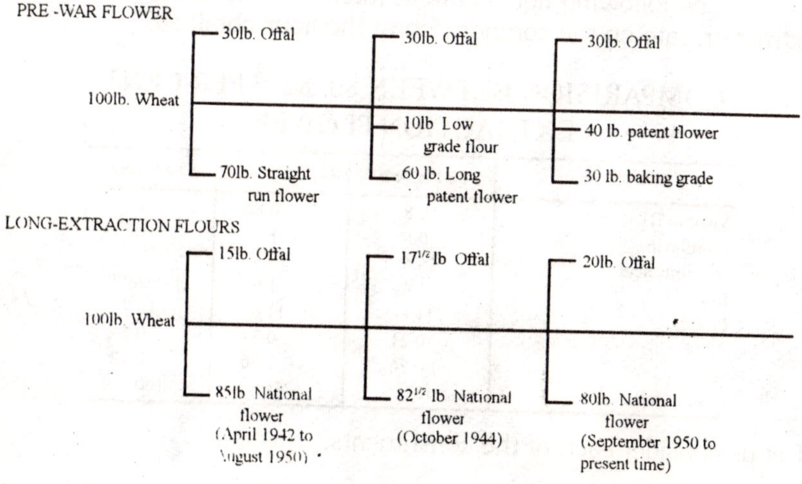

Fig. 4

Constituents of flour. The constituents of flour are as follows: (1) starch; (2) proteins (soluble proteins of the type of albumin and gliadin; insoluble proteins such as gluten in, one of the main constituents of gluten); (3) oil or fat; (4) sugar; (5) mineral salts; (6) moisture; (7) small amounts of cellulose.

The balance of these constituents is of importance when using flour for breadmaking purposes, because slight variations are associated with important differences in the quality or physical nature of the flour.

Typical analyses of flour can be obtained, and, speaking generally, for breadmaking purposes a flour should have about the following composition when of 73 per cent. extraction.

	per cent.
Gluten forming protein	11
Starch	69
Sugar	2.5
Soluble proteins	1
Fat	1
Mineral salts (or ash)	5.5
Moisture	5
Vitamin B-1	0.3 I.U. per g.

The following figures are of interest to show the influence of extraction rate on the composition of the flour obtained.

COMPARISION BETWEEN 80, 82 1/2 PER CENT EXTRACTION FLOWER

	80 Per cent.	821/2 Per cent.	85 Per cent
Vitamin B1	0.8	0.88	0.95
Riboflavin	0.8	1	1.3
Nicotinic acid	16.5	18	17
Iron	1.62	1.95	2.07
Protein	11.8	11.6	10.7
Fibre.	0.21	0.31	0.5
Ash	0.76	0.90	0.98
Colour index	13	41	100

Let us consider each of the constituents.

Starch. Starch of any kind is a coarse, white powder when examined with the naked eye, the degree of coarseness depending on the process of milling. Under the microscope, however, it is found to possess a definite structure, each different kind of starch possessing a structure, all itsown. Wheat starch is seen to consist of a number of concentric rings, the outer ring being very dark with a lighter zone round it, shading off to a dark grey in the centre.

In the milling of flour the particles can be ground to almost any size. In the production of special flours for cake-making purposes, much finer grinding is employed than for normal breadmaking flours. With such fineness in conjunction with a suitable acidity greater absorption is obtained when the flour is used in a cake-batter medium.

Wheat starch in common with other starches is gelatinized when heated with water. The ease with which this takes place depends on the type of wheat from which it is obtained. For instance, the starch from durum wheat is more easily gelatinized and also attacked by the enzyme diastase than that from Monitoba wheat.

Wheat starch will commence to gelantinize and swell at a temperature of 140°F., and at 158°a a good starch paste can be made.

As the temperature of baking is so much higher than this, the question is sometimes asked, Why does not the starch in a loaf galentinize completely during baking? The answer is, (a) the internal temperature of a loaf does not reach210°F. until the final stages of baking, (b) there is only a limited amount of water present sufficient to bring about a partial swelling, and (c) the time available is insufficient.

Proteins. The proteins in flour may be divided into four groups: (1) those which are soluble in cold water; (2) those soluble in a salt solution; (3) those which are soluble 75% in alcohol (4) those which are soluble in any of these solvents.

Soluble proteins. There are two substances which are typical-albumin, which is soluble in water, and globulin, soluble in a salt solution. There are also substances of a slightly more simple structure and composition called proteoses and peptones, which are utilized by the yeast as food.

Insoluble proteins. These constitute the substance gluten, which can be washed out from any wheaten dough. Gluten, itself is considered to be composed of gliadin, globulin, and glutenin, along with small amounts of oil, fibre or cellulose, and mineral salts.

Gluten is only formed when water is added to flour and a dough is produced. There have been many theories advanced as to its formation; the only one which has been accepted for a long time is what is termed the Hydration Theory, according to which the change is regarded as a colloidal one; the protein matter, being in a certain form, imbibes or takes up the water and becomes hydrated.

The gluten which can be obtained by washing from a dough is 'wet gluten'. This contains approximately two-thirds of its weight as water.

The amount of gluten obtained from a flour will depend on the nature of the wheats used in the grist from which the flour is milled. It will also depend on the grade of the flour, the higher the grade of flour the lower the percentage of gluten.

The two important proteins of gluten are gliadin and glutenin. It is considered that the gliadin in a gluten confers mellowness and elasticity on it, whilst the gluten in provides the structure. The greater the amount of gliadin, the softer the gluten.

The proteins of wheat -e not distributed uniformly through out the whole grain, as the bran and germ are much richer in proteins than is the endosperm. If the endosperm alone is considered, the centre is not so rich in protein as the outside portions.

Further, the gluten from wheats of the same class do not all posses the same physical characteristic. This is particularly noticed in English, Manitoban, and Australian wheats. Some wheats yield very much better gluten than others, whilst No. 1 Manitobas produce gluten with better gas-retaining properties than any other grade, although the actual quantity may be the same.

3

BREAD MAKING PROCESSES

BREADMAKING processes can be divided into two main classes, the straight-dough process and the sponge-and-dough process. There are many modifications of both of these, but the underlying prnciples remain the same.

Straight doughs. In English breadmaking practice the straight dough reigns supreme. With straight doughs the type of flour to be used is of as great importance as in the sponge-and-dough process used in scotland, for whilst home-milled flours will stand a bulk fermentation of 12 hours, which is generally the maximum time dough is lying in the trough after being made and before being scaled off, most are produced to suit shorter processes.

During a long fermentation the dough softens, and to counteract this softening effect it is always necessary to make the doughs tighter and to use a higher salt content and lower dough temperature. This prevents the dough from working too fast, and ensures that when it is ready for the table it has sufficient elasticity and spring for a bulky loaf to be obtained.

There are some advantages obtained from using long-process doughs: less yeast is used, 3/4-1 lb. per sack being sufficient; less moisture is lost during fermentation and baking than with loaves made by shorter processes, and the bread produced will eat much moister at the end of 24 hours than other bread, because of the different and more complete changes which have taken place in the gluten during fermentation. Further, long processes enable the baker to make up his doughs in the early evening and scale them off first thing in the morning, thus eliminating night work. This effects a great saving in light, fuel, and labour, and in the case of the smaller, baker, he can get his bread out for sale just as erarly as the large bakeries. Short-procress straight doughs are, however, very popular today, because they fit in with modern plant production procedure and, moreover, are under control the whole time, thus enabling a consistent fermentation to be maintained.

Temperatures of dough. It is very necessary to have the correct temperature, for temperature controls fermentation. For doughs which are to stand 10 to 12 hours, the initial temperature should be about 72°-74°F. Heat is produced as fermentation proceeds, which is retained by the dough. As a result, when the dough is ready for scaling the temperature is approximately 78°F., provided the bakehouse temperature is suitable.

Very frequently the temperatures are kept too low in order to prevent the yeast from working too fast and, if the yeast content is in adequate, and under-ripe dough and poor bread results.

There are two ways of calculating dough temperatures:
(1) Double the temperature at which the dough is required and subtract the temperature of the flour, the difference giving the temperature of the water. This is an approximate method but very useful when dough is being made by hand.

Thus, for example: Dough temperature to be 78°F. Flour temperature = 62°F. Temperature of water = 2 x 78°- 62 = 94°F.

(2) **'Major factor' method.** This method takes into account the flour, water, bakehouse temperature, and the heat produced by the machine. The method is that the temperatures of the flour and bakehouse are taken, then that of water which is suitable to produce a dough at 76°F. for a 3-hour dough, for example, with the particular dough machine being used; these temperatures are added together and give the factor. Then, for future working, this factor is always used and the difference in the temperature of the other components, flour or bakehouse, mean a corresponding change in the water temperature. For example, the temperature of the flour may be 64°F. and the bakehouse temperature 67°F. whilst the temperature of the water used was 89°F. If these conditions produce a dough at the right temperature and satisfactory bread

results, then they may be used for finding the fixed factor. Thus we get 64 + 67 + 89 = 220, and so long as a 3-hour process is used this factor is employed. When the flour and bakehouse temperature vary, as they will do in winter, then these are noted, and these two subtracted from the factor 220 give the temperature of the water to be used.

Thus flour temperature is 62°F., bakehouse temperature 58°F., then temperature of water is 220-62-58 = 100°F.

In most bakeries this method of calculating water temperature will be found most satisfactory. There will generally be a different factor for summer and winter conditions, but this will be determined in each bakery.

Sometimes this method does not take into account frictional heat developed by the machine, but it is advisable to do this, so as to simplify procedure for the doughmaker, since most bakeries make dough by machine today. All dough machines have a different heat factor which varies with the mechanical action of the machine and its capacity, i.e. wheather 1/2-1-, or 2 sack capacity. This may be from 4°-10°F., and unless allowance is made for this frictional heat doughs will be produced that are too hot.

Another factor which needs to be understood is heat of hyderation.

This has been found to be related to moisture content of the flour, the lower the moisture content the higher the heat of hydration, as shown below:

Moisture Content	*Heat of hydration (calories per g.)*	*Calculated increase in dough temperature (°F.)*
14	1.5	2.0
13	2.1	2.9
12	2.7	3.7
11	3.5	4.8
8	6.8	9.3

This can be of considerable importance in summer wheather

when flour may dry out if stored in warrm lofts, for some irregularities in dough temperature which occur at such times may be attributed to this factor and not only to irregular temperatures among the flour bags themselves.

A further point of interest is the influence of flour granularity on frictional heat in the dough, particularly when considered in relationship to meals. It will always be found that water for brown doughs should be taken from 2 to 4 degrees cooler than for white dough owing to the extra frictional heat development during the mixing of the coarser meals due to the influence of the branny particles.

With overnite doughs the bakehouse temperatures play a very important part because of the length of time the dough is in contact with it and the consequent heating up or cooling which may result from variations in it. In all bakeries some form of heating system should be used, particularly during winter months. A controlled doughroom temperature will at all times ensure regular fermentation. There is no other way of doing so.

Quantity of yeast for varying times. In practice, however, there are not many doughs made by processes between 5 to 10 hours, because they are difficult to work. An all-night dough has to be made late in the evening in order to be scaled off at 5 a.m. For a 10-hour dough it would be necessary to commence doughmaking, where machinery is used, at 6.30 p.m., and for an 11-hour dough at 5.30 p.m., which times are not so inconvenient. In small businesses this can easily be done, and very good bread can be produced as a result. With any other times the baker's leisure is seriously interfered with and a very early start is necessary.

BREAD MAKING
A FACTORIAL METHOD OF DETERMINING YEAST QUANTITIES FOR VARIOUS LENGTH STRAIGHT-DOUGH PROCESS

Dough time in hours	Quantity of Yeast	Dough Temp. (f.)	Quantity of salt (lb.)	Quantity of liquor (gals.)	Dough time * quantity of yeast
0	9 lb.	88	5	15 1/2-16	9
1	8 lb	84	5	15 1/2-16	8
2	41/2 lb.	80	5	15-151/2	9
3	3-4 lb	76	5	15-151/2	9-12
4	21/4-21/2 lb.	76	5	15-151/2	9-10
5	13/4-2 lb.	76	5	15-151/2	9-10
6	11/2 lb.	76	51/4	141/2-151/5	9
7	11/4 lb.	76	51/4	141/2-151/5	9
8	11/4 lb.	76	51/4	14-15	10
9	1 lb.	75	51/4	14-15	9
10	1 lb.	74	51/4	14-15	10
11	14 oz.	74	51/2	14-141/2	91/2
12	12 oz.	74	51/2	14-141/2	9

The table of yeast quantities has been drawn up from the practical experience of many people, and when examined shows that there is an obvious relationship between the quantity of yeast which is used for a process of breadmaking and the time for which each dough must stand to reach maturity on that process.

This will seem perfectly reasonable to every one who thinks the matter over for himself. There are, however, many people who are always at a loss to know how to determine the amount of yeast to use for an 8-hour process-for example, if at the present time they are using a 3-hour system-and who may have realized there must be some system of calculation but have not heard of it. When the quantity of yeast used is multiplied by the time of the dough it is found that the factor obtained is approximately 9 in all cases. Moreover, this factor 9 gives the maximum quantity of yeast which is advocated per sack of flour for no-time doughs. This is shown above.

During the war a higher salt content became the general practice, viz. 5 oz. per gallon instead of 4 oz. per gallon, and consequently more yeast had to be used and so this factor 9 was arrived at. In pre-war days with white flour, faster-working yeasts, and lower salt content, a factor of 7 was generally used. This, however, is too low for today's practice with National flour, but the white flour of 73 per cent. extraction or less the factor of 7 may be found necessary. For automatic plant work a higher factor is frequently used, and 10.5 is quite general today, whilst 12 is sometimes used.

Small mixings. With smaller batches more yeast is always required, because small doughs, instead of increasing in temperature during fermentation, only hold their own temperature, due to the greater surface exposed to the cooling effect of the bakehouse atmosphere. The factor 12 will be found satisfactory in most cases, but again minor adjustments may be necessary. It must be remembered that this factor is on the sack equivalent basis, so that for all batches the proportion of sack must be taken into consideration before dividing 12 by the lenth of dough time. For batches smaller than 1/2 half-sack use factor 12 on pound sack equivalent basis.

Thus 28 lb. dough = $1\frac{1}{10}$ sack.

For 3 hours : . quantity of yeast = $\frac{12 \text{ lb.}}{12 \times 3} = \frac{2}{5}$ lb.

In practice use 6 oz.

Small adjustments will be necessary according to the type of yeast being used, types of flour, and dough produced. This factor only works with dough at the temperature given in the table, i.e. those most generally used and, further, is only correct as long as the dough temperatured is maintained. For long processes where the bakehouse temperature is not constant, more yeast would be required to allow for the cooling down which would occur in the average bakehouse.

Cold doughs. Much have been written of the value of cold doughs, and many beneficial results have been obtained from their use. There are, however, many people who have never achieved any success because they have had little guidance in the necessary adjusting of yeast quantities for cold doughs. Further, they have not been given much guidance as to the temperature of the cold doughs.

Generally cold doughs refer to those at temperatures below 72°F., whilst those doughs at temperatures between 72°F. and 78°F. should be referred to as cool doughs.

In converting from existing systems of fermentation to cold

doughs between 72°F., then it is necessary to double the amount of yeast which would be used in the table, e.g. 7-hour dough at 76°F. use 2-1/2 lb. yeast per sack. ; 7-hour dough to be at 68%° F. use 2 $\frac{1}{2}$ lb. yeast per sack.

The quantities of yeast must be varied with the type of flour, and with the type of water in the locality. These processes assume the use of 5 lb. of salt with national flour in the short processes for those up to 6 hours in the through, of 5-1/4 lb. of salt with the longer process from 6 to 10 hours, and 5-1/2 lb. of salt for times exeeding 10 hours. More yeast and more salt can be used provided the correct balance is maintained; also more yeast and a lower temperature can be used where colder doughs are preffered. The quantities given refer to short doughs at 80°F. and longer ones at 76°-78°F.

In warm weather it is always advisable to make the doughs 2 degrees colder at least in order to prevent their working too fast, since the bakehouse temperature will affect the speed of fermentation considerably.

Quantity of water. The amount of water used for making a sack of flour into dough varies between 14-1/2 and 16 gallons, depending on the type of flour used and the type of bread being produced. Strong flours will always take more water than soft flours or flours already possesing a high moisture content.

For crusty bread 15 gallons to the sack is the average quantity, since a dough must be produced of such a consistency that it will retain its shape during proofing and also be able in the case of cottage bread to carry without flattening out a superimposed piece, which constitutes the top of the loaf.

For crusty bread, such as coburgs, splits, Danish, Collas, and pan cottage, a softerdough can be used, and for such types of bread 15 to 15-1/2 gallons of water per sack of flour is most suitable with good breadmaking flours.

For tin bread a softer dough still can be used, and with a strong flour 15-1/2 to 16 gallons of water to the sack can be used with ease, whilst with softer flours 15 gallons of water may be be sufficient.

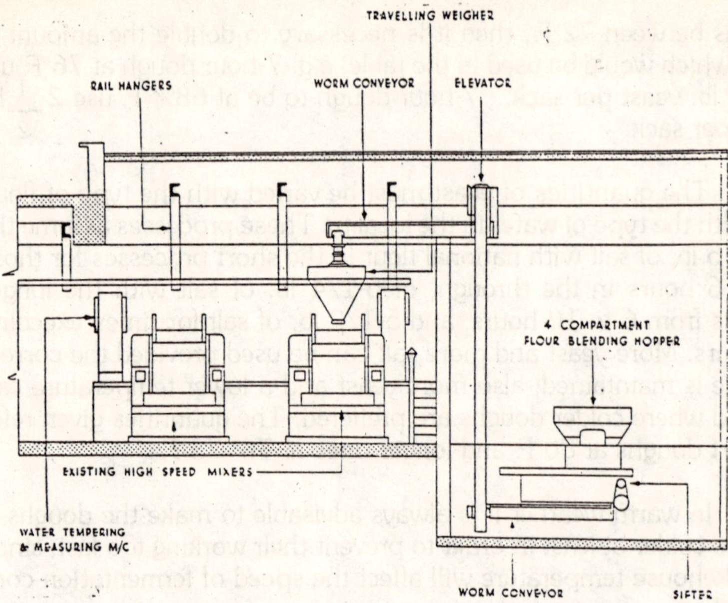

Line drawing showing layout of blender, weigher, and high-speed dough-mixers.

With some strong American flours it is possible to get even greater quantities of water incorporated into the dough with the production of good bread, especially when enriching agents are used.

Necessity for corrrect water absorbtion: keeping qualities of bread. Glutens differ in their capability of holding water, so that each particular type of flour requires special consideration if the best results are to be obtained. There are very few flours today which give the best types of bread on short processes with 14 gallons of water per sack; with many flours, if this quantity is adhered to, the bread produced rapidly goes dry and stale, becoming exceedingly solid in the crumb, and unpalatable.

Bread made from a dough in which the flour has been afforded suitable water absorption will keep much fresher than bread made from a dough in which this factor has not been considered. If too much water is used,that is, quantities of 17 gallons or more to the sack, the bread produced is very loose in the crumb, being light and fluffy unless the gluten has been treated in a special way. When water in excess of this is used, rapid deterioration takes place. Doughs which are to stand for periods upto 10 hours in the trough should be made tighter, and the time which the dough has to stand must be considered along with the water absorption.

Water absorption is the determining factor for the final consistency of short-process doughs, for they do not soften appreciably during fermentation, and in the case of plant production, adjustments need to be made according to atmospheric conditions, otherwise the dough will stick in the prover pockets and cause trouble.

With long-process doughs, however, considerable softening takes place as the dough ripens, and this must be allowed for. There is a need for more care in this matter even with long-process doughs, since an extra half-gallon of water would make all the difference between good and poor bread in so many cases; and yields must be controlled today to ensure a correct cash return per sack of flour, since all subsidies are based on a yield which is a fairly high average.

Addition of Salt. The quantity of salt as set out in the table given in previous pages, being based on the water absorption, is usually added to the mixer dissolved in some of the liquor. In all modern plants provision is made for this. The salt and yeast should never be placed together in the same liquor, since there is great risk of the salt damaging the yeast by coagulation. The damage which yeasts suffers when brought into contact with salt solutions has been found by the author to be directly proportional to the time of contact rather than concentration of brine alone.

Dry-salt method.Some bakers sift their salt in with their flour, and it was formery the practice for some Vienna bakers to make their doughs without salt, and dust it in afterwards. Satisfactory fermentation occurs if this is done, and should salt be omitted from a dough, it can always be added in this manner with very satisfactory results.

From this old practice has developed the modern technique of the dry-salt method in which the doughs are made without salt, but are not brought to normal development. They are partially mixed, being fully developed, and after they have fermented for two-thirds of total dough-time, the salt is sifted over the top of the dough and the dough is mixed for at least 8 minutes until it is thoroughly cleared. This time of mixing is allowed for in the fermentation time and at the end of the predetermined time the dough is scaled.

This system is usually only worked when open-pan mixers are used, in which the pans are used as fermentation bowls. It can be worked with any open-pan type of machine, but it may involve cutting the dough out of troughs and placing it back in the machine. The advantages obtained from the method justify this extra work, however. These are as follows:

- Better crumb color in the bread.
- Stronger crumb structure due to the toughening action imparted by the mixing in of the salt, and the stabilizing action of the salt on the gluten.
- Better fermentation, since bulk, fermentation proceeds without the action of the salt for two-thirds its total time.
- Better keeping qualities in the bread.

Short-process doughs. These include all doughs which are to stand fermenting in the trough for a period up to 5 hours. Actually short-process work should include only those doughs which stand in the troughs for periods between 1 and 5 hours, since those standing for shorter times are not fermented in the real sense of the word. Gas production is the main feature in such doughs, since few of those compounds which contribute to the flavour of loaf are produced in so short a period of time.

The temperature of the dough from the mixer should not exceed 78°F. for the 3-and 5-hour doughs, whilst 80°-82°F. may be necessary for those standing a shorter time. The use of malt products in quantities not exceeding 1 lb. per sack is sometimes advantageous, since they assist in the ripening. Normally, the temperature of a dough will rise to 82°F. or higher during the first 2 to 3 hours and then will recede until, when the dough is ready for scaling, the temperature is about 80°F. All doughs should be knocked back about 1 hour before scaling.

The 3-hour dough bulk fermentation process is the one employed in most large bakeries since this suits plant procedure, and for tin and crusty bread gives very satisfactory results.

No-time dough process. The principles involved are the use of high temperature and the thorough mixing of the doughs. The dough temperature should be as high as 1-86° F. The usual quantities of ingredients are used with yeast 2-1/2 per cent. of the weight of flour. The temperature should be 88°F. when the dough is turned into the trough: it is then ready to go to the dividing machines or to be divided by hand. All draughts should be excluded during this process, otherwise the dough will be chilled. Whatever. precautions are taken the temperature will drop to 84°.F., but it should never get any lower. The dough should be left to recover from the divider for from 11 to 18 minutes, depending on the type of bread being made; it will then be ready to be moulded into the desired shapes.

The bread now goes to the prover, the temperature of which is most important. It should be at 108°-115°F. and sufficient steam should be admitted to prevent the loaves becoming skinned. Too much steam makes the loaves sticky and, unless it is pan bread, difficult to handle. The proving times varies from 40 to 60 minutes, depending on the amount of yeast used and the temperature of the dough. Overproving should be avoided, otherwise poor bread is obtained. What is known as 'three-quarter proof' gives most satisfactory results.

There should be steam in the oven during baking, since this permitsof a more even expansion of the loaf, but the steam should only be added for the first 11-14 minutes, the time during which the maximum expansion takes place.

Advantages claimed:

- The necessity for relying on individual judgement as to ripeness of a dough is eliminated.
- Variations in the quality of the flour do not affect the process, since gluten quality does not enter to the same extent, softer glutinous flours giving better results.
- High-speed dough-mixing can be utilized without the necessary coolers and blowers, since a high initial dough temperature is actually required.
- The dough is not felled by machinery, since the elastic limit is not reached by fermentation.
- Fermentation losses are reduced, so that greater yield is obtained.
- Bread possesing good cutting qualities is obtained.
- A greater uniformity of products results.
- A short-eating crust is obtained.

Disadvantages:

- The keeping properties of such bread are not always good; a cut surface rapidly goes dry.
- Flavour depends on the use of quantities of milk, malt, fat, and sugar, so that a different type of bread is produced from that to which we are accustomised in this country. When no enriching agents are used the flavour disappears after the first few hours.

This system is most suited to brown bread of all kinds. Most of the proprietary brown breads such as Daren, Hovis, and Vitbe are worked on this system, and wholemeal can equally well be made.

The quantity of yeast used for wholemeal is the same as that used for germ breads, but an addition of 4 oz. of fat or oil to each 14 lb. of meal is advisable, whilst 4 oz. salt must also be used. The water will be about the same for all germ meals.

A slight modification of this process is to allow the dough to ferment for half an hour before scaling. This short fermentation period permits of a lower initial dough temperature used: 80°F. is high enough and allows of such gas production as will confer resiliency on the dough and aid the subsequent moulding by conferring more 'life' on the dough, particularly if the dough is to be machine moulded. The yeast quantities are the same as for no-time doughs.

This half-hour dough system can be employed for white and brown breads, whilst it gives excellent results for Vienna rolls.
Besides the straight-dough process there are two other systems which are used in English breadmaking practice which incorporate the ideas of older systems, but with the advantage that they still constitute short processes. These are sponge-and- dough and ferment-and -dough systems.

Sponge-and-dough systems. Whereas in the past it was customary for the sponge to stand for any period of time from 10 hours upwards, today short-period sponges are made, and these are of a much softer character than the old-fashioned sponges. Thus for a sponge-and-dough process to take 5 hours from start to scaling, the following quantities should be used:

140 lb. flour	2 lb. yeast
10 gallons water	1 lb. malt

This sponge should have a finished temperature of 76°F. and should fermented for 4 hours, at the end of which time the following ingredients should be mixed in:

140 lb. flour	4 lb. salt
5 gallons water	1 lb. malt

This dough should be finished at 80°F. and will stand for 1 hour before scaling. The type of flour used at the second stage may be slightly softer than at the first stage, because of the shorter fermentation. This process has the advantage that with a stronger flour a fuller fermentation can be given at the first stage because of the softness of the dough and the low salt content, whilst it is possible to make adjustments in the second stage if the fermentation has not been completed sufficiently in the first stage. The following advantages are produced by this process:

- The bread posseses a moisture crumb.
- The keeping properties are improved.
- The crumb color is improved.
- A more even oven spring is obtained.

In comparing this formula with the dry-salt method, it will be seen that the main difference between the dry-salt method and the sponge-and-dough is that in the former all the flour has a fuller fermentation without any addition of salt.

Ferment and no-time dough. This method is sometimes employed in an endeavour to poduce bread with better keeping properties and imporved flavour. It is called a ferment-and-dough process because all the liquor is present in the initial stage, whereas in a sponge only part of the liquor is used. This method consists in taking all the liquor, salt, yeast, and yeast food with approximately three-quarters of the flour and mixing these to produce a slack dough which will stand for a predetermined time. At the end of this period the remainder of the flour is worked in and the dough can then be scaled off immediately, or it may be left for 15 to 30 minutes, depending on such details as temperatures, yeast qualities, and the time to be given for the first proof.

With this process softer flours can be used for the final doughing stage. The following quantities would be used for a one-sack mixing to stand 4 hours before the final addition of flour:

210 lb. flour	.5 lb. salt
15 gallons water	1 lb. malt
2-1/2 lb. yeast	

Finished temperature 78°F. At the end of 4 hours, 70 lb. of flour are mixed in. If this flour has been standing at the dough-room temperature, the heat of the finished dough should be 78°F.

Both of these processes are only particiable when there are open moveable pan machines where the pans will be used as fermenting vessels.

For a two-stage process the dry-salt method is the one which commends itself most today, because although it is a two-stage process, there is only the salt to add at the second stage, and greater regularity of fermentation can be obtained by this method than with any of the others.

Barms. The use of barms has practically disappeared in english breadmaking, but it is still retained in many Scotch bakeries and on ships. The 'compound barm' found more favour in England than elsewhere, and can be made as follows:

Compound barm. Preparation. 2 or 3 oz. of hops are boiled in 5 gallons of water for 50 minutes and the liquor than cooled to 170°F.; 14 lb. of crushed malt is then added and the liquor kept at a temperature of 140°-150°F. for 4 hours. The liquor is now strained from the grain, and then stocked with barm, 3 pints from a previous batch being generally used. The barm is now kept at a temperature of 74°F. in summer and 80°F. in winter. If the barm has to be kept for a day or two, then salt should be added, 1/4 lb. being sufficient. As the barm ferments the temperature rises owing to the activity of the yeast cells, so that precautions have to be taken to control it. In cold weather it is very necessary to see that the temperature does not drop, otherwise acid fermentation will take place. During fermentation the amount of yeast increases and a foam is formed, but as it proceeds the liquid becomes less dense owing to the formation of alcohol, so that the yeast commences to sink, and as less gas is produced the liquid becomes clear. A slight scum is always produced, and when a clearness begins to show through, it is a sign of readiness. Barm generally takes at least 20 hours before it is ready.

In using the barms, the whole should be stirred well and all of it used for beadmaking, since the liquor has a ripening and softening effect on the dough, most probably due to the presence of the alcohol formed during the fermentation, and the acid produced by oxidation of the alcohol.

It is not advisable to use barms unless it is very difficult matter to obtain distillers' yeast, since great care must be exercised in their production, and then only on long processes.

Quantity to use. For a straight dough which is to lie from 8 to 10 hours from 3 to 4 quarts of barm should be used with the dough made at 78°F. The dough works very slowly for the first few hours, but after 3 or 4 hours it comes along very well, though the bread produced is not bulky. The flavour, however, is good. Barm cannot be satisfactorily for a short process since the quantity required to bring the dough along satisfactorily confers a charactersitic flavour on the bread, although the volume is fairly good and the bread moist.

Flour barms. Flour is frequently an ingredient of barms, but those containing flour are generally called 'Parisian' or 'Virgin' barms. They are used in Scotland. The ideas of bakers differ on the subject of the proportion of crushed malt that should be allowed to a gallon of water, but a fair proportion is 2-1/2 lb. For a small quantity of Parisian barm takes as follows: 2 gallons of water at 160°F.; put this in a wooden tub which has been warmed with hot water and then stir it into this 7 lb. of roughly crushed malt. Now cover it up and allow this mash to lie for at least 3 hours. It is very important that the temperature is maintained during this period. At the end of this time run off this liquor through a sieve, pressing the grains to get the maximum amount of liquor. To this 'wort' add sufficient very hot water to make the liquor upto 2 gallons at a temperature of 126°F. When large quantities are made it is frequently the custom to use less water for the mash so that more can be used with the wort.

Having obtained 2 gallons of wort at 126°F.. stir in about 30 lb. of flour, and have ready a supply of boiling water. Now add this, a gallon at a time, until 4 gallons have been added (sometimes more will be necessary), stirring all the time vigorously with a stout stick. The batter will thicken at first as the flour begins to scald, but will thin down gradually. The first process is termed 'prepairing the mash', the second is called 'making the scald'.

The scald is now left to cool and during this time the starch is slowly converted to sugar by the diatase of the malt. If artificial cooling was restored to, this change would be retarded. In summer, however, where large quantities are made, cooling coils have to be employed to cool down the scalds after they have lain for several hours. When the scald have cooled down to 80°F. it is stored or stocked with some barm from a previous brewing. The quantity of old barm should be about one-fourth of the liquor used, say 1 gallon in this case. The barm should be left for 3 days, when it will be ready for use. During fermentation this barm behaves like a thin ferment; the bubbles at first are white and opaque, and gradually they become clear, rising high in the tub. The barm should not be touched during fermentation.

When making large quantities great care has to be exercised to prevent the diatase of the malt from being destroyed, and so the last gallon of water is used cold. Temperatures must be watched closely, since the diatase can easily be destroyed by too hot water, whilst it is very necessary that the water should be sufficiently hot to gelantize the starch of the flour in the scald and that of the malt in the mash.

Such barms are used in most Scotch bakeries for making 'household' bread.

Quantity to use. When this barm is used for breadmaking, 1 gallon is generally allowed to a sponge that will make a sack mixing.

Malt extract barm method. This is a method worked out during the Second World War to meet emergency conditions in the event of a failure of yeast supplies. Take:

1 gallon water at 70°F.
1-1/2 lb. malt extract (preferably of low diastatic value)
5 oz. yeast or
1-1/2-2 pints old barm

Mix and allow to stand for 18 hours. This barm is in condition for baking from 18 to 48 hours after making. As with compound barm, the starter should be thoroughly mature, and better results will be obtained if the starter is 48 hours old. use starter in the ratio of one of starter to 4-6 of liquor. Keep sufficient of the barm from each making to start off the next. If dried yeast is used as a first starter, 2-4 oz. should suffice.

For 1-sack dough. Take:

280 lb. National flour	Fat (if used)
4 lb. salt	14-1/2-15 gallons water

Dough temperature: 82°F. Allow to stand 6 hours with a knock back at 2-1/2 hours.

Overnite sponge and morning dough (emergency process):
Take :

280 lb. flour
4 lb. salt
8 oz. yeast
15-16 gallons water, according to nature of flour

Dough temperature 72°F. when kneaded, rising to 80°F. as fermentation proceeds.

The above dough is ready for use as leaven 10 to 14 hours after kneading.

The sack batch as given is sufficient to leaven a further three sacks of National flour. One-third of the sponge is therefore added to:

280 lb. blour
4 lb. salt
15.16 gallons water

This dough may be made at 86°F. and scaled in 2 hours, or the dough may be made at 82°F. and scaled in 3 hours. Final proof for tin bread: about 45 minutes.

It will be observed that 8 oz. of yeast are used to ferment a total of 4 X 280 lb. sacks of flour, 1 sack in the sponge and 3 sacks in subsequent doughs, a yeast rate of 2 oz. per sack.

(4 stone) batch of bread using the above systems :

For those who had a smaller bread out put, details are given of a 56 lb.

14 lb. flour
3. oz. salt
1/2 oz. yeast

6-6 $\frac{1}{2}$ pints water according to nature of flour. Dough termperature when kneaded : 72° F.

In the above small batch it will be observed that the yeast rate is slightly increased, 1/2 oz. yeast to 4 stone of flour being equivalent to 2-1/2 oz. per sack. The final proof time is also increased since the temperature used for final prooving in the smaller bakery is seldom as high as the 90°F. (or higher) normal in an automatic prover.

These recipes have been made as simple as possible and as they stand will give reasonably good bread. But fat, yeast food, or other bread improvers can be added with advantage if they are available. Diastatic malt should not be included at more than 8 oz. per sack, as with National flour and less fermentation than usual the bread will be close and may be difficult to bake out.

Overnight sponge process. Since many small bakers can only maintain their production satisfactorily by the use of overnight methods of of fermentation, of the following process was worked out during the Second World War. It has been extensively used and most satisfactory bread can be produced.

It is based on the principle that the main value of the long fermentation system lies in the ripening and conditioning of the gluten. Gas production is of secondry impotance during the sponge stage, but is required at the final stages of proofing. Therefore a small amount of yeast is used in the sponge and a greater amount in the dough to produce the normal volume in the finished bread.
The method is a sponge-and-dough method.

One-sack mixing (280 lb.)

Overnite Sponge

4 gallons water	3 oz. yeast
70 lb. flour	12 oz. salt

Stand 16 hours (at least). Temperature 70°F.- 74° F.depending on bakery conditions and lenth of time sponge stands.

In the morning this sponge is doughed up with:

11 gallons water	1-1/2-2 lb. yeast
210 lb. flour	4-1/2 lb. salt

Stand 30-50 minutes. Temperature 78°-80°F.

Calculation of water temperature for sponge. Take temperature at which the sponge is to be finished, multiply by 2, and subtract flour temperature.

Example. The sponge to be 70°F. Flour temperature 60°F. the water temperature = 70°x 2 - 60°F. = 80°F.

Sponge method using dried yeast. Dried yeast can be used in an emergency as follows:
For a 1-sack batch
(a) Sponge
100 lb. flour
10 gallons of water
14 oz. yeast
To stand 16 hours. Temperature 70°F.

Note: yeast should be disapersed in some of the water for about an hour before sponge is made.
180 lb. flour
4 lb. salt
5 gallons water
Time to scaling 1-1/2 hours. Temperature 74°F.

The quantity of yeast can be reduced when longer sponge times are needed or for week-end work.

This dough should be handled in the usual way, and will give bread of normal volume in the usual proving time.

Scotch bread systems. These differ radically from the English straight-dough system. Sponging is not general practice today, but the two leading processes are the 'quater'-and 'half'-sponge systems. In these processes barm is used as the fermenting agent, but in the Scotch pan bread, which is made on a straight-dough system, and much of the batch bread, distillers' yeast is largely used today.

The quarter-sponge system consists of three processes. The

quarter-sponge is made up at night and lies about 13 hours as a rule, at the end of which it should have come up and dropped slightly (generally about 1 inch). It is now turned into a 'sponge' tub, which has a capacity of 48 gallons, and water is added, the 'quarter'being well broken down, aftre which salt and flour are added to make a thin sponge. This lies for 1-1/4 hours, and as soon as it commences to settle down it is doughed up. This dough then stands for 1-1/2 hours, being cut back once before being scaled off. This process is used for square batched bread and gives a loaf of fine appearence which can be equalled by no other process.

(a) Quarter-sponge for 1-1/2-sack mixing

28 lb. water	70 lb. flour
10 lb. barm	10 oz. salt
Temperature 80°F.	Time 13 hours

(b) Sponge

160 lb. water	2-1/2 lb. salt
126 lb. flour	
Temperature 78°F.	Time 1-1/4 hours

(c) Dough

20 lb. water	5-1/2 lb. salt
224 lb. flour	
Temperature of 78°F.	Time 1-1/2 hours

Bread produced by these processes has a flavour all its own of quite a pleasant acid nature, while the crumb of the loaf is so soft that it breaks down on the palate in a very pleasing way. For the sponges strong flours are required to withstand the long softening action of fermentation

Advantages of a sponge for breadmaking

- With a small amount of yeast it is possible to do a large amount of work provided there is sufficient time for the yeast to grow in a suitable medium.

- A sponge is in reality a dough, and as it ferments not only is there some reproduction of the yeast, but the character of the gluten is altered and, and from being a stable body, it is changed into an unstable compound by the degradation of the proteins. Considerable amounts of acid are also produced, together with compounds of organic acids and alcohols, which confers a flavour on the bread obtained. As a result of degradation of the proteins and the formation of acid, a sponge, when broken down and made into dough with more flour, salt, and water, ripens more quickly and very thoroughly. The nature of all the gluten is affected without any detrimental effects being produced, unless carelessness is displayed. The bread obtained possesses a softness and silkiness of crumb which can be equalled by no other process.

- A long sponge is much safer to leave overnight than a dough and will give better results as a rule, but such a sponge must be tighter than a short sponge.

- A flying sponge-such as can readily be used as preparatory to straight-dough methods-will not only save time on a short process but will produce a loaf with a moisture crumb, better volume, and better bloom. The disadvantage of a sponge process is that two or three stages are involved-thė making of the sponge and the breaking down of the sponge and the doughmaking; with a sponge, therefore, there is extra scope for mistakes to be made.

The dropping of a sponge must be considered in the same light as the dropping of a ferment, the main difference being the different consistencies of these two. The guiding principles are the same. The toughness of a flour plays a most important part, and for so long sponge processes it is very important to have suitable strong flour

Extra salt is generally used with sponges to prevent acid bacteria from, working, while, when the sponges are made into dough, 1 lb. of sugar is often used in order to provide suitable material for the yeast to ferment and so acid gas production during proving and in the oven.

Flying-sponge systems. Flying sponges are considered a great help in obtaining ripeness on short fermentation systems. The reason for the lack of adoption in many factory bakeriers is that the sponge introduces an extra factor in the control of fermentation which is not always justified by the results obtained. For the most part with scientific control of short processes equally good bread can be made by straight-dough methods as with flying sponges.

The system consists in taking a large proportion of the liquor generally all but 2 gallons of the total liquor-and an equivalent weight of flour, a 25 per cent. reduced yeast content, but no salt or only about 1 lb. per sack.

Such a sponge will stand for a period of 1-1-1/2 hours in the case of a 4-hour dough fermentation system.

A typical formula would be, for a 1-sack dough:

130 lb. water
140 lb. flour
2 lb. yeast
1/2 lb. malt
Sponge temperature 78°F.
Stand 1-1/2 hours

Dough up with
20 lb. water (varying with the type of bread)

140 lb. flour	Finished at 78°F.
4 lb. salt	Stand 2-1/2 hours

A system of breadmaking which has also been advocated for short processes is the use of a flying sponge followed by doughing and the scaling of the dough without any bulk-fermentation dough time.

A formula for such a process is as the follows

140 lb. water	1 lb. invert sugar
100 lb. flour	Sponge finished at 82°F.
4-1/2 lb.. yeast (fast)	Stand 1-3/4 hours

Dough up with
180 lb. flour
4-3/4 lb. salt
2 gallons water at 96°F.
4 lb. milk powder, 1 lb. invert sugar, 5 lb. fat } to be creamed up and added as a paste
Finished dough temperature 76°F.

For such processes a soft blend of flour should be used.

Leaven process. This is one of the oldest methods of breadmaking known and consists in using a piece of dough for the ripening of another batch. When working such a method it is usual to keep back about 30 or 40 lb. of dough at the end of day's working, and after breaking it down in the liquor, as is done with sponging, it is incorporated in a further quantity of flour as the fermenting agent. The volume of the bread produced is small and the crumb close and not very pleasing to eat, owing to the acid produced in such long doughs and the decreasing vitality in the yeast, although good bread can be produced for the first two days. This process is largely used on the Continent for the production of the various types of rye bread and is known as the 'sour dough' system.

The following system was advocated by the Ministry of Food technical experts. This leaven process will produce bread for a month or more if carefully controlled. The bread produced is not good commercial bread but it is palatable food, the only vital point in a case of extreme emergency. The process and the bread must be judged from this stand point.

Starter dough:

15 gallons water	8 oz. yeast
280 lb. flour	4 lb. salt
Dough temperature 72°F.	Time in dough 12 hours.

This dough is lightly mixed and the temperature should rise approximately 10° during the 12 hours.

First day without yeast. In the mornring there are two things to do. The first job is to make a dough for carrying on the fermentation from day to day. This dough lies for 12 hours and is made fairly cool, 72°-74°F., and the details are shown in the left-hand column below (b).

Recipe for leaven (a)	**Recipe for bread (b)**
280 lb. flour	280 lb. flour
15 gallons water	4-1/2-15 gallons water
4 lb. salt	4 lb. salt
140 lb. starter dough	140 lb. starter dough
Dough temperature 72°-74°F.	Dough temperature 82°F.
Dough lightly mixed, kept in a warm place for 12 hours so that the temperatures rises 5°-7°F.	Dough well mixed, and scaled at 3 hours and then proceed as usual, for the dough will be lively and give bread of normal volume

Twelve hours after the leaven is made the process has to be repeated, carrying on the fermentation by using the leaven which was made 12 hours previously in place of the starter dough in the recipe given above.

The fermenting agent for the process is then kept going as long as required, by making up a leaven from the preceding one every 12 hours, and this can conveniently be fitted in at the begining and end of each day's work.

Second day without yeast. The leaven is made up in the morning and evening of the second day, as stated above, and because of the acid which develops, bicarbonate of soda must be used to control it. The doughs for bread should from this day onwards be scaled 1 hour after mixing. The reason for this is that the doughs made with the leaven quickly develop acid and, although soda is included at doughing, it is important to scale the bread doughs after 1 hour, although the dough appears to have made with the very little movement. If the dough is left for two hours it will taste acid. It should be in the oven within 2 to 2-1/2 hours of mixing.

The recipe, then, for bread doughs on the second and all subsequent days is as follows:

280 lb. flour
14-1/2-15 gallons water
4 lb. salt
12 oz. bicarbonate of soda. This must be dissolved in water with salt.
140 lb. leaven

Dough temperature 86°F. Time in dough 1 hour

From this day onwards, in order to make good palatable bread, it is essential to bake it on the oven sole. Tin bread requires a very long proof, and is not satisfactory.

BROWN BREADS

Brown bread in its many varieties has had a greater appeal to the public during the past few years because of the activity of dietitians and propagandists.

Wholemeal breads. Types of meal. There are many varieties of meal on the market, from very fine meals to some which consist entirely of crushed wheat. Today much more attention than ever before is being paid to the production of meals which are likely to produce good-flavoured bread. Both coarse and fine meals find favour, and many meals, enriched with an extra amount of wheat germ, have been marketed.

It is frequently given in recipes that white flour should be mixed with wholemeal, because, with wholemeal alone,it is impossible to obtain volume. If volume alone is required, then wholemeal should not be used; a wheatmeal, which is a fine meal containing a high percentage of ordinary middlings, and white flour should be employed. On the other hand, if volume, crumb stability, and moisture-retaining qualities are desired, the addition of powdered gluten at the rate of 2-1/2 per cent. on the weight of meal will effect a remarkable improvement.

Wholemeal bread should possess the following qualities: (1) good, wheaty flavour; (2) good bloom and pleasing appearance; (3) moist crumb after 24 hours or more; (4) easy to masticate without any irritation in the throat.

Methods for making wholemeal tin breads. 14 lb. wholemeal, 5 oz. salt, 4 oz. yeast, 3 quarts 1-1/2 pints of water (more or less depending on absorbtion of meal). (This can be taken as unit and increased proportionately as required.)

The water for the dough should be taken at such a temperature that the dough when finished will be at 80°F. (78°F. for sack mixings). The dough should be thooughly cleared, should be free and well toughened by mixing, or pinching back if done by hand.

It should ferment for 1 hour, at the end of which time it should be knocked back, and after a further 1/2 hour scaled off, the total time in dough being 1-1/2 hours.

With this amount of yeast the dough will prove quickly and should not be allowed more than 1/2 hour; under-proof is always preferable to over-proof for brown bread.

Bake the bread in an oven at 450°F. allowing 35 minutes for 1-lb. sizes and 50-60 minutes for a 2-lb. loaf. Brown bread is not easy to bake thoroughly, so that a longer time must be allowed than for white bread, otherwise the centre of the loaf will be unbaked.

Reason for shot process. It is important to use a method which will produce the best possible flavour, and for wholemeal bread a short process is necessary, whereas for white bread a long process is desirable.

Wholemeal, consisting of the whole of the bran of wheat, along with the endosperm and germ, contains great amounts of active enzyme matter. As a result of this there are other powerful agencies, besides the yeast, bringing about changes in the dough during fermentation; consequently the ripening is quicker. It is true that if the dough is allowed to stand longer, being knocked back several times, a larger loaf will be obtained with a fine uniform texture; but it will be apt to cut crumbly and will also be devoid of a rich flavour. Long processes, besides producing bread devoid of good flavour, tend to produce sourness.

Many varieties of crusty wholemeals are made, and with these the addition of fat at the rate of 1 oz. to 3-1/2 lb. meal will improve the eating and keeping qualities. The liquor will be reduced, and a suitable formula is:

14 lb. wholemeal	3-1/2 oz. yeast
4 oz. fat	2 oz. sugar
4 oz. salt	3 quarts water

Dough to be finished at 78°F. Fermentation time 1-1/2 hours

Many varieties of wheatmeal breads are now made besides the standard wholemeal loaves and proprietary bread such as Allinson, and in such breads National flour is generally used in the ratio of 3 wholemeal to 1 flour.

GERM BREADS

The best known of this type of bread are Hovis, Daren, and Vitbe. Hovis is prepared by cooking the germ of wheat with salt and mixing this in with National flour in predetermined quantities.

Hovis bread. The method is as follows: 14 lb. of Hovis meal; 4 quarts of water; 4 oz. yeast. Most of the water is taken at 120°F., one pint at 90°F. being kept back in which to break down the yeast.

Some of the flour is added to the water at 120°F. and mixed well for 5 minutes until a rich golden colour is developed. The yeast liquor is now added, together with the remainder of the flour, and made into a soft dough. It is scaled off straight away, moulded, and proved for 30 minutes or more as necessary. It is then baked in a sound oven at 450°F. for the same length of time as wholemeal.

Observations. While this methods gives a loaf with the desired rich golden colour and texture of crumb, with small mixings, the quantity of liquor must be reduced on larger mixings as well as the dough temperature. In practice the dough is made at 80°F. and is allowed to stand for about 1/2 hour, so that some fermentation takes place, which results in a loaf of good volume and even-textured crumb which will keep moist for several days. The golden crumb colour is not quite so good, whilst the flavour is slightly different. That which is normally produced by the no-time dough method is due to the roasted germ, whilst in the fermented loaf this flavour is somewhat modified.

The use of salt is not necessary, as it is included in the meal, although it is sometimes added at the rate of 1/2 lb. per sack, whilst today the addition of fat at the rate of 2 lb. per sack is permissible to assist in the production of a shorter crust for slicing purposes.

Daren bread. The makers recommended: 14 lb. Daren flour; 4-1/2 oz. yeast; 4 quarts of water.

As with Hovis, the best results are obtained with a cooler dough and 1/2 hour's fermentation if a loaf with good keeping qualities is desired. If a longer process of 1-1/2 hours is used, then the yeast should be reduced to 3-1/2 oz.

Vitbe bread. For this germ bread the formula and procedure to be used is the same as for daren bread. A no-time dough produces very satisfactory results with this meal.

For all these breads the special tins supplied by the millers should be used and no addition of flour, meal, or other ingredients outside the given forrmula should be made. In all cases the dough should never be tight but always on the 'free' side.

Turog bread. This is a germ bread but quite different in character from those previously dealt with. The proportion of germ is smaller, and it is roasted at a much higher temperature so that a greater degree of caramelization is attained. This results in a pronounced rich brown colour in the crumb of the bread. No salt is present in this meal. The formula recommended is:

14 lb. meal	2 oz. yeast
4 quarts water	3 oz. salt

The dough should be finished at 80°F. and will stand 2-1/4 hours, knocking back at the end of 1-1/2 hours and again 1/2 hour later. The bread should be given three quarters proof and baked for 35 minutes in a solid oven at 450°F.

Unfermented wholemeal breads. This type of bread finds considerable favour in certain districts. It is generally made of fine wholemeal with which fat and milk are used in order to produce as moist a loaf as possible.

Method:

10 lb. fine wholemeal	4 oz. cream of tartar
10 oz.fat	3-1/2 quarts of milk (atleast)
4 oz. golden syrup or sugar	2 oz. salt
2 oz. bicarbonate of soda	A little black jack

This should be a soft dough and should be handled quickly, being baked under inverted tins. It requires moulding in plenty of flour and a nice extra finish can often be imparted by moulding-in extra coarse meal or crushed wheat. The amount of liquor is considerable because the dough must be free in order to enable the gas produced to give as much lift to the loaf as possible. Fat can be used as an improver in all wholemeal breads, but is especially necessary in this type.

Wholemeal farls. These are extremely popular and can be made as follows:

2 lb. wholemeal
1 lb. white flour } stand for 1 hour at 80°F.
3 pints milk (skim)

Dough up with

2 lb. wholemeal	5 oz. fat
4 oz. baking powder	2 oz. treacle
1-1/4 oz. salt	2 eggs

This is scaled off in 4-lb. pieces and pinned out as a round of scones and cut into four pieces. They should stand 20 minutes before being baked in an oven at 410°F. for 25 minutes.

Variations can be made by substituting crushed wheat in the dough to replace an equal weight of wholemeal. Alternatively fine bran can be used in half this amount.

The mixture of flour and milk is allowed to stand for the given period in order that lactic acid may develop which will aid in the maturing of the gluten in the finished dough. If about 1/8 oz. of yeast is added to the ferment, a much greater quantity of acid is produced and a better finished product results.

Malted breads. There are many malted breads on the market and many kinds can be made, from a lightly malted loaf to a heavily malted one, such as are now sold under proprietary names.
Below is given a recipe of a lightly malted bread. By varying the quantity of malt, different kinds of bread can be produced.

10 lb. fine wholemeal	4 oz. treacle
4 lb. white flour	4 oz. salt
8 oz. malt extract	6 oz. yeast
4 oz. fat	3-1/2 quarts water

This dough should stand for 2 hours at 78°F. and then be scaled off, proved, and baked under inverted tins. It is very necessary that the oven should not be too hot. An oven not above 420°F. is required. The pound-size loaves should stand for 40 minutes in such an oven.

Necessity for careful baking. This bread will contain a lot of sugar since more sugar is produced during fermentation and baking. This sugar has some solvent action on the gluten of the flour with the result that the centre of the loaf is very dense, and if too cold an oven is used a thick outer crust is formed and the penetrates too slowly to the centre and diastasis continues for too long a period.

Consequently, the centre is unbaked, very soft, and sticky, and the bread unfit for sale, since the loaf cannot be cut into slices. On the other hand, too hot an oven causes caramelization of the sugars and some dextrinization, as a result of which, instead of the sweet, malty flavour being produced, a bitter crust results which is not at all pleasing.

Bermaline bread. This is a lightly malted bread, sold under a registered name, the malted meal for which is sold under the name.

The following formula is recommended for making this bread:

	lb.	oz.	lb.
Bermaline meal	14	..	280
Lard	..	$1\frac{1}{2}$	2
Salt	..	4	4
Yeast	..	3-1/2-4	4
Water	..	3/4 gallon	15 gallons
Yield	410 loaves per sack		

Times and temperatures

Temperature of dough 80°F. Time in dough 2-1/2-3 hours
Knock back after 1-1/2 hours and again before weighing off.
Weigh into pieces of 16-1/2 oz. for 14-oz. loaf and mould.
Prove as usual 35-40 Minutes.
Bake in an oven at 450°F. to a rich golden brown.

A very plesing lightly malted loaf can be produced using Daren meal as a base, and the following formula recommended:

8 lb. Daren flour — 1-1/2 oz. yeast
1 gill malt extract — 2 quarts of water
2 oz. oil
Dough finished at 78°F. — Fermentation time 1 hour.

These loaves can be scaled at 13-1/2 oz. and baked under 1-lb. tins in an oven at 400°F. for 35 minutes.

There are many malted flours sold for the use of bakers. One well known bread is Carr's malt bread. This is made from the following formula:

14 lb. meal — 3 oz. yeast — 5-1/2 pints water

The yeast should be broken down in 1 pint of water at 90°F. and the remainder of the water taken at 110°F. The dough must be made stiff and this quantity of water is sufficient. The dough should ferment for 2 hours, being knocked back at the end of 1 hour. The bread should be baked in an oven at 440°F.

Owing to the number of ingredients to be weighted out for malted bread and the variations which occur in flour many proprietary meals have been marketed for use in the production of malted breads, and the following formula can be used:

3-1/2 lb. malted meal	2 oz. yeast
12 oz. sultanas (optional)	1-1/2 pints of water
Dough finished at 80°F.	Fermentation time 1-3/4 hours.
Prove 30 minutes.	Bake in oven at 440°F.

Malted fruit breads. Generally such breads as these contain sulatanas alone, since their flavour blends better with malt than that of any of the other fruits. A recipe which will produce a nice medium malted loaf is as follows:

6 lb. straight-run flour	6 oz. brown sugar
12 oz. dark malt flour	5 oz. yeast
4 oz. malt extract	3 lb. sultanas
1-1/2 oz. salt	1 oz. baking powder
3 oz. fat or oil	3-1/2 pints water
4 oz. treacle	

Dough finished at 82°F. Fermentation time 2 hours.

The loaves should be placed under inverted tins, proved till ready, then baked in an oven at 380°F. for 1 hour for a pound size.

Today the baker is well advised to purchase malted meals prepared specially for this type of bread. There are many such excellent meals on the market, and the methods of making are supplied by each manufacturer.

Procea white bread

Ingredients	Sack mixing	Small mixing
Flour	280 lb.	35 lb.
Procea gluten	40 lb.	5 lb.

Salt	5-1/2 lb.	10 oz.
Yeast (variation of yeast and salt according to local practice) . . .	5 lb.	4 oz.
Good fat or oil	2 lb.	4 oz.
Malt	1 lb.	2 oz.

Water-sufficient to give a slightly slacker dough than for ordinary bread.
Dough temperature 80°F.
Method. Ferment 1-1/2 hours, give a good knock back, and let lie for one hour. Then scale and allow 15 minutes in proof. Mould and tin up. Allow about 45 minutes in final proof, only a little steam is needed. Baking temperature 500°F. Baking time 25 to 30 minutes.
Scaling off weights—18 oz. for 1-lb. loaf.
16 oz. for 14-oz. loaf.
13-1/2 oz. for 12-oz. loaf.

CONVENIENT PLASTIC CLOSURES FOR BREAD BAGS-KWIK LOK LOK JOIN HANDS WITH BIOFOODS

In recent time, customers have not only started demanding quality products at affordable prices but their preference for hygienic, attractive, efficient, easy to open & easy re-close packs which keep the products fresh long time has also grown many folds. He becomes more choosy & critical about these aspects when products are food items. Studies have clearly shown that consumers want food packages that are easy to open and easy to re-close. The modern bottle cap is a prime example. The cap is easily removed and can be used to re-close the bottle, preserving the beverage's effervescence. Reclosability ranks high on the list of consumer food packing requirements. Smaller family units and high food costs lead to slow food consumption creating a greater probability of spoilage if the package cannot be effrcitively reclosed.

Limited shelf life or ready to eat Processed Foods have eniticed the customers to necessarily look for 'Best Before date' the packages of items they purchase for themselves & their family. Mention of 'Best Before Date' has gained so much importance that Ministry of Health & Welfare vide it's notification no. GSR 380 (E) dtd. 25th June'98 had to enact an amendment within the preventation of Food Adulteration Rules 1955 providing **'Best Before Date' mandatory on the packages of various food items including bread.**

Indian bakery industry till recently had no answer to these needs of customers, partially answering to cinsumer need of 'Easy to open and easy to re-close, the industry which is mostly dependent on heat sealing method of bag closing came out with 'Wire ties', 'Tapes' and or "Rubber band" options. Unfortunately these method have not been able to come up to the expectations of the customers for reason given henceforth. Wire ties are prone tocause injuries while tightening it around the bags & they cinfront the consumer of which direction to twist in order to open the package. Re-closing in case of wire ties & rubber band requires repeated twisting while holding the package, a cumbersome task. Tape, once opened, can stick itself or the bag. Some tapes stick so tightly on the bag that is must be torn open, increasing the probability of freshness loss because torn open bags can not be properly re-closed. Also, dirt & other foreign substances collected on tape's adesive are repulsive to customers for use with a food product.

Moreover, with none of these options it would be possible to print 'Best Before Dte' on the packages at the time of packiing the bread.

Looking at the emerging needs of the consumers & statutory requirement of the Government, **Biofoods Private Limited**, manufacturer of **'STAR'** brand **baker's yeast** since 1982 have joined hands with **Kwik Lok** the leaders in Plastic Bag Closing System. The system is a time tested and well established one.

Today the presence of Kwik Lok is seen not only in developed markets of USA, Australia, Newzealand, South Africa, Europe and Japan but also in the Middle East and the developing markets of India and Sri Lanka. In India few national and regional bakeries have already adopted the Kwik Lok bag closing system.

Kwik Lok & Poly bag combination is an example of packaging that meets the customers requirements in the most satisfying manner. **The packages is easy to open & to re-close, thus maintaining the freshness of the product and prevent the premature spoilage.**

The Kwik Lok Bag Closing System consist of Bag Closing equipment/applicator machine & plastic clips/closures. The bag closing machines range from simple hand operated Semi-automatic models (recommended for small bakeries) to high speed, high tech, assembly line units which are fully automatic and **capable to close 110 bags** per minute. The machines are simple to use and adaptable to all type of bagging machines/systems. Clips/closers made of Food-grade polystryleneretain their original shape, insuring convenient reuse as many time as needed.

The system has additional advantage which makes it possible to print "manufacturing date/use by date Best Before Date" on the clips or closures at the time of packaging of bread. This feature ensures imjplementation of 'Best Before Date' provision of the PFA Act. Other information such as price, code, batch no. etc. can also be printed on the closures.

Kwik Lok also offers range of machines which have typical applications in snacks, vegetable, meat, courier, spare parts, milk packing & many other industry.

BUN GOODS

For the production of those goods which come under this heading both the straight-dough and the ferment and dough systems are used.

There are advantages in both methods. If satisfactory results are to accrue, fermentation must be carried out so that ripeness is obtained in the finished dough. This can be obtained in different ways, and for this reason no one process alone is used.

There are, however, points peculiar to each. With straight-dough systems more yeast is used and from the same percentage formulae as for ferment and dough systems the doughs obtained are always softer. In seeking an explanation for this difference the author has studied several factors which may influence the dough characterstics. One explanation seems to be that the acid prroduced during working of a ferment plays its part in stabilizing the dough when made. To test this out, lactic acid has been added to straight doughs to give the same initial dough acidity. Although some slight improvement resulted, the doughs were not of the same consistency as that from using a ferment. Further investigations have shown that a ferment will lose moisture during the period of fermentation at the rate of 1 oz. per quart ferment for each half-hour it stands. By making allowance for this and correcting the acidity, doughs of similar consistency were obtained. These however, did not ferment in quite the same manner, the reason probably being the yeast has gained activity from its working in the thin medium of the ferment.

Setting a ferment. For a ferment the following quantities may be taken as a unit:

1 quart of water at 108°F.	3 oz. of yeast
2 oz. milk powder	8 oz. of flour
2 oz. of sugar	

(This quantity of sugar can be replaced by malt extract if the flour used is stronger than usual. Such an alteration will result in a more through ripening of the dough than would be otherwise obtained.)

The milk powder and sugar should be dissolved in the water by whisking, the yeast is then thoroughly broken down and the flour mixed in so as to produce a clear batter. This is then thoroughly aerated by whisking in order to stimulate the action of the yeast. The ferment should be at a temperature of 90°F. and should be left for not longer than half an hour. The ferment can be worked at the same temperature all the year around, but in the winter it is necessary to warm the dough ingredients, otherwise the finished dough temperature of 82°F. will not be obtained.

Taking the ferment. The old idea, which still holds today, is to let the ferment drop before taking it; this is not only unnecessary, but unwise in some cases. Whether a ferment will drop or not depends on many factors, since some ferments can be left for hours before dropping.

● **Shape of vessel used.** The shape of the vessel in which the ferment is placed must influence the dropping of a ferment. If a sponge bowl is used, a great surface is exposed as the ferment rises, and the curved shape also has a marked effect. It will be seen that the time that the ferment takes to rise before it drops will depend on how long it can keep the 'head' on the ferment as one mass. If, for instance, a tub were used, the surface of the ferment would be relatively small and, morever, the head on the ferment would be prevented from dropping by the straight sides of the tub until a point had been reached when it was absolutely incapable of holding together and retaining the gas any longer. This may take any period from half an hour to several hours.

● **Temperature.** The temperature at which the ferment is made is a factor exerting a considerable influence on the ferment. Yeast works increasingly faster at high temperatures than at a low one within certain limits, bit in doing so it soon becomes exhausted. At a low temperature the yeast works slowly and takes more time to produce gas, but while doing so it retains its vitality. A ferment working at a high temperature will produce gas very quickly and soon drop, while one working at a lower temperature will take a much longer time before it drops, but be in better condition for using in a dough.

● Type of flour. This is a factor of primary importance when dealing with a substance which depends on flour for its body. In the ferment given, the quantity of flour is small, but it is sufficient to provide a medium in which the yeast can work and become acclimatized to the surroundings in which its work must be perfored.

A soft flour with a small amount of gluten of a poor quality will not be able to retain the gas which is produced by the yeast, and so a ferment containing such flour will soon drop.

There are some flours with glutens of a sticky nature that will retain gas for a long time; a ferment made with such a flour will frequently only drop after a blow has been imparted to the vessel.

A fairly strong flour will produce a ferment which will hold the gas produced for a considerable time before breaking and causing the ferment to drop, whilst a strong flour will cause the ferment to drop fairly quickly.

● Milk powder. Most types of milk powders affect the flour of the ferment, rendering the it more elastic and so capable of stretching and retaining the gas for a longer period. It is quite possible for this reason that in a ferment it does affect the time taken for a ferment to drop.

● Quantity of flour used. In the ferment given, 1/2 lb. of flour is used to a quart of liquor. Sometimes 1 lb. is used, and then the time taken for such a ferment to drop is bound to vary, since the consistency is different; the denser the ferment, the longer will it take to drop, because of the greater amount of flour used.

Objects of using a ferment

● One object is to make the yeast capable of doing a large

amount of work by the multiplication of the yeast cells in it.

● Acclimatizing the yeast to the medium in which it is to work, since yeast is affected to some extent by flour and so works best when stimulated by the use of a ferment to commence with.

● A bun dough is very much richer than an ordinary bread dough since it contains considerable amounts of fat or oil, sugar, and fruit. Yeast requires sugar to ferment, but with greater quantities it finds difficulty in working and in ripening the dough. In a bun dough at least 12 oz. of sugar are used to a quart of liquor, which represents a 30 per cent. sugar solution. Yeast works most satisfactorily in a 10 per cent. sugar solution, so that in a dough it finds itself in the presence of a high concentration of sugar and so works slower, unless stimulated by means of ferment.

● Oil or fat has a retarding effect on the yeast. Yeasts works by surface action, absorbing all its food through the cell wall; consequently there might be a tendency for the oil or fat to become emulisified in the dough and to form a thin film round the yeast cell wall. If oil or fat is whisked into a ferment no retarding action is noted, the ferment coming along in the normal time. If the ferment is whisked several times the yeast still works in a normal manner and the dough produced from it ferments in the usual time and produces articles of normal volume. Unless the particles of oil become smaller than the yeast cells it does not seem likely that any clogging action would occur. A ferment stimulates the activity of the yeast, and good, fresh yeast should always be used, in greater quantities than for ordinary bread.

These are the combined forces tending to operate against the yeast, so making it advisable to use the ferment. When taking a ferment, the head need not be knocked down; this should be left until actual doughmaking takes place, when the incorporation of the ingredients with the flour brings about this action.

Time for ferment to stand. It is best to allow the ferment to stand for 20 minutes to half an hour at 90°F., for the yeast will then get a good start in a suitable medium. This time is not sufficient to spoil any ferment.

Straight-dough processes

Straight-dough processes are today extensively used for all types of bun goods, dough time ranging from 40 minutes to 1-1/2 hours. Although the buns produced by this process are attractive in appearance they are not always mellow eating nor do they possess good keeping properties.

The following are suitable mixings for different types of bun goods, in all of which the standard ferment is usec.

Currant buns

Ferment	Dough
1 quart water	4-1/2 lb. flour
2 oz. milk powder	1/2 oz. salt
2 oz. sugar	12 oz. fat or oil
3 oz. yeast	10 oz. sugar
8 oz. flour	1 lb. currants
Color as required	2 oz. peel
	2 eggs

The dough should stand 1-1/2 hours at 80°F., being knocked back once during this time. It should then scaled off in pieces suitable for the divider, moulded, proved in steam, and baked in an oven at 460°F. for 10 minutes.

For hot-cross buns the same recipe can be used with the addition of spice, sultanas, and peel. Liquid spice is very convenient to use since it does not discolor the bun, but it must be used in small quantities.

Currant bread. There are many kind of currant bread, from lightly fruited to more heavily fruited loaves such as are exhibited in the competitions. For general commercial work a lightly fruited loaf finds more favour, and the following recipe gives a nice loaf. Using the standard quart ferment, dough up with either A or B:

A	B
4-1/4 lb. flour	4-1/4 lb. flour
8 oz. fat	8 oz. fat
3/4 oz. salt	1/2 oz. salt

8 oz. sugar	8 oz. sugar
12 oz. currants	2 lb. currants
4 oz. mixed peel	4 oz. mixed peel

The A dough should stand for 1-1/2 hours and the B dough for 2 hours, and then be scaled, moulded into tins, proved in steam, baked in an oven at 460°F., and finally washed over as withdrawn from the oven.

In both the doughs it is best to warm the fruit slightly or it will take up heat from the ferment, producing a cold dough.

Currant tea cakes

Ferment	Dough
1 quart	4-1/4 lb. flour
	3/4 oz. salt
	6 oz. fat
	6 oz. sugar
	2 oz. peel
	8 oz. currants
	2 eggs

The dough should stand 1-1/2 hours and then be scaled off, moulded round, and pinned out to an appropriate size and washed with egg.

When proved they are set in the oven and baked until just set and begining to colour. The tea cakes are all turned with a palette knife, and baking is finished. This gives a flat tea cake with a good glazed surface and pleasing appearance.

Bath buns

Ferment	Dough
1 quart	$4\text{-}\frac{1}{2}$ lb. flour
	$\frac{1}{2}$ oz. salt
	14 oz. fat
	8 oz. sugar

The dough is allowed to stand for 1-1/2 hours, when the following amount of fruit is mixed by tearing it in the dough:

12 oz. sultanas
6 oz. peel
8 oz. sugar-nibs
1 gill eggs

The dough should be now left for 15 minutes to recover from the toughening, then placed in lumps on tins as for rock cakes, when the London Bath bun is desired, or moulded round for the original Bath bun.

The lumps are then proved in a slightly humid prover, and when ready for the oven are egg-washed with a very soft hair brush and few sugar-nibs are placed on each bun. Bake in an oven at 420°F. for 15 minutes. Should the oven be too hot, it is advisable to double-tin, or the sugar-nibs will melt and caramelize.

For a richer bun for better class-trades, butter can be used instead of fat, and a much superior flavour will be obtained.
It is customary, sometimes, to make Bath buns off an ordinary cookie dough: in this case the following quantities are used:

6 lb. of bun dough
12 oz. sultanas
6 oz. peel
8 oz. sugar-nibs
1 grill egg yolks

Work in the same manner as with the recipe given above.

Chelsa buns. The following recipe will give a good quality bun:

Ferment	Dough
1 quart	4-1/2 lb. flour
	8 oz. fat or butter
	8 oz. castor sugar
	1 gill eggs
	1/2 oz. salt

The dough is fermented for 1-1/2 hours and then divided into 2 equal portions. Each piece is taken and pinned out 24 inches square and on each piece are spread:

4 oz. butter or margarine
5 oz. castor or brown sugar
6 oz. currants

Each piece is now folded separately like a single fold for puff paste, and then pinned out at least 36 inches long and 10 inches wide.

The piece is now rolled up as for swis roll, only slight moulding takes place with the rolling. To finish off the roll the edge is wetted and sealed.

The whole roll is now brushed over with oil and then cut into slices 1 inch thick. These pieces are then placed on a baking sheet, spacing each one and each row equally, so that, as they prove, they will produce a square bun. When they are almost touching, bake in an oven at 440°F., and withdrawal wash over with egg and dust with icing sugar.

Where only a small trade is being done, 4 lb. of the ordinary bun dough can be taken, pinned out to this size, and the above amounts spread on it with the exception of the currants.

Sometimes it is more convenient to melt the butter or margarine and brush it over the piece, whilst brown sugar will not only improve the flavour but also the general appearance of the bun. Care must be taken in baking to see that the buns are thoroughly cooked as the centre ones require more than the outside ones, being batched.

STRAIGHT-DOUGH SYSTEM FOR BUNS AND FRUIT BREAD

Currant buns

1 quart of water	12 oz. fat or oil
4-1/2 lb. flour (medium)	3/4 oz. salt
2 oz. milk powder	1 lb. currants
12 oz. sugar	4 oz. yeast (fast)

Dough to be finished at 82°F. Fermentation time 1-1/2 hours.

Yorkshire tea cakes

Wholemeal	Plain
1 quart water	1 quart water
3 lb. wholemeal	4-1/2 lb. flour
1 lb. white flour	2 oz. milk powder
6 oz. fat	1 oz. salt
2 oz. sugar	7 oz. fat (lard)
1-1/4 oz. salt	2 oz. sugar
2 oz. yeast	3 oz. yeast (fast)

Currant
1 quart water
4-1/2 lb. flour
2 oz. milk powder
1 oz. salt
7 oz. fat (lard)
7 oz. sugar
12 oz. currants
2 oz. peel
4 oz. yeast

These doughs should be fermented for 1 hour at 78°F. The tea cakes are generally scaled off at 4 oz., proved with sufficient steam to prevent skinning, and baked in an oven at 460°F.

Ingredients in bun doughs. Sugar. A high sugar content is necessary since such articles possess a degree of sweetness varying with the type of bun being made. When extra sweetness is required such as in Bath and Chelsea buns, the sugar is added at the end of the fermentation period. By doing this a fuller fermentation is obtained with the dough because the sugar content is not unduly heavy at this stage, whilst the sweetning power is not affected by inversion. For Bath buns, sugar-nibs are used as they do not dissolve until they have reached the baking stage in the oven, whereas if other sugars were used they would cause the dough to flow during proving since the stability of the gluten would be affected.

Eggs are an ingredient by no means generally used in bun goods. They are, however, an excellent improver and they improve the dough-handling properties by stabilizing the dough (the lecithin of the egg-yolk being no doubt largely responsible for this). As a result increased volume and boldnes are obtained, and in fruit bread, greatly improved cutting qualities.

A dough containing eggs should always be worked soft and knocked back twice during fermentation, and extra time or yeast is generally necessary.

Fat. The quantity of fat used varies with the richness of the buns. Only the best-quality fats or oils should be used, whilst for special types of buns butter is necessary to confer the desired flavour. For the plainer types of bun, oil may be used since it is so uniformly distributed and produces a silkness of texture not obtained with fats when used in smaller quantities.

Fruit. In many varieties of buns and fruit breads the fruit is fermented in the dough itself, but frequently recipes are given, particularly for exhibition work, where the fruit is worked in afterwards. This is done for two reasons: (a) to minimize the risk of the fruit bursting whilst the dough is being handled and so staining the dough, and (b) to enable the dough to be well fermented without the retarding influence of the fruit.

Commercially, the first method is to be preferred, since if a reliable formula is used the correct degree of ripeness will be obtained, even when the fruit is present in the dough.

Rich fruit bread

4-3/4 lb. flour	10 oz. sugar
1/2 oz. salt	2 oz. milk powder
8 oz. fat	1 quart of water
4 oz. peel	1 gill eggs
1 lb. currants	5 oz. yeast
1 lb. sultanas	

Dough to be finished at 82°F. Fermentation time 2 hours.

These heavily fruited breads find favour in many parts of the country, and sometimes go by the name of doughcakes. They can be made up as a straight dough or by taking a fermented dough and working in the fruit. The loaves should be baked in an oven at 440°F. This temperature is most suitable for such bread, since the amount of sugar in it gives it a tendency to take on too much colour if a hotter oven is used.

If an ordinary bread dough is used for such bread, then, taking 6 lb. of dough, the following quantities of ingredients should be used.

8 oz. fat or margarine	1 lb. sultanas
6 oz. peel	8 oz. sugar
1 lb. currants	Spice optional

These must be well worked and the dough then allowed to prove for an hour. This is necessary since there is less yeast than in the other formula: consequently, unless extra fermentation and proof are given, a badly aerated loaf will result. As the bread is withdrawn from the oven the loaves should be well washed over with a sugar-and-egg wash to give them a bright glaze.

Sultana bread

1 quart water	4 oz. sugar
2 oz. milk powder	2-1/2 oz. yeast
3/4 oz. salt	2 lb. sultanas
8 oz. fat or oil	4-1/4 lb. flour

Finished dough temperature 80°F. Fermentation time 2 hours

Sultana bread of the above type has only a limited appeal and the use of sultanas with a brown flour finds more favour. Thus Hovis sultana bread is quite popular and is made as follows:

5-1/2 lb. Hovis meal	4 oz. sugar
6 oz. fat	2 oz. yeast
6 oz. sugar	3 pints milk and water

Dough temperature 78°F. Fermentation time 1/2 hours

Doughnuts. For doughnuts a Swiss bun or cookie mixing can be successfully used. Great care should always be taken in the frying of the doughnuts and the finishing of it attractive buns are to be result. The following points should be noted:

- The temperature of the fat should not exceed 380°F.
- The best-quality fat should always be used. Hydrogenated shortenings should be used since their smoke point is very much higher than 380°F. Thus there is no objectionable odour while frying.
- After frying the doughnuts should be allowed to cool down before being rolled in sugar or filled with jam. As the doughnuts cool down steam is given off and if they are rolled in sugar immediately on withdrawal from the fat this moistre is absorbed by ther sugar and a wet, sodden coat is formed. This spoils the appreence and also uses a much greater quantity of sugar.
- Doughnuts absorb 3 oz. fat to each dozen during frying.

Bun washes. There are many mixtures used for this purpose, and preparations are now sold which require only the addition of warm water to produce a liquid which can be used as a glaze. One of these which has been examined is nothing more than ordinary powdered glue, and whilst producing a glaze, gives an unpleasent hard surface and bitter flavour to the bun.

The following glazes will give satisfactory results:

- An egg-and-water glaze, consisting of two parts egg to one of water, thoroughly whisked.

- One egg, a gill of water, and 1 oz. of sugar, all thoroughly mixed. This will produce a good gloss, but will be slightly sticky.

- Stock syrup in which 1 oz. of gelatin has ben dissolved will produce a good glaze. Stock syrup alone produces an extremely sticky glaze and should only be used in those districts in which such a glaze is desired.

SPECIAL BREADS AND SMALLS

Milk bread.

140 lb. flour	$3\frac{1}{2}$ lb. fat
2 lb. salt	1 lb. yeast
1lb. sugar	7-3/4 gallons of water
$2\frac{1}{2}$ lb. Milk powder	

This dough should stand for 2-3/4-3 hours, reaching a temperature of 80°F. when finished, and be knocked back at least during this time.

Butter should always be used as the fat in milk if a genuine milk loaf is to be obtained. This, is however, is not possible while butter is rationed.

This same mixing can be used for rich Vienna rolls, but for these the dough should be worked softer, so that if a strong flour is used 8 gallons of water would be required, for the dough must be well toughened.

BREAD MAKING PROCESSES

TABLE 1. TABLE OF QUANTITIES OF VARIETIES OF BUNS

	Flour	Sugar	Oil or fat	cur-rants	Sul-tanas	Peel	Eggs	Butter	Dem-erara sugar	Sugar-nibs	Salt	Yeast
	lb.	oz.	oz.	oz.	oz.	oz.	gills	oz.	oz.	oz.	oz.	oz.
Currant buns												
*(A)	41/4	10	10	16	. .	2	. .	. .	. .	. .	3/4	. .
*(B)	41/4	12	12	16	. .	2	1	. .	. .	. .	1/2	. .
*Tea cakes	41/4	6	6	8	. .	2	1/2	. .	. .	. .	3/4	. .
Current bread	4											
*(1)	41/4	8	8	12	. .	4	. .	. .	. .	. .	3/4	. .
*(2)	43/4	8	8	32	. .	4	. .	. .	. .	. .	1/2	. .
†*Fruit bread	41/2	10	8	16	16	4	1	. .	. .	. .	1/2	5
*Chelsae buns	41/24	8	8	12	. .	. .	1	8	10	. .	1/2	. .
*Bath buns		8	7	. .	12	6	1	7	. .	8	1/2	. .
*Swiss buns	4	8	8	. .	. .	. .	1	. .	. .	. .	1/2	. .
*Doughnuts	4	8	8	. .	. .	. .	1	. .	. .	. .	1/2	. .
*Hot-cross buns	41/4	10	8	16	8	4	1		liquod spice as required (1/4oz.)	. .	1/2	. .
*Cookies	41/2	10	10	. .	. .	. .	2	. .			3/4	. .
†*Bridge rolls	41/4	2	2	. .	. .	. .	. .	. .	. .	. .	3/4	21/2

* Used in conjuction with a standard ferment. † Used in conjuction with a quart of liquar.

Cheese bread. This is a type of bread introduced in America and which found favour over here before the Second World War. Kraft cheese, which is sold specially prepared, is mixed in the dough at doughmaking, and then fermentation proceeds as usual.

The bread produced is rich, has a pleasant flavour of cheese, and will keep moist for a very considerable time owing to the fat that is present. Such bread takes on a good colour the oven, so must be baked at a lower temperature, 380°-400°F. being very suitable.

The following mixture given by the Kraft Cheese Co. gives a very nice eating loaf:

10 lb. flour (white)
2 lb. Kraft baker's cheese
2 oz. salt
4 oz. yeast
5-1/2 pints water
Dough to be finished at 80°F.

The dough is made and left for $1\frac{3}{4}$ hours, being knocked back once during this time. It is then treated in the usual way: generally 14-oz. loaves are made and baked in an oven at about 400°F. for 35 minutes.

A modification using wholemeal flour makes a most attractive loaf using the following formula:

10 lb. wholemeal
2 lb. Kraft baker's cheese
2 oz. salt
4 oz. yeast
5-1/2 pints water
Dough temperature 78°F. Fermentation time 1 hour

Walnut and pecan-nut breads

4-1/4 lb. flour
1 quart water
2 oz. milk powder
12 oz. sugar
10 oz. oil
1 oz. salt
1 lb. pecan-nuts or walnuts
1 lb. sultanas
4 oz. yeast
Dough temperature 80°F. Fermentation time 1-1/2 hours.

A straight-dough process is used.

The walnut halves should be chopped into quarters and the loose chaff used for dusting the moulded loaves. On the top of each moulded piece two walnut halves should be placed. Scale off at 14 oz. and bake under wholemeal tins for 30 minutes in an oven at 400°F.

Pecan-nuts are to be preferred to walnuts since they are less bitter and such a shape and size that render them suitable for cutting in the bread.

Egg and milk bread

4 lb. flour	4 oz. butter
2 oz. milk powder	1 oz. sugar
5 eggs	$1\frac{1}{2}$ lb. water
1 oz. salt	2 oz. yeast

Dough temperature 80°F. Fermentation time 2 hours

This dough should be soft and well toughened. Fresh eggs should be used since they impart a characterstic flavour to the finished loaf. Nine ounces of such a dough will be sufficient under a 1-lb. brown bread tin. It should be baked in an oven at 420°F. for 25 minutes.

Tomato bread

5 lb. flour	2 oz. sugar
$1\frac{1}{2}$ lb. tomato puree	1 oz. salt
2 oz. milk powder	2 oz. yeast
4 oz. fat	34 oz. water

Dough temperature 82°F. Fermentation time 1-1/2 hours.

Scale at 13-1/2 oz. and bake under 1-lb. brown bread tins in an oven at 440°F. for 30 minutes.

HOT-PLATE GOODS

Only those fermented hot-plate goods such as crumpets, muffins, and pikelets can be dealt with in this volume.

Crumpets

9 lb. flour (medium)	$3\frac{1}{2}$ oz. sal
4 oz. yeast	4 quart milk and water (half of each)
1 oz. sugar	

The water is taken about 106°F. and placed in a bowl, the yeast is broken down in it, and the sugar and salt dissolved. The flour is then added until a smooth batter is obtained which should be placed in a prover for 1-1/2 hours or until it has risen and droped. Three gills of water are now added in which $1\frac{1}{2}$ oz. of bicarbonate of soda has been dissolved, and the batter is well stirred. It should then be left for 10 or 15 minutes, when it will be ready for the hot-plate.

While this is going on, hoops are prepared for the plate, greased slightly, and the hot-plate temperature adjusted. The hoops are filled with a ladle to two-thirds their height and when the batter has begun to hole nicely the goods are turned over with a palette knife and left until the top commences to colour.

They are removed to cool and the hoops replaced in position. It will be found that the hoops require greasing after every second or third round, but much time is saved by having a duplicate set. This mixing will give 14 dozen standard-size crumpets.
For successful working the top of the plate must be kept polished, otherwise the crrumpets will stick, and when ladling the batter see that no drops fall on the plate.

Pikelets. These are made in a similar manner, but the batter is thinner, extra water, upto half a pint, being used. They are baked on the plate without hoops, the batter being poured on. When finished they should be 6 inches in diameter.

Muffins. A quick process is very satisfactory for these since the dough must be kept warm all the time or else bad results are obtained. The following recipe gives satisfactory results for small quantities:

$3\frac{1}{2}$ lb. flour $2\frac{1}{2}$ oz. yeast
1 oz. salt 1 quart or more water,
depending on flour
$\frac{1}{2}$ oz. sugar

The yeast is broken down in the liquor, the sugar and salt dissolved, and the flour then added and well tooghened. The dough should be kept in a warm place and, after about $1\frac{1}{4}$ hours, turned out on to a table, scaled off at 3 oz., and moulded round.

The muffins are then proved on warm trays, well dusted with cones so as to prevent sticking; they must be placed well apart during proving, othewise they will touch and so be spoilt.

Whilst the muffins are proving, the hot-plate should be got ready and the hoops set in position so that they will be warm when the muffins are ready to set. When setting, the muffins must be lifted carefully with a scoop so as to conserve all the proof, baked until half-cooked and then turned and baking finished.

A good muffin should be quite square at the edges, of a golden brown colour, and, when broken, be of a nice, light, open texture.

A good, strong flour is required for muffins, otherwise a light, open texture will not be obtained. For crumpets an ordinary high-grade patent home-milled flour will give satisfactory results, but all flours require treating in such a way as to bring out their best qualities. For this kind of work experiments must be carried out with each consignment of flour in order to find out the best mode of treatment, the water absorption, time of fermentation, and baking; when all this has been determined, such flour should be kept for this particular work.

Fermented scones

(1)	(2)
4 lb. flour	$4\frac{1}{2}$ lb. flour
8 oz. sugar	12 oz. sugar
$\frac{1}{2}$ oz. salt	$1\frac{1}{2}$ oz. salt
8 oz. fat	12 oz. fat
3 oz. yeast	3 oz. yeast
1 quart skim milk at 96°F.	6 eggs
	1 quart skim milk at 96°F.

Make up a ferment, using all the milk, 1 oz. sugar, and 1 lb. flour, anrd let it stand for $\frac{1}{2}$ hour. Then dough up with the remainder of the ingredients. At the end of 1 hour knock back the No. 1 dough and $\frac{1}{3}$ hour later scale off at suitable weights. With No. 2 dough it will be found necessary to let it stand $\frac{1}{2}$ hour after the knock back. Pin out and cut into triangular pieces and bake on the hot-plate. For the richer mixing the plate must be cooler, otherwise the scones will take on too much colour before being correctly baked.

Gluten bread. This is a type of bread consumed by people suffering from diabetes, indigestion, or obesity.

Method:

$1\frac{1}{4}$ lb. flour $\frac{1}{2}$ pint water

$1\frac{1}{4}$ oz. salt $\frac{1}{2}$ oz. oil

This is made into a dough and left to stand in water for 1 hour, at the end of which the starch is removed by working the dough well in the hands. The washing waters containing the starch and soluble constituents of the flour can be used for ordinary bread-making. The gluten when washed out, is left in a basin in a cool place for 12 hours at least, during which time it softens to some extent. At the end of this time the gluten is taken and 2 oz. of an English wheat flour are worked into it. The dough obtained is scaled off at 4 oz., moulded round, and then made into batons about 8 inches long. These should be allowed to stand for 15 minutes and then baked in an oven at 440°F. When small quantities are made, a cream-bun pan is the best for baking the batons as it is essential that they should be baked in their own steam in order to obtain an even expansion and attain a maximum volume. An oven at 440°F. is suitable since too hot an oven will cause slight decomposition and produce undesirable odours and flavour in the bread.

A baton of this weight should be about $1\frac{1}{2}$ inches in diameter when finished.

Slimming breads. There is a demand for a type of gluten-enriched bread which may be sold as a dietetic loaf or under proprietary names. The following recipe will produce a satisfactory loaf:

14 lb. white flour 4 oz. salt
2 lb. wet gluten 4 oz. yeast
1 oz. malt extract $\frac{3}{4}$ gall water
4 oz. fat
Dough temperature 80°F. Stand $2\frac{1}{4}$ hours.

From such a dough a voluminous loaf will result. The dough after scaling is treated in the normal manner.

American bread

The following formula produces bread of a somewhat different nature to the ordinary commercial bread, but with a very pleasing and appetizing taste.

For the production of this bread a high-class Canadian or American Spring wheat flour is necesary.

Flour	100	parts	280 lb.
Water	60	,,	17 gallons
Milk powder	1.5	,,	$4\frac{1}{4}$ lb.
Yeast	1.5	,,	$4\frac{1}{4}$,,
Salt	1.75	,,	5 ,,
Malt extract	1	,,	3 ,,
Sugar	2	,,	6 ,,
Oil	2	,,	6 ,,

Dough to be at 78°. when finished. Time of fermentation $2\frac{1}{2}$ hours.

This dough should be throughly mixed for 15 minutes and then should lie for $1\frac{1}{4}$ hours. At the end of this time it should be knocked back again, and finally after a further 45 minutes scaled off. After scaling it should be left 15 minutes to recover and then be moulded into the tins.

Proofing must be carried out carefully so as to maintain a velvet like surface on the loaf. The loaves will stand from 50 minutes to 1 hour's proof and should then possess three-quarter proof. In any case they must be set in the oven on a rising proof and baked throughly.

The temperature should not be above 450°F. or too much colour will be imparted to the crust. The finished loaf should have a golden brown colour.

Rye breads. In many seaport towns there is a demand for rye bread and the following formulae will produce different types. Some people prefer the type made from sour dough while others prefer the Kummelbrott which contains caraway seeds. Short-process doughs are always used because of the active nature of rthe enzymes in rye. Both straight doughs and sponge processes are used.

Wheaten rye bread. Straight-dough formula.

Straight run flour, 65 lb.
White rye flour, 35 lb.
Water (variable), 59-63 lb.
Salt, 2 lb. 6 oz.
Caraway seed (optional), 1 lb.
Yeast, 1 lb. 12 oz.
Yeast food, 4 oz.
Malt extract, 1 lb. 8 oz.
Shortening (optional), 2 lb. 8 oz.

Mixing: low speed, 15-20 minutes
Temperature when mixed: summer 78°F.; winter 81°F.
Consistency on bench: medium firm
Time: 1st knock back, $\frac{3}{4}$ hour; 2nd knock back, 1 $\frac{1}{4}$ hours; to bench, $\frac{3}{4}$ hour.
Total time, 2 $\frac{3}{4}$ hours.

Smaller test mixings can be made from:

1 lb. strong Canadian flour
1 $\frac{1}{2}$ lb. rye (white) flour
$\frac{1}{2}$ lb. sourr dough
$\frac{1}{2}$ oz. treacle
Dough temperature 78°F.
$\frac{1}{4}$ oz. caraway seeds
1 oz. yeast
$\frac{1}{2}$ oz. salt
1 pint $\frac{1}{2}$ gill water
Bulk fermentation 1-1/2 hours.

Glaze the loaves before setting with a rye-flour scald made by scalding 1 $\frac{1}{2}$ oz. rye flour with a pint of boiling water.

Sponge dough forrmula

Sponge

Straight run flour, 10 lb.
White rye flour, 35 lb.
Water (variable), 38-40 lb.
Yeast, 1 lb. 8 oz.
Yeast food, 4 oz.
Malt extract, 1 lb.
Shortening (optional), 2 lb. 8 oz.
Caraway seed (opotional), 1 lb.

Mix sponge 4 minutes high speed.

Dough

Straight run flour, 55 lb.
Water (variable), 20-23 lb.
Salt, 2 lb. 6 oz.
Malt (optional), 12 oz.

Sponge temperature when mixed 77 °F.

Sponge fermenting time $3\frac{1}{2}$ -3 $\frac{3}{4}$ hours.
Dough mixing time 7-8- minutes high speed.
Dough temperature when mixed 80°F.
Dough fermenting time 10 minutes.
Total time, 3 hours 40 minutes to 3 hours 55 minutes.

Sour rye bread. *Straight and sponge dough formule.*

Straight dough formula

Medium rye flour, 10 lb.	Yeast, 1 lob. 6 oz.
White rye flour, 18 lb.	yeast food, 3 oz.
Straight run flour, 65 lb.	Shortening (optional), 1 lb.
Water (variable), 58-60 lb.	Caraway seed (optional), 1 lb.
Salt, 2 lb. 4 oz.	Preparatry sour, 14-15 lb.
Malt extract, 1 lb. 8 oz.	

Mixing: high speed, 8-9 minutes.
Temperature when mixed 79°F.

Time: 1st knock back, 1 hour; 2nd knock back, 1 hour; to bench, $\frac{1}{4}$ flour.
Total time, 2 $\frac{1}{4}$ hours.

Sponge dough formula
sponge

Straight run flour, 8 lb.	Water (variable), 30 lb.
Medium rye flour, 10 lb.	Peparatory sour, 14-15 lb.
White rye flour, 18 lb.	Yeast, 1 lb.

Mix sponge 10 minutes slow speed.
Tempeature 76 °F. Ferment 3-1/2 hours.

Dough

Straight run flour, 57 lb.	Shortening (optional), 2 lb.
Water (variable), 22-24 lb.	Caraway seed (optional), 1 lb.
Salt, 2 lb. 6 oz.	

Mix dough 20 minutes on low speed. Temperature 79°F. Rest 15 minutes. Total time, 3 hours 45 minutes.

The preparatory sou for use in the above formula is made as follows:

Prepapatory sour

Dark rye flour, 7 lb. Yeast, 5 oz.
Water (variable), 7-8 lb. Salt, 1 oz.
Temperature when mixed 78°F. Ferment 12-14 hours.

Retarded dough system. A considerable amount of work has been carried out on a retarded system of fermentation for both rolls, buns, and bread with varying degees of success. In all cases certain fundamental conditions must be observed.

First of all, the refrigerator mustr be designed to bring down the temperature of the mass of dough to about 35°F. as rapidlly as possible in order to retard yeast activity as quickly as possible. Unless this is done, extended proofing will occur and the crumb and texture of the loaf will suffer. Secondly, the humidity of the chamber must be sustained so as to give a relative humidity of 85 per cent.

Thirdly, the temperature of the dough must not exceed 70°F., otherwise the dough pieces will undergo too much proof before reaching the refrigeration cabinet.

Fourthly, the yeast content of the dough must be adjusted so as to ensure adequate volume in the finished goods in the shortest possible time, when the goods are withdrawn after the period retardation, which may be for 12-18 hours or even longer.

Fifthly, the period of bulk fermentation must be adjusted to suit the process, some workers advocate 30 minutes' bulk fermentation using $2\frac{1}{2}$ per cent. of yeast, whilst other workers have used 2 hours' bulk fermentation.

In the case of oven-bottom bread ($1\frac{3}{4}$ lb.) the loaves should be placed in the cabinet as soon as moulded as any proof will cause the dough to flow and produce bread from which the crust tends to break away. With tin bread, upto 20 minutes may be given depending on the dough.

With buns and rolls a similar technique is followed, but in all cases 15-20 minutes' proof can be given provided the bulk dough temperature does not exceed 70 °F.

On withdrawal from the refrigerator after 14-16 hours' retardation the bread or rolls should be transferred to a steam prover, but the temperature should not exceed 85°F. and there should not be excessive amounts of heat, only sufficient to maintain a moist surface.

A slow final proof is essential, otherwise blisters will occur, and it is a good practice to allow the trays of rolls or buns to stand in the bakery and slowly come up to room temperature before transferring them to the steam-press. This will ensure freedom from spots or blisters.

Finally, baking should be carried out in an oven at 440°F. since the retarded dough pieces take on more colour in the oven and the use of higher temperature will cause excessive coloration.

Breads, rolls, andr buns produced by this method possess a good, even texture, free from large gas holes, a mellow eating crumb which is soft and resilient, an attractive rich outside appearence, and a nice short-eating crust.

4

BISCUITS, COOKIES AND CRACKERS

Biscuits, cookies and crackers are important bakery items and are used all-day and are not restricted to any particular time of the day. They have very long shelf-life as they are not prone to distruction by fingers etc. They are quite popular.

BISCUITS

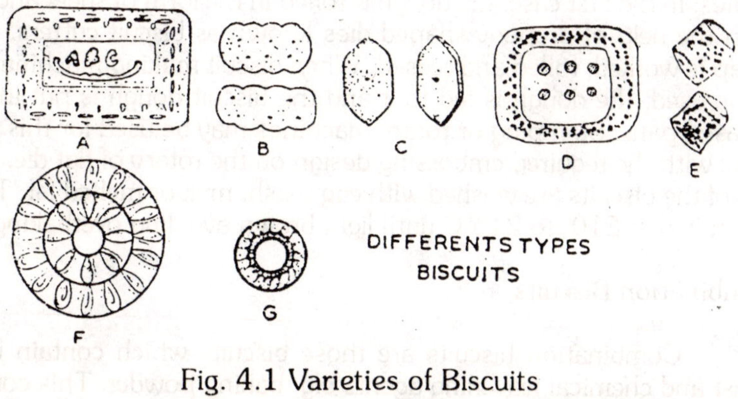

Fig. 4.1 Varieties of Biscuits

Usual ingredients e.g. flour, sugar, salt, milk, shortening and leavening agents are used in making biscuits. Eggs, butter and other ingredients are also sometimes added for variety. They improve quality but raise the cost. Addition of eggs improve volumes, taste and flavor of the biscuits; due to the natural leavening effect of eggs the chemical leavening agents are appropriately reduced. Biscuit doughs are mixed for complete development to get a soft, cake-like interior. The recipes which are richer in fat content, are mixed like a pie crust.

The fat and flour are rubbed together and the dissolved sugar and salt are added with the liquid and folded in very gently. This makes a flaky type of biscuit. These biscuits should be handled carefully because the dough becomes tough very quickly. These biscuits also tend to lose some of their shapes and bake somewhat flatter than others. A typical biscuit recipe is given below:-

Flour	56 parts
Sugar	8
Salt	0.5
Shortening	8
Milk powder	4
Eggs	4
Baking powder	3
Water	32

Sugar, salt, milk powder and shortening are blended into a smooth paste. Eggs are then added and blended well followed by addition of water with stirring. Flour and baking powder are added and mixed to a smooth dough. Biscuits may be made by hand or on machines. In the first case, the dough is rolled in the form of sheet and cut with the help of properly shaped dies known as biscuit cutters. The scrap is worked, rolled and reused. When biscuit making machinery is to be used, the dough is fed to it and the biscuit dough is put in the greased pans. Stamping or rotary machines may be used for this purpose with the required embossing design on the rotary of flat die. The top of the biscuits are washed with egg mash, milk or melted fat. They are baked at 210° to 215°C until light brown avoiding overbaking.

Conbination Biscuits

Combination biscuits are those biscuits which contain both yeast and chemical leavening agents e.g. baking powder. This combination results in a biscuit of lighter texture and grain with a variation in taste and appearence. The dough should be allowed to relax for $\frac{1}{2}$ hr. before makeup thus permitting the yeast to condition the dough. The conditioning time is controlled by the temperature of water or milk. A typical recipe of combination biscuit is given below:

Flou	58 parts
Sugar	10
Salt	1

Milk powder	4
Shortening	8
Eggs	4
Yeast	4
Baking powder	1
Water	32

Sugar Biscuits, salt, milk powder and shortening are blended together to a smooth paste followed by the mixing of eggs and 16 parts water. Flour and baking powder are added with stirring. Yeast dissolved in 16 parts of warm water is added and the dough is developed until smooth. It is kept in a warm and moist place to rise keeping it covered to prevent crust formation. It is rolled and cut in suitable shape of biscuits with a hand cutter, reusing the scrap or moulded with the help of stamping or rotary biscuit machine. The biscuit pieces are placed in greased pans, proofed, washed with egg-wash or melted fat and are baked at 200-210°C.

Cinnamon biscuits are made by rolling the dough in sheet form $\frac{1}{2}$ thick. The sheet is brushed with melted fat and sprinkled with cinnamon sugar. The filled dough is rolled up and brushed with melted fat; and cut into round slices $\frac{3}{4}$ thick. The pieces are put in greased pans, half proofed, egg-washed and baked at 200°C. After this the biscuits are washed with syrup and when mildly warm, iced with simple icing.

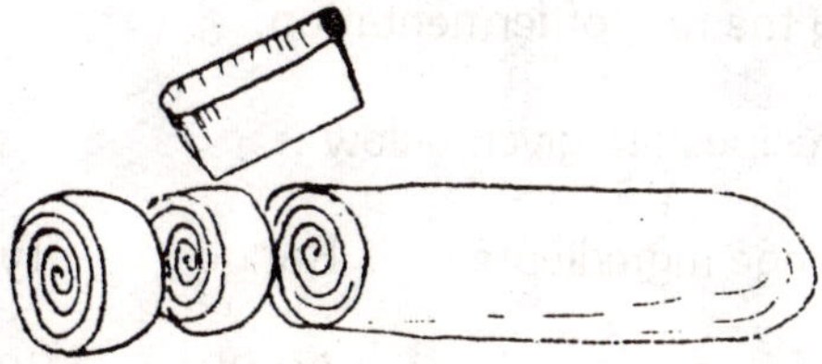

Fig. 63. Cutting of Brushed Rolls with Scraper.

Fig. 4.2 Cinnamon Biscuit

SODA CRACKERS

Soda crackers are cheaper items hence higher quantities of flour and salt are used in these formulations, keeping in view the cost and quality factors.

Ingredients

Soda crackers contain upto 80% or more of flour, hence its quality is. important particularly for texture. Specifications for cracker flours are narrower than those cookies flours. The sponge flour should be stronger, unbleached and with an ash content of 0.39-0.42% and protein content of 8.5-10%. The dough flour should be weaker with 0.4% ash and 8-9% protein content. Strong flours tend to increase oven spring and give tougher crackers while weak flours give lesser spring and tender cracker. Lard gives better flavor and tenderness while vegetable glue has the advantage of improved spring.

Sometimes emulisifiers are added, topping salt is also required apart from the salt in the dough. Salt with special particle size is used for this purpose and about 2.5% of salt based on dough weight is required for topping. Amount of fines in the salt should be minimum. Rapidity of fermentation depends on dough temperature, absorption, quantity of salt, and sugars. Increase in the quantity of water increases the rate of fermentation while higher quantity of salt reduces it. Sugars in the form of corn syrup, sucrose or invert syrup serve as yeast food thus increasing the rate of fermentation.

Soda cracker recipes are given below :-

Sponge ingredients	Range	Typical
Flour	60-80	70 parts
Yeast	0.1-0.5	0.2
Water	23-34	30
Shortening	0.8	4
Diastatic malt	0-0.1	0.002

Dough ingredients

Flour	40-20	30
Shortening	0-10	5.8
Salt	1.3-1.6	1.4

Sodium bicarbonate	0.5-0.7	0.6
Malt syrup	0-1.5	0.9
Water	0-2	0.8

Sponge time is about 16-20 hrs. and fermentation time about 3-5 hrs. at a temperature of about 25-30°C.

All the crackers are made from laminated doughs with the help of automatic laminators when required. At least 6 to 7 layers are preferably put. In contrast to puff pastry no interleaving ingredient is put between the layers; but in the case of cream crackers a mixture of flour and shortening may be put between th dough sheets. Shortening is usually added to the sponge, as this ensures adequate dispersion of the shortening, and if any crust form on the sponge, it gets softer by the shortening. Ever rancidity is also decreased, while fermentation is not appreciably affected by the fat. The amount of sodium bicarbonate in the dough is adjustable depending upon the pH required in the baked crackers.

COOKIES

Cookies are one of the most important bakery items. Various types of cookies are made and the basic principles of their production are being given here:-

Ingredients

As usual sugar, salt, flour, shortening, milk solids, eggs, leavening agents and cocoa and flavors are the basic ingredients for making cookies. Flour, water, milk solids, eggs and cocoa or chocolate products are binding materials and toughers. Water assists in gluten formation; milk solids are not very effective due to low quantities used and egg whites are better binders or toughners than whole eggs. Sugars are most important tenderising materials while shortening leavening agents and egg yolks are less important. Baking acids, oat flour, soy flour act as toughers and ground raisins, ground dates etc. act as tenderisers, corn flour acts as tenderiser but only minor amounts are used otherwise an off-flavor is imported. Starch is a good and cheaper tenderiser.

Flour supplies the continuous structure to the cookies. Strong flours require more shortening and sugar to obtain an acceptable texture. Strong flour gives hard texture and coarse grain and surface appearance. Soft cake flour results in too much spread and loss of design. Cake flour (weak flour) is used in recipes containing egg whites. Wafers are made with egg whites and when yolks are also added, strong flour should be used. If the quantity of flour is reduced too much or when more enriching ingredients are added the cookies, will lack body and will become very fragile. Coarse or fine sugar or their blends may be used in cookies to adjust spread and machining properties. Coarse sugar requires longer mixing period and results in too much spread thereby making the cookies difficult to handle. It also results in more breakage during finishing and handling. Fine sugar produces close, dense grain, mixes quickly but may result in separation of fat from the mix, while bagging out, which will produce greasiness and toughness in the baked product. Sugars and especially syrups in large amounts tend to make the dough sticky and harder release from dies and wires. Invert syrup should be used with care, it makes wire-cuts, especially wafers, soft, light, and spongy with an open texture; the crust color is often brighter and develops earlier in the baking.

Milk solids suppress harsh flavors and are used at 5% of the flour weight. It improves the crust color and gloss. It binds water and makes the dough stiffer and stickier. The toughening effect is quite mild. Most cookies are rich in fat. The bagged out creamed cookies may contain upto 65 to 70% fat based on flour. Fat improves taste, tenderness and keeping qualities when used in increasing qualities. Vegetable glue is usually employed but a mixture with butter is the best. Too much shortening may lead to a greasy, smeary cookie which is susceptible to rancidity because the fat soaks into the package, this necessitates the use of cellphone overwraps. The natural flavor of butter will impart its flavor to the neutrae flauer of the shortening. Ideal amounts of shortening and sugar vary with the kind of method used for cookies, e.g. for cutting machine 15% shortening and sugar variable, rotary machine-30% shortening and 30% sugar, wire-cut-50% sugar and 50% shortening based on flour weight. If amount of shortening is increased too much higher than the indicated amounts then problems arise in the case of rotary and cutting machines.

Use of egg yolks as part of whole eggs will give a tender cookie with excellent eating quality but the grain or internal structure of the cookie may not be as good as with whole eggs. Use of eggs imparts natural flavor, taste and keeping qualities. Egg whites are generally whipped to a wet peak rather than a dry peak when nuts, flour and other ingredients have to be folded into the beater whites. They blend in more easily and avoid overmixing without loss of volume. Salt is added in the formulation of biscuits upto 1% based on flour, in cracker doughs it is based upto 1.5% of flour weight. In the recipes containing nuts etc., or more fat, even higher quantities of salt may be used. Based on fat weight salt may be used upto 3%. Addition of lecithin increases the shortening effect of fats and the tendency for the fat to cover or spread among sugar, flour etc. particles. Lecithin make rich sweet doughs seem drier thus improving their machineability. Particularly it ensures better die release from rotary cutters and improves impression and reduces cripples. Lecithin reduces mixing time thereby improving tenderness by minimising gluten development particularly when strong flour are used.

Formulation Aspects of Different Cookies

One of the most important formulation aspects of cookies is the 'spread'. The cookie should have the desired spread. Too much spread will result in cookie becoming too big for the package while too little spread will result in slack fill in breadth and excess height. Toughners usually decrease spread while tenderisers increase it. Increased amounts of leaveners, use of finer sugar, increased amounts of shortening or water result in greater spread. Spread can be decreased by using stronger flour, increasing the mixing time and using cold water.

Too much salt can reduce spread while increase in the amount of sugar often increases it. When other methods fail, 0.12% pottassium carbonate may be added to increase spread. Increasing the temperature in the first oven zone tends to decrease spread while reducing the temperature spread increases.

The amounts of major ingredients in cookie doughs depend on the method of production employed. In the case of rotary molded cookie doughs 5-15% water, 10-40% shortening, 20-45% sugars and 0-20% syrups may be taken based on flour. In the case of stamping cookie doughs 10-25% water, 5-20% shortening, 15-50% sugars and 0-20% syrups are recommended. In the case of wire cut cookie doughs 10-40% water, 10-50% shortening, 40-85% sugars and 0-20% syrups are recommended. The average amounts of these ingredients are 22.2%, 33.7%, 43.7% and 16.9% respectively based on flour weight. The method of production used influences the texture apart from the affects on formulation.

Deposit cookies are similar to the hand bagged cookies. They contain 35-40% sugar, 65-70% shortening and 15-25% whole eggs. In the case of wire-cut cookies the dough composition is not so narrow. The dough should be quite cohesive, non-sticky and short enough to be separated cleanly after being cut by wire. The dough may contain upto 100% shortening and even more of sugar based on flour. The doughs may be as soft as cake batters or too stiff to be moulded by hand. Wire cut cookies have more open grain and softer texture than the deposited cookies and have more uniform shape; but have less potential for making surface design and less uniformity of size and shape than cookies made by rotary molded cookies.

For rotary molded cookies, the dough should have such a consistency that it feeds uniformly and readily fills all the crevices of the die cavity. The dough blank should be capable of being extracted from the cavity without distortion, but it must be adhere to the die roll long enough to prevent the piece from falling out before it reaches the extraction roller. The blank should not break before or after baking and the finished cookies should have smooth surface. Spread and rise should be controlled so that design does not get distored. Doughs formulated to meet these requirements are usually fairly high in sugar and shortening and low in water. Lecithin at about 0.4% level improves machineability. One stage mixing is quite satisfactory but a creaming operation with most of the minor ingredients added before the flour goes in ensures the freedom from lumps in the cookies. For rotary sandwich bases 20-30°C dough temperature is quite suitable.

Making up of cookies

The dough for making cookies should be properly mixed, otherwise the cookie shall become tough. Proper mixing or creaming of the mix is essential before adding the flour. Short doughs do not require creaming but good blending before adding flour is essential. Flour is folded in gently to avoid development of gluten, otherwise tough cookie will be obtained. In over mixed short doughs the dough becomes tougher to roll and stretches and is not tender. In the case of doughs containing egg whites a dry peak will not permit easy absorption of flour and will result in toughness. Each cookie should be of the same size and evenly spaced on conveyor or greased pans. Pans should be greased evenly and with minimum of fat. Excessive greasing results in too much spread while lack of greasing results in sticking and little spread. Garnishing should be done just after being put on the pans otherwise crust formation will prevent the nuts or fruit pieces from sticking.

Baking

Cookies being small in size require short baking period and lower oven temperature. Cookies containing 35% or less sugar, based on flour, require higher baking temperature than the cookies low in fat and high in sugar content. An oven temperature of 190 to 200°C is quite satisfactory. Special care should be taken in the baking of wafer type cookies and those which are to be rolled and filled after baking. Overbaking will cause them to crack and break while they are being rolled; they should be rolled while slightly warm. The cookies shall be taken out of the oven just before the desired stage of baking, as baking continues outside the oven due to the heat in the cookie and the pan.

Decoration and Finishing

Addition of food color is desirable in the cookie, to supplement the natural color obtained due to baking and caramelisation of the sugar on the surface. Deep colors should be avoided as they affect the flavor and taste by dominating the natural color and flavor. Combination colors and flavors should also be avoided. The cookies should be properly finished. They may be dipped in or decorated with chocolate of the first drying type containing an emulqsifier, and lesser quantity of natural cocoa butter. For sweetening purpose additional 20-25% sugar may be added. Due to the lesser amount of cocoa butter it will not have the defect of graying. It is not as good as natural fine-grade sweet chocolate. Chocolate should be dissolved in a double jacketed vessel taking care not to exceed the temperature of 40°C. Cookies should be given an even and equal dip. Dipping temperature should be carefully controlled as at lower temperature it gets thickened and the coating becomes thick.

When fudge icing is to be applied, the fudge should be warm and should firm up when cool. Fat must be added to those fudge icings which dry quickly and crust too heavily, for this purpose emulsified fat is the best. If jam is not used for sandwiching the cookies, fudge should be used, it is tasty and prevents separation of cookies. A fine grade jam should be used instead of flavored jelly otherwise the product will be ruined. Nut garnish or fruit garnish may be applied on the top of dipped or bagged out cookie. A whole or half nut e.g. cashewnut may be put at the center of the cookie. Variety in the types of nuts and fruit pieces will increase the variety of the cookies.

Production Apects of Different Cookies

In the case of short Dough Cookies the dough is chilled before rolling on a flour dusted canvas cloth. Excessive dusting flour is avoided and the scrap dough is folded into the fresh dough after each rolling of the dough to avoid toughness fron excessive scrap dough. In the case of Bagged-out cookies, the cookies are bagged out evenly in size and shape; even and enough space is allowed for cookies to spread in baking. Cookies are garnished before they dry or develop a crust and if jelly or jam is used they shoud be used in small amounts. For Ice Box cookies the dough is chilled before making various designs, too much color should be avoided and should be evenly blended. The madeup units are frozen before slicing into even thickness with a sharp knife. Cookies are allowed to return to the room temperature before baking.

In the case of coconut Macroons the mix is heated in a double jacketted vessel to avoid scroching, mixing is carefully done to avoid scorching and creation of own or burned spots. The mix is bagged out while warm; if it cools, reheating is required. Marcoon is garnished before drying Macroons are allowed to dry and form a crust before baking on paperlined pans. For chocolate coconut macroons cocoa is blended with sugar before adding it to the egg whites. When making chocolate macroons additional egg whites are added to allow for the absorption of the cocoa. For almond Macroon cookies the paste is blended with a little egg white to remove lumps or dried pieces before adding the sugar. Egg whites are added gradually to ensure proper blending. Canvas bag is moistened with cold water before filling with the mix. Parchment paperlined pans are used and cookies are garnished before they get dried. Cookies are allowed to dry and form a crust before baking. Plain macroons are allowed to dry overnight. Overbaking should be avoided. 3 to 5% of corn syrup based on weight of sugar may be added to the mix to keep the cookies fresh and soft for a longer period. The cookies are washed with a hot glaze just after the removal from the oven.

Sugar Cookies

Following formulation is quite suitable for these cookies:-

Weak flour	64 parts
Sugar	32
Salt	0.5
Milk powder	2
Glucose or corn syrup	2
Eggs	8
Baking powder	2
Water	12

Sugar, salt, milk powder, shortening and syrup are creamed together, followed by creaming in of eggs. Water is added with vanilla. Flour and baking powder are folded in, avoiding overmixing, otherwise the cookies will be tough. Dough is chilled before using. Dough is rolled to 1/4" thickness. Egg wash, water or milk wash is given to the dough. Granulated sugar is sprinkled over it and cookies are cut in the desired size and shape, e.g. round, heart, diamond, square etc. Dough may be left unwashed and cut cookies may be dipped into a pan of sugar. They may be garnished with jam or nuts before baking at 200°C until golden brown. For chocolate sugar cookies 6 parts cocoa is added and flour is reduced by 5-6%. 0.25 part of baking soda is added and baking powder is reduced to 1.5 parts.

Coconut Cookies

Flour	28 parts
Sugar	28
Salt	0.5
MIlk powder	1.5
Shortening	16
Baking soda	0.25
Eggs	6
Water	12
Coconut powder	26
Baking powder	0.25

Sugar, salt, milk-powder, shortening and baking soda are creamed with eggs; water and vanilla and then added followed by coconut powder. Finally flour and baking powder are mixed until smooth. Cookies are bagged out on lightly greased pans and baked at 190°C until golden brown.

Jumble Cookies

Flour	39 parts
Sugar	24
Salt	0.5
Milk powder	2
Glucose	2
Shortening	21
Macroon paste	8
Eggs	19
Water	8
Baking powder	1.5

Macroon paste and 1/6th egg are blended until smooth and then rest of the method is as usual. For chocolate jumbles 5 parts of dark natural cocoa is added to the flour. Flour is reduced to 35 parts. 0.25 baking soda is also added, and baking powder is reduced to 1.25 parts.

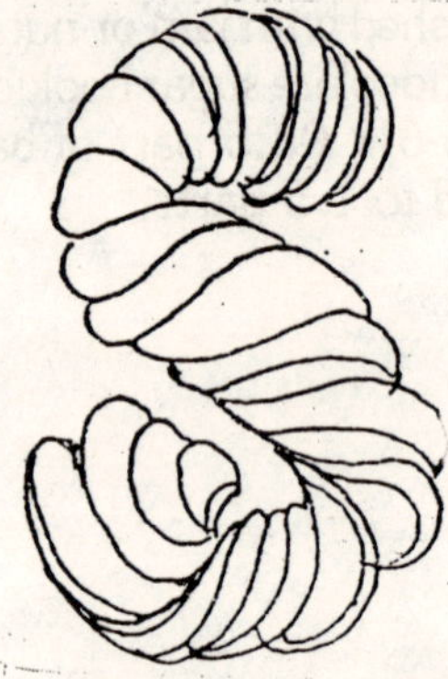

Fig. 4.4 'S' Shaped Jumble

Fig. 4.5 Ring Shape Jumble.

Thus with slight variations in the cookies formulation and method of making different types of cookies may be produced.

Ice Box Cookies

Flour	56
Confectionery sugar	24
Salt	0.5
Shortening	36
Glucose or corn syrup	2
Eggs	10
Vanilla	1

Method of mixing is as usual. All or part of this dough may be colored by blending color in the required amount of dough. Melted chocolate or fudge base is best used for making the dough chocolate. The addition of cocoa causes toughness and cracking when the dough is handled for makeup. Each colored piece of dough is kept separate from the rest. The dough is refrigerated before making up the cookies. Water may be used to adhere different layers of dough but egg whites or regular egg-wash have better adhesive qualities. Before slicing the made up rolls of dough or checkboard shapes it is chilled. Each layer is cut with a sharp knife to even thickness. The cookies are allowed to come to room temperature and are caked at 190°C, avoiding overbaking.

Anise Cookies

The cookies are called anise cookies due to anise flavor. Ground anise is used for this purpose.

Flour	64 parts
Ground anise seed	1
Sugar	64
Salt	0.5
Eggs	48

Eggs, sugar and salt are whipped and to this flour containing ground anise seed is gently folded in. Overmixing is avoided. The bagged out cookies are left overnight to get dried, this also forms a crust which cracks during baking at 190°C. The cookies will have a white crustlike effect and will be slightly brown around the edges.

Spice Drops

Flour	72 parts
Honey	48
Brown sugar	8
Eggs	4
Oil	3
Salt	1
Cinnamon	1
All spice, Ginger, cloves	0.2 each
Water	12
Baking soda	1.5
Ammonium bicarbonate	1.25

Honey, sugar, eggs, oils, salt, spices are mixed until smooth, to this soda dissolved in ammonium bicarbonate is added with good stirring. Finally flour is added and the dough is mixed until smooth. Small amount of molasses may be used in place of some honey. Spices should be carefully weighted and excess should be avoided at all costs. To make the dough easier to handle it may be cooled. The dough is rolled to 1/4" thickness and cut into strips of 1" length. Each piece is rolled into a ball form and put on paper-lined pans about 1" Part. They are baked at 180°C avoiding overbaking. Otherwise they will become hard. The cookies are put in a bowl and hot syrup is poured over them, with gentle stirring, to coat them with syrup. The syrup is made by boiling 100 parts of sugar with 25 parts water at 115°C to a soft ball. Cookies are then placed in a pan filled with confectionery sugar and rolled until coated with it. The sugar may be colored pink or green for variety.

Sugar Wafers

The sugar wafer base cake contains only small amounts of leavening agents e.g. ammonium bicarbonate or soda and the major leavening action is due to steam. Structurally sugar wafer mix is a dehydrated starch gel with a supporting gluten network. The batter is closely confined so that the steam cannot readily escape, thus its leavening effect is much greater than it would be if the thin sheet were exposed to the atmosphere, sugar shortening fillings are used with sugar wafers, as presence of excess moisture will ruin the texture of the base wafer. The wafer batter is a quite thin mixture of flour and water to which small amounts of other ingredients are added. Appropriate amounts of color and flavor are also added. Vanilla is used upto 0.025 to 0.05% as flavor. Chocolate or dark colored wafers sometimes do not contain any cocoa products and are colored with caramel or food dyes. For chocolate flavor about 10% cocoa may be added together with additional 15% water.

Previously enriching agents like milk, sugar and eggs used to be added but they result in carbon deposit on the plates which causes the wafers to stick. Small amount of lecithin and some shortening, e.g. coconut oil, are added to facilitate release of the wafer. Addition of some starch makes the wafer tenderer and improves the texture. General formula for the sugar wafer is given below:

Flour	100 parts
Water	125-150
Sodium bicarbonate	0.2-0.7
Ammonium bicarbonate	0-0.5
Milk powder, skim	0-5
Whole milk powder	0-3
Starch	0-5
Dried egg yolks	1.2-2.5
Salt	0-0.7
Lecithin	0-0.4
Coconut oil	0-2

A typical formulation is given below :

Flour	100 parts
Water	140
Sodium bicarbonate	0.5
Salt	0.5
Lecithin (optional)	0.1
Coconut oil	1

If the flour used is too weak the wafer will have a too dense or too close texture while a too strong flour will result in a hard and flinty wafer. The dry ingredients are first blended and then water is added gradually while mixing, shortening if used, is blended in while the mixture is still of a doughy consistency. If eggs and milk solids are to be used, they are added to the mixer at the start with about half of the water, followed by other dry ingredients and finally the remaining water is added.

Special wafer ovens are used for baking sugar wafers. In these ovens pairs of plates or continuous bands travel with the batter confined between them. The baking time is about 2 minutes. When cream is applied the wafer should contain less than 2% moisture for best strength and crispness.

The basic principles used in making the flat, cream-layered sugar wafer are also used in making ice-cream cones or waffle cones and novelty cream filled shapes such as circles, hemispheres, half cylinders and peanut shell etc. These may be filled with cheese-flavored or other fat based fillings instead of usual sugar-shortening mixture.

BISCUITS

Almond Biscuits

Serves 6-8 minutes
Preparation time 30 minutes

Ingredients

- 2 cups flour
- $1\frac{1}{4}$ cups ground sugar
- 2 tsp. almond essence
- 20 almonds blanched
- warm milk for kneding
- $\frac{3}{4}$ cup butter
- 3 tbsp. ground almonds
- $\frac{1}{2}$ tsp. baking powder

Method

- Sieve flour and baking powder together. Mix ground almonds to it.
- Mix sugar, butter and almond essence nicely in a large bowl mixing bowl.
- Add flour mixture to sugar mixture and knead to a hard dough with warm milk.
- Keep covered in the fridge for $\frac{1}{2}$ hour.
- Knead the dough again and roll out into $\frac{1}{2}$ cm thick sheet.
- Cut round biscuits. Place one almond in the centre of each biscuit.
- Place biscuits in a tray leaving space in between. Prick the biscuits with fork.
- Bake in a preheated oven at 180°C for 15-20 minutes.
- Cool for 2-3 minutes and remove from the tray.
- Cool completely.

Variation

- Instead of almonds you can use cashewnuts.

Chocolate Biscuits
Serves 6-8
Preparation time 30 minutes

Ingredients

2 cups flour
1 cup ground sugar
1 egg
Milk for kneding.
$\frac{3}{4}$ cup butter
2 tbsp. cocoa powder
$\frac{1}{2}$ tsp. baking powder

Method

- Sieve flourr and baking powder together.
- Mix sugar, butter and egg nicely in a large mixing bowl.
- Add flour to egg mixture and knead with milk to a hard dough.
- Divide the dough into two parts.
- Add cocoa powder into one part and leave other as it is.
- Keep the doughs covered for $\frac{1}{2}$ hour in the fridge.
- Knead both the doughs again and roll them out into thin sheets.
- Place one over the other and roll slightly more.
- Cut biscuits of any shape and put in a greased tray leaving space in between. Prick them with fork.
- Cool them in the tray for 2-3 minutes.
- Remove from tray and cool completely.

Variations

- When hot you can sprinkle some sugar over the biscuits.
- You can put some nuts also at the top of biscuits while baking.

Coconut Macaroons
serves 6-8
Preparation time 25 minutes

Ingredients

2 eggs white
1 cup powdered sugar
1 $\frac{1}{4}$ cup desiccated coconut powder

Method

- Beat the egg whites until stiff and peaks form
- Fold-in (mix slowly) sugar and coconut. Mix well.
- Grease a baking tray.
- Put table spoon fulls of mixture on the tray, leaving space in between.
- Bake in a preheated oven at 160°C for 20 minutes.
- Cool for 5 minutes. Remove from the tray and cool completely.
- Store in an airtight container.

Variations

- You can also put a glazed cherry in the centre of each macaroon while baking.

2.Instead of coconut you can use grround almond or ground peanuts also.

Dates Biscuits

Serves 6-8

Preparation time 30 minutes

Ingredients

2 cup flour	1 cup ground sugar
1/2 cup butter	1/2 cup chopped dates
1/2 tsp. baking powder	1/2 cup warm milk

Method

- Sieve flour and baking powder together in a large mixing bowl.
- Mix butter and sugar to flour till nicely mixed. Add chopped dates to it.
- Knead the flour and dates mixture to hard dough with milk.
- Keep covered forr $\frac{1}{2}$ hour in fridge. Knead again.
- Put in a greased tray leaving space in between. Prick them with frok.
- Bake in a preheated oven at 160°C for 15-20 minutes.
- Cool for 3 minutes.
- Remove from tray and cool completely.

Variations

- You can add chopped walnuts along with dates.
- You can put the date's paste between the two rolled layers of dough

and make stuffed biscuits.

Orange cream biscuits
Serves 6-8
Preparation time 40 minutes

Ingredients

2 cups flour	$\frac{1}{2}$ cup butter
1 cup ground sugar	4 tbsp. orange juice
1 tsp. finely grated orange rind	$\frac{1}{2}$ tsp. baking powder
2 tbsp. milk powder	1 tbsp. icing sugar
A few drops of orange colour	1 tsp. butter

Method

- Sieve flour and baking powder together.
- Mix butter, sugar, orange juice and rind in a large mixing bowl.
- Add flour to it and knead to a hard dough.

round biscuits and put in a greased tray. Prick with fork.

- Keep covered in the fridege for $\frac{1}{2}$ hour.
- Knead again & rool out the dough in to $\frac{1}{2}$ Cm. thick sheet
- Bake biscuits in a preheated oven in 180°C for 15-20 minutes.
- Cool for 2-3 minutes and remove from tray. Cool completely.
- Make a hard paste of milk powder, butter, colour and icing sugar.
- Put the paste between two biscuits and press lightly.

Variation

- Instead of orange cream, lemon juice and lemon rind can be used to make lemon cream biscuits.

flour	2 tbsp. butter
1 cup grated cheese	Pinch of soda-bicarb
$\frac{1}{2}$ tsp. salt	2 tbsp. milk for kneding

Method

- Sieve flour, soda bicarb and salt together in a lareg mixing bowl.
- Mix butter and cheese and add flour to it and knead to a hard dough with milk.
- Knead well and keep for $\frac{1}{2}$ hour in the fridge.

- Knead again and roll out is the dough as thin as possible.
- Grease a baking tray. Put a thin pastry in it.
- Mark the cuttings into small squares.
- Bake in a preheated oven at 160°C for 10 minutes.
- Remove from the tray and cool completely.

Potato salties
Serves 6-8
Preparation time 20 minutes

Ingredients

1 cup flour
1 cup boiled arnd mashed pototoes
2 tbsp. butter
2 tbsp. cummin seeds
Pinch of soda bicarb
$\frac{1}{2}$ tsp. salt
Milk for kneding

Method

- Sieve salt, soda bicarb and flour together in a large mixing bowl.
- Crush the cummin seeds slightly
- Mix mashed potatoes, butter and cummin seeds together.
- Knead flour and potatoes mixture into a hard dough with milk.
- Keep in the fridge for $\frac{1}{2}$ hour.
- Knead again and roll out the dough $\frac{1}{2}$ cm thick.
- Cut into desired shape and sprinkle little cummin seeds over the biscuits. Prick the biscuits with frok.
- Grease a baking tray, place biscuits into it and prick with frok.
- Bake in a preheated oven at 180°C for 15-20 minutes.
- Remove from the tray and cool completely.

Variation

- Instead of cummin seeds you can put some sesame seeds over the biscuits.

Jam Biscuits
Serves 6-8
Preparation time 30 minutes

Ingredients

2 cups flour
1 cup ground sugar
$\frac{1}{2}$ tsp. baking powder
$\frac{3}{4}$ cup butter
$\frac{1}{2}$ cup mixed fruit jam
Milk for kneding

Method

- Sieve flour and baking powder together.
- Mix sugar, butter and half of the jam together in a large mixing bowl.
- Add flour to sugar mixture and knead to a hard dough with warm milk.
- Keep covered in fridge for $\frac{1}{2}$ hour.
- Knead again and roll out the dough into $\frac{1}{2}$ cm thick sheet.
- Cut oval shaped biscuits. Prick them with frok.
- Put little jam over the biscuits and put them in greased trays.
- Bake in preheated oven at 180°C for 15-20 minutes.
- Cool for 2-3 minutes and remove from tray.
- Cool completely.

Variation

- You can use strawberry or cherry pulp instead of jam.

Christmas Cookies
Serves 6-8
Preparation time 50 minutes

Ingredients

2 cups flour
1 cup ground suga
1 egg
2 tbsp. grated milk
2 tbsp. chopped sultanas
Milk for kneding
$\frac{3}{4}$ cup butter
$\frac{1}{2}$ tsp. baking powder
1 tsp. vanilla essence
$\frac{1}{2}$ cup mixed peels finely chocolate chopped
2 tbsp. chopped walnuts

Method

- Sieve flour and baking powder together in a large mixing bowl.
- Add chocolate, sultanas, walnuts and peels to flour mixture.
- Beat egg, butter and sugar well. All vanilla essence to it.
- Mix egg mixture with flour mixture and knead to a hard dough with milk.
- Keep covered in the fridge for $\frac{1}{2}$ hour.
- Knead again and roll out the dough 1 cm thick.
- Cut the cookies, place in a greased baking tray and prick with frok.
- Bake in a preheated oven at 180°C for 15-20 minutes. Cool for 2-3 minutes and remove from the tray.
- Cool completely.

Variations

- Instead of walnuts you can add almonds or cashewnuts.
- Instead of mixed peels, chopped glazed cherries can be used.

5

SPONGE CAKES AND ALLIED PRODUCTS

Pounds cakes, Sponge cakes, and chiffon cakes are examples of products based on whole egg foams and containing shortening. They are always much more dense than angel food cakes.

Pound cakes were traditionally based on the very old formula of one pound each of flour, butter, whole eggs, and sugar. Modern formulas have departed considerably from this archetype. Most present-day commercial versions include at least some baking powder though the amount is usually considerably less than in layer cakes so as to retain the relatively dense and firm but tender and somewhat crumbly texture expected in pound cake. Other changes which have occurred in the formula have been decrease in eggs and butter accompanied by the an increase in sugar to give the sweeter, more tender cake acceptable to modern tastes. Very frequently some or all of the butter is replaced by vegetable shortening to decrease the ingredient cost.

An example of a simple modern formula which does not rely on baking powder is :

	Lb.
Cake Flour	25
Shortening, emulsifier type	8
Sugar	28
Salt	1
Milk, liquid whole	12
Eggs, whole	17
Butter	9

Whipping improvers (other than emulsifiers) and acidifying agents are not used. The quality of the eggs has a marked effect on the volume, texture, and flavor of the finished product. Cake flour meeting the usual specifications is satisfactory for pound cake.

The usual procedure for making the batter involves the following steps : (1) Cream the flour, shortening, and butter. (2) Add the sugar, salt, and milk and mix well. (3) Gradually add the eggs, and beat for about 5 min.

There are many modifications of the mixing procedure which have advantages under certain circumstances.

Some minor variations in the formula include the addition of a few percentages of invert sugar syrup or a small amount of glycerire to increase moistness of the crumb, the use of additional yolks or additional whites to secure desired textural improvements, replacement of some of the sugar with corn syrup of high De, use of MSNF and water instead of fresh whole milk, and addition of baking powder. Many flavor variations are possible. Excellent chocolate flavored cakes can be made by replacing a few percentages of the shortening with chocolate liquor or by adding a good grade of cocoa. Marzipan cakes contain 5-8% of almond paste, or combinations of almond paste and kernel paste. Nutmeats can be added alone or in combinations with almond and kernel pastes to give interesting flavor and texture variations. Raisin pound cakes are well-linked in some areas.

Major variations in the formula include:

- The Genoise, a speciality of the french cuisine, calls for melted and clarified butter as the shortening ingredient and requires a complicated mixing technique involving beating of the whites before they are mixed with the yolks and (in separate steps) with the flour and butter. This overrated cake can easily be replaced by pound or sponge layers wherever it is called for as a component of pastries.

- White pound cakes require only egg whites instead of whole eggs, and might be compared to angel food batters to which butter or other shortenings have been added.

- Fruit cakes, with a substantial part of the finished product consisting of nuts and glace fruit. Pound cake formulae are regarded as preferable for this type of cake because the batter is viscous and relatively dense so that the fruit does not sink to the bottom during baking.

Pound cakes can be used as the basis for tortes, petit fours, jelly rolls, lady fingers, and trifles ; but it is more common to use sponge cake for these purposes.

Sponge cakes can be regarded as a part of the continuum which starts with the original formula for pound cake and continues through sponge and chiffon cakes to layer cakes. It is very common to find baking powder or soda and some acidic ingredient in sponge formulae, and the shortening content is less than in pound cake (sometimes none). A formula not containing shortening is given below:

	%
Sugar, granulated	32.1
Whole eggs	20.0
Cake flour	26.5
Milk whole or skim	21.0
Salt	0.4

For maximum volume, the eggs can be beaten separately, the sugar, milk and salt mixed in, and then the flour folded in with minimum agitation. If baking powder is to be used, it should be added in the final stage. Satisfactory results can generally be obtained by a one-stage mixing procedure, employing the wire whip at high speed to aerate the batter.

Many variations are possible. For loaf, sheet, and layer cakes, it is desirable to use substantial amounts of short ening.

Variations in flavors are similar to those suggested for pound cake. Sponge cape batters are well accepted as the basis for jelly rolls, lady fingers, tortes, berry shells, and the like.

Chiffon cakes are similar to angel food cakes in that leavening occurs mainly as the result of whipping the egg whites. In addition to the egg whites, flour, and sugar found in the batters of angel food, chiffon cakes contain egg yolks and added fat, the latter in the form of vegetable oil. Baking powder is often used to assist the oven spring. A typical formula is:

	%
Egg yolks	10.7
Salad oil	10.7
Egg whites	32.0
Salt	0.4
Granulated sugar	16.0
Cake flour	14.0
Powdered sugar	16.0
Cream of tartar	0.2

The egg whites and salt are whipped until they develop a soft foam, then the cream of tartar and sugar are added and beating is continued until a soft peak is obtained. The egg yolks are whipped in separate equipment until thoroughly blended and aerated. The egg yolk and oil mixture is carefully folded into the meringue using minimal agitation. The sugar and flour are sifted together and then folded into the eggs. If baking powder is to be added, it goes in with the flour.

Although chiffon cakes may be used in many of the same combinations suggested for pound and sponge cakes, the greater difficulty of making them and their somewhat coarser and less resilient structure reduces their utilization in these items. Flavoring preferences are similar to sponge cakes, although orange and lemon chiffon cakes seem to be the most common. Chocolate flavored varieties are also well accepted.

The preferred temperature for baking sponge-type cakes is around 350°F. Scaling weight, pan conformation, and batter characteristics will determine the baking time, but as first approximations, allow 40 min. for tube cakes, 20 min. for sheets, and 30 min. for loaves.

PIE CRUSTS

The most important representative of the class of unleavened bakery foods is pie crust. Puff pastry and certain types of cookies are also unleavened in the sense that no chemical or biological leavening agents are included in the formula, although an appreciable volume increase occurs in puff pastry during baking. It is true that some formulae for pie crusts call for small amounts of baking powder, but the conventional and typical recipe omits such as ingredient and it is not required to secure finished products having desirable eating qualities.

Pie crusts are low in moisture and high in fat. The ratio of ingredients together with the method of preparation prevent the formation of a continuous gluten network throughout the dough mass and result in baked products that are more or less friable or flaky. A porous structure such as typifies all leavened bakery products is not desired because pie crusts must support and retain without leakage fillings of moderate viscosity and high moisture content.

Pie crusts are generally divided into three classes based upon their "flakiness." The latter term can be defined loosely as the tendency of the crust to separate into strata or layers when it is broken.. Flaky or long-flake crusts when broken tend to exhibit fracture along different lines at different levels, and to show separation in layers to parallel to the surface. Mealy crusts can be broken in a straight line and show a fracture surface more like that of cookie. Short-flake or flaky-mealy crusts exhibit characteristics intermediate between the two extremes.

The flaky crust is esteemed by connoisseurs and by trade experts, but it shows the abuse of handling more quickly than the mealy type and it posses difficulties in serving. It is also more difficult to process than the mealy type. Mealy crusts can be cut readily, using support fillings adequately, and are not particularly sensitive to processing conditions. Most manufacturers catering to the general public make pies with mealy! type crusts. Home recipes are generally designed to produce flaky crusts, but most packaged mixes yield the mealy variety.

The basic formula for pie crusts requires flour and water for structure formation, shortening to provide the desired textural qualities, and salt to enhace the flavor. Usually sugar is added to ensure adequate coloration. The amount of water used, the kind of shortening, and the method of of mixing are the chief determinants of crust characteristics.

The weakest flour available is suitable for pie crusts. Any factor tending to strengthen the gluten structure is to be avoided. In practice, this means that the flour used in pie crusts should be unbleached with a protein content of 7.0-8.5, ash content of 0.38-0.48 per cent, and a MacMachael viscosimeter reading of 30°-40° (Cook 1953). Struckmann (1956) recommends even narrower limits of 7.0-7.25% for protein, and 32° for viscosity. The flour should be milled from a soft white winter wheat and should be slightly granular. Soft red winter wheats yield somewhat stronger flours which may or may not be satisfactory for the purpose, depending upon how critical the finished requirements sare.

Shortening for pie crust doughs is used at a level of about 70-75% (FWB) in household recipes, about 50-60% in commercial pie crusts, 50% or less in doughs made with liquid shortenings, and as little as 35% in fried pie doughs. The type of shortening determines the amount which must be used. Elling (1952) listed the following shortening values for some common fats:

Totally hydrogenated shortening	100
Partially hydrogenated shortening as generally used in bakeries	110
Partially hydrogenated lard	110
Open-kettle plasticized lard	125
Special grainy type lard	130-135
Oil	150

These shortenings were evaluated by preparing crusts from a uniform recipe, varying only the type and quantity of fat. Woerfel (1959) claims that vegetable oils are generally lower in shortening value than is lard. Lard is frequently called for in household recipes and some prepared mixes include hydrogenated lard from which part of the lard oil has been removed. Lard is also much used commercially and and the tough, fibrous variety is preferred over the soft, grainy type. The former gives a short and tender crust without greasy effect. Emulsifiers should not be used in pie crust shortenings.

Salt is used at levels of from 1.5-4% of the flour weight. It should be dissolved in the absorption water, otherwise its solution may be excessively slow at the temperatures and water concentrations present in pie dough.

Sugar, corn syrup, or dextrose are commonly used in proportions of about 3-8 lb per 100 lb of flour. These amounts give adequate coloration without contributing a sweet taste to the crust. Sometimes the sugars are dispersed in the absorption water along with the salt and the milk solids, if the latter is used. Whey or MSNF can be included for much the same purpose as sugar. That is, the lactose in whey and milk powder contributes to the browning. Spray-dried milk solids are preferred to roller-dried material. Wheat or corn proteins may be added to ensure good machineability of the dough and crispness of the finished product. Propionates are frequently included in the formula at about the 0.2% level to retard mold formation.

The flaky crust is obtained by mixing all of the shortening with all of the flour for a period just sufficient to reduce the shortening to small lumps. The recommended size for the fat pieces varies somewhat according to the authority consulted and the type of shortening employed. Generally all of the ingredients are refrigerated, and in any case the flour and water are brought to 35°-40°F before mixing. The doughs are invariably refrigerated before being rolled and cut in order to keep the shortening particles discrete.

In preparing doughs for mealy crusts, the shortening may be completely dispersed in the dough. Consequently, processing conditions are less critical. It is usually convenient to mix the flour-shortening blend until the fat is completely absorbed and the flour particles are coated. Refrigeration of ingredients and doughs is of no particular value in that case.

Large amounts of scrap dough are generated in the cutting of pie crust circles, and the problem of economically disposing of this scrap is of great concern to pie manufacturers. Most authorities recommend that scrap dough be blended into fresh dough in quantities not exceeding 50% of the total. Use of scrap dough in this manner is essential in most operations, but it does adversely affect texture. Some bakers restrict the use of scrap blends to bottom crusts, while other operators believe that it is more desirable to take advantage of the greater dilution of scrap which is possible when it is blended into both the bottom and the top doughs.

The two steps common to nearly all pie dough mixing proceses are:
(1) blending the shortening and the flour until the fat has reached the desired degree of subdivision, and (2) adding the water and water-soluble ingredients to the fat and shortening mixture and agitating until the water has been absorbed. As stated previously, flaky crusts require a short first stage which leaves the shortening in the form of discrete lumps while mealy crusts are thoroughly mixed during the first stage so that the flour particles are completely coated by the fat. Intermediate types of crusts may be prepared either by reducing the shortening to very small lumps, e.g., about the size of peas, or by a two-stage addition of fat during one stage of which the fat is thoroughly

dispersed while in the other step mixing is carried out only to the point where the fat has been broken down to fairly small uniform particles.

Most processing instructions call for the water to be chilled. Not infrequently the flour is also brought to refrigerator temperatures before use. In addition, the dough itself is usually chilled for several hours after mixing. This cool rest period allows the water to distribute itself more thoroughly in the dough mass and hardens the shortening so that it is less likely to liquefy during subsequent handling and shaping operations. These chilling steps are particularly important in the manufacture of dough for long-flake crusts. Mealy-type doughs should come out of the mixer at about 65°F and be held (covered, of course) at this temperature for about 3-4 hr.

Elling (1952) gives a formula and procedure for making a 221-lb batch of long-flake dough suitable for use during the warm weather months. He indicates that the same formula can be adapted for producing short-flake or mealy crusts if the processing techniques are changed appropriately.

Long-flake Crust

(1) Mix smooth but do not cream:
45lb steam rendered lard
15lb partially hydrogenated vegetable shortening

(2) Add the following ingredients to the above and mix until the fat is in pieces the size of walnuts:
100lb soft pastry flour at refrigerator temperatures
6lb nonfat milk solids

(3) Add the following to the flour, fat, and milk solids and mix just enough to blend thoroughly
38lb ice water
4lb salt
3lb corn sugar

Struckmann (1956) described the production of doughs yielding a short-flake crust suitable for fruit pies.

Fruit Pie Dough

(1) Place in arm-type mixer and blend the following together until the shortening and flour are well incorporated:
100lb flour
25lb margarine or low melting point

(2) Continue to mix the flour and margarine until it attains the

appearance of a coarse streusel with no raw flour spots in evidence, and then add 45lb of lard.

(3) After mixing has reduced the lard to chunks about the size of eggs, add:

4 lb spray skim milk powder
3 lb calt
2 lb corn sugar dissolved in
28 lb ice cold water

(4) Continue the mixing until all of the ingredients are thoroughly dispersed. Stop mixing when the pie dough is dry with no wet spots evident and the shortening is in tiny lumps well distributed throughout the entire batch.

Struckmann also gave a formula and procedure for making a mealy-type crust especially suitable for small individuals pies and custard shells.

Dough for Mealy Crusts

(1) Place in mixer and blend thoroughly:

100lb pie flour
45lb pie flour
20lb margarine or low melting point shortening

(2) When the above is thoroughly mixed and no raw flour spots are visible, add:

3lb spray dried nonfat milk fat
4lb corn sugar, and
3lb salt dissolved in
24lb ice water

(3) Continue to mix until the water has been completely taken up.

Freazier (1947) recommends using 6-1/4 oz. dough for the bottom crust and 5-1/4 oz. for the top crust of 9-inch pies containing 26-28 oz. filling. Crusts for 9-inch cream pies should be scaled at 7 oz. However, Elling (1952) suggested a 6-1/2 oz. scaling weight for both crusts of 9-inch pies and 4-1/2 for both crusts of 8-inch pies. The filled pies are baked 28-32 min at 450°F.

There is a considerable difference of opinion regarding the merits of "washes" for the top crusts of pies. Washes of egg or milk, or combinations of these, result in glossy and relatively dark crusts. Some bakers regard this appearance as highly desirable while others consider it to be somewhat artificial. Struckmann (1956) suggested the application of a spray of skim milk to the top crust of pies just before they enter the oven. This gives a golden brown crust color and a drier and crisper texture. Cook (1953) indicated that some bakers spray the crust with melted shortening to give a flake on the top of the product.

Fried pie crusts present some special problems. The all-important characteristic in this case is structural strength since the crusts of fried pies are not supported by pans during their transportation from the factory to the point of consumption. According to Keathley (1956), the basic formula for fried pie is:

100 lb pastry flour
35 lb vegetable shortening
35 lb water
3 lb salt
4 lb corn sugar

Lard is not recommended for the dough or as the frying fat. Mixing procedures and equipment are similar to those used for baked pies except that fried pie doughs may be mixed a little longer and to a smoother consistency than those used for baked pies. The securing of flakiness is generally not a primary consideration with these products.

Dietrich (1957) has given a specific formula and procedure for fried pie crusts.

Dough for Fried Pies

(1) Blend together thoroughly:
100 lb pie flour
25 lb hydrogenated shortening
100 lb dough scraps from previous production

(2) Blend together the following, and then add to the above:
30 lb water (variable)
2 lb salt

(3) Add and mix until a smooth dough results:
1 lb corn sugar (optional)
3 lb wheat or corn protein
3 oz. mold inhibitor

This dough can be made up of immediately if desired, but holding does not cause it to deteriorate. After mechanical or hand scaling into pieces of desired size, the dough is sheeted by mechanical or other means. Dietrich described some ingenious automatic panning and forming devices for preparing fried pie crusts, but these machines are apparently not available commercially.

About $1\frac{1}{2}$ oz. of dough or 2 oz. of the filling is the recommended scaling weight for fried pie crusts. The pies are fried submerged at a temperature of 375°-380°F for about 3 min and then are thoroughly cooled by forced air before wrapping.

Dietrich described variations in processing of fried pies which yield special characteristics. In one operation, fried pies were dipped into a kettle of constantly boiling water immediately after frying. This set the crust and floated off excess cooking fat. Such pies kept well during the summer months and had a slight gloss. In another variant process, the crusts were made up with high protein spring wheat flour. Then, prior to frying, the pies on the screen were dipped quickly into boiling water and then immediately transferred to the frying fat. Pies prepared by this method had less greasiness of crust than most

Causes of Faults in Pie Crusts

For trouble-shooting crust problems, the following suggestions (Anon. 1958) may be helpful:

- Excessive shrinkage of crusts may be caused by: (a) Not enough shortening. (b) Too much water. (c) Dough worked too much. (d) Flour too strong.

- Crust not flaky. May be caused by: (a) Dough mixed too warm. (b) Shortening too soft. (c) Rubbing flour and lard too much (overmixing).

- Bottom crust soaks too much juice. May be caused by: (a) Insufficient baking. (b) Crust too rich. (c) Oven too cool.

- Tough crusts may be caused by: (a) Flour that is too strong. (b) Overmixing the dough. (c) Use of excess water.

- Soggy crusts may be caused by: (a) Not enough bottom heat. (b) Oven too heat. (c) Using a filling that is too hot.

PUFF PASTRY

Puff pastries, in their conventional form, are not very well adapted to mass production and so are, in the strictest sense, outside the scope of this volume. However, a brief discussion of these foods is included at this point for general information purposes.

The principle underlying the preparation of puff pastry is very similar to that on which the manufacture of true Danish pastry is based. Layers of fat are interleaved between layers of dough so that upon baking a separation of dough strata occurs. However, in Danish pastry yeast leavening action plus the inclusion of auxiliary ingredients result in a relatively soft and porous structure in the baked dough layers. In the preparation of both of these products the main precaution to be observed is the maintenance of cool doughs so that the shortening will not melt and then be incorporated into the crumb.

A traditional method of preparing puff pastry dough is illustrated by the following method and procedure.

Dough for Puff Pastry

(1) Mix the dough consisting of:

5lb bread flour or a mixture of 8 parts bread flour and 2 parts pastry flour.

$2\frac{1}{2}$ oz. salt
$2\frac{1}{2}$ lb special puff paste shortening
1lb water

(2) Roll the dough out into a rectangular shape and place it in the refrigerator. After the dough has cooled down, sheet it out to one-third inch in thickness, retain the rectangular shape as much as possible.

(3) Spread $2\frac{1}{2}$ lb of puff pastry shortening over $\frac{2}{3}$ of the sheet and fold it over so that three layers of dough are separated by two layers of shortening. Roll the mass out to a thin sheet and again fold into three layers.

(4) Refrigerate for about 1 hr. and then roll out and fold over as before. Repeat the sheeting and folding and then refrigerate once more. For best results, the sheeting and folding repeated once or twice after

this refrigeration stage.

(5) After cooling down the dough, cut it into the desired shapes and bake at 350°-375°F for 35 min.

Development of highly specialized puff pastry shortenings has allowed the use of procedures which do not include the tedious rolling-in steps of the traditional method.

Rapid Puff Pastry Method

(1) Mix together just enough to incorporate the shortening:
10 lb bread flour
2 lb puff pastry shortening (cold)
3 oz. salt

(2) Add 6lb (variable) of water at about 40°F. and mix with the batter beater at high speed until the dough forms a ball. Scrape the dough from the bowl sides.

(3) Add 2lb of cold water and develop the dough.

(4) Scrape the dough away from the sides of the bowl and add 8lb of puff pastry shortening. Mix at low speed until the shortening has just been blended in. This is the critical step and overmixing here will destroy the puff pastry characteristics of the product.

The special shortenings developed for puff pastries are generally compounds of meat fats, vegetable oils, water, and salt. Lecithin and mono glycerides may be included. Sometimes the water is replaced by skim milk or cultured milk. Butter was originally the shortening of choice for puff pastries, but many of the new compounds improve on the performance characteristics of the dairy product.

AIR-LEAVENED BREADS

Matzos

Although matzos or matzoth, the Jewish speciality which is traditionally consumed at Passover, is an unleavened bread in the sense that no fermentation is permitted, it does undergo a moderate amount of oven expansion to the entrapped air bubbles. If it were not for this leavening effect, the product would be much less palatable.

The formula for matzos is essentially flour, salt, and water, although some varieties flavored with onion and garlic have been offered commercially. The product is baked in very thin sheets at a moderately high temperature until a moisture level of about 2-5% is reached. It is desirable to have a substantial contribution of radiant (top) heat in the oven to brown the top of the wafers so as to produce some flavor in this otherwise quite insipid product.

Beaten Biscuits

Beaten biscuits are a southern specialty especialty popular in Maryland. These biscuits have a crisp texture somewhat resembling that of soda crackers or ship's biscuits and the crust is pale in color, almost white. The method of preparation resèmbles in some respects the preparation of puff pastry without the use of roll-in shortening. They are prepared entirely without yeast or chemical leavening, the air bubbles being incorporated by repeated folding and thinning out of the dough piece. The "sheeting" is usually done by pounding the dough with a rolling pin or similar implement, although sets of rollers driven by a crank can be purchased for home use.

The formula is very simple,consisting of flour, salt, lard (a small amount), and water. A little sugar is sometimes added. The flour should be strong and a minimum amount of water added to make a very stiff dough. The dough should be developed before the beating and folding process begins. The dough piece should be folded and sheeted out perhaps 20-30 times. If sheeting rollers are used, the dough will break down and tear long before this many steps are reached unless rest periods are provided for it.

Small round pieces, about $1\text{-}1\frac{1}{2}$ in. in diameter and $\frac{1}{8}$ $\frac{1}{4}$ in. thick, are cut from the dough sheet, an indentation is made in the centre and the top is docked with several holes. The dough pieces are placed (separated) on an ungreased baking sheet and put in a 325°-250°F oven until substantially dried out (about 5% moisture remaining). They are generally cold, and should be stored in a closed container to delay moisture absorption.

Home preparation has greatly declined in the last few decades because of the difficulty of preparation and lack of general appeal, apart from tradition. Attempts have been made to commercialize the product, which is inexpensive and easy to prepare using a dough brake, but there has been little demand for the product except as a novelty. When home recipes are used, the biscuits become ranchid rather quickly, because of the instability of the lard at the low moisture levels.

Eclair Shells, Cream Puffs, and Popovers

These products typically have an extremely coarse grain, the interior being formed of a few large cells. Steam contributes the greater part of the leavening action. Popovers are a type of hot bread while eclair and cream puff shells are components of desert foods.

Popover batters are made by a simple formula and procedure. In an average formula about 85-130 parts by weight of liquid whole eggs and 200 parts of milk will be used for each 100 parts of flour. Small amounts of shortening, salt, and flavorings constitute the remainder of the batter. Bread flour is generally used and it should be sifted.

To prepare popover batters, the eggs are beaten until light, the milk is added, then the flour is slowly added with moderate agitation until a homogeneous mixture is obtained. The butter or other shortening is melted and added last. The finished batter should be quite fluid, about the consistency of heavy cream.

Popovers can be baked in muffin tins or in specially designed pans. These utensils should be heavy walled to provide an initial source of heat. Before the batter is added, the pans are greased and placed in the oven to heat. The cavities are filled about one-third full of the batter.

The baking conditions are very critical in the successful production of popovers. The filled pans should be placed in a hot oven (about 450°-475°F) so as to form steam rapidly and expand the piece before the crust is set by radiant heat. After the expansion has reached its maximum, the temperature of the oven should be reduced to about 350°F to dry the popover and finish setting it without burning the crust. As the pastries are removed from the oven, the shells are punctured to allow steam to escape and drying to continue. When properly baked, the crust will be crisp in texture and medium dark in color, while the interior will be nearly dry but not tough or crumbly.

Grated cheese, rye meal, whole wheat flour or other flavoring materials can be added to the matter without ruining the popovers if the batter is kept at a very fluid consistency and the total fat content is low.

The preparation method for cream puffs and eclair shells is unusual in that the batter is cooked before it is deposited and baked. This socalled pâte à chou has a fairly simple composition of about 150-200 parts of liquid whole eggs, 100 parts flour, 100 parts shortening, and about 200 parts of water. Part of the whole eggs can be replaced by egg whites, but some egg yolk is needed because the eggs not only contribute to the structure of the finished shell, but also, emulsify the fat so that it does not leak out of the batter during baking. The quality of the eggs has an important influence in both flavor and appearance of the cream puff.

The shortening (e.g., butter) and the water are brought to a boil, then the heat is reduced, and the flour and salt are added in one portion. The mixture is stirred until a ball of dough is formed. The source of heat is then removed, and the ball of flour paste is allowed to cool slightly so that it will not cause coagulation of the egg proteins. The eggs are added gradually with vigorous beating. At the completion of mixing the paste should be stiff enough to remain in a peak when a spoon is drawn out of it. The egg content may have to be adjusted to attain this consistency. The batter must be homogeneous, lumps, being a distinct liability.

Mounds of the paste are extruded onto a lightly greased baking sheet from a pastry bag, or by any equivalent method. A hot oven temperature (450°F) is generally recommended although some authorities indicate 375°F is satisfactory. The pastries are baked until they are golden brown and beads of moisture are no longer seen, and then the heat is turned off and the sheets are punctured to allow the escape of trapped steam. The puff cases are allowed to dry out in the oven for a few minutes.

Eclair shells are made in exactly the same way except the paste is extruded in strip form.

COOKIES

Many kinds of cookies are made with only small amounts of leavening and several varieties contain none. Perhaps the most straightforward example of this type is the sugar wafer base cake. Small amounts of ammonium bicarbonate or soda are often added, but the major leavening action is due to steam.

Sugar Wafers

The base cake is entirely different from any other cookie. It has many similarities in texture and structure to puffed snack foods. Structurally, it is a foamed, dehydrated starch gel with a supporting gluten network. Most of the leavening action results from the evolution of steam during the baking process. The batter is closely confined so that the steam cannot readily escape, and its leavening effect under these conditions is much greater than it would be if the thin sheet were exposed to the atmosphere.

The basic principles used in making the flat, cream-layered sugar wafer are also used in manufacturing ice cream cones (waffle cones) and novelty cream-filled shapes such as circles, hemispheres, half-cylinders, peanut shells, etc. Some of the novelty shapes are filled with cheese- flavored or other savory fillings instead of sugar-shortening mixtures. All of the fillings are essentially fat based, however, since any appreciable amount of moisture completely ruins the texture of the base cake, causing it to collapse.

The batter is a very fluid mixture of flour and water to which small amounts of other ingredients are are added. Generally, no sugar or other sweeteners are present. Table 1 summarizes six formulae found in the recent literature. To the base formula may be added colors and flavors selected to be compatible with the process. A yellow color, egg shade, is commonly added to the vanilla or plain base cake. Flavors should be added sparingly, since the predominant flavor is expected to come from the filling. Vanillin at the 0.025-0.05% level is a suitable flavoring. Chocolate or dark colored wafers sometimes do not contain any cacao products and are colored with caramel or food dyes. For a chocolate flavor, about 10% of cocoa (preferably the high fat or breakfast type) may be added to the formula. This addition will necessitate of increase of around 15% in water.

Old-style formulas contained enriching ingredients such as milk or eggs, and sometimes even sugar, but batters made with these components tend to cause excessive build-up of carbon on the oven plates, especially at the corners. Carbon deposits will cause sticking of the sheet with consequent difficulty in ejecting the sheets from the plates. Shortening, usually 76° coconut oil, is added to facilitate release of the wafer. The function of lecithin is to help prevent sticking, but its effectiveness in the simple batters must be questionable. Corn starch, when added, is intended to improve the texture, i.e., to make the wafer tenderer.

The flour should be a short extraction soft wheat flour. Flour from white wheat is sometimes used. Both bleached and unbleached flour

TABLE 1
SUGAR WAFER BATTER FORMULAS

		Range		
	Average (Parts)	High (Parts)	Low (Parts)	Recommended (Parts)
Flour	100	100	100	100
Water, variable	135	150	125	140
Sodium bicarbonate	0.38	0.75	0.2	0.5
Ammonium bicarbonate	0.22	0.5	0	0
MSNF	1.8	5	0	0
Dried whole milk	0.5	3	0	0
Corn starch	1.7	5	0	0
Dried egg yolk	0.96	2.5	1.25	0
Salt	0.32	0.75	0	0.5
Lecithin	0.13	0.4	0	0.1
Coconut oil	0.8	2	0	1

have been used successfully. Any speckiness shows up clearly in white wafers. The amount and quality of gluten seem to have some effect on expansion, so that a very weak flour may give too dense or too close textured a piece. On the other hand, gluten also affects the texture so that a strong flour causes the wafer to be hard and flinty. The protein content or strength of the flour should be chosen to achieve a a compromise between excess hardness and excess fragility or denseness. The precise specification will depend upon the kinds and amounts of other ingredients, the type of end product desired, and the characteristics of the equipment. As usual, water is varied, the amount being chosen to give a batter viscosity which will enable it to spread rapidly over the plate and between the plates while still retaining a substantially uniform internal structure without large voids or other defects.

Other ingredients which have been suggested for sugar wafer shells include heat-treated defatted cottonseed flour and determinated white corn flour. Such materials add viscosity to the batter without increasing the possibility of gluten separation during mixing. Ammonium bicarbonate is often added in addition to soda. Leavening acids are rarely used, but the small amount of soda included in the formula is neutralized by the flour so that satisfactory pH's are attained. Color, especially of white shells, may be improved by adding cream of tartar or other leavening acid in an amount sufficient to bring the pH slightly below 7.0.

Mixing is a simple procedure. Any equipment which can produce a smooth, lump-free batter is suitable. The dry ingredients are first blended, then the water is added gradually while mixing. If shortening is used, it is blended while the mixture is still of doughy consistency. Some recommend using melted shortening. Eggs and milk solids can be added to the mixture at the start with about half of the water, and rehydrated before the remainder of the dry ingredients are added. Finally, the rest of the water is gradually brought in.

Batters are preferably mixed at high speed although there are numerous cases where low speed horizontal mixers have been used successfully. Under certain conditions, as when overmixed, the gluten may develop into strands and separate. Setling-out is also a problem and some agitation is necessary while the batter be being held for depositing. Mixing batches of the smallest possible size is highly recommended. Holding for longer than 30 min is definitely not recommended.

The baking devices for sugar wafer bases are ovens through which travel pairs of plates (books) or continious bands with the batter confined between them. The baking time is usually about 2 min. For maximum strength and crispness, the wafer should be at 2% moisture content or less at the time the cream is applied. The pH should be between 6.8 and 7.8 with the lower ranges preferred.

The original Scotch shortbread, actually a kind of cake or cookie, rather than the kind of "bread" we are familiar with, contained no liquid ingredients or leaveners in the formula, and was dense and very short in texture. Some formulae adapted to modern tastes include a small amount of egg and specify longer and no more vigorous mixing to give a slight aerating effect. A traditional formula is

1 Cup butter
$\frac{3}{4}$ Cup powered sugar
1 teaspoonful vanilla
2 Cups sifted flour
$\frac{1}{2}$ teaspoon salt

The butter is creamed with the sugar and the vanilla added. The flour and salt are mixed in just enough to distribute them uniformly. The paste is rolled to desired thickness, usually about $\frac{1}{2}$ in., cut in shapes, and baked at 300°F for 20-25 min.

There are many other kinds of cookies which contain little or no leavening substance. For a complete discussion, the reader is referred to cookie and cracker technology (Matz 1968).

Cakes

In cakes chemical leavening agents e.g. mixtures of sodium bicarbonate and leavening acids are used for the expanding effect during baking. The mixing stage during cake manufacture, is the most important, if mixing is not done according to the set procedure, the product obtained shall be poor even when the recipe is excellent.

Functions of Various Ingredients

Various basic ingredients present in a cake mix perform some special function. Amounts of these ingredients are interlinked and when amount of any or more of the ingredients is varied the quantities of the remaining ingredients have to be balanced to get the best results. The following is a classification of various cake ingredients according to their functions:--

Tougheners : Flour, milk solids, egg whites and other binding ingredients come under this category. They provide the structure and bind the cake.

Tenderizers : Sugar, shortening, egg yolks, chocolate and other fat containing ingredients provide softness and shortness to the cake.

Moistners : Milk, water, eggs, syrups and other liquids provide moisture and impart keeping quality.

Driers : Flour, milk solids and starches etc. absorb and retain moisture and provide body to the cake.

Flavorers : Cocoa, chocolate, butter, eggs and other natural flavor-bearing ingredients provide flavor to the cake.

The functions of these ingredients have been elaborated as under:

The wheat flours used in cakes are weaker, i.e., they contain lower quantity of gluten and also as compared to bread the quantity of flour used is itself smaller in the recipe. Thus the cakes have denser structure than the breads. Apart from sweetening effect sugars have a tenderizing effect and also impart good color to the cake crust. Invert sugar and glucose imparts better color to the crust than cane sugar. Usual sugars help in retaining the moisture thereby reducing the staling of the crumb; glucose and invert sugar exert better effect than cane sugar.

Increasing the concentration of sugars in the cake recipes makes the latter more fluid and thus less air is entrained during whipping.

Shortening apart from tenderizing the crumb and imparting it some flavor, helps in entrapping air during mixing of the latter. The entrapped air bubbles give the leavening effect and help control the grain size. It has to be confirmed that all the air bubbles are enclosed in the layers of fat; which is known as creaming action of fat. Emullsified shortenings increase the amount of water which can be used, this improves tenderness and the resistance to staling. Addition of egg whites compensates the otherwise poor ability of the cake flours to support the formation large cells. Angel food cake, for instance, the entire leavening effect is obtained from the air enclosed by the egg white during vigorous whipping. Egg white does not contribute to the texture. Eggs impart flavor and color. Egg yolks have emullssifying and tendering effects. Thus eggs are the important ingredient to compensate or the excessively weak flours.

Addition of milk improves crust color. Skim milk somewhat toughens the crumb but the whole milk has no such drawback due to the presence of milkfat which compensates it by imparting tenderness and lubrication. Milk also contributes to flavor and its lactose content helps in retardation of staling.

MIXING OF CAKE BATTERS

The mixing stage of cake making is very important and should be carried out according to the set procedures. Proper mixing helps in achieving a uniform mixture of the ingredients, incorporation of minute air-cells and in developing a desirable grain and texture in the baked product. Various techniques of mixing the cake batters are employed. Some of the more important are given below:

Creaming Method

In this method sugar and shortening are beaten to get a light and fluffy or creamed mass. During this stage small air cells are formed and then incorporated into the mix; its volume increases and consistency becomes softer. The eggs are then added while creaming is continued at medium speed, and finally milk and flour are added alternately, in small portions. For best creaming fat or shortening should not be below 20°C and also their temperature should not exceed 45°C otherwise the fat will be too fluid to hold much air hence volume increase shall not be as high as desired. Speed of the mixer should be controlled properly. Sugar and shortening are best creamed at medium speed until soft and light.

Addition of eggs should be slow otherwise if eggs are added too quickly or if milk is added in one lot the mixture will curdle. Addition of the flour alternately with the liquid i.e. milk when the mix is creamed will eliminate the tendency to curdle.

Blending Method

In this method flour and shortening are blended in the bowl until the flour particles are thoroughly coated by the fat. The remainder of the dry ingredients are then added and the batter mixed until homogeneous. Finally the remaining liquid is added in portions and mixed to get the desired result. Sometimes sugar and eggs are beaten together to form a foam before they are added to the flour and shortening mixture.

In this method also curdling has to be avoided. For high-ratio type mix a high-ratio shortening should be used. The emullsified fat enables the cells formed in mixing to hold the large percentage of moisture and sugar without curdling. As usual temperature of fat is important. When high percentage e.g. 140% or more is to be used it is best to dissolve it in the liquid before adding to the mix, so as to eliminate the possibility of incomplete blending of sugar ; this modification will result in a more tender crust of the baked cake.

Whipping Method

Generally most of the sugar is added to the eggs used in sponge cakes before beginning whipping. Whipping introduces air cells which cause leavening without the need of baking powder. Eggs and sugar heated to 40° to 45°C before whipping. If some egg yolks are also added, the foam formation is improved. When large amounts of sugar are used compared to that of eggs, part of the sugar is dissolved in the liquid e.g. milk and then folded in after the eggs have are been whipped e.g. if the sugar is above 100% part of it is added later. In the case of leaner sponge cakes, less amounts of eggs are used the liquid e.g. milk or water, is added after the eggs are almost completely whipped and the whipping is completed. In whipped type cakes, the flour should be sifted and folded gently in stages, if added too much at a time, loss in aeration will take place resulting in poor volume of the baked cake.

In the case of Angel cake egg whites are whipped slightly to a foam and then slowly sugar is added. As amount of sugar used is high, all of it is not added there. Otherwise maximum aeration will not be obtained. Part of the sugar is sifted with the flour and then folded in gently. Both over-whipping and under-whipping of the eggs should be avoided. Mixing machine speed is also important for best whipping. First machine is run at full speed and when whipping is almost complete the speed is reduced to second place to ensure maximum aeration. If high speed is maintained at final stages, there will be loss in volume as the air cells formed will rupture due to high speed.

Creaming and Whipping combination Method

As the name itself suggests this method is a combination of the whipping method and creaming method. In this method flour and shortening are creamed until soft and tight. The eggs and sugar are whipped as in the whipping method. The two mixtures are gently combined by folding the whipped eggs and sugar into the creamed flour and shortening. Leavening is mostly obtained by aeration and sometimes chemical leavening agents may also be added in small quantities. Care must be exercised in folding in the whites. Otherwise overmixing shall result in loss of volume, large holes and uneven grain of the cake. As usual over-mixing should be avoided.

Choice of Mixing Method

Creaming method allows entrapment of a maximum number of air bubbles in the fat with the result that grains of the finished product are better; and also flour gluten is not developed as much as in other methods, thus texture of the cake is somewhat better. The blending method of mixing is used primarily in the making of high ratio type cakes. The chief advantage of the blending method is that it permits a very thorough dispersion of the shortening throughout the batter. This results in a very fine and uniform grain in the product. The whipping method of mixing is mainly used in the preparation of sponge and angel cakes and also in the whipping cream etc. The combination method of mixing is very often used in the making of pound-cake, and also for wonder cakes and cheese cakes.

FORMULATIONS AND BLEACHING OF CAKE RECIPES

Various ingredients and their functions in cake recipes have already been given. They have effects on each other and also some of them have opposite effects hence in balancing a cake recipe, it is a must to have proper proportions of toughners and tenderisers, and the driers and moisteners, so that the cake obtained may be of the desired characteristics.

At first a type of pound cake was made by mixing equal parts of sugar, butter, eggs and flour. With the refinement in mixing methods and experience various types of cakes with excellent quality are nowadays manufactured. In general following guidelines may be let in mind while formulating the cake recipe. Taking the weight of flour as 100 parts, the sugar may be kept at about 110-160 parts in yellow layer and white layer cakes, and at 110-180 parts in Devil's food and chocolate layers. Eggs as liquid eggs should be equal to or more than the shortening. The total liquid in the recipe (including water in eggs and milk) should be more than the amount of sugar by 25-35%. Amount of shortening should be about 30-70 parts, sodium bicarbonate should be 1.2-2 parts and salt should be 3-4 parts. If in a formula the quantity of sugar is to be increased, the egg content should also be equally increased. When quantity of eggs is to be increased, shortening is also increased.

Rich formulas used less chemical leavening agent as during mixing more air gets incorporated. Rich formulae thus have low sp. gravity and are baked at lower oven temperature. Batters to be baked in large sizes require less water in the recipe and also less leavener than those baked in smaller sizes.

Balancing of Pound Cakes and Creamed Cake Mixes

Usually the weight of sugar is equal to that of flour which in the leaner cake mixes the weight of sugar should be less than that of flour. The weight of shortening or fat should be equal to that of flour or sugar and the total weight of eggs and milk should be equal to the weight of sugar or flour. If the quantity of sugar and\or flour is more than eggs milk is required for moistening and baking powder has to be incorporated for supplementing the leavening power of eggs. In other words if the total of sugar and flour is more than double of eggs, than 2/3rd weight of the difference is added as milk, but milk is not a leavening agent as is eggs hence baking powder is required otherwise the cake will have poor volume and very dense grain.

In the case of wine cake the structure has to be more porous than that of the pound cake. Thus in creamed cake mixes for every 100 parts of liquid milk or water 6 to 9 parts of baking powder should be added. The quality of flour used also affects the recipe balance. A strong flour necessitates the incorporation of extra baking powder in the recipe. If some acid-containing ingredient, such as cocoa, is present in the recipe, then some baking soda has to be used for part of baking powder.

Balancing of High-Ratio cakes

In the recipes of high-ratio cakes the quantity of sugar should be equal or more than that of flour and the amount of eggs should be more than that of fat or shortening. The weight of the liquid (eggs and milk) should equal or exceed that of sugar. As mentioned earlier special or emulsified high ratio type shortening should be used for these cakes and fine cake flour should be used so that it may absorb and retain moisture and also provide structure. In high-ratio yellow cakes sugar may be as high as 1.5 times that of flour white in chocolate cakes it may be as high as 1.65 times. Due to this higher quantity of sugar more liquid will be required to dissolve it and also to gelatinise the flour starch; thus more milk and eggs have to be used in the recipe.

Eggs supply moisture and also toughen the product due to the protein content. Apart from this they function as emulsifier also. To compensate for the toughness of the eggs the fat used should not be much less than the quantity of eggs. Egg yolks contain neutral emulsifier (lecithin); hence when yolks are used small amount of emulsified shortening will be required. Emulsified fat helps in carrying the added liquid without curdling. Any change in the quantity of sugar must be compensated by adjustment in the amount of flour and liquid. Excess of sugar and liquid will result in a cake of dense grain and poor volume. In high ratio cakes amount of leavening depends on the weight of flour; for 100 parts of flour depending upon the amount and types of eggs 4 to 6 parts of baking powder may be used.

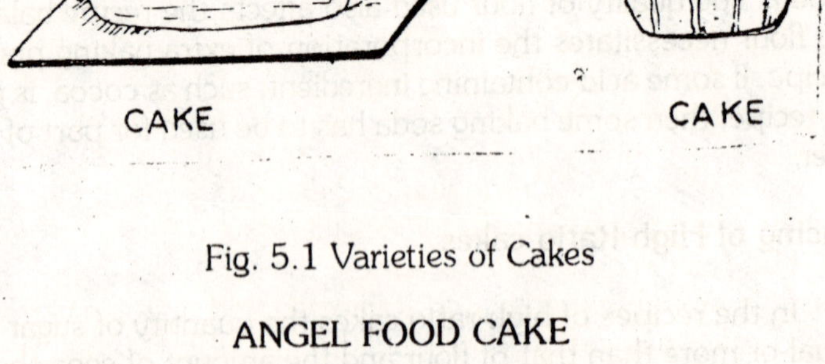

Fig. 5.1 Varieties of Cakes

ANGEL FOOD CAKE

Angel food cakes are based on egg whites, sugar and flour, and do not contain any shortening; other ingredients present are salt, cream of tartar and flavor etc. The ranges of the main ingredients used are flour 20-40 parts, sugar 80-100 parts and egg whites 100 parts.

Ingredients

Egg white is the critical ingredient of angel food cakes. Usual whites or dried albumen may be used. They affect the whiteness of the crumb, crust appearance, texture and flavor. Thinner whites can be whipped quickly but give less stable foam than the viscous whites. Sometimes water is added to the whites (upto 10%) to get additional moistness and closer grain in the finished cake but some reduction in volume may take place. Usual cane sugar may be used in the mix, but fine grain sugar is preferably due to ease of dissolving in the egg whites. The flour used should be quite weak and for this reason weak soft wheat flour is used, replacement of part of flour with wheat starch shall give excellent cake. Egg whites and sugar act as toughners by contributing to the strength or resilience to the foam structure. Due to the absence of shortening, the function of sugar as tenderiser is much more pronounced.

Whipping aids are necessary to improve the foam properties of the albumen, for this purpose cream of tartar, i.e. potassium hydrogen tartrate is very good imparting the cake a fine texture; it imparts a brighter color to the crumb. Some acids like acetic acid, malic acid, citric acid and tartaric acid also improve the cake structure and color but are inferior to cream of tartar, hence the latter is used upto 1-2% in the formulations. Emulsifiers like triacetin, sodium oleate, oleic acid and triethyl citrate are used for improving the whipping qualities of dried albumen. Flavors free from fatty materials are used in angel food cakes. Vanilla, almond extract and imitation rum extract are suitable for this purpose. Citrus fruit juices may also be used for this purpose but due to acidity the cream of tartar should be somewhat reduced to compensate. Spices may also be used but presence of oil will affect the cake volume. Cocoa is sometimes added but it has some collapsing effect on the bubbles due to melting in the early stages of baking. Nut pieces may be used but they are not popular due to their unacceptable texture. The basic recipe remains almost the same but with variation in flavoring materials chocolate, fruit flavored and marbled varieties of angel food cake may easily be produced.

Method of Manufacture

Angel food cake is a product very sensitive to changes in preparation method. One method is the two-state one, in which case the egg whites containing the cream of tartar are whipped with or without a part of the sugar, followed by the mixing in one of the remaining sugar with continued beating. In the second stage flour is folded in with least disturbance while ensuring good distribution, this keeps the collapsing of the bubbles to the minimum. In a different procedure egg whites are whipped at medium speed until a soft structure is obtained and to this 50-60% sugar is slowly added with continued whipping, when wet peak is obtained, flavor, remaining sugar and flour are added with continued intermittent, and lowest speed of mixing, until uniform. Whipping is a critical step, under-whipping results in low volume and texture while over-whipping results in low volume and coarse crumb due to collapse of bubbles during baking. Best whipping temperature is 15-20°C and whipped sp.gr. is 0.15.17 with sugar.

Angel food cake pans should be free from grease and if they are slightly wetted before filling with batter, the crust color will be lighter due to delay in the dehydration of the surface. Aluminium or thin steel pans are preferred. The best baking temperature range is 175-200°C, the higher temperature limit being used for smaller cakes.

Formulations

A typical formulation for Angel food cake is given below:

Eggs whites	8 parts
Sugar	8
Cream of tartar	0.06
Salt	0.06
Cake flour	3
Vanilla	0.12
Almond flavor	0.06

Egg whites are whipped to a froth. Half of sugar, cream of tartar and salt are sifted together and added as a steady stream during whipping of eggs, until a wet shiny peak is obtained. Flavors are folded in gently followed by gentle addition and folding in of remaining sugar and flour. The batter is baked at 175°C in most ungreased, clean, pans. The cakes are trained upside down to cool them. They may be finished with a thin covering of fondant icing, before that the cakes may be filled or left plain. Icing may have the required color and flavor.

It chocolate angel cake is to be prepared the quantity of the flour is reduced to 2.5 parts instead of 3 parts, and 1 part of natural cocoa is incorporated in the last stage with the flour.

POUND CAKE

The name pound is due to the fact that these cakes were traditionally formulated using one pound each of flour, butter, whole eggs and sugar but now-a-days better formulas are employed. As distinct from angel's food cake they contain shortening and whole eggs.

An old fashioned pound cake formulation is given below:

Shortening	10 parts
Butter	10
Cake flour	10
Bread flour	10
Sugar	20
Salt	0.3
Eggs	20
Vanilla	0.4

Flour is mixed carefully with fats and cream until soft and light. Sugar, salt and eggs are whipped until light. Vanilla is then added. Whipped sugar and eggs are added into the creamed fat and flour, taking care to avoid collapsing the bubbles. Baking is carried out at 175°C.

A modern high ratio pound cake may have the following typical formulation:

Sugar	20 parts
Salt	0.4
Milk powder	1
Cake flour	20
Emulisified shortening	12
Water	7.5
Eggs	12
Falvor	0.4
Baking powder	0.2

Sugar, salt, milk powder, shortening and water are blended to get a soft, smooth paste, at medium speed for about 7 minutes. Eggs are added in 3 stages blending well after each addition, with this addition flavor and baking powder are also added. Rapid mixing should be avoided as it gives lumps and heavy, thin consistency. Blending method gives smaller air cells than those obtained with creaming. Baking is as usual carried out at 175°C.

As can be seen from above these pound cake formulations do not contain whipping improvers and acidifying agents (cream of tartar). Modern formulations contain some baking powder but the quantity is kept low to retain the dense, firm, tender and crumbly texture; quantity of eggs is lower but sugar is more to make it more sweet and tender. Replacement of butter by vegetable shortening reduces cost. Pound cake formulations may be used as the basis for tastes, petit fours, jelly rolls and trifles also but usually sponge cakes formulations are preferred for this purpose.

Varieties of Pound Cakes

In above formulations a few percentage of invert sugar syrup or glycerine may be added to increase moistness of the crumb, more yolks or whites may be added for the desired textural improvement. In place of part of sugar corn syrup of high DE may be used, white pound cakes require only egg whites instead of whole eggs.

Good chocolate flavored cakes can be made by replacing a few percentages of the shortening with chocolate liquor or by adding a good grade of cocoa. Marzipan cakes contain a few percentages of almond paste or combinations of almond paste and kernel paste. Fruit Pound cake is obtained by mixing some diced nuts, raisins, glace fruit, or orange peel. Raisins and other fruits, but not nuts, are dusted with flour before adding to the mix. All these materials are added at the final stages of mixing to avoid smearing and discoloration of the cake.

WHITE LAYER CAKE

White layer cakes contain egg whites while yellow layer cakes contain whole eggs. They usually contain a high percentage of sugar as compared to other types of high ratio cakes. In high ratio cakes i.e. in the cakes containing a high proportion of sugar to flour, high emulsifying shortening is used. In white layer cakes usual flavor is vanilla (extract or artificial) at about 0.5 to 1% level. Almond flavor may also be added. A typical universal white layer cake mix is given below:

	%
Cake flour	37.5
Sugar	41
Dried egg whites	3
Dried skim milk	2.5
Shortening, with emulisifiers	13.7
Sodium bicarbonate	0.55
Sodium acid pyrophosphate	0.15
Monocalcium monohydrate	0.55
Salt	0.9
Powdered vanilla	0.15

To dry this mix is added 35 to 40% water depending upon the quality of the flour and emulisifier efficiency. This formulation is very versatile and is immune to failure even when other than usual mixing procedure is used.

A typical formulation of high ratio white layer is given below:

Cake flour	11 parts
Sugar	12
Skim milk powder	1
High ratio shortening	5
Salt	0.2
Water	7
Egg whites	7.5
Baking powder	0.6
Vanilla	0.25

Sugar, salt, milk powder, flour and shortening are mixed together, to this 4 parts of water is added with mixing at medium speed for about 5 minutes. This is followed with the addition of remaining water and mixing until a smooth paste is obtained. Egg whites are added in three lots, in the last lot baking powder and flavor are also added. If desired about 0.1 part of almond flavor may also be added. Cakes are baked at 175-180°C. To reduce the alkaline effect of the egg whites, about 0.05 part of cream of tartar may also be added, this will impart a softer cake structure.

YELLOW LAYER CAKE

Yellow layer cakes contain whole eggs as compared to white layer cakes which contain egg whites only. Due to the presence of egg yolks, yellow layer cakes are richer. Emulisified shortening is used in these formulations, a typical formulation is given below:

Sugar	12 parts
Cake flour	12
Milk powder	1
Emulisified shortening	5
Water	8
Whole eggs	6
Salt	0.25
Baking powder	0.6
Vanilla	0.25

Sugar, salt, milk powder, flour and shortening are blended at medium speed for 5 to 6 minutes, with 6 parts of water, the remaining water is added and blended at medium speed. Eggs are also blended in stages, with the last lot baking powder and vanilla are also incorporated. Baking is done as usual.

Yellow cakes are particularly suitable for the addition of special flavors. In spice cakes mixture of cinnamon, nutmeg, ginger and all-spice in the ratio of 8:6:1:1 are added. Further varieties of yellow cake can be made by adding pumpkin, apple sauce, or mashed bananas.

Filling and Icing

The cake is cut into layers of required thickness, with the help of a knife. Each layer is filled with butter-cream, jam, jelly or fudge etc; required number of layers are placed on each other and gently pressed to ensure sticking. Any icing which come out on the sides is used for giving, the sides of the cake, a thin covering. The cake is placed on cake liner and the top is covered with a layer of garnish, sometimes sides are also garnished with toasted cake crumbs, toasted nuts, sliced almonds or chocolate sprinkles etc.

CHOCOLATE CAKES

Chocolate cakes contain cocoa or chocolate liquor. Devil's Food cake described later also contains cocoa but the difference between the two is that of pH which affects the texture, color and flavor. Chocolate cakes are basic cakes to which cocoa or chocolate liquor has been added and their pH is almost same as that of yellow cakes. A typical chocolate cake (High-ratio) formulation is given below:---

Flour	12 parts
Sugar	13.5
Shortening	5
Milk powder	1.5
Cocoa	2.2
Baking powder	0.6
Salt	0.25
Water	12
Whole eggs	6

Sugar, salt, milk powder, cocoa, flour, shortening and 2/3rd water are blended at medium speed until soft and smooth. Remaining water containing small amount of soda is also blended, followed by 3-stage blendings of eggs containing the remaining soda in the last-stage. Vanilla is also added. The blend obtained should be soft and smooth and should pour like a thick gravy. The mix is baked as usual in the form of cupcakes, sheet cakes or loaf cakes. Marshmallow icing, whipped cream oir cream tapping is also applied when desired. The cake may be finished in the form of layer cake as described earlier. It may be garnished with chocolate cake crumbs, malted chocolate, fudge icing or long-shred coconut.

DEVIL'S FOOD CAKE

As mentioned above Devil's Food cake is also a cocoa containing cake. It contains extra soda and the pH is alkaline, thus the devil's food cake has a slightly reddish color, more open grain and it is somewhatleaner in fat content. The reddish tone is imparted due to the reaction between cocoa and baking soda. Chocolate cake formulation may be used as a base. The following is typical formulation for high-ratio Devil's Food Cake:

Cake flour	12 parts
Sugar	13.5
Emulisified fat	5
Milk powder	1.25
Salt	0.25
Natural cocoa	2.25
Water	12
Baking soda	0.2
Eggs	6
Baking powder	0.4

MIxing done as usual, baking powder and vanilla are added last.

SPONGE CAKES

Sponge cakes are primarily leavened with eggs, using the whipping method. In the mix some baking powder is also added:-

Cake flour	8.5 parts
Sugar	8
Glucose or corn syrup	1
Eggs	9
Salt	0.06
Water	1.5
Baking powder	0.12
Flavor	0.3

Eggs are whipped and to this sugar, salt and glucose are added and whipped, 2/3rd of the water is added slowly and whipped. Remaining water and flavor are added and gently mixed. Slowly, cake flour and baking powder are mixed in avoiding overmixing. Baking is done as usual. Lemon flavor may be used.

CHIFFON CAKE

Chiffon cake is somewhat similar to Angel's food cake as egg whites are used instead of whole eggs, due to the same reason it differs from sponge cake. The main difference between the chiffon cake and Angel's food cake is that the latter contains fat in the form of vegetable oil. Baking powder is added to assist the oven spring. Additional egg yolks are also added. Two typical formulations are given below:---

	1	2
Egg whites	32	20
Salt	0.4	0.5
Egg yolks	10.7	16
Vegetable oil	10.7	10
Sugar	32	27
Cake flour	14	20
Cream of tartar	0.2	0.1
Water	----	6.9
Baking powder	----	1

Egg whites and salt are whipped to get a soft foam then the cream of tartar and sugar are added with continued heating until a soft peak is obtained. The yolks are whipped separately until thoroughly blended and aerated. Egg yloks and oil mixture is added, to the previous foam, gently, sugar and flour as gently added. Baking powder if used is added with flour. Baking is done as usual. Orange and lemon flavored cakes are more popular while chocolate flavored cakes are also made.

FRENCH PASTRY

Frensh pastries are squarel, triangular, rectangular or diamond shaped pieces cut from cake sheets. The cake sheets are layered with fillings and creams. The cakes used may be of high ratio types e.g. yellow, chocolate etc., sponge or chiffon type. Two or more (usually 3) sheets are put one over other with filling e.g. cream filling and cut into pastries of above mentioned shapes.

The cake or pastry pieces are then iced and finished. The cake is made in sheets about $\frac{1}{2}$ thick. Light buttercream, combination of buttercream and jelly or jam, or fudge kind are used in between the layers. The total height should not be more than 2". The sheets stick to each other. The layered cake is then chilled and cut with sharp knife dipped frequently in hot water, to get the pieces of required size and shape. The sides of the pieces may be iced with buttercream or fudge and topped with finely ground cake crumbs or ground nuts or chocolate strips. The pastry tops are also decorated with neat design, proper color blend and garnish. The units may also be covered with warm fondant or dipped into the warm fondant.

The pastry pieces may also be cut from the layered cake sheets the top of which may already be decorated with buttercream before being cut into pastries.

Fig. 5.2 3-Layer Cake with 2 Fillings

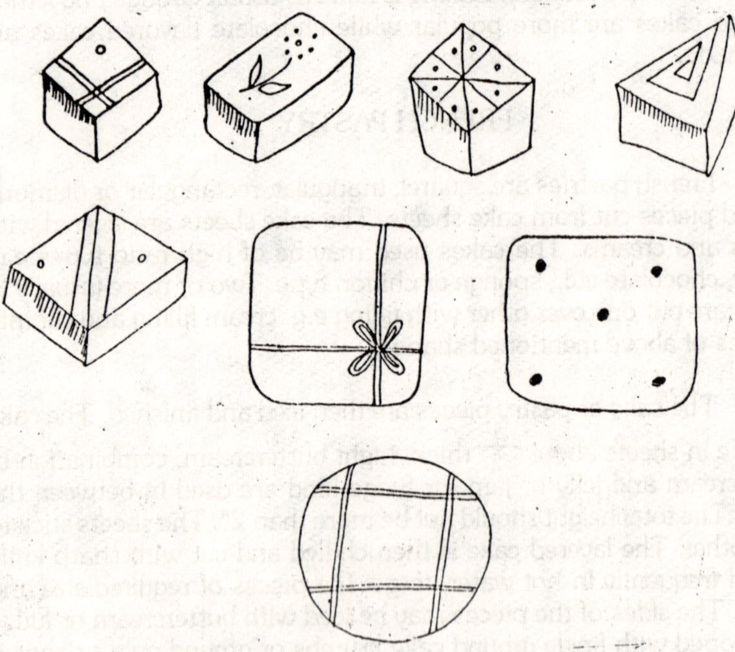

Fig. 5.3 Various Shapes of French Pastries

CAKES

Basic sponge cake (Fatless)
Serves 6-8
Preparation time 50 minutes

Ingredients

4 eggs
$1\frac{1}{2}$ cups flour
1 cup sugar
$1\frac{1}{2}$ tsp. baking powder
4 table spoon liquid milk
1 tsp. vanilla essence.

Method

- Sieve flour and baking powder together. Keep aside.
- Powder the sugar.
- Put sugar and eggs in a large mixing bowl. Beat with a spoon till thick frothy and turns whitish.
- Add liquid milk and vanilla essence. Beat well.
- Add flour slowly little by little and beating in one direction only.
- Beat for 10-15 minutes till light in texture.
- Take a round tin. Grease it.
- Pour the mixture into it. Bake in a preheated oven at 160°C for 35 to 40 minutes.
- Insert a knife in the centre. If it comes out clean the cake is ready, otherwise bake for another 5 to 10 minutes.
- Cool it for 10 minutes and remove from the tin.

Variations

- Instead of milk you can add curd
- You can use strawberry essence and 2-3 drops of red edible colour.

Basic Eggless Cake
Serves 6-8
Preparation Time 60 minutes

Ingredients

$1\frac{1}{2}$ cups flour
1 cup sugar
1 tsp. baking powder
$\frac{1}{2}$ tsp. baking soda (soda bicarb)

$\frac{1}{2}$ cup butter
$\frac{1}{2}$ tsp. vanilla essence
$\frac{1}{2}$ cup liquid milk
4 table spoons milk powder

Method

- Sieve flour, baking powder and soda bicarb together. Keep aside.
- Beat sugar and butter together for 5-7 minutes in a large mixing bowl.
- Add milk and milk powder to sugar and butter. Beat again for 5-7 minutes. Add vanilla essence.
- Add flour to butter and sugar a little at a time and beat for another 5-7 minutes.
- Grease a baking dish and pour the mixture into it.
- Bake in a preheated oven at 160°C for 35-40 minutes.
- Insert a knife in the centre. If it comes out clean, cake is ready. If not, bake for another 5-10 minutes and remove from the tin.

Variations

- Instead of milk powder and liquid milk you can add $\frac{1}{2}$ tin of condensed milk and reduce sugar to $\frac{1}{2}$ cup.
- You can add 1 tbsp of cocoa powder while sieving the flour and another 2 tbsp of liquid milk to give chocolate colour instead of vanilla essence.

Dates and Walnut Cake

Serves 6-8

Preparation time 60 minutes

Ingredients

3 eggs
$1\frac{1}{2}$ cups flour
1 cup sugar
$\frac{3}{4}$ cup oil
250 gms dates
1 cup chopped walnuts
$1\frac{1}{2}$ tsp. baking powder
5-6 walnut halves

Method

- Sieve flour and baking powder together. Keep aside,
- Remove the seeds from the dates and boil in half cup of water Mash them with a fork.
- Mix oil and sugar well in a large mixing bowl.
- Add half of the dates and chopped walnuts to oil mixture.
- Beat eggs till well blended.
- Add flour to it and beat for 5 to 7 minutes. Add oil and dates mixture to it. Beat and add the remaining walnuts and dates. Beat for 2 minutes.
- Grease a tin. Pour the mixture. Decorate with walnut halves.
- Bake in a preheated oven at 180°C for 15 minutes. Reduce the oven mark at 160°C and bake for another 20 to 30 minutes.
- Test with a knife. If it comes out clean, cake is ready.
- Cool for 5-7 minutes and remove from tin.

Variations

1. Instead of oil you can use butter.

2. You can boil and mash half the dates and chop half and add to the batter.

Plum Cake with Plum sauce

Serves 6-8

Preparation time 70 minutes

Ingredient

For cake	For plum sauce
3 eggs	250 gms fresh plums
2 cups flour	1 cup sugar
$1\frac{1}{2}$ tsp. baking powder	2-3 drops ad edible colour (optional)
2 tbsp. curd	$\frac{1}{2}$ cup cream
$\frac{1}{3}$ cup milk	
$\frac{1}{2}$ cup butter	
250 gms fresh plums	

Method

- Sieve flour and baking powder together.

- Beat eggs, sugar and butter till frothy.
- Add flour to egg mixture. Beat for 5-7 minutes. Add milk and curd to it and beat again for 5 minutes till light in texture.
- Remove seeds from plums and cut into pieces.
- Grease a cake tin. Sprinkle 2 table spoons sugar over it. Place plums over it in a single layer.
- Pour the cake batter and bake in a preheated oven at 160°C for 35-40 minutes.
- Insert a knife in the centre. If comes out clean, cake is ready.
- Loosen the sides of the cake with a knife and turn the cake over a plate immediately. Let it cool down.

Sauce

- Peel and cut plums.
- Boil with sugar at low heat till uniform mixture is obtained. Add colour and cool it.
- Mix cream to it.
- Cut pieces of cake and serve with sauce.

Variation

- Instead of cream in sauce, you can use thick curd also.
- In place of butter, you can use oil.
- It can be made eggless also by using 3 tbsp milk powder and $\frac{1}{2}$ cup milk instead of eggs.

Pineapple Upside Down Cake
Serves 4-6
Preparation time 70 minutes

Ingredients

3 eggs	$1\frac{1}{2}$ tsp. baking powder
$1\frac{1}{2}$ cups flour	3 tbsp. sugar for carmelisation
1 cup sugar	A few almonds
5-6 slices of pineapple (tinned)	2 tbsp. sour curd.
$\frac{3}{4}$ cup butter	

Method

- Sieve flour and baking powder together
- Grease a round tin. Place one pineapple ring in the centre and halved rings on the sides. Put almonds in the centre of the pineapple rings.
- Heat 3 tbsp. sugar and 1 tbsp. water in a small pan till it burns to a dark brown colour. Pour this immediately over the pineapple rings.
- Beat butter, curd and sugar together in a large mixing bowl. Break eggs into it, beat well and add flour to it. Beat for 10 to 15 minutes till light in texture.
- Pour the batter over decorated tin.
- Bake in a preheated oven at 160°C for 35-40 minutes
- Put a needle or knife in the centre of the cake. If it comes out clean, the cake is ready.
- Loose the sides of the cake with the help of a knife and turn on to a serving dish immediately. Cool and serve.

Variations

- Instead of butter, you can use $\frac{3}{4}$ cup of oil.
- Cherries can be placed in the centers of the pineapple rings instead of almonds.
- It can be served hot also.

Chocolate Sponge Cake
Serves 6-8
Preparation time 70 minutes

Ingredients
3 eggs
1 cup flour
1 cup sugar
$\frac{1}{2}$ cup cocoa powder
1 tsp. baking powder
$\frac{1}{2}$ tsp. soda bicarb
$\frac{1}{2}$ cup sour curd
2 tbsp. oil.

Chocolate icing
$\frac{1}{2}$ cup cocoa powder
1 cup icing sugar
$\frac{1}{2}$ cup butter

Method

- Sieve flour, soda bicarb, baking powder and cocoa powder together.
- Beat eggs, sugar oil and curd together in a large mixing bowl, add flour to it and beat for 10-12 minutes until light in texture.
- Grease a cake tin. Pour the cake batter into it.
- Bake in a preheated oven at 160°C for 40-45 minutes.
- Insert a knife in the centre. If it comes out clean, cake is ready; otherwise bake for another 5-10 minutes.
- Cool for 5-10 minutes and remove from the tin. Cool completely.
- Prepare icing by mixing butter, icing sugar and cocoa together. If too hard, put a few drops of milk.
- Spread icing on the cake and serve.

Variations

- You can grate milk chocolate over the icing.
- You can serve the cake without icing also.

Mango cake

Serves 6-8

Preparation time 70 minutes

Ingredients	For mango cream
2 eggs	$\frac{1}{2}$ cup mango pulp
2 cups flour	$\frac{1}{2}$ cup mango cubes
2 tsp. baking powder	2 tbsp. sugar (optional)
$\frac{3}{4}$ cup sugar	1 cup milk
2 apples	
2 tbsp. sugar	

Method

- Sieve flour and baking powder together.
- Peel and cut apples into circles. Remove the seeds. Boil with 2 tbsp of water and cook on low heat till tender. Sprinkle 2 tbsp sugar. Cook again for 5 minutes. Cool it. Mash half with fork.
- Beat sugar, butter and eggs till creamy in a large mixing bowl.
- Add half of the flour and mashed apple to egg mixture. Beat well for 5-7 minutes.
- Add remaining flour and beat vigorously till light in texture.

- Grease a cake tin. Pour the batter.
- Bake in preheated oven at 180°C for 5 minutes.
- Arrange the remaining apple slices over it and bake for 35-40 minutes at 160°C.
- Insert knife in the centre. If comes out clean, the cake is ready or bake for another 10 minutes. Cool and remove from the tin.
- To make apple sauce, peel and cut apple into pieces. Blend in mixi to make paste. Heat butter in a sauce pan. Add corn flour and cook for 2-3 minutes on low heat. Add milk and sugar and cook stirring vigorously. cool.
- Add apple paste and beat well.
- Pour this apple sauce over and around cake and serve.

Variations

- You can use oil instead of butter in the cake.
- Cake can be served hot also without apple sauce.
- In the apple sauce, you can use half cream and half milk.

Custard Cake with Custard
Serves 6-8
Preparation time 70 minutes

Ingredients

For cake
1 cup flour
1 cup sugar
$\frac{3}{4}$ cup butter
$\frac{1}{2}$ cup custard powder (vanilla)
3 eggs
$1\frac{1}{2}$ tsp. baking powder
$\frac{1}{2}$ tsp. soda bicarb
$\frac{1}{2}$ cup red and green peels

Decoration
A few glazed cherries

For custard
2 cups milk
2 tbsp. pink custard powder
2 tbsp. sugar

Method

- Sieve flour, custard powder, baking powder and baking

soda together.

- Beat eggs, sugar and butter till creamy in a large mixing bowl.
- Mix peels with flour mixture and add to egg mixture. Beat for 10-12 minutes till the batter is light in texture.
- Grease a baking tin. Pour batter into it and bake in a preheated oven at 180° for 30-40 minutes.
- Insert a knife in the centre of cake. If it comes out clean, cake is ready. Cool for 5-7 minutes and remove from the tin. Cool completely.
- Boil milk. Dissolve custard powder and sugar into 3 table spoon water and pour in milk. Cook stirring continuously till it is thick.
- Cut cake into two. Pour custard on both the pieces. Keep for 2-3 minutes, join together and cool.
- Cool the remaining custard and pour over cake.
- Decorate with cherries.

Variations

- Keep the cake plain and cut into pieces. Pour custard into individual plates and keep cake pieces over it at the time of serving.
- Instead of eggs, you can use 4 tbsp milk powder and $\frac{1}{2}$ cup liquid milk.
- You can mince cherries and add to custard while pouring in between cake layers and over the cake.

Rich Christmas Cake

Serves 8-10

Preparation time 90 minutes

Ingredients

2 cups flour
3 eggs
1 cup sugar
1 cup butter
$\frac{1}{2}$ cup mixed peels
1 cup raisins
1 cup currants
1 cup glazed cherries
1 tsp. baking powder
$\frac{1}{2}$ tsp. soda bicarb
1 tsp. all spices (ground cinnamon, ginger, nutmeg)
$\frac{1}{4}$ cup rum or brandy
$\frac{1}{2}$ cup water
15-20 almonds chopped

Method

- Mix all the fruits, put in rum and keep over night.
- Sieve flour, baking powder and all spices together.
- Heat water. Put butter and sugar. Cook on low heat till butter melts. Add soda bicarb and cool slightly. Add all the fruits to it.
- Add the flour mixture to the fruit-mixture. Mix well.
- Beat white of eggs till forthy. Add yolks to white. Add yolks to white. Add to fruit and flour mixture.
- Grease a cake tin. Pour the batter into it. Decorate almonds over it. Bake in preheated oven at 140°C for 1 hour.
  Insert a knife in the centre. If it comes out clean, cake is ready. Pour some rum over it.
- Cool for 5-10 minutes. Remove from tin and wrap into aluminium foil and keep aside for 10-12 hours to cool.

Variations

- Instead of rum or brandy, soak the fruits in fresh grape juice.
- You can add chopped walnuts also along with other fruits.

Banana Cake
Serves 6-8
Preparation time 60 minutes

Ingredients

2 eggs	1 tsp. baking powder
1 cup flour	$\frac{1}{2}$ tsp. soda bicarb
$\frac{1}{2}$ cup whole wheat flour	2 tbsp. green coloured peels.
$\frac{3}{4}$ cup sugar	
$\frac{3}{4}$ cup oil	
3 riper bananas	

Method

- Peel and mash bananas with a fork till well blended.
- Sieve flours, baking powder and soda bicarb together.
- Beat eggs, sugar and oil till creamy in a large mixing bowl.
- Mix coloured peels with mashed bananas and mix with flour.
- Add flour to egg mixture and beat for 10-12 minutes till light in

texture.

- Grease a cake tin and pour the batter into it.
- Bake in a preheated oven at 160°C for 40-45 minutes.
- Inset a knife in the centre of the cake. If comes out clean, the cake is ready or bake for another 5-10 minutes.
- Cool for 5-7 minutes and remove from the tin and cool.

Variations

- Can be served hot.
- Can be served with banana and fresh cream beaten together.

Bitter Coffee Cake

Serves 6-8

Preparation time 70 minutes

Ingredients	Icing
3 eggs	
1 $\frac{1}{2}$ cups flour	1 cup butter
1 cup sugar	2 tsp. coffee powder
1 cup butter	1 cup icing sugar
1 tbsp. baking powder	1 tbsp. warm water
1 tbsp. coffee powder	
3 tbsp. hot water	

Method

- Sieve flour and baking powder together.
- Dissolve coffee in hot water.
- Beat eggs, sugar and butter together till creamy in a large mixing bowl.
- Add flour to egg mixture and beat for 5-7 minutes.
- Add coffee to above mixture and beat till texture is light.
- Grease a round baking dish. Pour batter into it.
- Bake in a preheated oven at 160°C for 35-40 minutes.
- Insert a knife in the centre. If comes out clean, cake is ready.
- Remove from the tin and cool completely.
- For icing, dissolve coffee in warm water and cool. Mix butter, coffee and icing sugar. Sprinkle some coffee powder over it.

Variations

- You can put the icing in the centre of the cake by cutting it into two.
- Can be made eggless also by using 4 tbsp of milk powder and $\frac{1}{2}$ cup liquid milk instead of eggs.

Cold Chocolate Cake
Serves 6-8
Preparation time 20 minutes

Ingredients

250 gms marie biscuits
3 tbsp. drinking chocolate
3 tbsp. cocoa powder
$\frac{1}{2}$ bar milk chocolate
$\frac{3}{4}$ cup powder sugar
$\frac{1}{2}$ cup milk powder
$\frac{1}{2}$ cup butter
1 cup cottage cheese (paneer)

Method

- Break and ground the biscuits with a rolling pin.
- Beat sugar and butter lightly. Add cocoa powder, drinking chocolate, milk powder and $\frac{1}{2}$ cup of cottage cheese to it. Mix well with hand.
- Add the biscuit crumbs and make dough. Divide the dough into two parts.
- Put greased paper at the bottom and inner circle of the tin.
- Put one part of the dough at the bottom. Grate the remaining cheese over it and again the biscuit mixture. Press nicely with a spatula.
- Cool in the fridge for 1 hour.
- Remove from the tin. Tear off the paper.
- Grate milk chocolate over it and serve.

Variations

- You can put a layer of cheese at the top also before grating he chocolate.

Black Forest Cake
Serves 6-8
Preparation Time 60 minutes

Ingredients

For cake

3 eggs
1 cup flour
$\frac{3}{4}$ cup sugar
1 tsp. baking powder
$\frac{1}{2}$ tsp. soda-bicarb
4 tbsp. warm water
3 tbsp. cocoa powder

For syrup

3 tbsp. sugar
1/2 cup water

For icing

$\frac{1}{2}$ cup butter
1 cup icing sugar
$1\frac{1}{2}$ tsp. gelatine
3 tsp. warm water
1 small bar of milk chocolate

Method

- Sieve flour, baking powder, soda bicarb and cocoa powder together.
- Beat eggs, sugar and warm water in a large mixing bowl.
- Put flour mixture into it and beat for 10-12 minutes.
- Grease a baking tin. Pour batter into it and bake in a preheated oven at 180°C for 25-30 minutes.
- Insert a knife in the centre. If comes out clean, cake is ready. Cool for 5-7 minutes and remove from tin. Let it cool completely.
- Cut the cake into two halves.
- Make syrrup of sugar and water. Pour syrup on both the halves.
- For icing, dissolve gelatine in warm water. Beat butter, icing sugar and gelatine solution very well. Cool it in the fridge for 15 minutes.
- Put icing on the lower half of the cake. Put other half of the cake over it.
- Put icing over and around the cake smoothly.
- Grate milk chocolate over it.
- Cool and serve.

Variations

- You can put $\frac{1}{3}$ cup of campa cola or pepsi in place of wam water and soda bi carb.

● Glazed cherries can be put in between the two halves of the cake and at the top of the cake also.

Coconut Cake
Serves 6-8
Preparation time 70 minutes

Ingredients

Ingredients	Glazed icing
6 eggs white only	
1 cup water	1 cup icing sugar
$\frac{1}{2}$ cup corn flour	4 tbsp. water
$1\frac{1}{2}$ cups sugar	1 egg white
1 tsp. baking powder	
2 tbsp. white vinegar	
$\frac{1}{2}$ cup cream	
$\frac{3}{4}$ cup desiccated coconut powder	

Method

● Sieve flour, corn flour and baking powder together.
● Beat cream and sugar. Add vinegar. Add flour mixture to cream mixture and mix well.
● Put coconut and fold gently.
● Grease a cake tin. Pour batter into it.
● Bake in a preheated oven at 160°C for 35-40 minutes.
● Insert a knife in the centre. If comes out clean, cake is ready.
● Invert the tin and remove the cake immediately. Cool completely.
● Prepare glazed icing by dissolving sugarin hot water. Boil till sugar is dissolved. Cool it. Beat white of egg. Add sugar solution to it.
● Spread this icing over the cake anmd cool it.

Variation

●You can add desicated coconut powderand a few drops of a edible yellowcolour to the icing.

Black forest Crepe Cake
Serves 8-10
Preparation time 50 minutes

Ingredients

For crepes
2 cups flour
2 eggs
2 tbsp. oil
Pinch of baking powder
2 $\frac{1}{2}$ cups water
1 tbsp. cocoa powder
$\frac{1}{2}$ cup sugar

For decoration
1 cup cream
A few almonds
$\frac{1}{2}$ bar chocolate

For filling
1 tin glazed cherries without seeds
$\frac{1}{2}$ cup sugar
3 tbsp. corn flour
2 tbsp. butter
$\frac{1}{2}$ cup orange juice

Method

- Sieve flour, cocoa powder and baking powder together.
- Blend flour mixture with eggs, sugar and milk to make a thin smooth batter.
- Grease a hot fying pan. Pour 1 tbsp batter into it. Make crepes as thin as possible. Cook on one side only.
- Make about 15-20 crepes and cool them between kitchen towels.
- Prepare filling by heating butter. Put corn flour, orange juice, sugar and cherries with liquids. Bring it to boil and cook till thick. Cool it.
- Put filling between crepes. Press them.
- Whip cream and pour over cake. Decorate with roasted almonds and grated chocolate. Cool for 3-4 hours.

Variations

- For filling, instead of cherries you can use mixed fruit or strawberry jam.

● You can decorate the cake with strawberries also.

Pineapple Cake
Seves 6-8
Prepration time 80 minutes

Ingredients
2 cups flour
1 cup sugar
4 eggs
2 tsp. baking powder
$\frac{1}{4}$ cup milk
$\frac{1}{4}$ cup pineapple juice

Icing
1 cup fresh cream
1 cup icing sugar
8 slices of tinned pineapple
A few glazed cherries

Method

● Sieve flour and baking powder together.
● Beat eggs, sugar and butter till creamy.
● Add flour to egg mixture and beat for 5 minutes.
● Add pineapple juice and milk and beat again for 5-7 minutes till light in texture.
● Grease in a rectangular baking dish and pour the batter into it.
● Bake in a preheated oven at 160°C for 40-45 minutes.
● Insert a needle in the centre. If comes out clean, cake is ready.
● Cool for 5 minutes and remove from the tin. Cool completely. Cut into two halves horizontally.
● Prepare icing by beating cream and icing sugar over ice cubes till thick. Keep in fridge.
● Chop four slices of pineapple finely.
● Cream the lower part of the cake with icing and put chopped pineapple over it. Cover with other half of the cake.
● Put remaining cream at the top of the cake. Decorate with sliced pineapple and cherries.

Variations
● You can make pineapple pastries also. Cut the cake into rectangular pieces after putting the cream in between two pieces of cake and decorate each piece with icing, cherry and pineapple slice.

Indian Milk Cake

Serves 6-8

Preparation time 90 minutes

Ingredients

2 lts full cream milk

250 gms sugar

2 tsp. lemon juice

$\frac{1}{2}$ cup chopped pistachious.

Method

- Boil the milk in a heavy bottom sauce pan.
- Keep boiling till it reduces to half.
- Put the lemon juice and sugar.
- The milk should curdle slightly.
- Keep on boiling stirring till it becomes one lump and leaves sides of the pan.
- Grease a round or a rectangular dish.
- Put the cake in it. Pat with spatula or hand so that it is uniform.
- Cool in fridge for about an hour.
- Remove from the tin. Decorate with pistachios and press a little.
- Cut into square pieces and serve.

Variartion

1. Instead of pistachios you can use almonds or cashewnuts.

6

PIES AND PUFF PASTRIES

Pie crust and puff pastry come under the class of unleavened bakery products. This is due to the reason that no chemical leavening agent or yeast is included in the formula. Only rarely, a small amount of baking powder may be added to the pie crust recipe.

PIE CRUSTS

Pie crust recipes have high fat and low moisture content. The ratio of various ingredients and method of preparation are such that there is no continuous gluten network and the baked product has a friable or flaky appearance. Leavening agents do not added so that the crust does not become porous, as it has to securely enclose high moisture content pie fillings. Depending upon the flakiness, pie crusts may be deivided into three classes (1) Mealy (2) Medium flaky, which is more popular, and (3) the long flake type. Similar ingredients are used in all the three, but the amount of water, degree of mixing of shortening and flour differ. The mealy variety of the crust absorbs less water than either of the flaky varieties, it is due to the fact that the flour and shortening are blended to a degree where the flour is almost completely enveloped with shortening and less flour remains to absorb the water of the filling. When broken mealy type break in straight line like a biscuit while flaky varieties show a fracture along different lines at different levels.

Ingredients

Flour for the pie crust should not be high or very low in gluten. High gluten flours give tough doughs while the very low gluten flours give pasty, sticky doughs. A blend of 60% cake flour and 40% bread flour or high-gluten flour with 20% starch is suitable for pie crust. Flour containing 7-8.5% gluten is the best. Lard is very good shortening for pie crust but imparts a flavor (sometimes unacceptable). Vegetable ghee is the usual material for this purpose and is used upto 60-70% based on the weight of flour. Cold water has to be used and particularly in warm wheather ice-water should be used, this will prevent dispersions of the fat to a pasty, soft dough. 25 to 30% water based on flour is the usual quantity used.

Sugar, dextrose and corn-syrup are used to add color and sweetness to the crust but impart the tendency to absorb moisture causing sogginess; if used they should not exceed 2%. Milk adds richness and gives a better color to the crust, upto 2 to 3% dry milk may be used, in warm wheather it imparts tendency to become soggy. Salt is added to accentuate the flavor of the crust and other ingredients. For thorough blending it should be dissolved in water first, 1.5 to 3% of salt based on flour is the usual range employed.

Mixing Procedure

Pie crust ingredients are mixed in two steps. The sifted flour and shortening are mixed together for a period just sufficient to reduce the shortening to small lumps. If the fat particles are in small lump form the medium flake dough is obtained and if the blending is done to get a paste the result will be mealy crust. A cold solution of salt, milk and sugar are added, mixing lightly until the liquid is absorbed by the flour. Amount of water or liquid used is the critical factor in pie crust making and it should be very carefully measured. Dough is left at 10-15°C for several hours after mixing, this allows the water to distribute itself more thoroughly in the dough mass and hardens the shortening so that it is less likely to liquefy during handling and shaping. Chilling is particularly important for long-flake crusts. Mealy type crusts should be mixed at 15°C (using chilled water as the ingredient) and held covered at this temperature for 3-4 hours. The conditioning period helps in eliminating toughness, shrinkage and later soaking of the crust by the filling. Overmixing should be avoided.

When shortening is mixed to a peas size only flaky crust is obtained while for mealy crusts, the shortening is completely dispersed in the dough. In the latter case the processing conditions are less critical and in this case refrigeration of ingredients and dough is not of much value.

Pie Crust (for Apple Pie) Dough

Cake flour	48 parts
Bread flour	32
Shortening	40
Milk powder, optional	2
Salt	1.5
Sugar	3
Cold water	40

Flour is sifted and to this shortening is added and rubbed together into small lumps avoiding the mixing to be carried upto pasty stage. Sugar and salt are dissolved in the water and added to the flour shortening mixture. It is folded over lightly until the flour is absorbed. The dough obtained should be lumpy and sticky.

Long-flake Crust Dough

Lard	45 parts
Vegetable ghee	15
Flour	100
Skim MIlk powder	6
Water	38
Salt	4
Sugar	3

Both ther fats are mixed, to this flour and milk powder are added and mixed until the fat is in pieces. Salt and sugar are dissolved in water and blended with the above mixture.

Pie making

The dough is placed on a floured pan and shaped into a rectangle. It is refrigerated before using, to prevent the fat from sticking and to make the rolling easier, in $\frac{1}{8}$ thick and circular form. The dough is rolled slightly larger than the top of the pie tin so that the dough can cover the bottom and sloping sides of the tin. Pie is filled with the filling keeping it slightly below the pie rim. Pie rim or edge is washed with water. Egg wash may be used for better adhesion of the top and bottom crusts. Upper pie piece is also rolled and put over it and small hole is made in it. Rim of the pie tin is pressed to remove the excess crust. Pies are baked in an oven at 210 to 220°C. When the pie is shaken and the pie bottom moves freely in the tin, it is considered to be well baked.

The pies may be washed with milk, melted fat or butter or egg wash. Washes of egg or milk or their combinations of these gives glossy and relatively dark crusts. Spray of skim milk to the top crust before baking, gives a golden brown color and a drier and crisper texture. The crust may also be sprayed with melted shortening to give a flake on top of the product.

The scrap or the excess cuttings of the dough are usually employed for the bottom crusts of pies to be made later on.

PUFF PASTRY

Making of puff pastry cannot be mechanised. Layers of fat are interleaved between layers of dough; on baking layers separate out. Thus in puff pastry open network of crisp and flaky layers is obtained. Dough should be cold so that the shortening does not melt and thus does not get mixed up with the crumb.

Ingredients

Cream of tartar, vinegar, or lemon juice may be added to the water in making of the dough. These acidic substances will not affect leavening or flakiness but will relax the gluten making the rolling easier and quicker. It may be emphasised here that addition of these substances is not a must. Addition of salt improves flavor. Puff pastry flour should be of the strong type with good quality gluten. Strong flour is necessary to support the large amount of fat used, (upto100% of flour). Weak flour will yeild a paste rather than the layers of fat and dough.

The puff pastry fat should be firm and plastic and stiffer than the dough. Harder fats containing an animal fat have higher melting points and blending of such a fat with vegetable shortening tends to mellow the hardness and eliminate the greasy taste or feeling when eating the product. Lecithin and monoglycerides may also be added. Sometimes instead of water skim milk is used.

Making up

In one method of making pastry dough a small amount of fat is rubbed with the flour, water is added and the dough is well developed.

Pastry fat is distributed over $\frac{2}{3}$ rd. of the dough and rolled. Dough is allowed to relax between rolls to allow gluten to relax. During the resting period the dough is placed in a fridge to keep the fat firm and prevent running out during rolling. Large number of fat and dough layers are thus formed. In a different method all the fat is coated with the flour, water is added to form a lumy moist dough. The dough is rolled. The previous method gives better distribution of the fat without excessive use of dusting flour while in the second process more dusting flour is required resulting in toughness of the dough.

Sharp knife is used to cut the rolled-out dough. Scrap pieces of puff pastry should be folded between layers of leftover dough and then rolled out. The puff pastry units should be allowed to relax $\frac{1}{2}$ to 1 hr. before baking, this permits complete relaxation of the dough. The pieces should be eggwashed twice. First wash is given as soon as made up and second before baking. This gives a desirable crust color. Washing is very desirable as there is no sugar in the formulation to provide carmalisation for brown crust formation.

The units are baked in oven, the temperature is usually 200°C. During baking the steam released by the dough moisture pushes up the layers of the fat and dough, producing the laminated flakiness of the product. Cooler oven will give poor volume due to low rate of evaporation of moisture and a heavy product while a very hot oven will create an outside crust again resulting in poor volume, and the unit will crack due to pressure of the expanding steam of layers.

Formulations

(1)	Bread flour	64 parts
	Cream of tartar	1
	Salt	0.5
	Shortening	60
	Eggs	4
	Water	36

Flour, salt and cream of tartar are blended with some shortening. In place of cream of tartar lemon juice or vinegar may also be used. Water and eggs are stirred together and added to the above blend to get a smooth dough. The fat is put on $\frac{2}{3}$ rd of the rolled dough and given two folds to get three layers of dough and two layers of fat. After relaxing the dough it is rolled and folded again. This is repeated many times. The sheet is given a wash and cooled. The pastry units are cut into the desired shapes and baked.

(2)	Flour	80 parts
	Salt	2.5
	Shortening	40
	Water	16

Dough is made and rolled into rectangular shape and cooled. 40 parts of shortening is put over $\frac{2}{3}$rd of the sheet and folded over as above. Thin sheet is formed and is folded again into 3 layers. After cooling it is repeated twice. The puff pastry pieces are then cut into shapes and baked at 200°C.

Common Faults and their Removal

The product obtained shall be tough if the dough is over-worked or too much scrap is used. Shrinkage of the units indicates that the dough is tough and rolled too much without relaxation and the oven is too hot. If fat is not rolled in properly, or flour used is weak, or too hot or too cold oven, or if the dough is over-aged the fat runs out during baking. Poor volume is usually due to improper rolling in of fat, inadequate relaxation, improper fat, or too hot or too cold oven. If the edges of dough are not washed the product will show blisters and flaking.

7

BAKERY ADJUNCTS

Various adjuncts such as icings, fillings, frostings, toppings, creams, strensels, marshmallow and jellies etc. are actually related more to confectionery than to the bakery products, but still they are being given here as they are used with various bakery products.

ICINGS

Icings are sweet coverings or coatings in which sugar is the main constituent. They add to the attractiveness of the finished products. A properly prepared and applied icing adds tremendously to the sales appeal of the products and higher sales are registered even when the product is of inferior quality.

Ingredients Used in Icings

Powdered or confectioner's sugar is used in the preparation of flat or simple icings, fudge icings and butter cream icings. This type of sugar gives smooth icings without the grit of coarser sugars. If granulated sugar is to be used it has to be made into a syrup by boiling with water before adding other ingredients; this sugar is used for making fondant type of icing. The cream type icings neutral shortenings either emulsified or hydrogenated are used. In light cream icings e.g. fudge type (containing 15% fat) emulsified shortening is used. Hydrogenated shortening is used in butter cream icings which contain upto 40% fat. Both types of shortening provide gloss and softness to the icings. Part of butter may be replaced by vegetable shortening for better volume. As chocolate contains some fat, it also contributes to the richness and flavor of icings, particularly in butter-cream and fudge-type icings. Cocoa butter improves gloss and keeping qualities. In icings other than that of chocolate they improve setting properties of the icings.

Skimmed milk powder absorbs moisture, provides body and flavor to the icing. Fresh milk is not used as it quickly results in spoilage of the icing. Water should not be used to thin the icings containing more than 25% fat because it may result in curdling; simple syrup should be used for this purpose. Eggs (whole, white or yolk) add to the volume of creamed icings and also improve taste and flavor. Egg whites improve the shine of flat type icings. Various stabilisers e.g. gums, pectin and starches are used in the icings, to absorb excess water, avoid sugar crystallisation, and sticky condition in tropical weather. Various colors and flavors are used in the icings. Salt may not be used in icings but when used in small amounts, it improves taste and flavor of other ingredients e.g. sugar.

Various types of icings e.g. flat-icings, creamed-icings, and combination-icings are avilable and are being given below :--

Flat icings

Flat icings are the simplest type and are also known as sugar glaze, or water icing. They are essentially made with confectioner's sugar, water, corn syrup and flavor. Some fat of oil may also be added. These icings may be pourable or plastic and are used commonly on doughnuts, specially cakes etc. In making the icing all the ingredients are made into a thin paste and warmd to 41-45°C using double jacket heating. Addition of cocoa ar chocolate thickens it and creates a lusture or shine. If cocoa stiffens it simple syrup should be added. These icings loose moisture readily hence become dull and flake of in a short time. These defects can be reduced by adding stabilisers and hygroscopic sweateners. An example of chocolate doughnut glaze is given below:-

Fondant, 20% moisture	70%
Water 100°C	10
Glucose	6
Chocolate liquor, melted	14

The mixed ingredients are heated to 40°C with stirring. The water content is adjusted to give proper consistency. The icing is cooled down to 30°C. In this formulation fondant is used instead of powdered sugar to get better quality and to avoid grainy texture. Fondant is a mixture of sugar crystals and sugar syrup. The soft, creamy fondants can be used directly as centres for chocolate creams and the like and for icings, fudges etc. Other types of fondants can be used as bases to which other materials can be added to form the finished icings etc. Pasty fondants usually contain 10-12% water and can be used directly.

Creamed Icings

Cream icings are made from sugar, egg, milk powder, water, salt, flavor etc. The dry ingredients are creamed with the shortening. Other fats with continued creaming eggs are also added gradually, lastly water and flavor are incorporated. In fudge type of creamed icing an emulsified fat is used instead of creaming method. Egs whites are usually whipped with part of sugar and blended into the creamed fat to add to the lightness. When boiling syrups are to be added to whipped whites, the syrup should be boiled to about 110°-115°C and then added in thin stream to the whipping whites, machine running at medium speed. After the addition of syrup, speed is increased.

Combination Icings

It is a combination of flat-type and creamed-type icings.Fondant may be warmed with egg whites to 45°C and then whipped to a thick consistency; the fat and sugar are creamed until light, they are then blended with the whipped whites until smooth.

Cocoa is added to the icing by first blending it with the powdered sugar, this avoids the formation of lumps. When chocolate is to be added; it is first melted and then added; if this is not done, streaking will take place due to incomplete blending. Creamed icing should be stored in a cool place and kept covered to prevent the formation of crust. It tends to lose smoothness when left standing for some time, such icing should be placed in warm water bath and mixed until smooth before rising. When fruits, nuts and other toppings are to be added, overmixing of the icing should be avoided.

WHIPPED CREAM AND CREAM-TYPE TOPPINGS

Heavy cream contains about 40% butterfat, while the lighter one contains about 18-20%. Heavy cream is suitable for whipping. Cream is first aged for 1 to 2 days at 0°C, this will greatly increase whipping ability. Addition of cream helps in forming a froth in the first stage of whipping and also amount of milk may also be greatly increased. Heavy cream should be whipped until it has body and retains its shape. To avoid overwhipping the last stage of whiping should be carried out at medium speed, for every litre of heavy cream 50-60 gms. confectioner's sugar, and vanilla are added at this stage.

Whip-toppings are very useful and popular, they have slightly inferior taste than heavy cream but due to their body, stabilisers and emulsifiers they are useful for blending heavy cream with the topping. They give better variety and shelf life. Various fruit fillings and other fillings etc. may be blended into these toppings without running.

MARSHMALOW

Marshmallow is freqently used as an adjunct with cookies. It may be sandwiched between base cakes or may be placed on a single base cake in which case it is emrobed wiyh chocolate or coconut powder. Marshmallow used with biscuits is essentially a gelatin foam stregthened by the dehydration effect of a concentrated sugar solution. Other types of marshmallow are based on foamed egg white or processed proteins derived from soyabeans, milk etc.

Formulation

Cookie marshmallows are formulated with granulated sugar, corn syrup, gelatin, neutralised invert syrup and water. If the amount of water is decreased, the marshmallow will become more firm and harsh in texture. Increased amounts of sucrose or invert sugar result in shorter, less elastic structure while the increased amounts of corn syrup result in stringy and elastic texture. Thus a combination of the two is used. Composition of a biscuit marshmallow may be as follows:

Granulated sugar	0-60% preferably 30%
Corn syrup 40° Be'	20-85% preferably 25%
Invert syrup, 76% solids	0.85%
Gelatin 200-bloom strenth	1.25 to 2.25%
Water	10 to 20%

Corn syrup may be substituted by glucose and water. Higher amount of gelatin imparts better stability to the foam but, due to impaired aeration, results in heavier and hence firmer texture. Granulated sugar and/or invert syrup can be completely replaced by corn syrup but too much of it will give a heavier, less sweet and gummy product. Addition of glycerin will increase its moisture retaining properties. pH of marshmallow should be kept near to neutral, higher pH imparts yellowish tint but has favourable effect on flavor. pH may be adjusted with soda. Phosphoric acid may be used to reduce pH, this will improve foam formation during whipping, and also due to some inversion will improve moisture retention and hinder sugar crystallisation. Gums e.g. gum arabic or tragacanth, may be added upto 10% of gelatin to improve the structure of marshmallow specialities but are usually not employed for biscuit toppings. Two typical formulations for summer and winter are given below:

	Summer	*Winter*
Granulated sugar	23	9%
Dextrose	14	9
Corn syrup, 43° Be'	31	27
Invert syrup, 76%	15	40
Water	15.2	13.5
Gelatin 200-bloom strenth	1.8	1.5

The moisture content is usually kept at approx. 30%. Tapioca starch (1.5%) may be added to reduce the requirement of gelatin and to firm up the structure while retaining shortness. Even traces of fat present in the formulation adversely affect the whipping properties due to breakdown of foam hence some sodium lauryl sulphate (upto 0.1% of gelatin) should be added when traces of fat are present, to overcome the difficulty. Non-fatty flavors may be used such as vanilla, vanillian etc. while citrus oil, mint, chocolate, cocoa etc. are avoided.

Preparation

Marshmallow production starts with the preparation of syrup of all the ingredients in an unwhipped form. Various methods are used for this purpose. In the cooked process, all the ingredients except gelatin and flavor are boiled to ensure complete dissolution of sugar; this method is employed when the sucrose content of the formulation is high and syrup content is low. When sucrose content is not too high, the semicooked process may be used in which a clear solution is obtained by heating the mixture to 85-90°C. In both these processes the syrup is cooled to 60°C before adding the soaked gelatin. In the cold process sugar dissolution is ensured by agitation at 50°C for sufficient time, and later on slightly heated soaked gelatin is added to the syrup. Gelatin is soaked in 4 times its weight of water or more, for at least one hour. During this step agglomeration should be avoided.

After the incorporation of flavour and gelatin solution in the syrup, the mixture is whipped in a bowl type machine using a wire whip. Whipping should be carried out in such a way that air cells obtained are of small and uniform size with thin cell walls. This type of foam will hold up better and will have a firmer and shorter texture. This will also result in better taste of marshmallow.

Marshmallow should be protected from fungal, yeast and bacterial attack, it depends on the sugar concentration also. Inhibitors like sorbic acid may be also added for this purpose. The finished syrup may be held for 30 minutes at 65° to 75°C and equipments should be regularly and thoroughly cleaned for keeping the spoilage under control. A minimum total solids content of about 68% is required to assure protection against spoilage. Enrobed or open-faced marshmallow should be stored for at least 2 days at 20°-25°C to allow the deposit to firm up before transportation.

STRENSILS

Strensils are dry lumps or powders of non-uniform particle size which are sprinkled on the tops of unbaked goods, and partially coalesce and adhere to the surface while retaining their soft crumbly texture. An example of simple strensel tapping is cinnamon topping which may contain 93% sugar, 6% shortening and 1% cinnamon.

Composition and Formulation

A typical strensel contains about 50% flour, 25% sugar and 25% shortening. Use of some butter or margarine as shortening improves flavor, but due to the presence of water they make the flour slightly sticky and lumpy. Usually granulated sugar is used but brown sugar may also be used to get proper color and flavor. It is preferable to use 0.2 to 0.7% salt; also sometimes 4-5% of eggs or egg yolks to get some binding effect. Cinnamon flavor can be used usually upto 0.5 to 1.5%. Vanilla, lemon extract or oil, rum and almond flavor may also be used. In chocolate strenscls 6% of the flour may be replaced with a good flavored alkalised cocoa of 10-12% fat. Nuts may-be chopped and added in the mixture; chopped groundnut and coconut powder are particularly suitable; the latter may be used upto 10-25%. Use of peanut butter gives a mix of slightly softer consistency than pie dough. Honey may also be sometimes used upto 10-15% to get flavor variation or a slightly glazed appearance to the topping.

	Plain Strensel	*Chocolate Nut-Strensel*
Flour	45	40%
Shortening	25	12
Granulated sugar	15	24
Light brown sugar	14	--
Salt	0.5	0.5
Cinnamon	0.5	--
Egg yolks	--	5.5
Chopped peanut	--	12
Cocoa, dutched	-	6

Honey strensel may have the following composition, part of shortening has been replaced by butter or margarine:

Flour	46%
Butter or margarine	10
Shortening	11
Granulated sugar	23
Salt	0.7
Honey	9.3

In preparation of strensels, sugar and shortening are creamed, followed by mixing in of the flour to form a light paste which is chilled and rubbed through a $\frac{1}{2}$ sieve. When eggs are also to be added, they are also creamed with the sugars and shortening.

COATINGS

Chocolate coatings and other pastel colored coatings of similar texture are used on biscuits and cakes. The coatings may be sweet or milk chocolate, or compound type. Sugar and fat are the main ingredients of these coatings; while corn syrup solids, flavors, colors and emulsifiers are the other ingredients. Compound coatings have chocolate flavor with a suitable food color.

Sugar used should be finely powdered. Coconut oil is preferable while hydrogenated cotton seed and soyabean oils are also used. Vegetables butters used in the coating formulations should have blend flavor, because if any taste or flavor is present in it, the product will attract disfavor from the customer. Moisture content of the coating should be very low. Addition of a small amount of glycerin will partially offset tyhe adverse effect of the presence of moisture. Corn syrup solids, starches etc. may be added to reduce sweetness and also make it somewhat cheaper. Viscosity can be lowered, for easy enrobing, by adding more of cocoa butter or hardened vegetable oil; viscosity control is possible by varying the lecithin content, which acts as an emulsifier and antioxidant. Contact of coatings with copper is undesirable as its traces accelerate oxidant and rancidity; this can be controled by adding a small amount of citric acid.

Formulations

A few typical coating formulations have been given below:

	Vanilla coating	*Dark chocolate coating*	*Coconut coating*
Natural chocolate liquor	--	41	--%
Hardened vegetable oil	34	--	34
Sugar	56	42	53
Cocoa butter	--	16.9	--
Coconut powder	--	--	15

Vanilla formulation may be taken as base for making colored coatings. Daru chocolate coating is quite costly due to the presence of large quantity of cocoa butter. It also contains natural chocolate liquor which may create a fat bottom or loss of gloss unless carefully tempered.

	Cocoa coating	*Peanut coating*
Hardened vegetable oil	32	27
Sugar	44	33
Powdered milk	10	12
Lecithin	0.3	--
Vanillin	0.1	--
Salt	0.1	0.1

Natural cocoa	13.5	--
Groundnut flour, 12-14% oil	--	28

For light cocoa formulations amounts of cocoa and vegetable oil are reduced while milk powder and sugar are increased; for dark cocoa formulation it is vice-versa.

Coating Method

When chocolate liquor is used in the formulation, carefully controlled tempering is required. Fat is melted at 45°C and cooled with constant stirring to about 28°C followed by heating again to about 32°C. The cookies are passed through the enrober at 20°C; excess chocolate is blown and shaken off. The enrobed pieces are passed through a cooling tunnel where chilled air is blown. The cookies are then stored at about 22°C to avoid blooming and dull surface. With vegetables coatings of higher M. Pt. than cocoa butter different coating conditions are used. With cocoa powder and hard butters in place of chocolate liquor higher coating temperature should be employed; they require less care to get gloss.

FILLINGS

Fillings are required with pies and some sweet dough products.

Pie fillings

Pie fillings may in general, be classified as fruit fillings and cream fillings etc. The preparation should be thickened with starch so thst the soaking of liquid into the crust is reduced to the minimum and also the application is easier. Some fruit pie fillings are made from from fruit pulps thus due to their own viscous fluid, they do not require any additional thickner.

Custards are baked in the crust and form a firm gel while the cream fillings are cooked outside the shell and give a softer gel when completely set. A good quality cream base filling is given below:

Whole milk	29.2	parts
Salt	0.05	
Granulated sugar	10	

Corn starch	2
Egg yolks	2.5
Melted butter	1.25
Whipping cream	5

Corn starch is mixed with the milk. Remaining milk, sugar and salt are boiled together and the solution is mixed with starch suspension. It is cooked with stirring until smooth. Egg yolks, vanilla and butter are combined. The two mixtures are well mixed and beaten. The filling is cooked for about 4 minutes over hot water. Butter scotch can also be used as flavor and bananas, coconut and cherries may also be mixed in. A pumpkin custard pie filling formulation has been given below:

Pumpkin	100 parts
Sugar	65
Corn syrup	8
Starch	3
Spices	1
Melted butter	9
Whole milk	125
Whole eggs	32

The ingredients are blended toghether and heated slightly. The material is filled into unbaked pie shells. Pumpkin used here is canned type.

A straight cheese-custard type filling is given below:

Cake flour	32 parts
Sugar	128
Salt	4
Milk powde	64
Shortening	32
Cheese	320
Eggs	48
Water	160
Vanilla	4

Sugar, salt, milk powder and shortening are blended together to a smooth paste. Flour and cheese are mixed together and added to the above paste. Eggs are also added and blended well. Vanilla and water are added finally in stages and blended well. The fillings should have thick gravy consistency, this can be achieved by adjusting the amount of water. Baker's cheese is usually employed but cream cheese may also be used; other modifications may also be made. For pineapple and other fruit filled cheese pie, the fruit filling is placed in the bottom of the pie and then the cheese filling is poured on the top. Pie is baked at 210°C until the edge has a brown ringlike crust and the centre of the pie feels filled.

These fillings are similar to pie fillings but, as they are used in small quantities, they are formulated with intense flavor and color. Fruit flavored fillings may or may not contain actual fruit. In jellies pectin is used for the formation of gel. Gels should contain at least 60-70% sugar, 30-40% water, 0.7-1.25% pectin and acid sufficient to produce a pH of 2.2 to 3.5. Imitation fruit jellies based on pectin are cheaper than the true fruit jellies but their gel structure tends to break down easily when vigorously agitated, or heated. The following formulation is of cheep imitation fruit flavored filling:

Sugar	9.3
Corn syrup 43° Be', 32 DE	60
Water	28
Pectin	0.6
Algin	0.1
Phosphoric acid, 8%	2

Various types of cream type fillings are also prepared for use in sweet dough products. The basic filling may be either cooked or uncooked. The uncooked filling base is made of fat, sugar, milk, egg whites etc.

Powdered sugar	46 parts
Margarine or butter	36
Milk powder	9.75
Egg whites	9
Salt	0.25

The dry ingredients are mixed and egg whites blended until smooth. To this required amount and kind of nuts, fruits, flavors, spices, cheese, cocoa etc. may be added as desired. In cooked fillings starch is used as follows:

Starch	2.5 parts
Sugar	27
Cake crumbs	27
Margarine	6.5
Water	37

About 25 parts of water is boiled and to this starch slurry made with remaining water is added and cooked until clear. Sugar is added followed by cake crumbs and margarine until smooth. It is cooled before using. Various flavors, cheese, nuts, and fruits etc. may be added as desired.

8

SWEET YEAST DOUGH PRODUCTS (BUNS ETC.)

Sweet yeast leavened doughs may be classified into two major categories, namely, remix sweet dough and the straight sweet dough. Other doughs of this type are sponge dough (Babka) and roll-in (Danish) type. Sweet doughs are much richer, in shortening, milk and sugar, than the bread-type doughs and they usually contain whole eggs, egg yolks or whites. Commonly used flavors include spices, vanilla, nuts and nut pastes, peels or oils of lemon or orange, raisins, candied fruits etc. By varying the flavoring, filling, shape and icing an almost infiniate number of types of cakes and rolls can be made.

A typical basic formula of straight sweet dough is given below:-

Bread flour	80 parts
Cake flour	20
Sugar	20
Margarine	20
Whole eggs	20
Milk powder	5
Non-diastatic malt syrup	2
Salt	1
Compressed yeast	8
Water	45

Sugar, margarine or emulsified shortening, salt, eggs, malt and milk powder are creamed together. To this flours are added slowly with good mixing. Finally water in which yeast has been dissolved, is added and the dough is developed. The dough is usually fermented for about

$1\frac{1}{2}$ hours at 30°C. To prepare a remix sweet dough, after fermentation about 20-22 parts of a strong flour, 13-14 parts of sugar, 13-14 parts of butter, margarine or emullsified shortening and 13-14 parts of egg yolks are added and mixed at medium speed. No further fermentation is required, the dough is immediately scaled and made up.

The basic formula given above is quite rich. If a lean dough is desired, the enriching ingredients can be reduced even upto 50% or more. In that case yeast may also be decreased due to increase in its activity.

The enriching ingredients soften the texture of the product and make it flakier. They improve the taste and color and increase the nutritional quality of the product. Liquid skim milk may be used in place of powdered milk and water may be correspondingly decreased. Various dough improvers and yeast foods may be added as in the case of breads.

We shall now describe all the four types of sweet yeast dough products mentioned above.

BUNS

Buns are almost similar to bread. Their dough is comparatively leaver dough. Due to leaver dough, they can be proofed longer and baked at higher oven temperatures. A typical bun dough formulation is given below:

Flour	100 parts
Water	67
Salt	2.5
Sugar	15
Compressed yeast	4
Milk powder	10
Shortening	9
Malt syrup	1

Richness of the dugh can be varied, a richer dough gives better bun of better keeping qualities. A well balanced sweet yeast bun dough recipe is given below:

Cake flour	16 parts
Bread flour	48
Water	33
Sugar	12
Milk powder	4
Salt	1
Shortening	12
Eggs	8
Yeast	4

Sugar, milk powder, salt shortening and mace are blended to a smooth paste. Eggs are also blended in well followed by 24 parts of water. Flours are added to it and stirred followed by solution of yeast in remaining water. The dough is developed until smooth. Temperature of water is controlled to control the dough temperature. Dough is allowed to rise well in warm and moist place. When ready, it is punched and allowed to relax for 20 minutes. The dough is scaled, divided and rounded. The slightly pressed bun doughs are put on pans. The tops are washed with water, milk or egg wash. For better appearance buns may be sprinkled with Struessel topping. Buns are given $\frac{3}{4}$ proofs and baked at 200°C until the crust becomes golden brown. The buns are cooled.

Various types of of buns

Apart from the basic and usual type of buns described above other buns are also made differing in shape, size, method of preparation and fillings used. Cinnamon buns are made by rolling the dough in sheet form, brushing it with oil or fat, cake crumbs and cinnamon sugar and then rolling it up tightly. The roll is cut into pieces which are proofed and baked at 190°-200°C. The butterfly buns are also made similarly except that pieces are pressed at the centre with a thin rolling pin to cause the layers of dough to flange or spread out in the form of wings. After egg-wash the units are baked and cooled followed by putting some icing. Some of the buns are pressed at the centre with a round object, in this depression cheese filling, fruit filling, jelly, orange or lemon filling may be put. These buns are accordingly called cheese-buns, fruit-filled buns etc. After $\frac{3}{4}$ proofs the buns are baked at 190° to 200°C. The buns are then washed carefully with simple syrup, cooled and iced with simple icing. Twist buns are made by rolling the dough into sheets. The sheets are covered with melted fat or jam or jelly. The dough is then folded in such a way as to give three layers of dough and two layers of fillings. The dough is rolled again and cut into strips. The individual strips are twisted and baked.

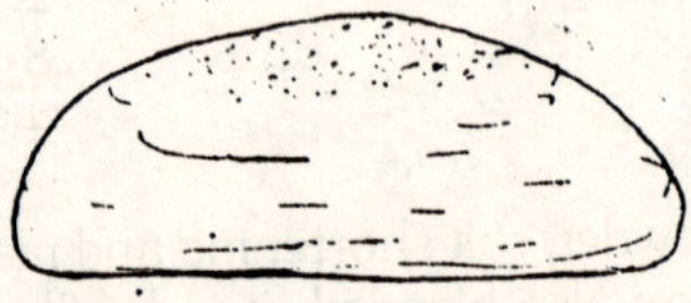

Fig. 8.1 Common Bun.

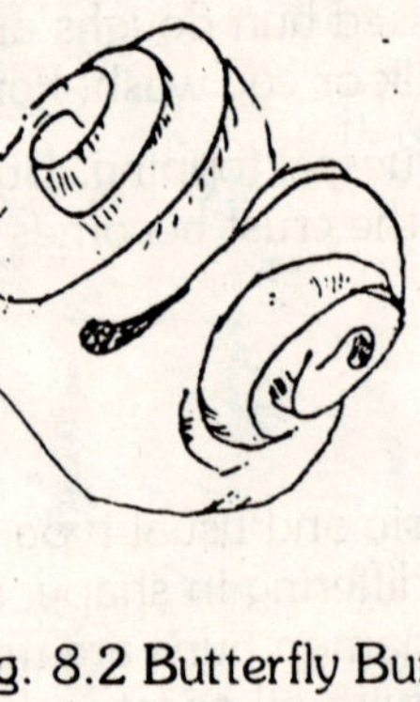

Fig. 8.2 Butterfly Bun

Fig. 8.3 Jelly-filled Bun.

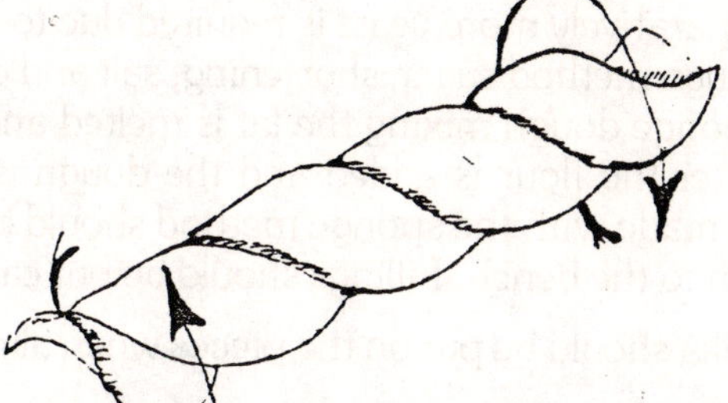

Fig. 8.4 Twist Bun

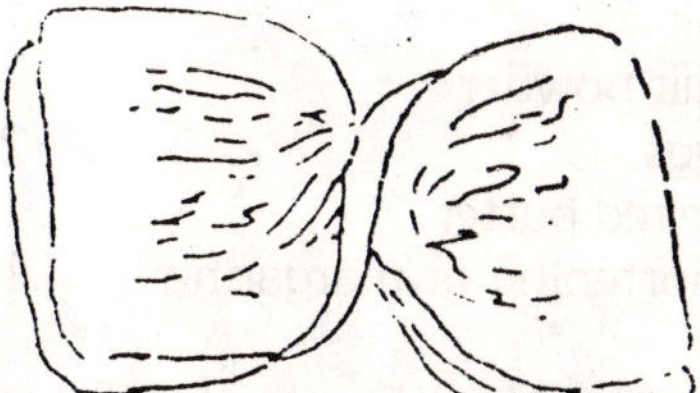

Fig. 8.5 Bow Tie Coconut Bun

Horseshoe-shaped buns may be made by washing the strips with egg wash and sprinkling with toppings. One side of the strips is given 5 slight cuts at one edge and then twisted and placed in a pan in horse-shoe shape, proofed and baked. Bow tie coconut buns are made by cutting the dough in the form of strips as in the case of twist-buns and then giving it one twist. The piece is egg washed, sprinkled with fine shread coconut, $\frac{3}{4}$ proofed and then baked at 200°C. Overbaking is avoided so that coconut topping may not become brown. The buns are then lightly washed with warm syrup, cooled and then iced with simple icing.

BABKA

Babka is a loaf-type cake made from a very rich sweet dough and is sometimes called 'coffee cake loaf' or 'Grand-mother's loaf'. Because of the added richness, the dough is made by the sponge dough method. Comparatively more yeast is required due to high richness. In the straight dough method sugar, shortening, salt and eggs are creamed together. In sponge dough mixing the fat is melted and drawn into the final dough after the flour is added and the dough is partially developed. Doughs made with the sponge method should be allowed to rise once and taken to the bench. Fillings should be put carefully. Toppings applied to Babka should be put on the pieces when almost $\frac{3}{4}$ proofed.

The use of butter, eggs, yolks and other enriching ingredients determines the quality. A typical Babka recipe is given below:

Bread flour	80 parts
Water	32
Yeast	8
Sugar	22
Salt	1.25
Milk powder	4
Eggs	24
Melted butter	16
Shortening or margarine	16

Yeast is dissolved in 32 parts of water and $\frac{2}{3}$ rd flour is mixed well. The mixture is allowed to rise well. Sugar, salt, milk powder, vanilla one part, cardamon 0.25 part, orange and lemon 1 part and eggs are added and mixed well. Remaining flour is then added and mixed. Melted fat is slowly added followed by fat. Dough is mixed until moon. It is allowed to rise well. This method is sponge dough method and gives more rapid fermentation.

The dough is sealed into oblong shape and after relaxing, it is rolled $\frac{1}{4}$ thich. It is smeared with melted butter, or melted chocolate and chopped nuts, cake crumbs, cinnamon, sugar or raisins are sprinkled over it and rolled gently. The sheet may be rolled or cut into strips and twisted in the required form. The pieces are put on well greased or paperlined pans, washed with melted butter, and $\frac{3}{4}$ proofed. Proofed units are sprinkled with struessel topping and then baked at

175° to 180°C.

DANISH PASTRY

Danish pastry has interleaving dough sheets and fat layers. The method of preparation of somewhat similar to that of puff pastry. In puff pastry the leavening action is that from the water vapors formed during baking while in the case of Danish pastry the leavening action is due to the yeast which gives it the required porous structure. The method of preparation results in separation of layers in the product. The fat layers are melted during baking and get absorbed into the dough layers, thus fat layers do not appear in the finished product. The amount and type of fat used is important. Butter is expensive but gives the best product. Butter and margarine in equal proportions is also a good fat for this purpose; vegetable glue is also satisfactory.

The fat used should not be too hard or too soft. In the first case it will tear the dough layers during rolling resulting in large uneven pieces, and in the latter case the fat tends to run out of the sides of the doughs causing stickiness and other problems also crop up.

Since it is important to maintain separation of the dough layers until the product is baked, Danish pastry dough is rolled while cold. The shortening is spread over a freshly thick piece of dough, it is folded over rolled again, folded again and repeated until a many layered structure has been developed. Refrigeration is desirable after each sheeting operation to dissipate the heat resulting from the rolling action; otherwise the fatty layers shall melt and dough layers shall merge. Usually four times rolling is sufficient. Too much rolling will make the layers of fat and dough so thin that they will blend togehter. Danish pastry doughs do not ordinarily recieve much fermentation. An initial short period of 20-30 minutes in the refrigerator before the fat is rolled in, allows some gas and flavor to be developed. Dough is cooled between each series of sheetings and in each of these cases some fermentation will take place.

Danish pastry doughs are carefully proofed otherwise the units may tear during baking, or may become greasy, flat or lack volume. When toppings, such as coconut or fruit toppings, are to be applied they are sprinkled after $\frac{1}{2}$ proof and then proofed upto $\frac{3}{4}$ profs. Baking is done as usual at the oven temperature of upto 200°C. Hot syrup wash is applied while the units are hot, and icing should be warmed to 45°C before applying. This will avoid stickiness in the cool product.

Method of Preparation

Sponge and dough method is employed for making Danish pastry. The first stage is called sponge and the second one is known as dough stage. The sponge usually contains $\frac{1}{2}$ to $\frac{3}{4}$ of the flour and all the yeast, yeast foods, and malt together with enough water to make a stiff dough. All or part of the shortening may be added here or later. $\frac{1}{2}$ to $\frac{3}{4}$ of the salt may be added to the sponge to control fermentation. The sponge is fermented until it begins to decline in volume i.e. starts dropping, this takes about 3-5 hrs. At the dough stage, the sponge is mixed with the remaining ingredients. The dough is developed to a peak and then proofed. The sponge and dough method is more cumbersome and time consuming than the straight dough method in which all the ingredients are mixed in the first mixing step. Some of the advantages of sponge method are about 20% saving in yeast; better volume, texture and grain; and greater flexibility.

Formulations

A typical formulation is given below :

Flour	64 parts
Sugar	16
Salt	1
Butter, margarine (Roll-in-fat)	16
Shortening	24
Yeast	4
Milk powder	4
Eggs	16
Water	32
Vanilla	1

Sugar, salt, milk powder, $\frac{1}{3}$ rd shortening and cardamon or coffee cakes flavor (0.12 parts) are blended to a smooth, soft paste. Eggs are added in two stages and blended well. Vanilla dissolved in 16 parts of water are added followed by flour which is stirred in slightly. Yeast dissolved in 16 parts of water is added and the mixture is developed to a smooth dough. Roll in fat and remaining shortening are mixed together and kept aside.

The dough is rolled in rectangular shape $\frac{1}{2}$ thick. After relax ing for 5 to 10 minutes fat is speard over $\frac{2}{3}$ of its surface and folded twice so that three layers of dough have two layers of fat in between.

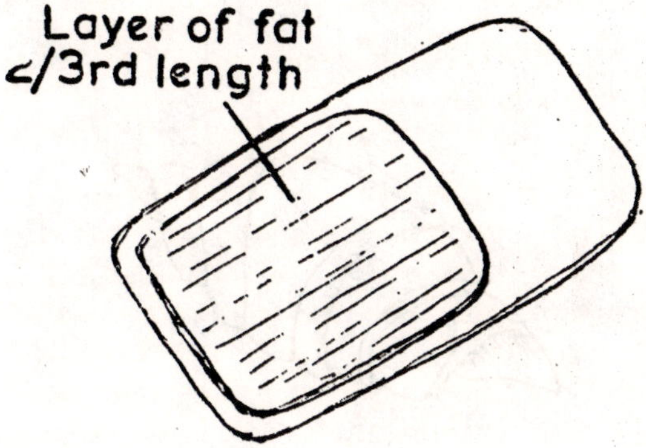

Fig. 8.6 Dough Before Folding

Fig. 8.7 Dough Folded Twice

After dusting with flour it is rolled again to $\frac{1}{2}$ thickness and spread again with fat and folded again. This procedure is repeated 4 times. With relaxing time (under refrigeration) of 15 minutes between each two rollings. The dough is then cut into shape and baked at 200°C to get the required specific Danish pastry product.

The dough pieces are finished with various sizes, shapes and designs to get specific Danish pastry products such as Danish Snacks, horns, twists, sticks, rings, miniatures, coconut rings etc.

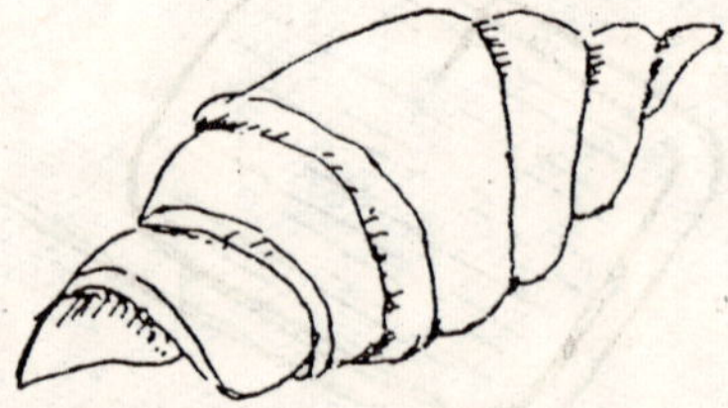

Fig. 8.8 Danish Horn

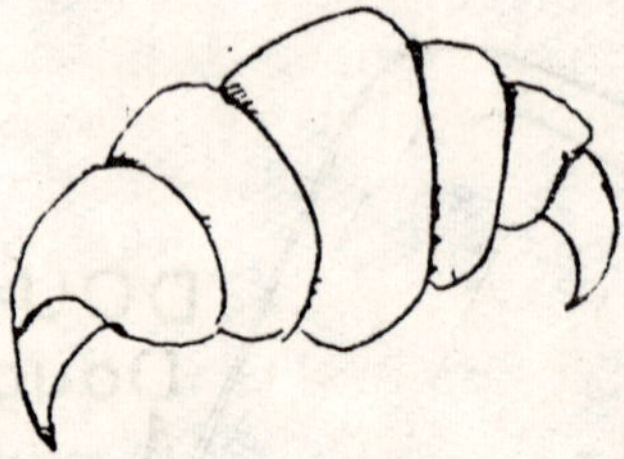

Fig. 8.9 Danish Crescent Horn.

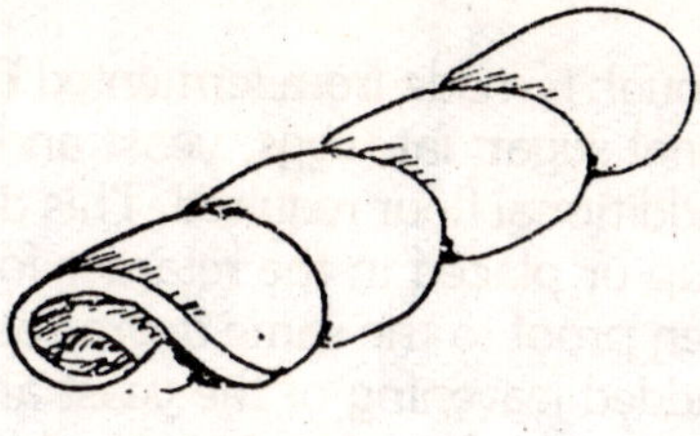

Fig. 8.10 Danish Pastry Stick

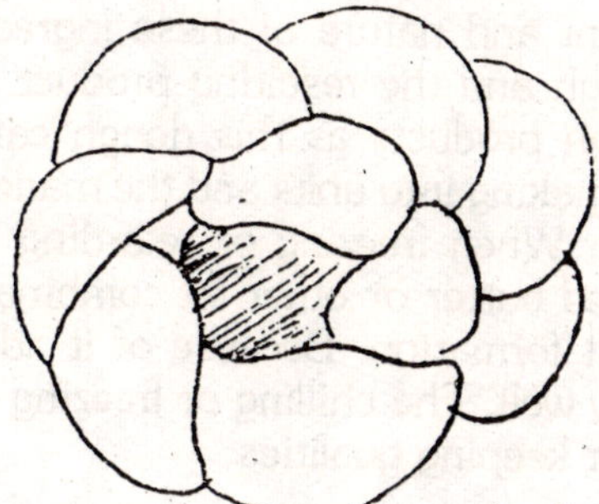

Fig. 8.11 Snail-Shape Danish

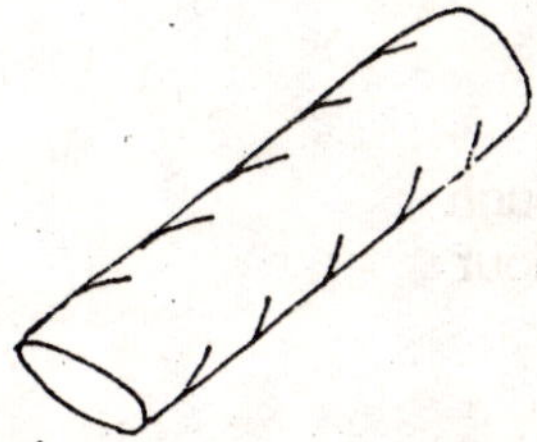

Fig. 8.12 Dough Strip Given cuts with Scissors.

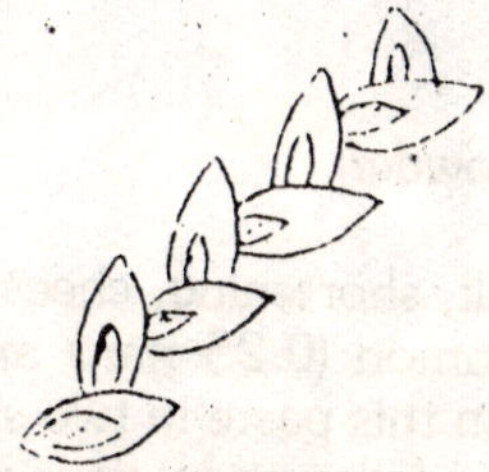

Fig. 8.13 Plam Leaf Strip Obtined After Baking.

FROZEN DOUGH PRODUCTS

Frozen dough is made from fermented Babka or rich bun dough as base. Additional sugar, fat, eggs, yeast and/or baking powder are added with the additional flour required. This dough is allowed to relax and then made up or placed in the retarder for later use. Since these units are not given proof to the same degree as Danish or Coffee cake because of the added leavening of the yeast and baking powder, they are allowed to relax to soften the gluten and half proofed before baking.

The amount and nature of these ingredients determine the quality of the dough and the resulting product. These products are called frozen dough products as this dough can be refrigerated for some time before making into units and the made up units can also be retarded or frozen. When freezing or retarding these units they are washed with melted butter or other fat combination before freezing, this prevents crust formation. Because of it added richness, frozen dough retards very well. The chilling or freezing of the added fat and eggs assures better keeping qualities.

A typical reasonably good recipe for frozen dough is given below:

Fermented Babka or

Bun Dough	64 parts
Bread flour	34
Sugar	24
Salt	0.5
Shortening	32
Baker's cheese	16
Eggs	20
Yeast	2
Water	4
Baking powder	1.5

Dough, sugar, salt, shortening, cheese (optional), vanilla (0.5 part) and mace or cardamon (0.25 part) are blended to a smooth paste. Eggs are blended in this paste in two stages. Yeast dissolved in water is also incorporated followed by flour and baking powder. The dough is mixed until smooth. The baker's cheese adds richness, taste and flavor to the dough. If cream cheese is used instead, then fat is reduced by 1 part for 2 parts of cream cheese. If frozen dough is made without any additional yeast, it will have closer grain and for leavening depend primarily upon the baking powder and the leavening supplied by the yeast present in the basic sweet dough.

The dough obtained should have medium soft consistency, if it is stiff more eggs may be added, if water is added it will make the dough leaner and baking powder will have to be increased. The dough is refrigerated to make it firm. For making pockets, the dough is rolled to 1/4" thickness and cut into squares. For filled Horns or Snecks melted fat is brushed on the dough before applying the filling, this will give added richness. Making up of units is done as usual. The dough is short hence units should be handled with care to prevent tearing the dough, particularly while making pockets. The made up units are washed with fat. They are topped with Struessel toppings, groundnut or sugar. After allowing the units to relax for 1 hour they are backed.

9

FORMULATIONS AND THE PROCEDURES FOR CHEMICALLY LEAVENED BAKERY PRODUCTS

Most bakery products depend upon the reaction of sodium bicarbonate and leavening acids for the expansive effect during baking. Such products from the largest percentages of cakes and cookies prepared in the homes or in bakeries.

CAKES

Function of the Ingredients

The gluten proteins of the flour serve as the basic structural element in chemically-leavened foods, just as they do in the bread. However, the use of relatively smaller amounts of flour, the weaker (less extensible) protein in the soft wheat flours which are customarily employed, and the lower amount of protein in the flour results in a softer, crumblier texture in cakes and similar products. In most chemically-leavened foods, the protein of the flour is inadequate in quantity and quality to support an expansion of the extent found in bread so that they are of higher density than the latter product.Formulations and the Produes for chemially leaving Bapena.

In addition to their obvious function as sweeteners, sugars have a tenderizing effect on the crumb and promote the coloring of the crust. Sucrose is less effective in coloring the crust than are invert sugar and glucose. The situation is thus different than in yeast-containing doughs, where the invertase of the yeast rapidly converts sucrose to glucose and fructose. No such action is observed in cakes and cookies, and the sucrose remains intact and nonreducing throughout the oven stage. Sugars retain moisture in the crumb and thereby retard staling. Once again, glucose or invert sugar are more effective on a weight for weight basis than sucrose because of their lower molecular weight and consequently greater osmotic effect. As the concentration of sugars is increased, the batter has a tendency to become more fluid. Less air is entrained under these conditions, but the batter can be conveyed more easily.

An important function of he shortening component of the batters is to entrap air during mixing. Not only do these air bubbles contribute directly to the leavening effect, but they also help to control grain size by serving as foci for gas evolution. Microphotographs of batters have shown that all of the air bubbles are enclosed in layers of fat. These observations demonstrate unequivocally the importance of the creaming function of shortening, regardless of whether or not the fat is creamed in a separate stage. Shortening also tenderizes the crumb and may contribute slightly to the flavor of the product. Emulsified shortenings increase the amount of water which can be used and thus contribute to the tenderness and resistance to staling of the finished product.

As mentioned before, the gluten of flours used in cakes has characteristics not conducive to the formation of large cells or thin cell walls. These deficiencies are remedied to some extent by using egg whites in the formula. Proteins of the egg form the vesicle wall in combination with gluten and permit the entrapment of air during mixing. In angel food cake the entire leavening effect is obtained from the air enclosed by the egg white during vigorous whipping. Egg white proteins themselves do not have sufficient mechanical strength, when in thin films, to withstand oven expansion or handling after and do not contribute the texture excepted in cakes. These attributes must be obtained from flour. Eggs also contribute flavor, which may or may not be desirable, and are important sources of color. Egg yolks contribute emulsifying and tenderizing effects. Eggs are frequently the only material that can be used to compensate for an excessively weak flour.

General Rules for Formulating Cakes

There exist more or less traditional rules for assuring "formula balance" or the correct proportioning of ingredients. These will be summarized here, but it should be understood that slavish adherence to their limitations is not necessary. They have worked well in practice in the past, but the development of new ingredients and new processing methods may very well allow the "rules" to be disregarded in some cases.

On a flour weight basis, sugar should be 110-160% in yellow layers, 110-160% in white layers, and 110-180% in devil's food and chocolate layers. Eggs as liquid eggs should be equal or exceed the amount of sugar by approximately 25-35%. Shortening should fall in the range of 30-70%. Sodium bicarbonate should be 1.2-2% and salt 3-4%of the flour.

If the amount of sugar in a formula is increased, the egg content should be increased an equal amount. More shortening should be added when the percentage of eggs is increased. Additional water is usually not added when the formula contains dry milk, but if the formula water is not sufficient to equal the reconstitution water for the milk, add about 1% of water for each additional percentage of milk solids.

The following differences are usually found: Rich formulae need less chemical leavening because they incorporate more air during mixing, the batters display lower specific gravity for the same reason, and they perform better at a lower baking temperature. Batters baked in large piece sizes require less water and less leavener than those baked in small piece sizes.

Example of Cake Formulae

Most authors consider the yellow cake as the basic type, but it is probably more logical to allocate this spot to the white layer cake since the yolk solids the additional ingredient in yellow cakes--do not contribute any essential property to the cake or the batter.

A formula for very lean white cake made in our American military installations for troop feeding (Anon. 1950) is shown below. Although this recipe is important as an approximate lower limit of "richness," cakes including considerably more enriching ingredients are desirable from a taste and texture standpoint. An example of a formula for a rich white layer cake which is considered basic from our point of view is also given. It is essential to use high emulsifying shortening in cakes which have a high proportion of sugar to flour, the so-called "high ratio" cakes. Of course, flavoring materials must be added to the basic formulae. In the case of white layer cakes, the flavor is nearly always vanilla. About $\frac{1}{2}$ of 1% of single strength vanilla extract or artificial vanilla is a common level of addition.

White Layer Cake

	%
Flour	25.6
Sugar	25.6
Shortening, Hydrogenated	11.2
Egg whites	16.0
Evaporated milk	10.2
Baking power	1.6
Salt	0.6
Water	9.2

Rich White Layer Cake

	%
Sugar	29.5
Flour	21.0
Shortening, emulsified	11.5
Egg whites	16.0
Milk, whole	20.0
Baking powder	1.3
Salt	0.7

The author developed for the Armed Forces a "universal" cake mix which is very versatile as a result of its assistance to failure even when rather high levels of flavoring ingredients are added. It also performs fairly well even when considerable deviations from the recommended mixing procedure occur. The formula is given here as an example of a basic white layer cake prepared from all dry ingredients.

Universal Cake Mix

	%
Flour, 6% moisture	37.51
Sugar	41.00
Shortening, high stability with added emulsifiers	13.70
Dried egg whites	3.00
MSNF	2.50
Sodium bicarbonate	0.54
Sodium acid pyrophosphate	0.15
Monocalcium monohydrate	0.55
Salt	0.90
Powdered vanilla	0.15

About 35-40% water will be added to the above dry mix, the exact amount depending to some extent on the quality of the flour and the efficiency of the emulsifier.

The principle difference between yellow layers and white layers is that the former contain whole eggs instead of egg whites. In other words, the "additive" to our basic mix is egg yolks. A possible formula would be the rich white layer cake recipe given above to which 12-13% whole eggs are substituted for the egg whites and about 2-3% additional milk is included to supply necessary moisture. Rumsey (1959) gives a formula range which will include most satisfactory recipes. Below is a slightly modified version of his formula.

Formula Range for Yellow Layer Cakes

	%
Flour	21-23
Salt	0.5-0.75
Shortening	8-12
MSNF	2-3
Baking powder	1-1.5
Whole eggs	10-14
Water	22-25
Sugar	24-32

The recipe which follows was developed to take full advantage of the special properties of whole eggs.

Typical yellow layer cake

	%
Flour	21.5
Sugar	30
Shortening, emulsifier added	11.5
Whole eggs	12.5
Whole milk	22.4
Baking powder	1.3
Salt	0.8

Yellow cakes are particularly adaptable to the addition of special flavors. Spice cakes are essentially yellow layer cakes to which, for example, mixtures of cinnamon, nutmeg, ginger, and allspice in the ratio of 8:6:1:1 are added. Pumpkin, applesauce, and mashed bananas may be added to spice cakes to furnish additional varieties. The above formula will support moderate additions of these adjunctions without failing. Larger quantities may necessitate increases in the flour and eggs.

Gingerbreads may deviate considerably in taste, texture, and appearance from yellow cakes, but they are usually formulated in accordance with much the same rules. The basic flavors in gingerbread are molasses and spices, and a coarser texture is acceptable and usually desired.

Typical Ginger bread Formula

	%
Cake flour	21.1
Sugar	8.4
Molasses	33.5
Shortening	9.4
MSNF	2.1
Whole eggs	8.4
Salt	0.5
Sodium bicarbonate	0.2
Baking powder	0.5
Cinnamon	0.5
Ginger	0.5
Allspice	0.2
Water	4.7

A small amount of soda in addition to that contained in the baking powder is included in the above formula in order to neutralize the natural acidity of the molasses.

Cakes containing cocoa (or chocolate liquor) can be divided into two classes, devil's food cakes and chocolate cakes. The difference is principally one of pH. Texture, color, and flavor are affected by the pH changes. Chocolate cakes may be considered as a basic cake to which cocoa or chocolate liquor has been added, and their pH is close to that of a yellow cake. Devil's food cakes are made with extra soda and have a crumb pH which is definitely alkaline. The next two formulae will illustrate the differences in preparation.

Chocolate cake

	%
Flour	18
Sugar	27.5
Shortening	10.6
MSNF	2.5
Chocolate liquor	3.5
Baking powder	1.0
Salt	0.8
Whole eggs	15.0
Water	21.2

Cocoa takes up a considerable amount of water when added to batter. This effect should be compensated by the addition of moisture to the base formula. As a rough rule of thumb, add water equivalent to 75-100% of the weight of cocoa. Most authorities recommend reduction of the shortening by an amount equal to the cocoa butter contained in the cocoa or chocolate liquor. It is doubtful that this change is imperative in any but the delicately balanced formulae. If it is desired to account for the cocoa butter in this manner, consider the chocolate liquor to contain 50% fat which has a shortening value $\frac{1}{2}$ that of hydrogenated vegetable oils. Thus, addition of 10% chocolate liquor would call for a reduction of $\frac{2}{1}$ 2% in the shortening.

Devil's Food Cake

	%
Flour	17.3
Sugar	26.8
Shortening	9.6
MSNF	3.8
Whole eggs	9.7
Egg whites	2.9
Water	24.1
Cocoa	3.8
Salt	0.8
Baking powder	0.7
sodium bicarbonate	0.5

Chiffon cakes, which derive a considerable portion of their leavening from an egg white foam, can be discussed here since they require chemical leavening agents to attain the required volume.

Chiffon Cake

	%
Flour	20.0
Sugar	26.5
Vegetable oil	9.5
Egg yolks	16.0
Baking powder	1.0
Salt	0.5
Water	6.9
Egg whites	19.5
Cream of tartar	0.1

The above formula indicates a separation of egg yolks and egg whites. In the usual batch mixing process, the egg whites and part of the sugar are beaten to a stiff foam and then the remainder of the ingredients are folded in. It is possible to mix and aerate the complete batter at one stage with some of the new continuous mixers. Flavors which can be added to chiffon cakes, include vanilla, almond, and citrus flavors, particularly the latter.

Principles of Processing Chemically-leavened Goods

There are perhaps five major categories of mixing methods for batters although, admittedly, what constitutes a minor modification, is very much a matter of opinion. The five categories discussed here are: (1) single-stage mixing; (2) two-stage mixing; (3) creaming methods; (4) blending, or flour batter, method; and (5) sugar-and-water method.

The single-stage mixing process is the simplest of them all and consists of dumping all of the ingredients into the mixer bowl and beating them with the wire whip or batter beater until they are homogenous. Usually, the batter is beaten at low speed for 1-3 min, or until the dry ingredients have been wetted, and then the mixer is turned to high speed or second speed for 5-8 min. Variations of this method include adding the leaveners near the end of the mixing period, or adding the eggs near the end with a total mixing time much reduced from the normal. The obvious advantage of this process is the saving of time which results. Disadvantages are said to be poorer grain, texture, and volume in the finished product.

Two-stage batters are mixed by placing all of the dry ingredients and part of the liquid materials into the bowl and mixing until a homogenous or creamed mass results. The remainder of the liquid is then added, usually gradually, and the mixing completed. Variations in this method usually involve changes in the stage at which the eggs are added.

The creaming process requires that the sugar and shortening be beaten until a light and fluffy (creamed) mass is obtained. The eggs then added while creaming is continued at medium speed, and finally the milk and flour are added alternately, in small portions. This method allows entrapment of a maximum number of small air bubbles in the fat with a consequent good effect on the grain in the finished product. It also does not develop the flour gluten as much as some of the other methods and this improves the texture of the cake somewhat.

The blending method requires the placing of flour and shortening in the mixing bowl and blending them together until the flour particles are thr-oughly coated by the fat. The remainder of the dry ingredients is then added and the batter mixed until it is homogenous. Finally, the remaining liquid is added in portions and the mixing continued for a predetermined period. A modification which is frequently used requires that the sugar and eggs be beaten together to form a foam before they are added to the flour and shortening mixture. The chief advantage of the blending method is that it permits a very thorugh dispersion of the shortening throughout the batter. This results in a very fine and uniform grain. On the other hand, the blending method does require more time and the use of more equipment than, for example, the single-stage method. Pyler (1952) says that cakes made by this method are tougher and have lower volume.

In the sugar-water method, all of the sugar and $\frac{1}{2}$ of its weight in water are placed in the mixing bowl and beaten for 30 sec at medium speed in the first stage. Next, the shortening, flour, dry milk, salt, and baking powder are added and the bowl contents beaten at medium speed for about 5 min. The leaveners must be reduced by $\frac{1}{4}$ and superglycerinated shortening used for best results by this method. Advantages secured by this procedure are better crust color, tenderer crust, and improved volume as compared to cakes prepared by other methods.

As a general rule, layer cakes are baked at oven temperatures of 360°-400°F. Cooler ovens tend to give cakes which are flat on top and exhibit excess shrinkage around the circumference. The cakes may also be too tender. Higher temperatures result in peaked cakes with cracked centers. In addition, more holes and tunnels develop in the crumb and the products may be tough and low in volume.

Cake Faults and Their Remedies

(1) Volume Too Low.- This can be caused by the use of insufficient amounts of leavening agents, in which case the remedy is obvious. If the batters are allowed to stand too long at too high temperatures, an initially addequate leavening action may be lost as a result of premature reaction of the bicarbonate and the leavening acids. This can be true even when delayed action leaveners are used. Undermixing can cause low volume because of reduced aeration of the batter. An excessively high oven temprature can set the structure of the cake before the full effect of the leavening gases has been exerted. Improper balance of ingredients, or improper types of ingredients, especially the flour or shortening, can reduce the expected volume markedly.

(2) Deffects of Texture.- Gumminess, doughiness, or chewiness are often the result of underbaking or improper cooling before packaging. Such faults are readily corrected by increasing the baking time slightly or by thorough cooling before wrapping. If these faults are due to improper formulation, the exact cause may be harder to spot although the percentage of water and the type of quality of shortening should be checked first.

Toughness may be due to use of too strong a flour, overbaking, inadequate amounts of water, overmixing with consequent overdevelopment of the gluten, not enough sugar, inadequate amounts or wrong type of shortening, or underscaling.

(3) Defects of Crust Appearance.- Spotted crusts can be due either to a nonhomogenous batter or to bubbles in the crust. The former problem can be corrected by using a different sequence of mixing, longer mixing, or more severe mixing conditions. The latter difficulty may be the resilt of unsuitable types of leaveners, batters which are too viscous, or excessire oven heat.

Bursting of the crust may also be due to high baking temperatures, or to overmixing, too much flour, or flour too much strong.

Pale crust color can result from a baking temperature which is too low. The oven as a whole may be set at too low a temperature or the heat distribution may be faulty with inadequate radiant heat reaching the crust. Conversely, crust colors which are too dark may result from undesirably high oven temperatures. In adition, pale crust colors can result from underscaling with resultant shielding of the top crust from radiant heat by the pan sides. Too much sugar, and particularly too much reducing sugars such as are found in corn syrups or in honey, can cause darkening of the crust even though baking conditions are correct as judged by the condition of the interior of the cake.

(4) Coarse or Irregular Grain.- Tunnels and large holes at the bottom of the cake may result from excessive bottom heat during baking. Too cold an oven can cause the grain to be open. Wet streaks are often use to underbaking. Undissolved spots of material in the crumb are not always the result of undermixing, although this is probably the usual cause. Some ingredients, particularly milk solids when improperly stored, will form agglomerates which are virtually indestructible by the usual procedures.

Both undermixing and over mixing can create a coarse, open grain in the finished product. An excessively close or fine grain is more often due to overmixing.

Cookies

The formulae for some types of cookies are very similar to those for layer cakes. Infact, some layer cake batters can be used to make quite acceptable cookies. For commercial production, however, the limitations of the equipment restrict the range through which the rheological properties of the dough can be permitted to vary, and these, in turn, limit the range of variations of the ingredients in the formula.

Functions of the Ingredients

The ingredients might be classified as bining or tenderizing materials depending upon their expected effect on the finished product.

Binding materials or tougheners: (1) Flour. (2) Water--beccause it assists in forming gluten. (3) Milk solids--not very effective in amounts found in cookie doughs. (4) Egg whites and whole eggs--the former more so. (5) Cocoa or chocolate products.

Tenderizing materials: (1) Sugars more important. (2) Shortenings. (3) Leavening--soften flour protiens, $NH\text{-}_4HCO\text{-}_3$, and $NaHCO\text{-}_3$. (4) Egg yolks.

In addition,lists baking acids, oat flour, and soy flour as tougheners and ground raisins, ground dates, etc., are listed as tenderizers. Corn flour acts as a tenderizer, but more than minor amounts contributes an off-flavor. Starch (corn or wheat) is a convenient and inexpensive tenderizer. Generally, nonreactive substances act as tenderizers.

The continuous structure of the cookie arises from the flour. The basic framework is tenderized by sugar, invert sugar, egg yolk, ammonia, soda (or baking powder), and shortening. It is firmed or toughened by water, cocoa, egg white, milk solids, and the leavening acids. Flavors and spices are usually not present in sufficient quantity to affect texture. Salt is usually considered to be a toughener.

Sugars and especially syrups in large amounts tend to make the dough sticky and hinder release from dies and wires. Shortening is one of the principal agents for increasing tenderness, at least so far as the rich, sweet biscuits are concerned. Too much shortening may lead to a greasy, smeary cookie which is susceptible to rancidity because the free fat soaks into the package, although these effects can be largely overcome by using plastic trays and cello over wrap . Too much sugar leads to hardness and excessive sweetness in the finished cookie.

Flours.- A wide variety of flours are being used, from a soft cookie flour to a rather strong sponge flour. The stronger the flour, the more shortening and sugar mjust be used to obtain an acceptable texture. High protien contents lead to hardness of texture and coarseness of internal grain and surface appearance. Chlorine bleached flours are not recommended for soft type cookies where relatively large amounts of tenderizing and moisture-retaining ingredients such as sugar, shortening and egg yolk are used. If the percentage of flour is decreased too much, as when large amounts of enriching ingredients are added, the cookie will lack body and may become too fragile.

Eggs.- Whole frozen eggs contribute a better structure and a more delicate texture than do dried eggs, especially in semibatter wire-type cookies. Frozen eggs seem to give greater volume and a more open grain Whole eggs either fresh or frozen cream readily and seem to provide better structure in drop cookies. Use of egg yolk as a part or complete replacement for whole eggs (using a smaller percentage than whole) will produce a tender cookie with excellent eating quality, but the grain or internal structure of the cookie may not be as good as with the whole egg.

Shortening.- There exists ideal relationship of shortening and sugar in three types of dough as follows: cutting machine, 15% shortening and sugar variable; rotary, 30% of each of these ingredients; and wire cut, 50% sugar and 50% shortening, all on a flour weight basis. Problems in machining are encountered when the shortening content is raised much above that indicated for rotary and cutting machine doughs, but this is not necessarily so far wire-cut doughs. Modern techniques have altered some beliefs; for example, it is possible to run certain shortening-free doughs on cutting machines.

Liquid shortening is in frequent use and oleo is the most common variety. For creaming, a hydrogenated vegetable shortening is recommended. Regular lard will not cream sastisfactorily, but the rearranged types are acceptable. In rotary doughs, lards will tend to "oil off" on the back roll and may streak both light and dark doughs. Substitution of liquid shortenings for plastic usually calls for less shortening in the formula plus the addition of cold water or ice to adjust the dough temperature to the proper level.

Lecithin.- Lecithin seems to increase the shortening effects of fats. It also promotes a tendency for the fat to cover or spread among slightly moist particles of sugar, flour, etc., which would otherwise repel the fat. Because of the emulsification effect, lecithin makes rich sweet doughs seem drier, thereby improving their machineability. Especially on rotary pieces, better release fron the die makes a cleaner impression and cuts down cripples. Lecithin also speeds dispersion of the fatty and aqueous components of the dough so that mixing time can be reduced. In turn, the reduced mixing time improves tenderness by minimizing gluten development, especially when strong flours are used.

Salt.- Except for topping, a salt of small crystal size should be used. Most biscuit formulae call for about 1% salt (FWB) or even less. This seems to be on the low side of the acceptable range. The usual cracker dough or batter can take 1-1/2% of salt (FWB) without the occurence of an unpleasent saline taste in the finished product. Rich or nut-containing doughs may be able to use slightly more. One guideline which has been suggested is to add salt up to 3% or the fat weight.

Sugar.- Granulated, fine granulated, and powdered can be used alone or in combination to adjust spread and machining properties. For better uniformity of spread a specific granulation should be established. No two suppliers of sugar have the same screen analysis even though the nomenclature is the same. Finer sugars require less mixing than do the coarser varieties and they may reduce sticking to the band. A fine granulated sugar creams better than powdered. Dextrose can often be substituted for upto 20% of the sucrose. Invert syrup must be used with care. It makes wire-cuts, especially wafers, soft, light, and spongy, with an open texture. The crust color is often brighter and develops earlier in the baking.

Milk.- Milk blends or ameliorates harsh flavors without contributing much flavor of its own. About 5% of the flour weight as skim milk powder (MSNF) is a good average figure for securing the full benifits of the ingredient. Crust color and gloss are generally improved. The protien components bind water and make the dough stiffer and somewhat stickier. The toughening effect on the finished product is minor, in most cases.

Whey has similar results, except that the stiffening , water-binding, and toughening effects are neglibile.

Proportions .-The range of contents of major ingredients in three kinds of cookie doughs are shown in Table 1

Spread

The control of cookie spread is one of the most serious problems confronting the production man. Minor variations in appearance, flavor, and texture are usually accepted with little complaint, but a cookie which spreads so much that it cannot be filled in the package, or one that spreads too little, causing slack fill or excess height for the package, can create havoc on the packaging line and generate large amounts of scrap. Happy is the lot of the production man who is dump packing his cookies.

TABLE 1
CONTENTS OF MAJOR INGREDIENTS IN THREE KLINDS OF COOKIE DOUGHS

	Water %[1]	Shortening %[1]	Sugars %[1]	Syrups %[1]
Rotary molded	5-15	10-40	20-45	0-20
Cutting machine	10-25	5-20	15-20	0-20
Wire cut 10-40	10-50	30-85	0-50	
Range	0-61	9-98	9-98	0-85
Average	22.2	33.7	43.7	16.9

[1]-Based on flour as 100%.

There are then flous :- (1) Michigan white, straight flour; (2) Indiana Ohio soft, red straight; and (3) a cracker sponge version of the soft, red straight. He also increased and decreased sugar in 5% increments to a maximum change of 15%. For width and thickness, the curves were a straight line function of the percentage of sugar change, except at the increase of 15% sugar there appeared to be a slight regression of width. However, Johnson belived that at a slightly lower baking temperature the straight line relationship has been retained. At the lowest sugar the tops shows fine hairline cracks and a light color,while at highest level wide deep cracks appears.

When ammonia carbonate or bicarbonate incremants are added in addition to the regular amount of soda, the spread is nearly a straight line function of the percentage of ammonia. Cracks became wider, and there is faster bake-out as shown by darker color.

When ammonia (0, 0.25, 0.50, 0.75, 0.1, and 1.25%) is used without soda, the width is a straight line function of ammonia. Height is also directly related with the exception of the no-ammonia sample. With no ammonia or soda, a very thick nonspreading soda, with large flat plateaus and heavy craks are obtained. As ammonia was increased, finer cracks were observed, and spread increass. At the upper level cracks again deepened, spread increased, and the color darkens.

With soda but no ammonia, a rapid increase in width occurrs between 0 and 0.5% soda, then very little change between 0.5 and 1.1%. When 1.1% is exeeded there is again a rapid increase in width. Thickness is affected in a similar manner except that with *no* soda and *no* leavening a relatively thin cookie results. Appearance of the cookies is similar to those in the ammonia series except that at higher levels they become much darker in color. At 0.4% soda the pH is near the maximum consideres desirable, yet added amounts of soda give additional spread without seemingly hurting appreance. Johnson did not comment on the flavor of these latter samples.

The pH is a critical factor, and once the optimum pH for a particular piece has been established, any change in the leavening system should be balanced so as to maintain that level. Means leading to a change in the pH (as by addition of soda without compensating amounts of acid) should not be used to modify the leavening effect or spread.

In the experiments mentained water gives no appreciable variation in width as it is increased (in the range considered). As water is decreased there is fairly steady reduction in height. Stiffer dough has a less well-developed system for retaining leavening gases plus a greater resistance to expansion. On the whole, it appears that changing the water content is a poor method for controlling spread though it does affect hieght. The water series show little change in appearance throughout.

Temperature variations (dough) seem to have minor effects on cookie width. Thickness, however, increased with increases temperature at lower levels, say to 75°-80° F; then at higher levels, to about 90°-95° F, thickness remains constant.

Working with a simple sugar snap formula showed that the amount of shortening (25-35% range) affected spread very little. However, the spread was directoly proportional to the amount of sugar added (50-80%) at each level of ammonium bicarbonate added to each level of granulated sugar.

Less than 55% sugar gave inferior top grain. An addition of 0.5% ammonium bicarbonate produced as much increase in diameter and change in top grain as 7.6% of granulated sugar. The optimum quantity of ammonium bicarbonate differed markedly for different wheat varieties. The pH of cookies increased from 7.3 with no am monium bicarbonate to 7.9 at 2.25% of this leavener, but further increases were without effect on pH.

Based on the preceding evidence, we can list some factors which might be varied to increase or decrease the spread. Those ingredients described as tougheners will usually decrease spread while tenderizers will often (but by no means always) increase spread. Increased spread will also result from increasing the amount of leaveners, using a finer granulation of sugar (within limits), or by adding more water or more shortening to the formula. However, powdered sugar will actually decrease spread and tenderness, while brown sugar contributes less to spread than does granulated. The spread can also be decreased by using stronger flour, increasing the mixing time, and bringing the dough from the mixture at a lower temperature (using chilled water or ice if necessary). Too much salt can reduce spread. Some authors have suggested the use of 1/8% pottasium carbonate to increase spread when all else fails.

So far as oven control is concerned, increasing the temperature in the first zone tends to decrease spread, while closing the dampers in the first zone will often increase spread.

Types of Cookies

Cookies are generally classified according to the kind of equipment used to form the individual pieces. Stamping machines, rotary cutters, rotary molders, wire-cut machines, and depositing equipment are used for over 90% of the cookie production in the United States. The equipment has a strong influence on the texture of the cookie and limits the formula variations which can be used.

Deposit cookies are the machine-made counterparts of the hand--bagged cookie and many of the formulae for the latter can be successfully adapted to automatic production. Deposit cookies will contain about 35-40% sugar, 65-75% shortening, and 15-25% liquid whole eggs. The flour should be milled from soft wheat, and it should be unbleached, with 8-8.5% protein and 0.35-0.40% ash. It should have a viscouity of 40%M or more and a spread factor of 79-80.

Wire-cut cookie equipment permits a wider variation in dough composition than any other type of machinery. It is necessary to have the wire-cut dough sufficiently cohesive to hold toghether as it is extruded through an orifice, and yet it must be relatively nonsticky and short enough so that it separates cleanly as it is cut by the wire. Formulae may contain upto several 100% sugar based on the flour, and shortening upto 100% or more of the flour. Doughs may be almost as soft as some cake batters, or too stiff to be easily molded by hand. The very soft doughs overlap deposit doughs in consistency, while the other extreme is close to the texture expected in rotary molded type doughs. Advantages of the wire-cut cookie over rotary molded cakes are more open grain and softer texture, and, as compared to deposit goods, a more uniformly shaped cookie. Disadvantages over the rotary molded piece are the lack of potential for making a surface design and somewhat less uniformity of size and shape.

The principal distinguishing feature of stamping machine or rotary cutting operations is that the pieces are cut from a continuous web of dough by a cylindrical die or reciprocating-motion cutter. A rether large range of dough types can be handled by these types of equipment, but it is necessary that the dough be sufficiently cohesive to form the continuous sheet from which the blanks will be cut and to hold the scrap (if any) toghether as it is lifted from between the blanks. Reciprocating cutting machines, or stamping machines, are often discussed as though there were many points of similarity between them and rotary cutters. In fact, there are so many differences between the two types of equipment that is not particularly informative to consider them toghether.

For rotary molded cookies, the dough consistency must be such that it will feed uniformly and readily fill all of the crevices of the die cavity under the pressures existing in the feeding hopper. The dough blank must be capable of being extracted from the cavity without undergoing distortion or forming tails of appreciable size, but it must adhere to the die roll long enough to prevent the piece from falling out before it reaches the extraction toller. The blank must have sufficient cohesion to hold toghether and not break up at any of the transfer points before or after baking. The dough must flow very slightly or smooth out during forming and baking so that woodiness or undesirable irregularities in the surface pattern are not apparent in the finished cookie. Usually, the spread and rise should be minimised so as not to blur or distort the design. Doughs formulated to meet these requirements are usually fairly high in sugar and shortening and low in moisture. Development of the gluten is definitely to be avoided.

Most manufacturers use flour of about 8.1-8.2% protein for rotary base cakes, although a range of 7.1-9.2% has been reported. Ash should be about 0.415, with a known range of 0.33-0.47% being used satisfactorily. Oleo shortening added in the liquid condition is suitable for most of these doughs, but vegetable shortening can also be used. Powdered sugar and sugar syrups are the preffered sweetening ingredients. MSNF are often added, but it is thought that condensed milk is preferable since the liquid ingredient removes any possibility of lumps appearing in the finished cookie. Lecithin at about the 0.4% level will improve machineability.

One-stage mixing is often perfectly satisfactory, but a creaming operation with most of the minor ingredients added before the flour goes in gives added assurance that lumps of undistributed ingredients will not appear in the cookie. Dough temperatures from 72° to 90° F are being used for rotary sandwich bases.

10

BAKERY MACHINERY

The question of bakery machinery is rather peculiar in the sense that when one thinks of bakery industry, he either visualizes a home scale unit where operations are carried out totally by hand or hand tools with brick oven, or a completely automatic and sophisticated plant comes to the mind. Thus there is a contradiction, while modern machinery is not available indigenously, there is surplus capacity in the bakery machinery industry. There is no standardization in this field. Particularly, the biscuit making machinery ia a neglected sector.

Important systems and machinery for bakery industry have been given in this chapter.

BULK HANDLING OF INGREDIENTS

Bulk handling systems of various ingredients are employed only in very big industries, therefore only a brief outline will be given here.

Flour can be mechanically conveyed or in more modern installations pneumatic transfer systems can be employed which may be either negative pressure systems or positive pressure systems or may even be their combinations. In the positive pressure system air under pressure pushes the flour while in the negative system vacuum pulls the flour forward. The flour bins can be horizontal or vertical. Bulk handling of sugar is usually mechanically occasionally pneumatic. In mechanical system screw and bucket-type elevators are used for to and fro bins; for long distances belt conveyers may be used. Liquid sugar materials can be handled with pumps and pipes as usual. Shortening, is bulk-stored in tanks equipped with temperature regulating arrangements, and is handled in a way common to other liquids. Conveying pipe should be electrically, steam or hot water traced to prevent solidification and blockage of the pipeline.

The bulk handling systems described above are, suitable only for very large scale bakery only, where ingredients at a rate of a few tonnes per hour are consumed. These installations are highly capital-intensive.

FLOUR SIFTER

Flour received in the plant contains some impurities such as bran, insects, germs, husk and gunny threads etc. which have to be removed to get quality food products. During melting much care is not exercised, also during storage extraneous matter gets mixed up with the flour, this is removed by sifting. Sifting can be carried out by hand using sieves, if the production is less than about 500 kgs./day. For bigger plants sifters are used. The size of the sifter is chosen according to the capacity of the plant. Sifters with capacities of even higher than 100 kgs./min are available.

Sifting apart from removing the extraneous matter, blends the flour and also loosens and aerates the flour.

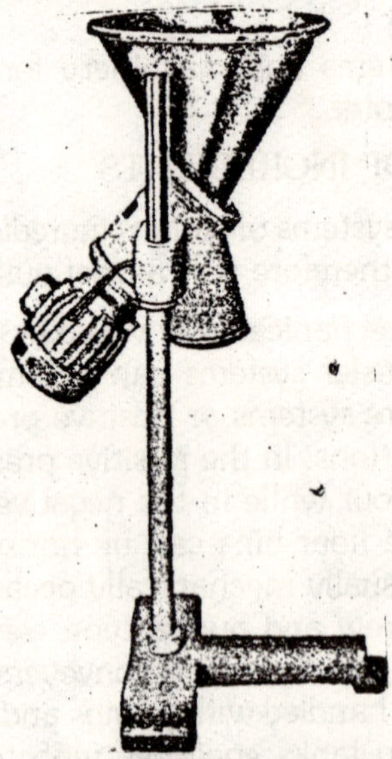

Fig. 10.1 Flour Sifter

The bulk flour sifter has even higher sifting capacity. It is suitable for high capacity plants with bulk handling systems.

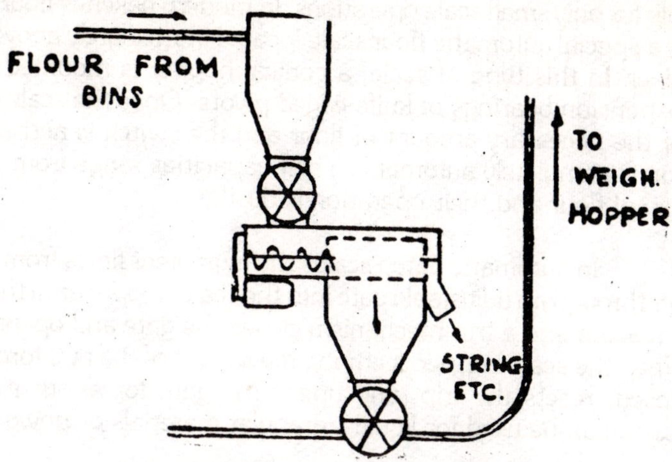

Fig. 10.2 Bulk Flour Sifter

WATER TEMPERING TANK

The quality of the bakery product depends on the dough temperature also, which can be adjusted suitably with the help of water as the temperature of ingredients other than water is not that easy to regulate. Water temperature can be regulated using a water tempering tank which is a graduated metallic tank, with the help of ice or warm water as required. The water thus obtained is then used in mixing with other ingredients. In a small scale or cottage scale bakery unit this tank is not necessary and graduated plastic buckets may be used instead.

WEIGHING & MEASURING MACHINES

Hand scaling using balances are now obsolete except for cottage scale units. Automatic weighing and measuring is a must in bulk handling systems. Everybody is familiar with water meters and they can be used for other liquid ingredients also. Powders and granular materials are measured by weighing while liquids are measured by volumetric methods. The latter method is very easy, simple and least expensive.

Weighing machines may be of the balances and force-deflection system types. Simple balance is not suitable for large capacity plants. Platform with dial type balances are more popular but are suitable for only small scale operations. In modern bakeries flour is weighted by a special automatic flour scale located immediately above the dough mixer. In this type of scale, a conical hopper is mounted on 4-point suspension bearings of knife-edged pivots. Once the scale beam is set for the necessary amount of flour and the switch is activated, operation is completely automatic. Their capacities range from 100 to 500 kgs. of flour and their operation is dustless.

In automatic batch scales the ingredient flows from a feed hopper through an adjustable gate into the scale hopper until the set weight is reacted and a trip mechanism closes the gate and opens the outlet. When the scale hopper is empty, the weight of the tare forces the door closed, resets the trip, and opens the gate for another cycle, such scales can be used for liquids, granular materials or powders.

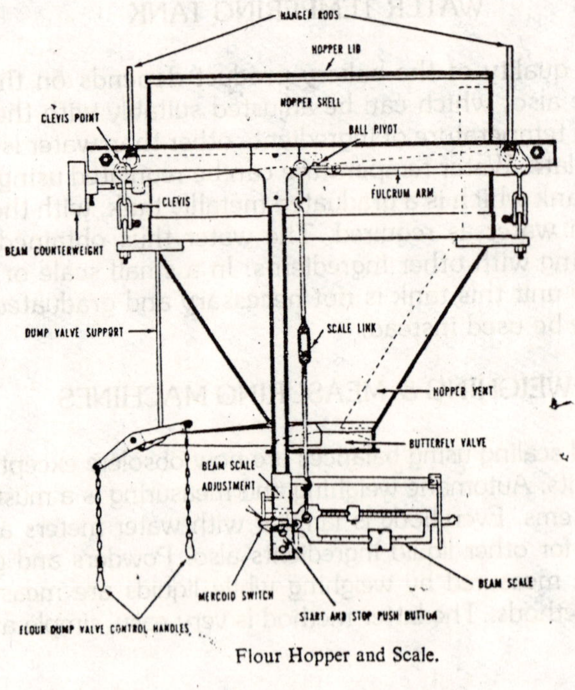

Flour Hopper and Scale.

Moving belt type weighers are used for continuous weighing and constant feed rate. Loss in weight type feeders also give controlled continuous feed; here the entire feed hopper is mounted on a scale which controls the rate of removal of material from the hopper.

Liquids are weighed volumetrically using flow meters based on orifice plates, ventures, screws or vanes etc. etc. Continuous measurement of streams can be carried out using displacement meters based on nutating discs, reciprocating pistons and rotating vanes etc.

MIXERS AND KNEADERS

Mixers and Kneaders are the equipment necessary for proper blending or mixing of the various ingredients. Liquids can be easily blended using propeller type agitators in the tank. For blending of premixes or preparation of adjuncts ribbon blenders, twin-cone and V-shell blenders are usually employed when dry ingredients are to be mixed.

Dough mixing can be carried out using horizontal, vertical, reciprocating agitator of continuous mixers as per the requirements. The horizontal type may have fixed bowl or tilting bowl while the vertical type may be planetary or fixed spindle type. The continuous mixers may be of agitator-in-tube type or rotor or stator heads type.

Horizontal Dough Mixers

These mixers can be used to mix various mixtures ranging in consistency from thin batters to tough doughs. They are a must when gluten development is desirable e.g. in bread making. These mixers have a horizontal U-shaped bowl mounted on the rigid frame with drive motor etc. Their capacities range from 10 kgs. upwards. Bowls are usually made of stainless steel or stainless steel clad mild steel. Bowls are sometimes provided with jackets for circulation of cold or hot water.

High speed mixers for gluten development usually contain single axle on which two or more arms parallel to the front of the mixer are mounted. The limited clearance of the jacket wall by the agitator bars causes the dough to be repeatedly stretched and kneaded resulting in quick gluten development. These mixers can usually be operated on two speed ranges viz. 30-60 and 40-80 r.p.m. In the slow speed mixers agitators of various forms e.g. 8, Z etc. are employed with 1 or 2 set of axles.

The agitator configuration and its speed affects the action. Slow speed Z or Eight-arm mixers have a speed range of 14 to 60 r.p.m. and 25 r.p.m. on an average.

The high speed horizontal mixers are also called kneaders and may contain bars projecting from the axle at right angles to it and also the bowl has radical bars intermeshing with axle bars. This construction gives a very efficient dough kneading particularly suitable for tough doughs.

The dough is discharged from these mixers by tilting the bowl so that top is brought to a forward facing portion. In some models the front of the bowl consists of a tightly fitting door which can be raised and lowered independently of the other immobile section of the bowl and the dough is discharged through this door. The bowl tilting mechanism may be hand operated or it may be operated by a separate low horsepower motor. A 40 to 50 kgs. capacity machine requires main drive of 2 to 2.5 HP motor while the tilting mechanism motor may be of 0.5 HP.

Vertical Mixers

Vertical mixers consist of a movable bowl or trough with one or two vertical shafts which may be stationary or may have planetary movement. Agitators may themselves be of various sizes and configurations. Most important design in the vertical mixers is the Planetary Mixer which is particularly suitable for mixing batters and for adjuncts such as icings. The agitator is called planetary as it, apart from revolving around its own vertical axis at relatively high speed, also moves in circles as it rotates round the bowl. Thus motion ensures beater action throughout the bowl contents. The agitator may be provided with variable speed mechanism and the bowl can be raised and lowered by separate drive of low HP. The agitator may be of any of the various types available e.g. simple curved single arm, wire meshing, and gate type.

The hook type agitator gives a good kneading action to the dough resulting in development of gluten with minimum of tearing. The wire mesh type agitator gives a good beater action with maximum air incorporation. The paddle type agitator ensures good mixing coupled with scrapping of the bowl sides. Bowls are usually provided with covers to prevent splashing or dusting. Capacities range from 10 kgs. upwards.

Spindle type mixers are used mainly for biscuit doughs. Their special advantage is with saltine doughs, in which case they are adapted for mixing in special mobile troughs used for fermenting doughs. Thus sponges and doughs need not be transferred in and out of the mixer between the various stages. Speed of spindle is usually low and spindles can be raised to allow the trough to be rolled into place under them. The mixer blades are so designed as to give a cutting action rather than a kneading or stretching action to the mix thus toughening effect on the crackers or biscuits is avoided.

In reciprocating Agitator or Revolving Bowl Mixers, a pair of agitator arms travels through intersecting elliptical paths in shallow slowly revolving bowl. These mixers are useful in mixing temperature sensitive doughs and also where nuts and raisins of the mix are to be kept unbroken. Their output is usually low compared to horizontal mixers; and are particularly suitable for pie doughs and puff-pastry. A single arm rotary bowl-kneader is shown here.

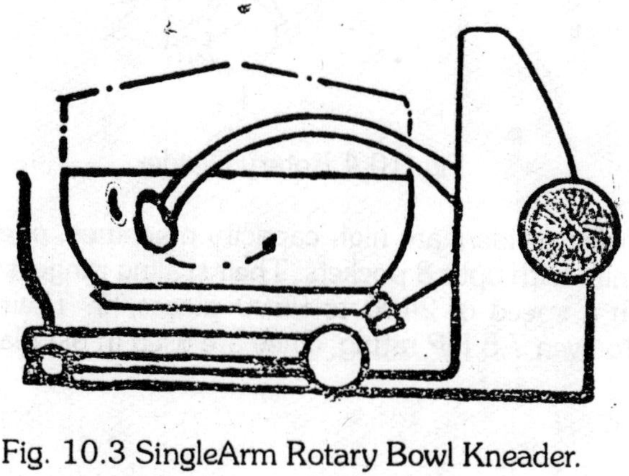

Fig. 10.3 SingleArm Rotary Bowl Kneader.

DOUGH DIVIDERS

To get loaves of uniform weight and size the mixed dough has to be sealed in lumps of required weight. This may be done manually using ordinary scale or balance, or may be done with the help of a machine known as dough divider. These divider machines are based on volumetric scaling as it is difficult to design machine which will subdivide dough on a weight basis. The basic principle of the machine is that the dough is forced into spaces having known volume (adjustable according to requirements), the pocket contents are cut off from the main dough mass and the dough pieces of constant volume (i.e. constant weight, when density is substantially constant) are ejected to be sent to rounder.

The divider machine are of several types varying from 1 to 8 pocketed. A small scale unit cannot afford to have the machine costing about 15 to 20 thousand rupees (single pocket) and only units with output of above 6 tonnes/day can afford it. Divider may be of rotary, ram and knife, and pocket type.

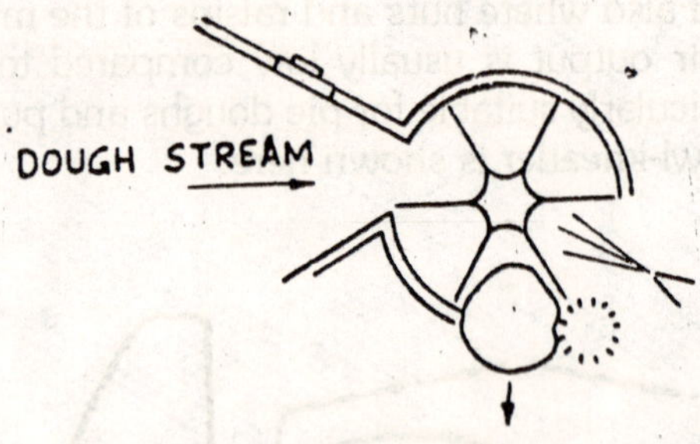

Fig. 10.4 Rotary Divider.

Pocket dividers are high capacity machines, operating at 25 strokes/ min. with upto 8 pockets. Their scaling range is 175 gms. to 1 kg. with a speed of 2400 to 9600 pieces/hr. Their drives have motor upto even 7.5 HP rating. They are used in big plants only.

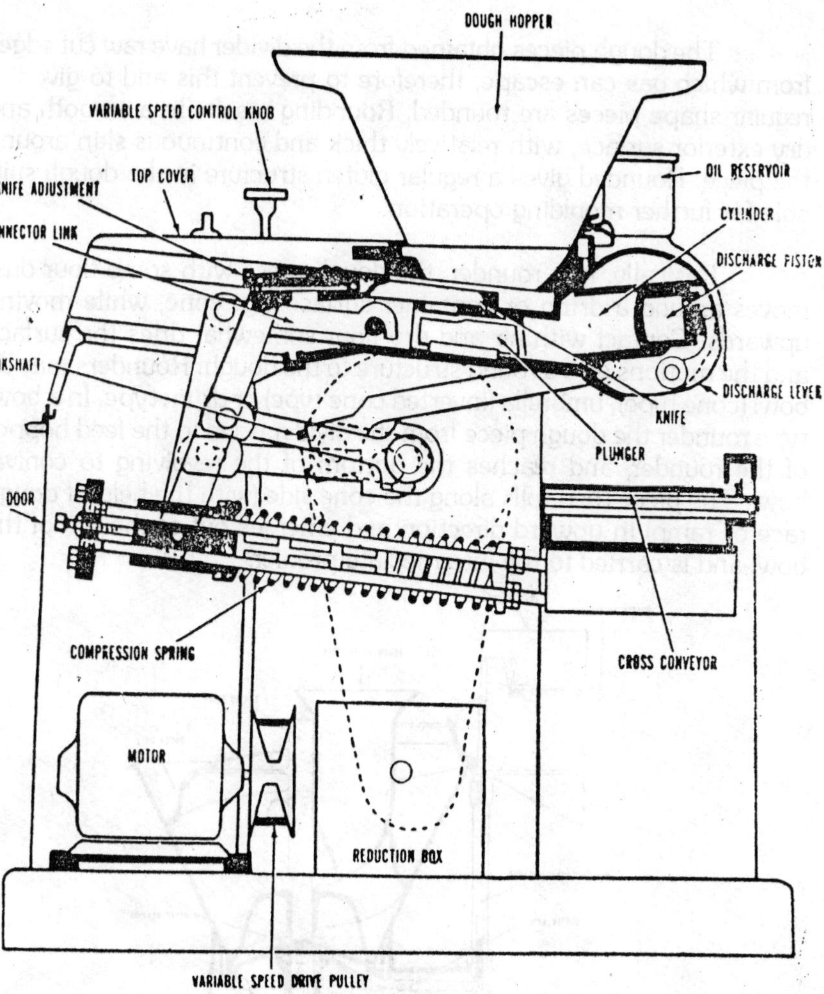

The working of a simple single dough pocket/dough divider is as follows. Dough is put in the hopper which is received by suction in the lower chamber from where it is pushed to the dividing chamber which divides the dough at the desired adjusted weight and deliver it to the moving canvas. It has variable speed drive of 1 or 2 HP motor, and output of 15 to 25, to 25 to 50 pieces/min. of 100 to 500 gms. to 250 to 1000 gms. respectively for single and double pocket machines.

ROUNDING MACHINE

The dough pieces obtained from the divider have raw cut edges from which gas can escape, therefore to prevent this and to give it a regular shape pieces are rounded. Rounding results in a smooth and dry exterior surface, with relatively thick and continuous skin around the piece. Rounded gives a regular gluten structure in the dough suitable for further moulding operation.

Basically, in a rounder, the dough piece with some flour dust moves around a drum or container surface e.g. cone, while moving upwards. Contact with air and dry flour somewhat dries the surface and the motions give a round structure to the dough. Rounders may be bowl (cone type), umbrella (inverted cone type) or drum type. In a bowl type rounder the dough piece from the divider is fed to the feed hopper of the rounder, and reaches the bottom of the revolving to conival bowl. The piece then rolls along the cone side (with the help of dough race or ramp) in upward direction and emerges out of the top of the bowl and is carried to the intermediate proofer.

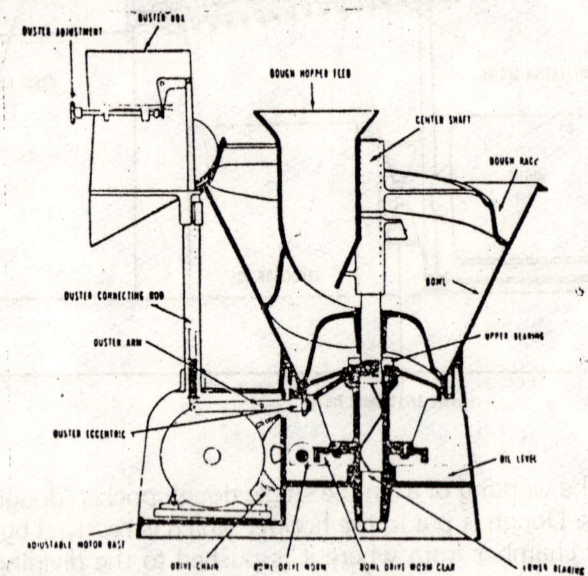

Fig. 106 Schematic Diagram of a Modern Bowl Type Rounder

A small machine with capacity of 100 to 1000 gms. dough pieces (50 pieces/min.) will require a drive of about 1 HP.

Umbrella or inverted cone type rounder has the bowl in inverted form and the dough piece is fed at the bottom i.e. at the larger diameter of the cone, and it moves upward to the apex. The ramp is at the outside of the cone. In the drum type rounder the cone has almost vertical sides, hence the speed of dough movement is almost uniform.

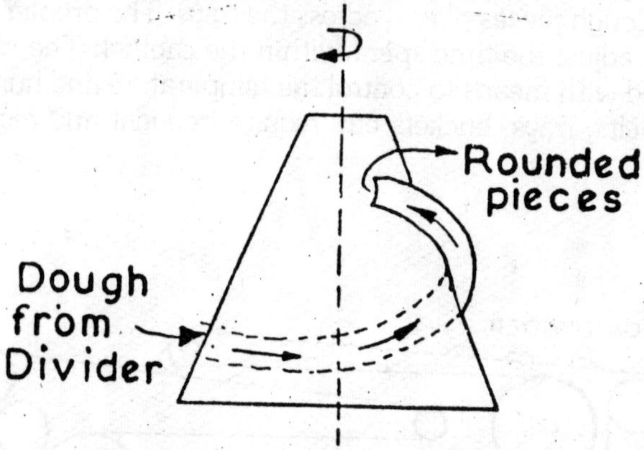

SCHEMATIC DIAGRAM OF UMBRELLA TYPE ROUNDER

Fig 10.7

The race or the ramp should be kept as close to the bowl as possible without creating friction. This is built up of a layer of dough and it should be carefully removed during shutdown using hardwood or plastic scrapers.

INTERMEDIATE PROFFER

The dough pieces receive some handling in rounders. So degassing takes place there, hence they are susceptible to tearing and lack extensibility and easy mouldability. Thus the rounded pieces are left for a few minutes before moulding. This is known as intermediate proofing, and is carried out by letting the dough balls travel through an enclosed cabinet for a few minutes, in mechanized bakery units. The dough pieces coming out of the intermediate proofer are bigger (due to fermentation and gas accumulation), more pliable and extensible, and their skin is firmer and drier. Intermediate proofers are of two types, namely, belt type and tray type.

Belt type intermediate proofers contain a series of endless belts enclosed in a cabinet , in such a way that dough pieces from one belt fall to the other end of the lower belt moving in opposite direction and so on until they reach the exit. Tray type intermediate proofers are the equipments in which dough moves in metal pans, troughs or buckets, wooden trays or canvas loops. The proofer trays may contain spaces for 1 to 8 dough pieces placed across the trays. The proofer speeds are variable to adjust the time spent within the cabinet. The cabinet may be provided with means to control the temperature and humidity. The pockets, belts, trays, buckets etc. require frequent and regular cleaning.

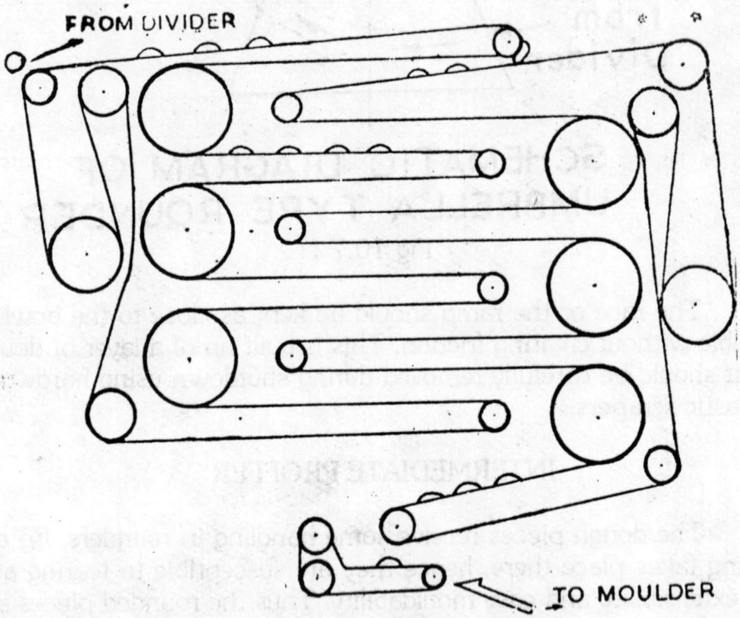

Fig. 10.8 Belt-Type Intermediate proofer

MOULDERS

Dough Moulders for Bread

The piece of dough from the intermediate proofer is fed to a moulder which shapes it into cylindrical shape ready to be placed in the oven. The moulder fattens, curls, rolls and seals the material. The dough is thus first pressed, in the machine with the help of two or more pairs of rollers, to make it flat. The flat sheet is then curled up into a loose cylinder, with the help of a set of rolls or by a pair of canvas belts. Next the cylinder is somewhat elongated to slightly more length than that of the pan, the entrapped air between the dough layers is expelled and the dough piece is sealed; so that it can expand into the typical loaf shape when proofed. Usually this is done in a moulder by rolling the dough cylinder between a large drum surfaced with canvas and a semi-circular compression board having a smooth surface. Fing 10.9 Shows a graphic representation of the moulding operation in a drum moulder. The clearance between the drum and board is gradually reduced along the route of dough travel so that the piece is constantly in contact with both surfaces and gradually becomes compressed.

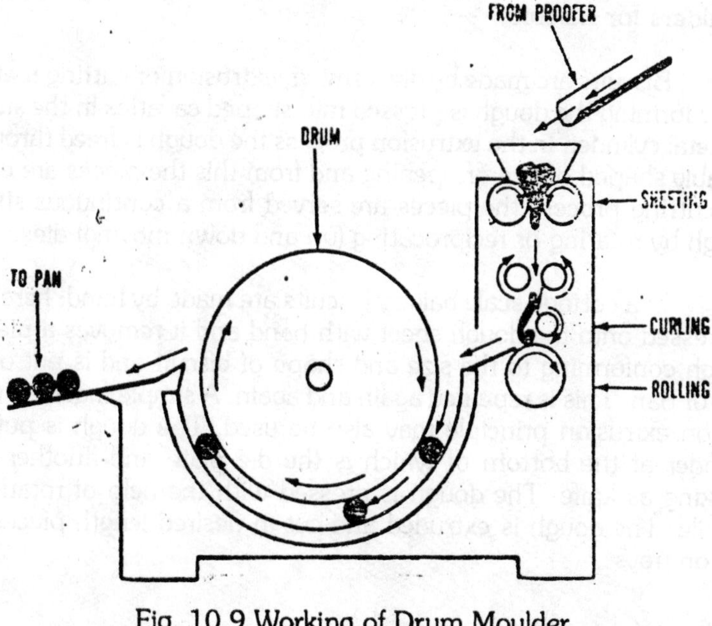

Fig. 10.9 Working of Drum Moulder.

Another system of moulder consists of a flat pressure board and a powered belt which gradually squeeze the dough cylinder into shape as a result of the gradually decreasing distance between them. Length of pressure boards range from 50 to 125 cms. Boards made of rubber covered with canvas may be used or thick pieces of canvas belting may also be used as pressure boards.

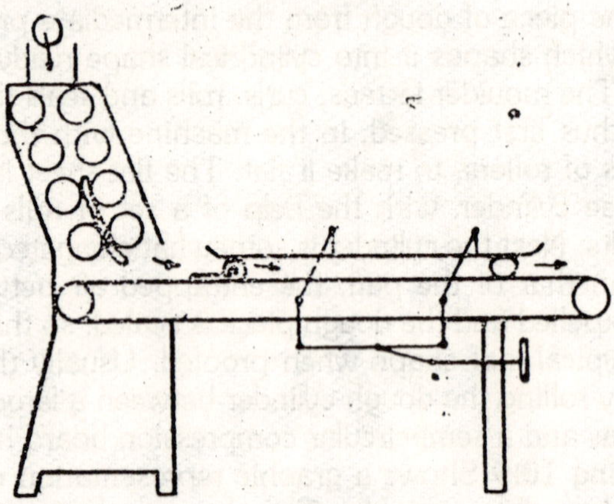

Fig. 10.10 Working of Flat Board Moulder

Moulders for Biscuits

Biscuits are made by die forming, extrusion or cutting method. In die forming the dough is pressed into shaped cavaties in the surface of metal cylinder. In the extrusion process the dough is freed through a suitably shaped orifice or opening and from this the pieces are cut. In the cutting process the pieces are served from a continuous strip of dough by rotating or reciprocating (up and down moving) dies.

In a cottage scale bakery biscuits are made by hand; here a die is pressed onto the dough sheet with hand and it removes a piece of dough conforming to the size and shape of biscuit and is put on the tray or pan. This is repeated again and again. A simple machine working on extrusion principle may also be used. The dough is put in a cylinder at the bottom of which is the die plate and another plate working as knife. The dough is pressed with the help of rotation of handle. The dough is extruded and cut in desired length pieces and put on trays.

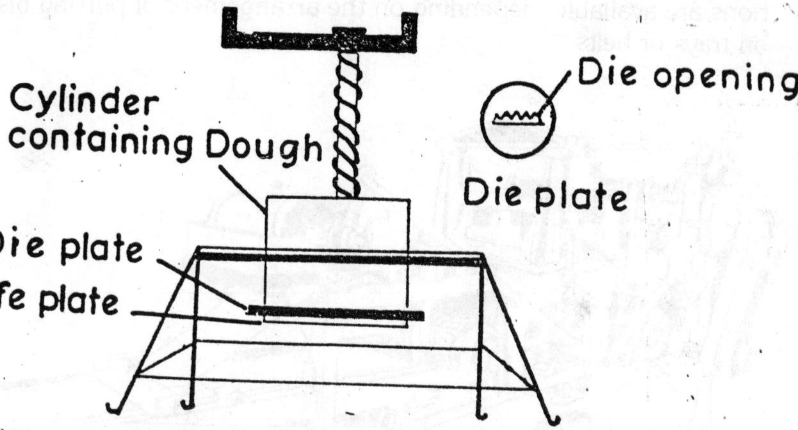

Fig. 10.11 Biscuit Machine.

Soda crackers, club crackers, saltines and the like are formed by a reciprocating die which cuts pieces out of a continuous strip of dough that has been formed by laminating and sheeting. The scrap is pulled of the belt and returned to the sheeting machine. The biscuit dough is 'docked' or perforated by pins in order that the crackers will not expand excessively during baking.

Thus the dough is converted into a sheet of desired thickness with the help of a sheeting machine known as Biscuit Rolling Machine, which may be operated by hand or power. It essentially consists of two heavy perfectly smooth roller. The gap between the rollers can be adjusted to obtain the desired sheet thickness. The biscuits are cut from the sheet with the help of hand dies, roller dies or reciprocating dies.

The sheet of dough is then fed to a biscuit moulding machine. In Rotary Biscuit Machine the dough passes under a metal (brass or stainless steel) cylinder having the surface covered with engraved pockets. The pockets fill with the dough which is cut from the sheet, the pieces are ejected on to a conyenor belt or tray series leading to an oven. In this type of machine a separate biscuit rolling machine (i.e. sheeter) is not required, from one side of the machine dough is fed and biscuits ready for baking come out of the other side. This type of machine requires least amount of labour and production rate is quite high. Different types of machines of this type with some modifications are available, depending on the arrangement of putting biscuits on trays or belts.

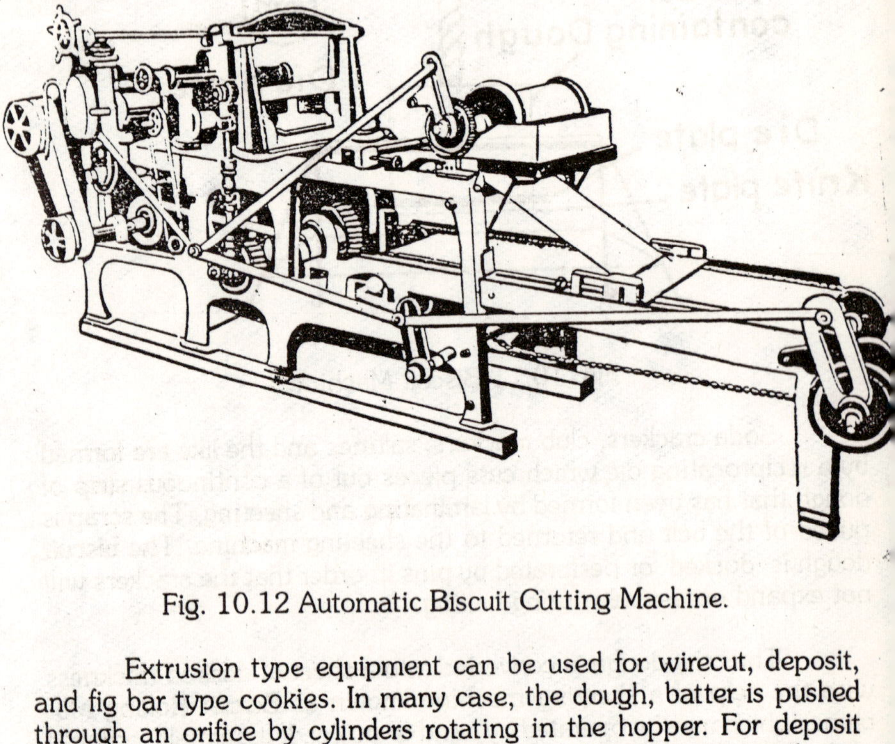

Fig. 10.12 Automatic Biscuit Cutting Machine.

Extrusion type equipment can be used for wirecut, deposit, and fig bar type cookies. In many case, the dough, batter is pushed through an orifice by cylinders rotating in the hopper. For deposit cookies, the individual pieces are separated from the constantly extruding strand of batter by moving the hand i.e. the baking surface, up and down beneath the orifice. In the wire-cut method, the strand of dough is served by a wire or tape that is moved back and forth across the face of the orifice. Fig bars and some other cookies, involve the simultaneous extrustion of two types of pastes which are baked in continuous strips and then cut by knives moving across the hand.

A combined cutting and rotary moulding machine may also be used for making all types of biscuits. For example, when glucose type biscuits are to be made the rotary moulder is in operation and for Marie type biscuits sheeter and stamping (i.e. cutting) unit will be in operation. This is essential where continuous production of different varieties of biscuits is being done; and it avoids the setting up of two different machines.

Roll-Formers

Buns may also be formed using equipment similar to those for bread. Divider, rounder, proofer and moulder may be combined in a single bun-machine. The machine consists of a horizontal cylinder containing cavities, which rotates below a hopper containing the dough. The dough is sucked into the cavities by pistons and the pieces are expelled onto the rounder conveyer where the pieces rotate and are rounded thus. The rounded pieces fall into trays of the proofer from where they enter the moulder, to be formed into the desired shapes, e.g. hamburger buns, hot dog rolls etc. Some of the parts, of all these sections of the combined machine, are coated with Teflon to ensure that dough pieces do not stick to them.

Piecrust Formers

Piecrusts may be formed by either sheeting the dough and cutting out the crusts, or pressing the dough to shape between two dies. The first method gives better texture but generates some scrap which has to be reworked, while the latter method does not normally produce any scrap. In sheeting and cutting machine the dough is first divided into two rectangular pieces (which will become the bottom and top crust) which go to the crust rollers, the bottom crust is sheeted and deposited into the pie tin. A measured quantity of fruit filling is deposited into it, and over it a sheeted dough pie is put and the two parts are sealed. If desired a wash or glaze is automatically sprayed onto the top crust. Trimmings are reworked.

In stamping type of machine the dough is not rolled but pressformed into desired shape. Measured amount of dough is formed and placed in a pan and filling is dispensed into it. A die formed pastry cover is placed over the pan and its edges crimped to the bottom crust. All this takes place automatically.

Machines for Doughnuts

Doughnuts are produced by extrusion of mixed dough through a circular orifice or cutting of hexagonal pies from a dough sheet. These pieces are proofed on cloth type proofer with some heating to speed up the leavening action. The doughnuts are then fried, finished and packed. Thus an automatic doughnut production line would include mixer, extruder for yeast raised doughs, automatic proofer, an automatic cake doughnut cutter, an automatic fyer a fat melter and leveler, a sweep conveyer, an automatic glazer and screen loader.

OVENS

Oven is an extremely important and indispensable item in a bakery unit. As regards its size, cost and importance, it is the main equipment in a bakery unit; other associated equipments are loaders, unloaders, coolers, depanners and conveyrs etc. Selection of a particular type of oven and its proper use both are very important. Different types of ovens, namely, brick oven, reel oven, rotary oven, deck oven, traveling tray oven, band oven etc. are available. The medium of heating i.e. fuel could be wood, coal, gas, fuel oil, electricity and infrared heat waves etc.

Brick Oven

The brick oven is the type of oven used by cottage scale bakeries but they are a crude design. The design described here is an improved one for better heat efficiency and quality of the product. First the four side walls each of 45 cms. thickness and 1 meter height are constructed and left to set for 4 days, sprinkling water twice a day. Length and breadth of the oven may be taken as per capacity requirement and usually 3 m x 2.1 m is sufficient to bake more than 100 loaves at a time. Brick pieces are filled upto a height of 45 cms. followed by 15 cms. of sand, 16 cms. of broken glass and 15 cms. of rock salt. Each layer is pounded to set properly. A layer of fine cement is spread over salt and fire bricks are arranged over it without leaving any gap between them. Over it a very thin paste or fire cement is spread and is left to set for 2-3 days, sprinkling water 2-3 times a day.

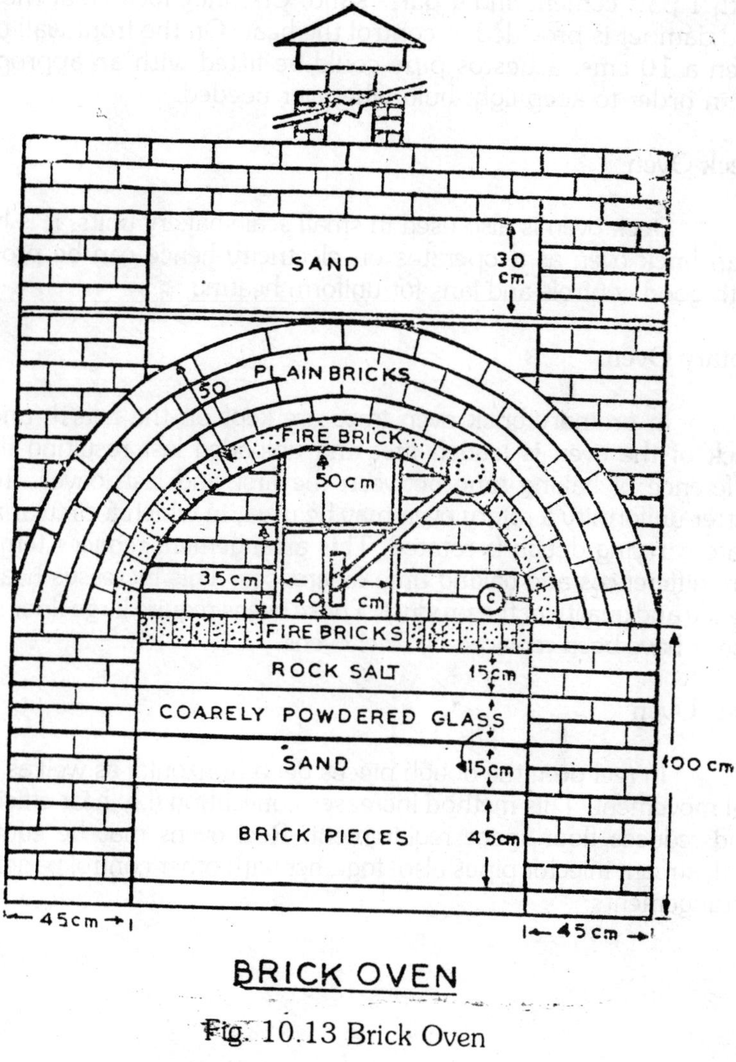

Fig. 10.13 Brick Oven

A false dome structure is first erected over which 10 cms. thick mud plaster followed by 0.5 cm. thick sand layer. Over it a thick layer of plaster of fire cement is put followed by fire bricks. Fire cement layer is put on the layer of bricks, so as to fill all the gaps between the bricks. The structure is allowed to set for 4-5 days with occasional sprinkling of water. When this dome is set the false dome is pulled out. Fire cement plaster is made using 5 parts of fire cement to 1 part sand while the ordinary plaster is made with 1 part cement and 4 parts sand. Chimney located at the rear, and damper is provided to control the heat. On the front wall of the oven a 10 cms. asbestos pipe could be fitted with an appropriate lid in order to keep light bulb wherever needed.

Deck Oven

Deck oven is also used in small scale bakery units, it is better than brick oven as it operates on electricity hence can be provided with good controls and fans for uniform heating.

Rotary Oven

In ordinary brick oven trays are kept on the hearth and the back of the oven is loaded first and unloaded last resulting in last difference of baking time between the first and last loaves. To get better uniformity a rotary oven may be used, in which a circular metal plate carrying dough is rotated. This arrangement reduces temperature differences and baking time differences. This increases heat efficiency and quality of the product. These ovens require large floor space hence have been replaced by Reel ovens.

Reel Oven

In reel oven the dough pieces get a horizontal as well as vertical movement. This method increases convention (i.e. heat efficiency) and reduces floor space requirement. Reel ovens may be equipped with stream injector pipes also, together with other control panels and arrangements.

The chief disvantages of Reel ovens are the difficulty in automating the loading and unloading operations and the inability to provide zone heating. Therefore in bigger bakeries tray ovens are used. In these ovens trays holding several pans are permanently fixed to a conveying chain. Trays are pulled by the chain from front to back of the oven, then moved to a lower track and continue baking on the return trip to the front, where they are unloaded. Small sized traveling trays ovens may be operated as batch or multicycle equipment; after the oven is loaded, the pans take two or more trips required for complete baking before unloading. In longer ovens, one cycle is enough for complete baking and in this case oven can be operated continuously, automatic loaders and unloaders can be used.

Band Ovens

Band ovens are continuous traveling hearth type ovens, in which hearth is one uninterrupted strip of metal. The band may be solid, perforated or woven. Doughs can be deposited directly on the hearth, as in the case of biscuits and cookies etc., sometimes pans are also used. Baking surfaces are made of either solid steel bands, perforated steel bands or wire mesh bands. The earlier mesh bands had a fairly open weave, but modern equipments have finely textured closely woven structure. Perforated bands and wire mesh allow steam to escape from the bottom also, thus help prevent gas pockets and distortions. The steel bands are made of low carbon alloy steel.

To prevent sticking of the dough, the bands are oiled or greased lightly at the first run. The band is powdered by a variable speed motor. The time of baking is adjusted by varying the speed of the band. To avoid sideways movement of the band, band guides are provided. Oven chamber consists of a frame supporting the necessary roller, guides, burners and the like, together with insulation on top, sides and bottom. Vents with dampers, clean-out doors and observation ports are also provided.

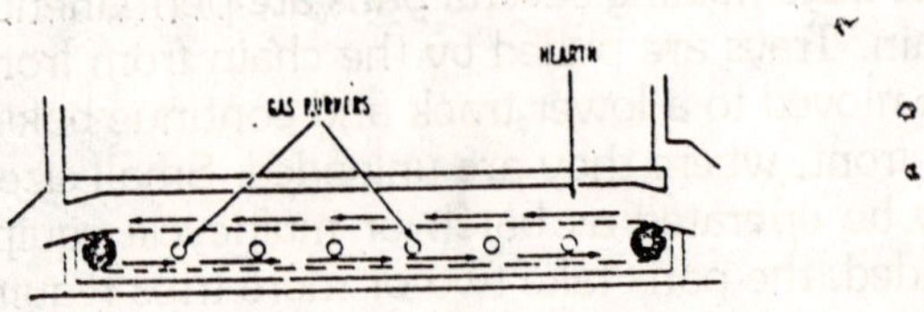

Fig. 10.15 Travelling Hearth Oven.

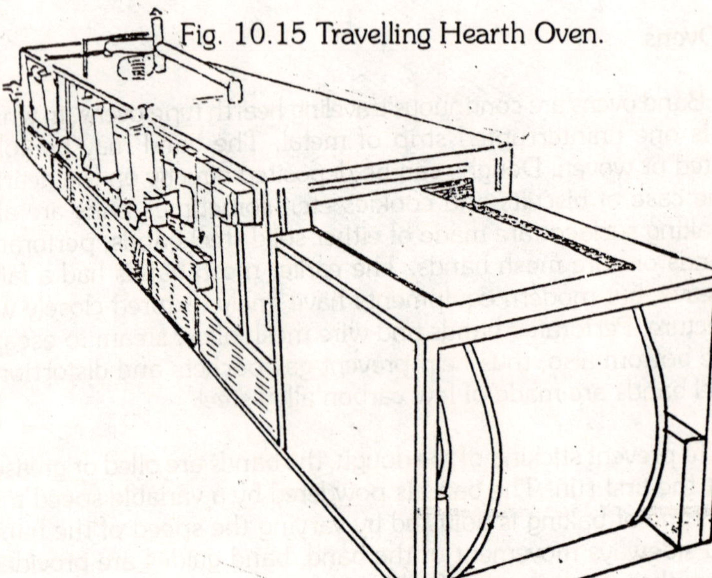

Fig. 10.16 Biscuit Banking Oven.

Other Ovens

In electronic ovens heat is generated in the dough itself with high frequency radiation. In dielectric heating frequency of 30-40 Mc and in microwave systems higher frequencies are used. For sugar wafer cookies travelling book ovens are used in which sets of 2 plates each are mounted on travelling chains and the top plate is hinged to the bottom plate. The books open automatically to accept a charge of batter, then close and lock. The closed books are carried through the baking chamber when they again reach the front of the oven, the books open, the baked sheet is ejected and the hook receives its next charge of batter. These wafer ovens are made in 12 to 30 plate models.

Usual ovens are fuelled by gas, oil or electricity. when gas or oil is used as fuel burners are employed, .which may be located in the baking chamber itself or outside it. In travelling hearth type evens baffles can be placed in the chamber to restrict heat circulation so that different temperatures can be applied to the product at different times in its baking cycle. This system is known as zone control. Provision for steam introduction in the oven is also made to modify crust chargteristics.

Loading and Unloading

In small scale operations loading of the oven is done manually but in larger factories this is accomplished by mechanical means. In one loader system the troughs moving on conveyer (right angle to oven) from final proofer are pushed to a series of rollers at right angles to the conveyer and parallel to the oven door. When a series of pans the width of tray or hearth has collected, they are pushed into the oven. A retractable metal bar prevents additional pans from coming onto the leading platform while the pusher bar is operating.

Unloading of the baked items is also done mechanically. In some of the tray ovens, trays are tilted just before they reach the unloading position, so that the pans slide by gravity onto a cross conveyer at a lower level. In horizontal unloaders pusher bars move the pans off the trays. This method causes lesser mechanical damage to the bread. Better unloaders are available for products like pies etc.

Depanning

In small scale units baked goods are taken off the pans by hand but in continuous production system, depanners are used. In one kind of depanners the baked loaf is dislodged by jerking the inverted pan. In vacuum depanners a series of suction cups lift the loaves or rolls, from the pans; but in this case special type of pans are required.

Coolers

The loaves coming out of the pan (after depanning) are quite hot viz. at a temperature of 125° to 150°C. They have to be cooled before slicing and wrapping. The pans themselves have to be cooled to below 35°C before loading of fresh dough pieces in them. The breads may be cooled by straking in racks and to facilitate fans may be provided. This method takes much floor space, labour and time hence high capacity baperies use conveyorised coolers. These coolers are equipped with a fan system which draws in air at the discharge end and moves it past the loaves, exhausting at the top. Other type of coolers e.g. vaccum conditioners are also in use. In any case excessive air circulation pans or the circulation of dry or warm air should be avoided so that the loaf will not dry excessively.

PANS

The pans form an important item of equipment requiring sizable investment. Their construction, color, reflectivity, confirmation etc. affect the finished product, handling efficiency and speed of baking etc. Pans are made of black iron, tin plate, aluminium, aluminized steel, and stainless steel. Black iron pans get heated up quickly and are almost rustproof due to the presence of an oxide coating. Usually tinplated iron pans are used in bakeries. New pans of this type are heated at 200°C for several hours to get an oxide film. Aluminum is a good conductor of heat but suffers from easy mechanical damage; in aluminised steel this deficiency is removed. Stainless steel is free from corrosion and mechanical damage but is very costly.

The new bread pans have to be conditioned prior to use. The new pans are wiped with dry cloth and heated at 200-225°C for 8-12 hours. After this they are greased with shortening and heated for second time, after which they are ready for use.

BREAD SLICERS

There is a great demand for sliced bread. Slicing by hand is laborious and time consuming. Hence bread slicers are used. Three types of slicer machines are avilable using circular blades, straight blades and continuous band blades. Circular blade slicers are suitable for rolls and buns etc. The other two types of machines are suitable for bread slicing.

Disc Slicers

Disc slicers essentially consist of horizontal disc blades with serrated edges driven by motors. They are used primarily for slicing hamburger buns and hot dog rolls so that meat can be inserted easily.

Straight Blade Slicers

Straight blade slicers or reciprocal slicing machines are quite commonly used in India due to low cost, trouble free operation etc. The blades are kept above $\frac{3}{8}$ for bread slicing. The blades are held taut by the force exerted by a heavy spring. Different frames are used for each slice thickness. The frame as well as a few blades can be replaced in a short time viz. a few minutes. These slicers usually have 20-40 minutes loaves/min. capacity.

Band Slicers

Band Slicers are high speed machines using continuous blades. They do not create vibrations, have less frequent need for blade sharpening and continuously slice thickness, within limits. One type of endless blade slicer requires that the bands be placed around steel cylinders and crossed in the center so that they form a figure eight as viewed from the side of the machine. The bread contact area is at the point where the blades cross. Slicer bands are made of chrome vanadium-steel conforming to close specifications of uniformity, hardness, dimensions, smoothness and accuracy of rounded edges.

GRANULATED MATERIALS, POWDERS AND OILS APPLICATORS

Various types of machinery are avilable for applying granulated materials like sugar, salt and coconut etc., powders such as starch, and oils to the bakery goods. A salt applicato shown here, it consists of an automatic recovery system for depositing on a non-continuous product e.g. round biscuits. The pitch and reciprocating strokes of accumulating and distributing plates are controlled to get uniform salt distribution. First, a measured amount of salt is deposited on the accumulating plate, from there it spreads uniformly onto the distributor plate. The salt from these fals on the product as a uniform curtain. Sugar applicators also function similarly.

Automatic coconut topper deposits a continuos, uniform layer of coconut topping material and the excess material is recovered.

Flour brushes remove excess flour or starch from the top of dough sheets as they travel on a conveyor to the cutting machine. Bristles are made of white nylon in cylindrical cross-section. In contrast to this machine flour dusters apply flour to the dough. In simple machines small hoppers extended across the width of conveyor drop flour. The hoppers have perforated plate, at the bottom, and flour movement is facilitated by a rocker arm. Rotary spindles below the plate ensure uniform flour distribution. Spinder and rocker arm are activated by a motor. Modern starch dusters which deposit a cloud of starch powder on the pieces, in slightly vacuumised chamber are also avilable.

Dough oilers are used to apply the required quantity of oil to the product. This may be done bu applying the oil from a roller soaked in oil, or by spraying the oil in the form of fine mist, on the dough, or by passing the product or dough pieces through a curtain of oil. Oil is a costly material hence an equipment depositing only the required amount of oil should be employed. Thus a sprayer unit is the best. Oil temperature añd pumping pressure should be carefully conpoued sharayer designed and kept free of debies to prevent clogging. A mist of small and uniform droplets of oil is created near the object to be coated, the excess oil is recycled. Oil losses to the atmosphere are thus minimum.

FILLINGS DEPOSITORS

Fillings depositors are machines used to deposit incings, fillings, frostings, fains, and jellies etc. on the product. Paste like icings can be deposited by hand also using a cloth with a hole through which it is squeezed out by hand on to the product. Jam, jellies etc. can be extruded on the dough sheet in the form of stripes. Spral screws in a cylindrical chamber may be used for this purpose. The machine will be having a wiper blade also to smooth and spread and deposit. For intermittent or semi-continuous deposit, fruit depositor may be used; pistons beneath the hopper are actuated by the vertical rods.

Multiple rosettes of whipped toppings or jellies can be extruded through die plates by air pressure in the closed hopper. If the filling is stringly in consistency, but still coheres slightly, e.g. buttercream, it can be extruded from large cylindrical pistons and cut off by a wire as discs which are then deposited on the cake. The deposit of cream filling onto sandwich biscuit bases is done in a different way. The filling is pumped to the centre of a rapidly rotating cylinder of small diameter. Extrusion takes place through orifices in this cylinder and the dies are usually ring shaped to give a deposit with a central hole. The extrusion is continuous and amount of deposit is controlled by adjusting the speed of the pump. The extruded material is sliced off by a stationary wire as the orifice passes above the base cake. Centrifugal force plays a part in detaching the disc of filling from the extruded mass.

SANDWICHING MACHINES

Sandwiching machines are used to make sandwich biscuits by applying a layer of cream filling between two biscuits. A modern sandwiching machine works in the following manner. Simple biscuits from the cooling conveyors are fed to the machine. Vibrating conveyors jog the rows into a stacked-on-edge position. Half the rows have the embossed design while the other rows have the opposite sides facing. They enter the magazines in the proper position for sandwiching and are removed, one at a time, by means of double pins or double chains. Biscuits travelling with design facing down recieve deposits of cream extruded through a rotating slieve with shaped orifices. At the second set of magzines, the top biscuits are dropped onto the deposit. The sandwich thus formed is gently pressed together to get good adhesion and uniform thickness of the sandwich biscuit. The product can then be packaged automatically.

ENROBERS

Enrobing machines are used for putting on a layer of moisture-free fatty material on the biscuits etc. Usually chocolate-flavored coatings are used for this purpose. Chocolate coating is usually recieved in slab form, which is melted in a drum maintained at about 35-40°C with the help of a thermostat control. In modern plants a special chocolate melting and conditioning unit is used for this purpose. The enrobing or coating machine consists of a jacketed coating tank with an agitator, a flow pan, a wire mesh conveyor belt for carrying the product through a curtain of coating, an agitator device for the take away section of the conveyor belt, a water jacketed heat exchanger, a bottomer, and other necessary auxiliary items e.g.

pumps, motors, controls etc.

The wire mesh belt carries the product through the coater, where double curtain of coating coats the product. Beneath the belt is a bottoming pan which recieves the excess coating which is recycled. Excess coating on the cookies is removed by high pressure blower system. Temperature control and precise control of chocolate temper is necessary to get glossy coatings and to avoid bloom. The coating is heated high enough to destroy all crystals, cooled to the temperature at which stable crystals develop and then reheated to production temperature and maintained there during the run. The coated product is cooled to solidify the coating, and then packed.

11

Confectionery Manufacturing Process

(1) HARD CANDIES

Modern confectionery, that is western type sugar confectionery, includes hard boiled sweets, candy, caramel and toffee and comfits. The basic manufacturing processes of some of the well known confectionery items is described in this chapter.

(a)Hard Candies:- The simplest form of candies are the hard candies which can be identified by their hard brittle texture. Typical hard candies are lemon drops, lollypops and china balls. These are essentially based on sugar. A water solution of sugar is boiled in an open pan or under vacuum until the described consistency is reached. During the cooling stage, additives such as colourants, flavouring and other optional ingredients or additives are added, and the mass is poured into moulds. Those that are directly moulded give clear hard candies with a minimum of moisture.

There are various recipes for different varieties of candies but thier manufacturing process is almost similar.

First, the sugar is heated with water in a copper pan, stirring occasiaoally. After boiling syrup, glucose is added but stirred until it has dissolved. Then a cover is placed on pan and is allowed to boil in this way for about 5 minutes. The cover is removed and a thermometor is placed in the boiling sugar. When the thermometer records 149 C, it is removed. The pan is taken out of the stove and is stirred in the sliced butter. The pan is again replaced and is brought to boil. Again the pan is removed, flavour is added and the baten is poured into frame of an oiled, water cooled slab. It is

VACUUM COOKER

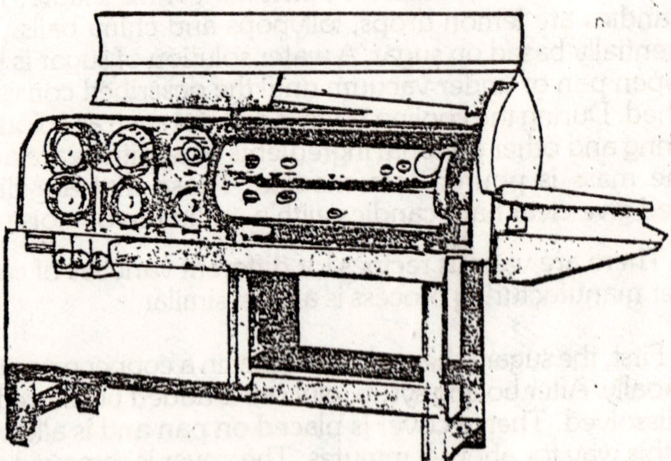

STICK CANDY PEPPERMENT

Cut in to shape by frame cutters. In the open fire boiling process a certain amount of caramelisation takes place which imparts a characteristic flavour of the product. For mass production, the mix is passed as a thin film over heated coils in a steam jacketed cooking tube, then to a revolving cooling table, wherefrom to drops rollers.

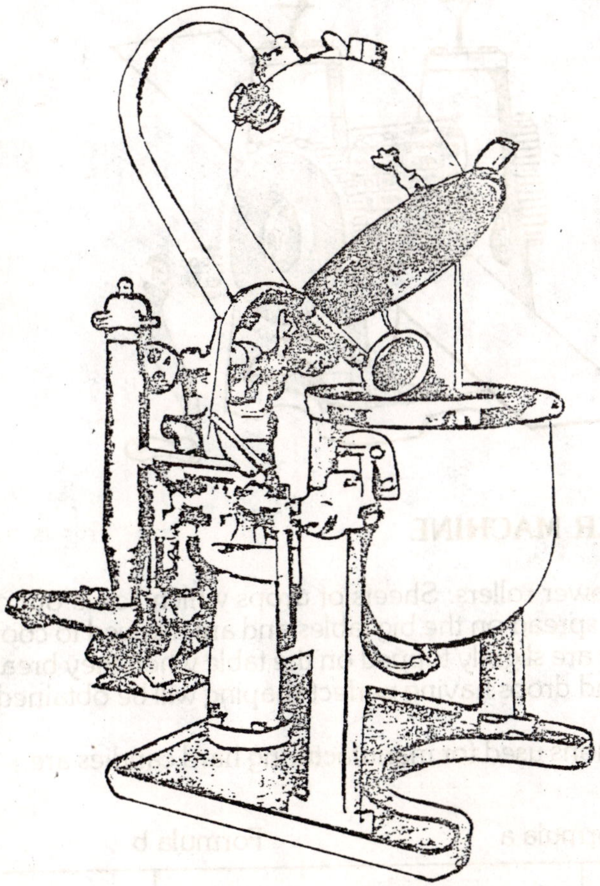

VACUUM COOKER
D-3 SIMPLEX OPEN-KETTLE

For making candies with the drop roller machine the above flavoured and coloured mass is made up in to a number of lumps for easy handling. Eachof the lumps are then flattened out to approxim- ately uniform thickness, and the breadth of the sheet is kept about 7 inches which is equal to the length of the drop rollers. These warm and soft sheets are fed into the hand and as the sheet passes between the rollers, bearing the half models of the design, it is at ince converted into a batch of symmetrical drops. The upper and lower half of each drop are moulded by the corresponding hollows of

DROP ROLLER MACHINE

the upper and lower rollers. Sheets of drops which come out of the machine are spread on the big tables and are allowed to cool. When cold these are slightly topped on the table when they break up into pieces and drops having perfect shaping will be obtained.

Formulations used for manufacturing hard candies are

Formula a		Formula b	
Ingredients	Quantity	Ingredients	Quantity
Sugar	25 kilos	Sugar	25 kilos/
Liquid glucose	5 kilos	water.	25 kilos
Water	25 kilos	cream of tartar	6 tea spoonful
cooking temp.	330 °F	cooking temp.	320 °F

HOW TO TAKE TEMPERATURE

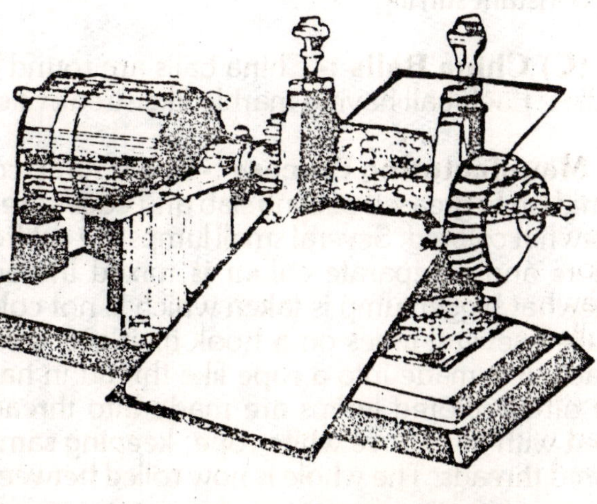

POWER OPERATED DROP ROLLER MACHINE

(b) Lollypops :- Toy candies or lollypops are made with a small hand press having two or three dies, for different shapes. Manufacture of these candies is a time consuming operation and should only be attemped when a good demand exists. The soft mass is immediately wrapped in rubber sheets to conserve its heat and to keep in plastic form. While wrapping in rubber sheet, one end is kept open from which the operator takes small bits out of the mass, the bit kept in the die of lollypop machine, together with a small thin stick of bamboo and upper portion of the die is pressed. The mass forms into the shape engraved in the die and comes out with a portion of bamboo stick embedded in it.

Formulation

Ingredients	**quantity**
Sugar	40 lbs
Glucose	10 lbs
Watrer	6 litres
Citric acid	2 oz
Colour	2 tea spoonful
Perfume	as desired

Manufacturing process :- Sugar, water and glucose are heated in a copper pan till sugar and glucose are dissolved. When it starts boiling a cover is placed on the pan and a thermometer is fitted to it. When thermometer records 165°C, the pan is removed from the fire and allowed it to cool, and other ingredients are added with constant stirring.

(C) China Balls :- China balls are round ball shaped hard candies. Each ball having marble like streak of several colours.

Manufacturing Process :- Sugar syrup cooked to 320°F is poured on to greased cooling slab and edges are folded to make it somewhat colored. Several small lumps are cut from it with a sharp scissors and a separate colour is mixed in each lump. Now a somewhat bigger lump is taken which is not coloured. The lump is pulled several times on a hook till it gets a white and shining surface. It is made into a rope like thread in hands, at the same time other colored lumps are made into thread-like shape and joined with the above white rope, keeping same space between colored threads. The whole is now rolled between palms to make

LOLLIPOP MACHINE

LOLLY POP PRESS

a long rope taking care not to twist it. Now pieces of about one foot length are cut from the long rope. Three pieces are kept in the machine at equal distances and the upper portion of the machine is moved back and forth. Beautifull coloured china balls will come out of the machine.

(d) Lozenges :- Lozenges are prepared by cold mixing of icing sugar, gum arabic, gelatine or stearine and flavouring materials. Two types of lozenges are produced. Plain lozenges are made by cutting pieces from a sheet of dough and drying them in air. Cut lozenges are made from mixtures are rolled or extruded into sheets, cut into required shapes and sizes, and hardened by heating. Colouring and flavouring materials are introduced at the time of kneading or during hardening. Compressed lozenges are prepared with stearine and gelatine as binding agents. The same procedure is employed in the production of medicated produ ts.

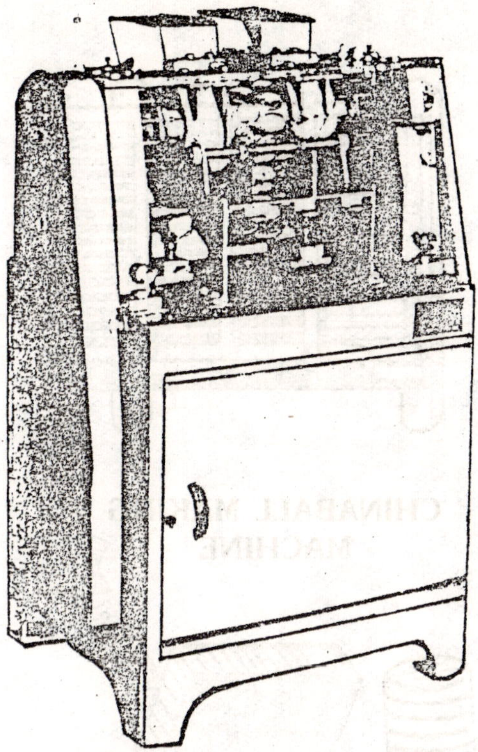

SUCKER (LOLLIPOP) MACHINE

Lozenges should have good snap or brittleness for which thorough and intimate mixing of dough is essential. The drying temperature should not exceed 105°F. and lozenges should not be left longer than is necessary in the drying stores.

(e) Fondant :- Fondant is a mixture of invert sugars prepared by heating sugar and water to a temperature of from 240o to 245°F and adding glucose or a week acid to accelerate the inversion. Fondants have the same composition as hard sugar boilings such as sugar 60%; water 20%; and corn syrup 20% The mixture of sugar, corn syrup and invert sugar (or cream of tartar) is cooked at 234-240°F. If the cooking is properly carried out, the syrup produced, when dro-pped into cold water, forms a soft ball which flattens on removal. The supersaturated solution from cooker is care fully cooled and whipped for 3 - 5 minutes to induce the

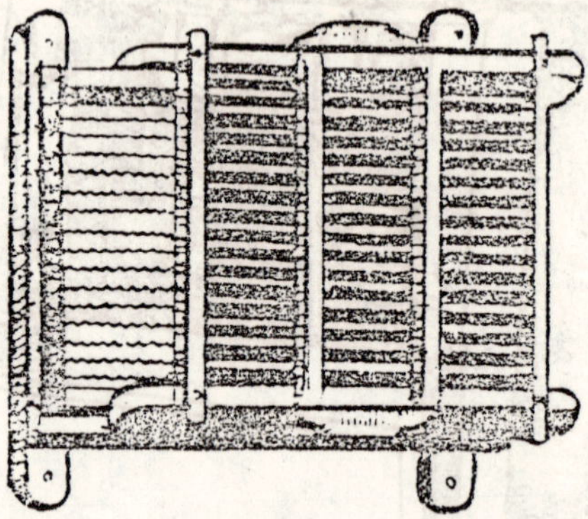

CHINABALL MAKING MACHINE

PEPPERMENT LOZENGES CUTTING PUNCH

formation of minute crystals of sucrose. it is then thinned with sugar syrup, cooking it all the time to remove the heat of crystallisation. The product is ripened or cured for 24 hours or more when the water present distributes itself uniformly throughout the mass. Acid fondants are obtained when acid is added to invert part of the sugar and glucose fondants are obtained when corn syrup is used.

The texture of the fondant varies according to the graining of the supersaturated sugar solution. The nature of the grains produced depends upon the degree of sucrose inversion, concentrations of dextrose and invert sugar present, cooking time and temp-erature, mani-pulation of fondant mixture, addition of colloidal ingredients e.g, egg albumin and

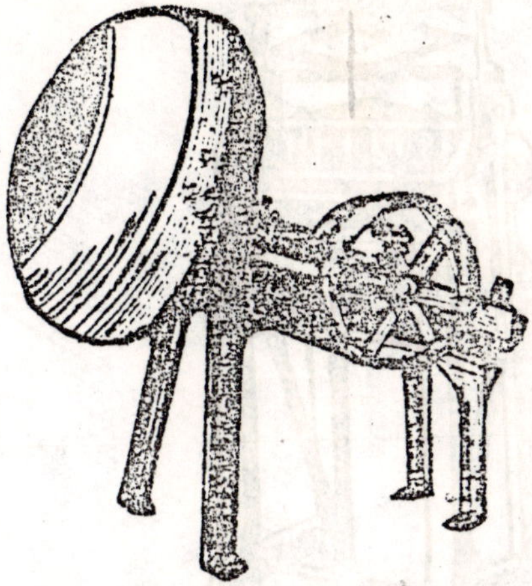

REVOLVING COMFIT PAN

gelatin, and the period of curing or ripening. All the sugar must be thoroughly dissolved before boiling. During boiling, the solution should be stirred to prevent caramelisation, it should not be stirred after boiling as it facilitates crystallisation.

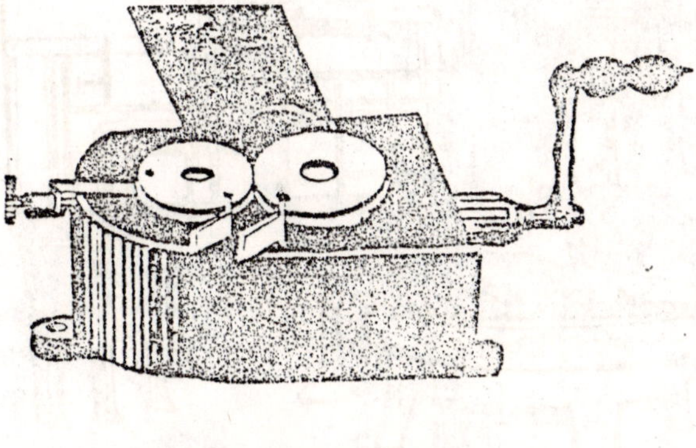

SIZING MACHING

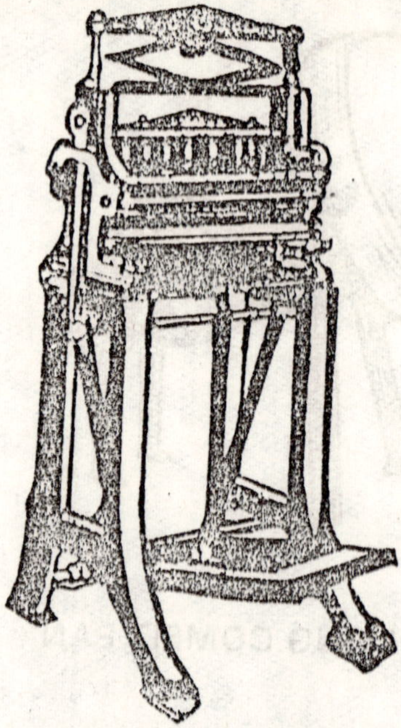

FOOT PRESS
FOR SEAMLESS DROPS

VACUUM UNIT, WITH A PRECOOKING
KETTLE AND OPEN CREAM BEATER

FORMULATIONS OF MORE CONFECTIONERY ITEMS

1. FRUIT AND NUT BARS

Ingredients	Quantity
Sugar	7 lbs
Corn Syrup	3 lbs
Water	1 qt.
Raw almonds	1 lb
Dates	1 lb
Figs	1 lb
Citron	1 lb
Glazed cherries	1 lb
Glazed pineapples	1 lb
Sliced coconut	8 oz
Cinanminor pearls	2 oz

Process :- The slab is greased and lined with iron bars 3 feet long, 4 inches wide, and $1\frac{1}{4}$ inches high. The fruits and nuts and the coconut are mixed and filled into the spaces between the bars. The red pearls are sprinkled on top.

The sugar, corn syrup and water are placed in a copper pan on the stove until dissolved. When the batch begins to boil, it is covered and allowed to steam for a few minutes. The sides are washed down and a thermometer is placed in the batch which is cooked to 290 degree F. The candy is then poured out evenly on the fruits and nuts on the slabs and allowed to cool for a few minutes. It is then loosened with a large knife, sliced with a sharp knife, and after cooling wrapped in moisture proof cellophane. It is then packed into tins.

This batch will yield approximately 20 pounds of candy.

2. FRUIT PUNCH CHOCOLATES

Ingredients	**Quantity**
Sugar	30 lb
Honey	2 lb
Fresh 18% light cream	16 lb
Salt	2 tea spoonful
Melted corn syrup	3 lb
Marshmallow whip	3 lb

Melted Bitter chocolate	3 lb
Assorted Diced Fruit	3 lb
Chopped pecans	2 lb
Roman punch flavour	3 tea spoonful
Invertase	2 tea spoonful

The sugar, honey, cream and salt are placed in a copper pan on the stove and stirred untill dissolved. The sides are washed down and stirring is continuud. The batch is cooked untill it forms a rather soft ball, or untill it registers 242°F. The melted corn syrup is stirred rapidly to about 100°F. The marshmallow and chocolates are added, the beater is set in motion, and the fruits, nuts, flavour and invertase are added. Operation of the beater is continued untill the batch is creamed to a lump. It is then allowed to sweat back for 10 minutes and then kneaded untill sift and put through a cut roll machine. The small centers are coated with high quality milk chocolate and after they are set, they are packed in the usual manner.

This formula will yield approximately 55 pounds of centers, or 75 pound of hand dipped chocolates.

3. BUTTER CREMAM CHOCOLATE

Formulation

Ingredients	**Quantity**
Sugar	3 tea spoonful
Water	10 qt.
Salt	3 tea spoonful
Butter	4 lbs.
Marshmallow whip	2 lbs.
Vanilla flavour	2 tea spoonful
Invertase	2 tea spoonful
Melted bitter chocolate	4 lbs.

The sugar, water and cream of tarter are placed in copper pan on the stove and stirred untill dissolved. When the batch begins to boil, it is covered and allow to steam for a few minutes. The sides are washed down and a thermometer is placed in the batch is stirred continuously while being roasted.

(ii) SOFT CANDIES

Continuous Process For Manufacture of Soft Candy

Soft candies are prepared by continnuous process which comprise the following steps:

1. Ingredients such as sugar, glucose, fat, gelatin and water were mixed and quickly concentrated to avoid formation of inverted sugar and was formed a homogeneous mass, which was free flowinig at high temperature.
2. The free flowing mass was cooled to a paste consistency.
3. The paste was induced to form crystallization nuclei.
4. Mixing, further homogenization under pressure, and shaping into a paste web, was done.
5. The paste web was cooled to an intermediate temperature below the temperature of the paste and the room temperature.
6. The mass was further mixed and homogenized under pressure and was extruded into a shape of suitable size for packaging

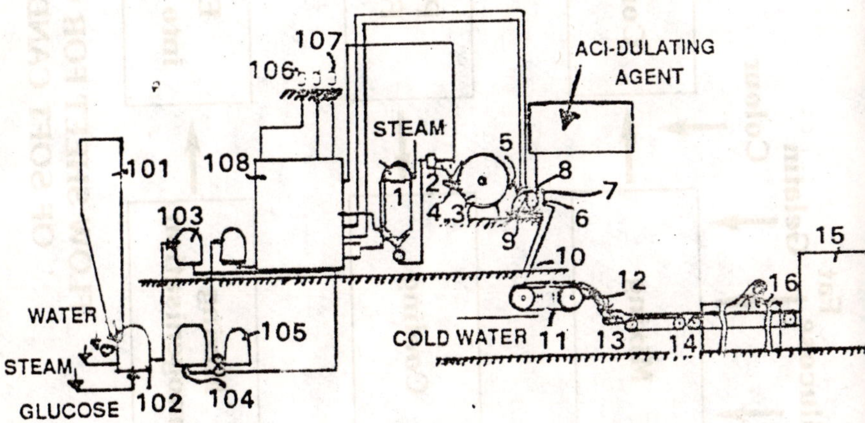

Continuous Process for Manufacture of Soft Candy

7. The rod was cooled substantially to room temperature and cut into suitably sized candy units.

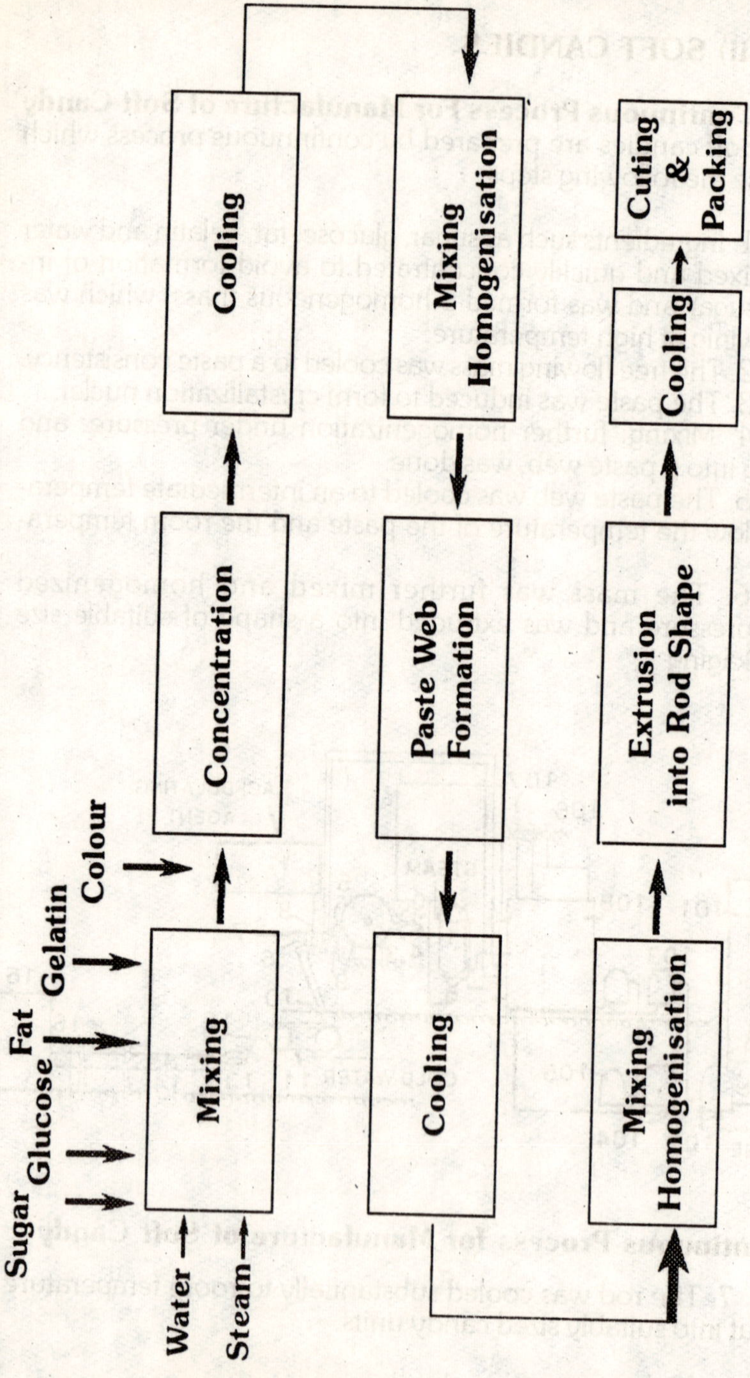

FLOW SHEET FOR CONTINUOUS PROCESS OF SOFT CANDY MANUFACTURING

Addition of colouring matter, flavouring agents and acidulating agent was done at any stage in the sequential steps, under such condition that the product was satisfactorily distributed through the mass so as to provide a homogeneous paste.

Automatic Soft Candy Manufacturing Process

Code No.	Process Equipment
101	Silo
102	Dissolver
103	Stock tank
P	Pump
104	Stock tank
105	Mixer
106	Stock tank
107	Stock tank
108	Volume metering system.
1	Concentrator
2	Feeding chute
3	Rotating drum
4	Doctor blade
5	Doctor blade
6	Mixer extruder
7	Strirrer blade
8	Feeder
9	Feed screw
10	Extruder
11	Belt Cooler
12	Blade
13	Extruder
14	Cooler
15	Cutting Machine

From the silo sugar is fed to dissolver along with water, glucose and steam. The solution from the dissolver is fed to stock tank. A solution of gelatin and water is prepared in the mixer and fed to stock tank as shown in figure. Bottom stock tank contains fat, and upper three small stock tank contain coloring matter and flavouring agent. The sugar syrup, fat, glucose, gelatin solution and the colouring and flavouring materials from the respective stock tanks are fed to volume metering systems which feed the required amount of each component to the subsequent portions of the system. A sugar syrup blend, gelatin solution and fat are fed to a thin film condenser . This condenser concentrates the mixture of components to a paste of desired concentration. To avoid the invert sugar formation excessively, it is necessary to concentrate the mixture in a short period.

The concentrated paste at 130° C temperature, is discharged from the concentrator-and fed to a feeding chute, which discharges onto the external surface of a rotating drum. Cooling of drum is done by a flow of water through the interior. The paste is spread on the drum by a doctor blade, in order to cool the paste to approximatly 70 degree C so as to provide a crystallization in the paste. On the other side of drum there is another doctor blade which strips the paste web from the drum and directs it to the mixer extruder. This extreder preferaby has a double wall and stirrer blade which is effective both for blending and stretching of the paste in the mixer. At this time this flavouring agent from metering system and acidulating agents from feeder are added. The paste temperature will increase to at least 70° C. The paste after the blending time is removed by the feed screw which homogenizes and pushes it through extruder. This extruder feeds onto a belt cooler, which is cooled by cold water. The web from the belt is stripped by blade and fed to futher extruder. In this extruder paste is further homogenised and comes out in the shape of rod. This is then passed through cooler and is discharged to cutting machine. Thereafter the candy can be packaged and bagged.

(iii) CARBONATED CANDY

Carbonated candy is a hard candy type containing carbon dioxide gas. It produces an entetaining popping sensation.

Formulation :

Ingredients	**Quantity**
Sucrose	16.200 kgs
Corn Syrup	8.700 kgs
Water	5.900 kgs
Food colour	8 gms
Artificial Flavour	31.5 ml.

A thick viscous melt is prepared mixing sucrose, corn syrup, and food colour in respective quantity in a kettle. This mixture is then heated to 320°F to remove water. This viscous mixtire is charged to a preheated autoclave and desired flavour is added to it. After sealing the autoclave, carbon dioxide at a pressure of 600 Psi is introduced to the headspace of autoclave. An agitator mounted vertically through the top portion of the autoclave is run for 4-5 minutes.

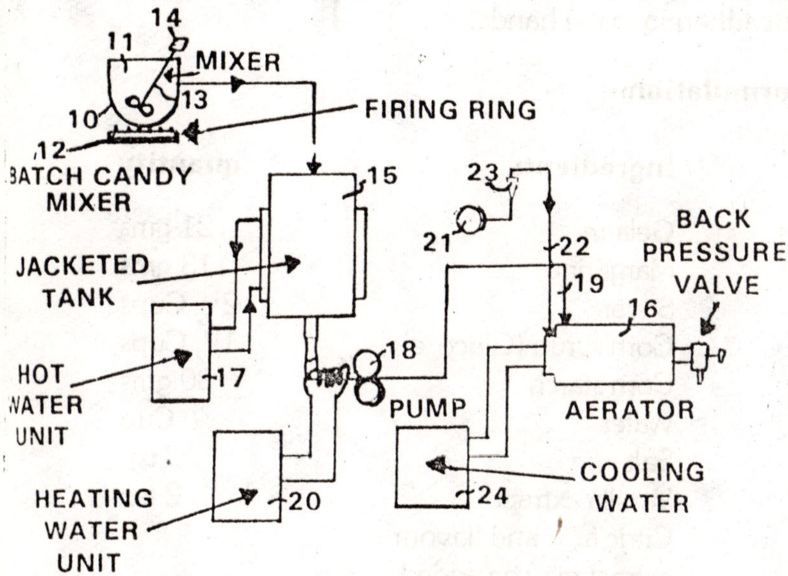

Diagram of Candy Aerating Apparatus

A jacketed cooling tube is vertically mounted adjecent to the autoclave and a jacketed line (1 inch) with a ball valve at its midpoints is connected to the bottom of the autoclave with the cooling tube. The ball valve is kept closed. The vessels are pressurized to 600 Psi with CO_2 and is allowed to complete the mixing The ball valve is opened. Then pressure in the autoclave is increased to 650 Psi and a needle valve which vents to atmosphere is slowly opened. So that all the viscous melt is transferred to cooling tube. Then ball valve and needle valve are closed. Cold water is circulated in the cooling tube jacket to reduce the temperature of product to 70° F. The product exists as the solid gas containing matrix at this temperature. The cooling tube is vented to atmosphere after cooling water and gas line are closed This suddenpressure chande in the tubes causes the matrix to shelter into granular particles of uniform size. This resulatant granular products is a hard candy containing carbon dioxide gas

(iv) SEED CONFECTIONS (POPCORN BALLS)

Popcorn balls are seed or nut type confection which can easily be stored, heated, handled and applied to the popcorn without adhering to the hands.

Formulation :

Ingredients	quantity
Gelatin	21 gms
Margarine	113 gms
Sugar	$2^1/_2$ Cups
Corn syrup (Glucose)	$1^1/_2$ Cups
Corn starch	30 gms
Water	$^2/_3$ Cup
Salt	2 tsp
Vanilla extract	2 tsp
Citric acid and flavour extract may be added if desired.	
Popped Corn	14 Quarts

In order to prepare this confection gelatin is dissolved in water by heat treatment. To this solution sugar is added and is heated to bring the mixture to a rolling boil then removed from burner and glucose and corn starch is added.

POPCORN MACHINE

This is mixed well and cooked at 200° F. To this margarine is added and allowed to cool. The remianing ingredients with flavour and colour are then added to it. The resulting confection is then packaged in heat resistant transparent envelopes and cooled for storage. Whenever requied, the the pouch confections are placed in boiling water upto melting and poured onto the freshly popped corn and stirred well to mix hot confection with the corn. Then popcorn are shaped into balls knows as popcorn balls.

a.

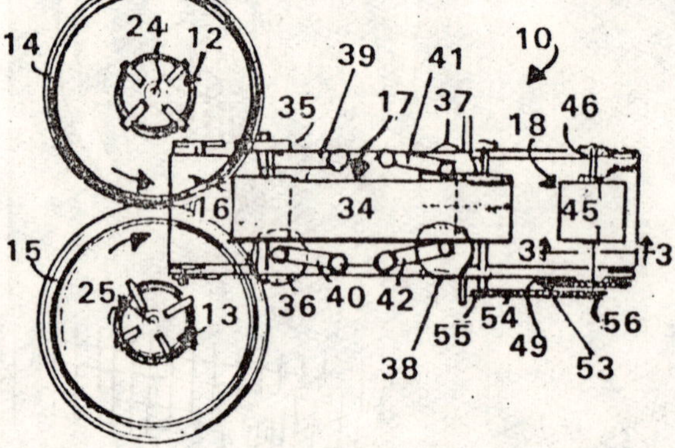

b.

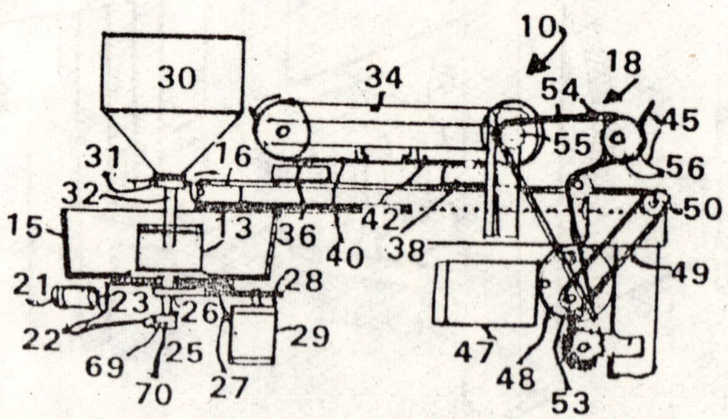

MACHINE FOR MAKING COTTON CANDY

(v) COTTON CANDY

Cotton candy is a type of candy extremely light in weight, a portion if it is like feather or a thin piece of cotton. Its production requires fully automatic machineries.

It is prepared by extrusion process. The molten sugar is extruded through small aperture in the cylindrical wall of a rapidly rotating extrusion head situated in the centre of a collection pass. The sugar strands are collected and bundled onto a stick or rod by continuously twisting the stick and passing it around the interior of the pass. This strands together like cotton.

This automatic candy making machine is accomplished by mounting one or more sugar spinning heads with collection pans adjacent to a conveyor belt moving continuously. The bundle of sugar strands pans. A plurality of sizing and compacting members near the top of the belt to compact the bundle of strands carried there through by the belt into a continuous bundle of previously determined cross sectional size and shape and then cutting of the compacted product into proper size and separating the sections by means of a rotating star blade cutter mounted above the conveyor belt. Then the product after cutting is automatically fed to an automatic packaging line.

(iv) COATED CONFECTIONS

Coated confections also knows as pan coated confections, comfits or dragees consists of nuts or seeds, or boilied goods or chewing gum, coated with a hard glossy sugar covering. The nuts or other centres are placed in a rotating coating pan and given an under coat of gum arabic orgelatine and sugar srup and a final coating of sugar. For the latter a supersaturated sugar solution is added in small quantities and the pan roated until the moisture from the syrup evaporates and leaves a thin sugar coating on the centres. The coating process is repeated a number of times until the required size is built up. The material is dried after each coating by hot air; dusting with flour or other starchy materials facillitates drying. High grade products are covered with sugar only. The polish and smoothness of the coated goods are due to continual rubbing against one another and against the side of the pan. They are finished in a polishing pan lined with heavy wax coated canvas. dried and packed.

(a) CHEWING GUM AND BUBBLE GUM

It is universally accepted that sucking and chewing is in fact a natural human instinct from infancy till old age. The habit of chewing in our country is mainly confined to betel and paan where as in western countries this instinct finds reflection in the common habit of chewing gum products. Chewing gum has proved to be a very aesthetic substitute for unaesthetic habits like smoking and chewing supari or betel nuts.

Gum chewing is also beneficial to teeth and jaw muscles and to the gums. Chewing gum has also been helpful in relieving the discomfort caused by varying air Bessure during air travel.

Chewing gum and bubble gum are originally made of the prime raw material natural gum. Sugar and flavouring agents were added to make the chew more palatable. With the increase in demand for these products, and the short supply of this natural gum considerable research was undertaken and several substitutes are developed in the country.

Essntial ingredients that are used in manufacturing chewing gum are the gum base either natural or non tixic synthetic, cane sugar. The optional ingredients comprise of glycerine, malt, milk powder, chocolate, coffee, gelatin food grade, flavour permitted in PFA rules, antioxidants, preservatives and other nutrients.

Chewing gum consists of two major portions masticatory and non masticatory. The masticatory portion usually called chewing gum lease and often includes filler, while the non-masticatory portion consists mostly of sweetening and flavouring ingredients. For along time natural water insoluble gums of vegetable origin, e.g., chicle were used for the major portion of chewing gum base. Unfortunately the natural gums are subject to substantial price fluctuations as well unpredictability of supply because of these reasons manufacturers have tried with varying degrees of sucess to duplicate the desirable properties of natural gums by means of synthetic resins, rubbers and other polymers. Atypical chewing gum base is formulated from natural and/or synthetic gums or elastomers, hydrophillic plactisizers, ester gums (elastomer solvent and hydrophobic plasticizers, oleagin plasticizer, emulsifiers, pigments and additives such as antixidants, stabiizers or preseratives. Examples of natural gums or elastomers are belater, sorva, gutta purcha, lichi caspe and jelutong. Examples isoprene copolymer and butadiene styrene copolymer. The hydrophillic placticizer is usually a synthetic resin.

Manufacturing process

The gum base is melted (temp 270°F) and placed in a standard dough mixer kettle equipped with sigma blades. The corn syrup and lecithin are added and mixed for 2 minutes at 200° F. At the time the mix is folding well, powdered saccharin is added and the mixture is mixed for another 2 minutes at 200° F. Thereafter about 1/3 of the sucrose is added and the mixture is mixed for 2 minutes. The sorbitol and remaining sucrose are added, mixed for 1 minute, and then spray dried flavour is added and the mixture is mixed for 1 minute. The gum is then discharged from the kettles, cut in 25 lb loaves and allowed to cool to 90° to 120° F. It is then rolled to a thickness of 0.178 cms on a standard gimpel machine and scored into strips 7.26 cms wide and 41.9 long, and cooled for 12 to 18 hours. The chewing gum product obtained is found to have pleasant sweet taste for upto 30 minutes and more without the bitter after taste normally asociated with free saccharin acid.

Formulation

Ingredients	Parts by Weight
1. Gum base	20
2. Corn syrup 44° Be	17
3. Powdered free sachharin and pulvirised to pass through a U.S. 140 mesh screen.	0.2
4. Powdered sugar (sucrose)	50
5. Dextrose	10
6. Peppermint oil	1
7. Lcithin	0.2

Formulation - II (*cherry flavour chewing gum*)

Ingredients	**Parts by weight**
Gum base	20
Sugar	50
Corn syrup	16
Dextrose	10
Lecithin	0.2
Citric acid	0.5
Fumaric acid	2
Free sachharin acid	0.2
Artificial cherry flavour	1
Gum Arabic coated cherry flavour	1.5

Formulation III (*Spearmint flavour chewing gum*)

Ingredients	**Parts by weight**
Gum base	21
Corn syrup	17
Sugar	49.8
Sorbitol	10
Flavour	1
Gum Arabic coated flavour	1
Lecithin	0.2

Formulation - IV

Ingredients	**Parts by weight**
Gum base	108.0
Sucrose	296.0
Corn syrup (44 dextrose equivalent)	90.0
Gum arabic	7.5
Peppermint oil	0.8
Poly oxyethylene (20)	
Sorbitan monostearate	0.2

Formulation for Sugariess chewing gum

Ingredients	Parts by weight
Gum base	330
Xylitol	60
Lecithin	1.5
Xanthan solution	5
Flavour	1

Formulation for Improved Shelf Life

1.

Component	Percent by weight
Sucrose	20
Sorbitol	40
Corn syrup	25.3
Gum base	14
Color and flavour	0.7

2.

Component	Percent by weight
Sucrose	30
Sorbitol	30
Corn syrup	25.3
Gum base	14
Color and flavour	0.7

3.

Component	Percent by weight
Sucrose	55
Sorbitol	3
Corn syrup	27.3
Gum base	14
Color and flavour	0.7

4.

Component	Percent by weight
Sucrose	30
Dextrose	30
Corn syrup	27.3
Gum base	12
Color and flavour	0.7

5.

Component	Percent by weight
Sucrose	30
Levulose	30
Corn syrup	25.3
Gum base	14
Color and flavour	0.7

Centre filled Gum containing a Humectant

Ingredients	Amount
Gum base lb	210 lbs
Glucose (corn syrup) lb	160 lbs
Plasticizer lb	19 lbs
Sugar (A X) lb	611 lbs
Oil of peppermint g	2,600 g
50% by weight glycerin and H_2O mixture, g	2,725 g
Titanium di oxide, g	850g

Industry in India

Though the confectionary industry has made considerable strides, the chewing gum industry is still in its infancy. Untill 1970 there was no unit manufacturing chewing gum bases and the entire gum base was imported. However int the early 70s, two units started manufacturing the gum base with foreign technial knowhow, and thereafter the chewing gum industry has made some progress in India. The supply of gum base is not adequate enough to achieve greater expansion and progress in the industry.

The chewing gum industry requires sophisticated plant and machinery such as mixers, extruders, rolling and scoring machine. Coating equipments and wrapping and packing machinery. The entire operations should be done under controlled temperature and moisture conditons, and naturally control air conditioning is absolutely necessary.

The technical knowhow and manufacturing process applicable in the chewing gum industry are entire different from those of the confectionary industry though certain operations such as wrapping and packaging are common. The gum base, which is the basic raw material for the chewing gum industry, has to conform to strict technical specification to make the produ:t a "good chew". The gum base to be incorprorated into the finished products should melt at body temperature; this essential feature make gum product easily susceptible to climatic vagaries, and the packaging used should affort sufficient shelf-life to the product till it reaches the consumer. In addition to the common raw material like sugar, liquid glucose and food colours, this industry requires special flavours which will linger as long as the product is chewed. Certain additional preservatives and chemicals have also to be incorporated.

Conclusion:- The future of the chewing gum industry depends very much on a reconsideration of the policy of reservation of this industry for the small scale sector.

(vii) TOFFEE

Introduction

The words "Toffee" and "Caramels" have no precise definitions. They include a veriety of products varying fro..ı hard butterscotch to soft eating caramels. Caramels and toffee contain milk and butter in addition to the usual ingredients, the former being softer in the commoner varieties. butter is partly or wholly replaced by coconut or cacao butter or margarine. In the manufacture of caramels, butter or milk are emulsified in a homogenizer to a creamy product and added along with other ingredients, icing sugar, corn syrup, corn flour or cashew powder to the boiling pan fitted with mechenical stirrers.

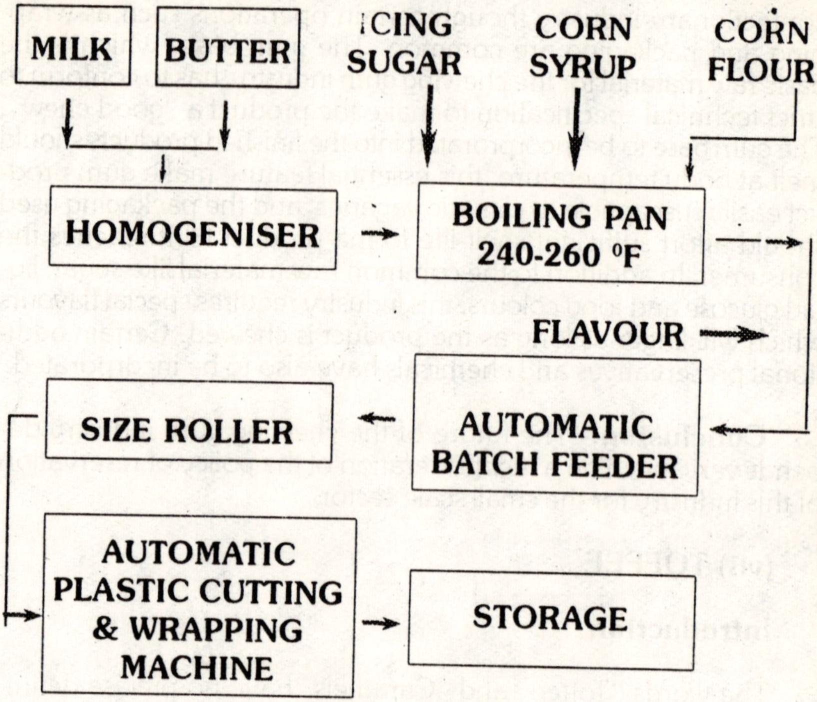

PROCES FLOW SHEET FOR MANUFACTURE OF TOFFEE

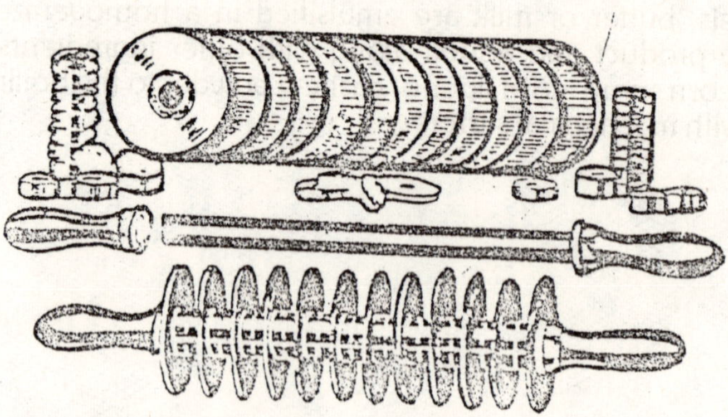

ADJUSTABLE TOFFEE CUT

HOW TO CUT TOFFEE BY TOFFEE CUTTER

Manufacturing Process

The manufacture of toffe and caramels can be divided into four stages:

(1) Preparation of the raw materials
(2) Cooking to the desired consistency
(3) Cooling and cutting into shapes
(4) Packing

For preparation of the raw materials all the ingredients ar

mixed in a mixing machine. The chief function of this stage is too bring about emulsification to the fat.

Formulation for a quality toffee is :

Ingredients	Quantity
Sugar	12 lbs.
Liquid glucose	8 lbs.
Salt	1 tea spoonfull
Water	1 1/2 qt.
Hardened coconut	4 oz.
Butter	1 lb.
Malted milk extract	1 table spoonfull.

The mixer used for this purpose generally consist of a horizontal cylindrical vessel, inside which rotates a number of arms fixed along the length of a horizontal axis. Babbles are fixed to break the flow. For loading there is a lid on the top, and for unloading a large diameter hole in the bottom fitted with a closing plate. In some cases, raw materials are prepared in the boiling pan prior to cooking.

In the boiling pan the mixture is cooked rapidly. The temperature of cooking is adjusted between (260⁰ - 280⁰ F). The steam pressure required for toffee boiling is upwards of 90 lb.

The toffee from the pans is cooled by pitching on to rectangular (usually 3 feet by 6 feet) cast-iron tables through cold water can be circulated. Its treatment on the tables varies according to the method of cutting to be adopted. In many cases the toffee is passed through rollers or by " levelling" the still liquid toffee on the tables. If it is to be made into slab toffee, steel frames are forced into the cooling mass and removed when the toffee has set.

In the case of roll pieces, they are put into automatic cut and wrap machines which produce 400 pieces of toffee a minute, wrapped in overstrip-aluminum foil laminated with waxed paper, cellulose film or waxed paper.

Formulation for Different Kind of Toffee

1. PLAIN TOFFEE

Ingredients	Quantity
Sugar	12 Kgs.
Glucose	3 Kgs.
Water	5 Liters.
Salt Butter	1 Kgs.
Flavour	Sufficient

Process :- The sugar with water is heated in a boiling pan with occasionally stiring. Glucose is added when the solution starts boiling, with continuous stirring untill it has dissolved. Then a cover is placed on the pan.

It is allowed to boil in this way for about 5 miniutes. Then the cover is removed and a thermometer is placed in the boiling sugar. When the thermometer records 149^0 C,it is removed and is placed in a jar or other vessel containing hot water which should be standing by the side of the stove. The pan is lifted from the fire and stirred in the sliced butter. The pan is again placed on the stove and again is boiled. After some time the flavour and colour are added in to the pan the whole mass is poured into a frame on an oiled slab. Then it is cut into appropriate size and wrapped in waxed paper.

2. BUTTER TOFFEE

Ingredients	Quantity
Sugar white	10 Kgs.
Sugar brown	2 Kgs.
Glucose	4 Kgs.
Butter	4 Kgs.
Water	5 Liters.
Flavour	As desired

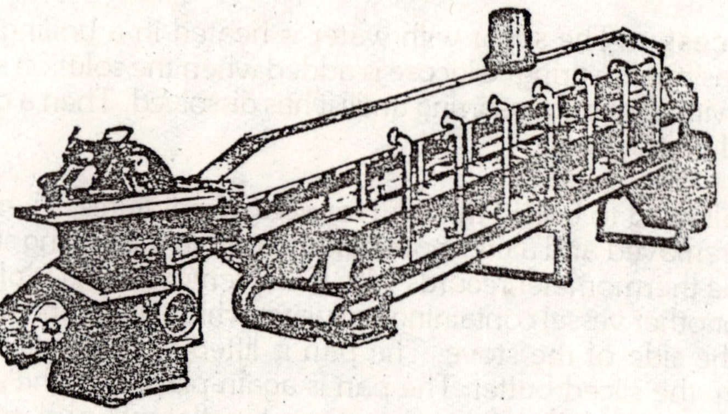

RUM BUTTER TOFFEE

3.. COCONUT TOFFEE

Ingredients	Quantity
Sugar brown	12 Kgs.
Glucose	3 Kgs.
Butter	1 Kgs.
Water	5 Litres.
Coconut chips	3 Kgs.
Essence coconut	15 c.c.

4. MILK TOFFEE

Ingredients	Quantity
Sugar	10 Kgs.
Glucose	5 Kgs.

Water	3.75 Litres.
Full cream sweetend	
Condensed milk	3 Kgs.
Salted butter	1 Kgs.
Saltd	15 Gms.
Butter milk flavour	15 c.c.

The butter is melted in a pan, then gradually stirred in the milk to form a paste. In another pan sugar syrup is prepared by boiling sugar and glucose in water to 151.50°C. The paste of butter and milk is added to the sugar syrup gradually with constant stirring, then the flavour is incorporated. Finally it is poured into slab to cool and is finishd as for other toffees.

5. MALT TOFFEE

Ingredients	Quantity
Sugar brown	9 Kgs.
Glucose	4 Kgs.
Water	3.75 Litres.
Full cream sweetend Condensed milk	8 Kgs.
Saltd butter	3 Kgs.
Malt extract	3 Kgs.
Essence vanilla	15 c.c.

6. PLAIN CHEW TOFFEE

Ingredients	Quantity
Sugar	11 Kgs.
Glucose	6 Kgs.
Water	5 Litres.
Saltd butter	1 Kgs.
Full cream sweetend Condensed milk	4.5 Kgs.
Sheet gelatin	90 gms.
Butter milk flavout	22 c.c.
Colour	q.s.

Generally a large pan is rquired in making chewing toffee. since the gelatin is apt to make the bulk froth and rise during the boiling process.

They gelatin is soaked in the water untill it is soft. Sugar is added to it. Then it is stirred over gentle heat untill the sugar is completely dissolved. It follows the addition of glucose and butter and boiling to 121°C. Milk is incorporated gradually and is continued to boil with constant agitation untill the temperature reaches 185°C - 188°C. Care should be taken of confectionary for which a moderate temperature is required. Then the mass is poured onto the slab to cool, flavour and colour are added when it is cool enough, the hook is pulled over as long as it is possible. Then it is removed to the slab and is kneaded well to press out the air. It is rolled out to the desired thickness. When cooled, it is marked and cut into suitable sizes and packed in wax paper.

7. CHOCOLATE TOFFEE

Ingredients	Quantity
Sugar	3 Kgs.
Sugar brown	3 Kgs.
Glucose	6 Kgs.
Water	2.5 liters
Full cream sweetend	
Condensed milk	3 Kgs.
Cocoa Butter	2 Kgs.
Cocoa powder	750 gms.
Essence vanilla	7 c.c.

Process :- Cocoa butter is melted and is worked out in the chocolate or cocoa powder to form a smooth paste using as little heat as possible. The sugar, glucose and water are boiled to 118.5°C. It is gradually added to milk with contiuous stirring. The batch is allowed to boil before adding the chocolate paste. When the temperature reaches 135° - 138°C. flavour is added and the whaole mass is poured into the prepared slab and is finished as other toffees.

8. PISTACHIO TOFFEE

Ingredients	Quantity
Sugar	10 lbs.
Corn syrup	10 lbs.
Condensed milk	8 oz.
Salt	1 tea spoonfull
18% fresh cream	$\frac{1}{2}$ qt.
Butter	3 lbs.
Choppened pecans	3 qt.
Pistachio flavour Green Colour	3 tea spoonfull

The sugar, corn syrup, coconut butter, salt, and fresh cream are placed in a copper pan on the stove and stirred untill dissolved. When the batch begins to boil, butter is added. The batch is stirred constantly and cooked untill it forms a ball when tested in cold water. The batch is then coloured green, the nuts and flavout are stirred in, and it is then poured out on a greased, cold slab between iron bars. The edges are folded together and the batch is cooled rapidly untill it is firm enough to handle. It is then cut the desire size and wrapped.

9. EVERTON TOFFEE

Ingredients	Quantity
Sugar	4 lbs.
Water	3 cup full
Cream of tartar	1/2 tea spoon
Butter	2 oz.

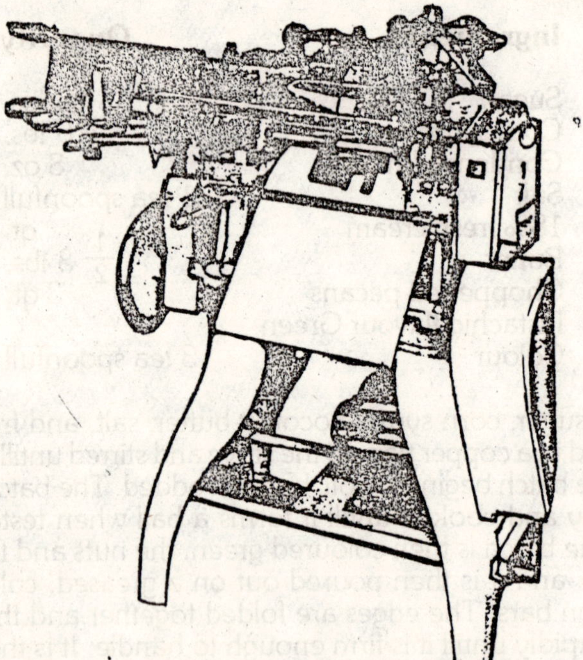

TAFFY & TOFFEE WRAPPING MACHINE

TAFFY & TOFFEE ERAPPING MACHINE

10. LICORICE TOFFEE

Ingredients	Quantity
Cane sugar	15 lbs.
Licorice syrup	8 lbs.
Cocoa butter	1 lb.
Corn syrup	13 lbs.

11. MOLASSES TOFFEE

Ingredients	Quantity
Molasses (High grade)	1 gallon
Brown Sugar	4 lbs.

Butter	1 lb.
Cream of tarter	1 tea spoon

12. MARMALADE TOFFEE

Ingredients	Quantity
Butter	60 gms.
Oranges	12
Sugar	2 lbs.

(viii) CHOCOLATES

The chocolate industry in India is of comparatively recent origin. Handmade fancy chocolate confectionary prepared from imported chocolate couverture had earlier been catering to the sophisticated taste of European population and of well-to-do Indians for some years and quite a few confectioners became household words in the big cities in India. However chocolate was made all the way from cocoa beans for the first time in India during world war II. A small beginning was made during the early part of the war when imports had come to a standstill and the requirement of cocoa powder as well as chocolate were met by indigenious product made in a small company in pune. Though small, the factory was well equipped with a destoner, ball roaster, winnowing triple stone mills, granite roller refiners, stone bed conches and moulding plant. Quality, particularly as it relates to particle size, may not have been up to day's standards, but was certainly good and acceptable.

Chacolate is a flavour that is enjoyed the world over and India is no exception. The Indian industry does produce a high quality cocoa powder for use in other products and to impart a chocolate flavour to other confections, foods and other medications. It produces a beverage-grade powder also which is sold as such or in its extended forms of drinking chocolates. However, such production is limited by the extent to which the industry can consume cocoa butter in making chocolate and chocolate confectionery. A substanial portion of the cocoa powder produced is use to make chocolate-flavoured malted milk food.

Chocolate is a first class confection and at the same time a first class food. It is known that the Indian diet is deficient in energy content. The per capita consumption of fat is also very poor. In these circumstances the nutritive value of chocolate, which contain milk solid, sugar and native cocoa fat or cocoa butter as easily assimilable vebetable fat with a melting point of 29.5^{0}C is pointed

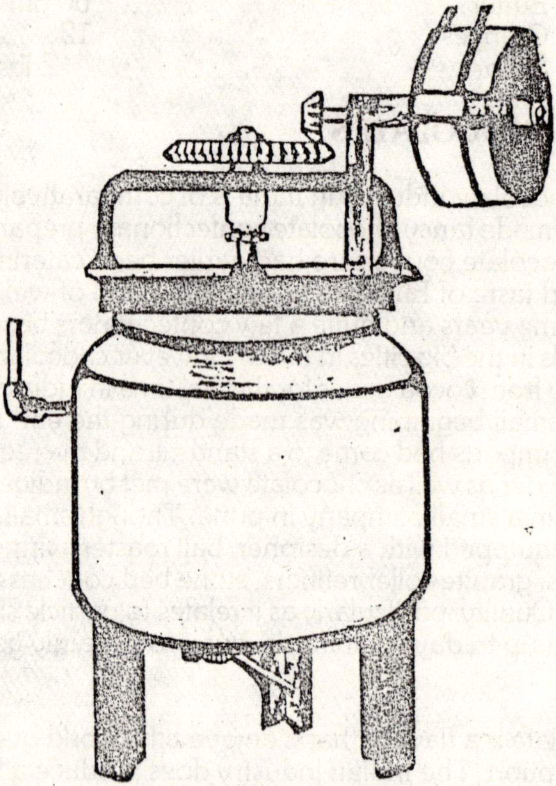

CHOCOLATE MELTING AND MIXING CATTLE

up. Cocoa powder also, with the mildly stimulant action, of the theobromine, the cocoa butter content and a high mlineral value, is an excellent food beverage.

Assorted chocolate in fancy packages are very popular the year around. Chocolate centers consist mostly of creams, chewy and hard masses, fruit jellies, and marmalades. Fruits and nuts usually top the assortment. In making and preparing these centers the confectioner should be quality minded. Whether they are starch cast or hand rolled, all creams should be made of fresh and pure ingredients under sanitary conditions. Only pure flavour should be used in centers. It is best to use pure extract rather than cheap imitations. In making cream centers, fresh fruit pulps supported by pure fruit flavours give best results. Hard and chewy centers should be made with fresh cream and butter and high grade nuts flavoured with pûre oil and extract. The finest glared and preserved fruits should be coated with the best dark sweet vanilla chocolate and the best pure milk chocolate.

Chocolate coating is a skilled practice. It takes endurance and patience, time and long practice to learn how to do it properly.

1. CHOCOLATE TOFFEE

Formulation

Ingredients	Quantity
Sugar	10 lbs.
Corn syrup	10 lbs.
Coconut butter	8 oz.
Salt	1 table spoonfull
Fresh cream	2 qt.
Evaporated milk	2 lbs.
Butter	21 lb.
Bitter chocolate	$2\frac{1}{2}$ lb.
Vanilla flavour	3 tea spoonfull

Process :- The sugar, corn syrup, salt, coconut butter, and fresh cream are placed in a copper pan on the stove and stirred untill dissolved. When the batch begins to boil, the evaporated milk is stirred in and the stirring is continued while the butter is added. The batch is cooked until it forms a medium ball when tested in cold water. The chocolate is then stored in and, while it melts, the vanilla is mixed in. The batch is then poured out on a greased, cold slab and the edges are folded together. The batch is cooled rapidly and, when it is firm enough to handle, it is cut and wrapped as usual.

2. CHOCOLATE COVERED BUTTER TOFFEE

Formulation

Ingredients	Quantity
Daily butter	$3\frac{1}{2}$ lbs.
Coconut butter	$2\frac{1}{2}$ lbs.
Salt	2 tea spoonfull
Sugar	25 lbs.
Corn syrup	5 lbs.
Eaporated milk	5 lbs.
Vannilla flavour	3
Oil of lemmon	1/4 tea spoonfull

The butter, salt and coconut butter are placed in a copper pan on the stove over low heat and stirred untill melted. The sugar and corn syrup are added and stirred until dissolve. When the batch begins to boil, it is covered and allowed to stream for a few minutes. The sides are washed down and a thermometer is placed in a batch, which is cooked to 290° C. The batch is then reduced with evaporated milk until forms a soft ball when tested in cold water. The flavours are stirred in and mixed through well. The batch is poured out on a cold, greased slab between iron bars and spread out to about 1/4 inch thickness. Then it is allowed to cool and, when hard enough, it is sliced and cut into small oblongs. These are coated with dark sweet vanilla chocolate. After they have been allowed to set in the trays, they are packed in the usual manner. The batch will yield approximately 60 pounds of chocolates.

3. CHOCOLATE ANNEX CARAMELS

Formulation

Ingredients	Quantity
Sugar	11 lbs.
Corn syrup	15 lbs.
Coconut butter	1 lb

Salt	1 tabie spoonful
Fresh 18% light cream	49 qt.
Evaporated milk	8 lbs.
Caramel paste	5 lbs.
Bitter chocolate (cut up)	4 lbs.
Vanilla flavour	3 tea spoonfuls
Dipping marsh allows	3 lbs.

The sugar, corn syrup, salt, coconut, butter, and cream are placed in a large copper pan on the stove and sitrred milk is stirred in gradually. Stiring is continued while the batch is cooking. The caramel paste is added and the batch is cooked until it forms a medium ball when tested in cold water. The batch is then removed to a stand, and the chocolate and flavour are added and stirred until completely melted. After adding the marshmallows and mixing well, the batch is poured out on a greased slab between iron bars and spread out evenly with a palette knife. It is allowed to cool until it is hard enough to handle. Then it is passed through a sizing machine, cut into square caramels and wrapped as usual. This batch yields 48 lbs of candy.

4. CHOCOLATE CARAMEL NOUGAT ROLL

Formulation

Ingredient	Quantity
Sugar	11 lbs.
Corn syrup	13 lbs.
Salt	1 table spoonful
Coconut butter	1 lbs.
Fresh cream	4 qt.
Evaporated milk	8 lbs.
Bitter chocolate	3 lbs.
Vanilla flavour	2 tea spoon ful
Honey Nought	12 lbs.

CARAMEL CUTTING MACHINE

Process :- The sugar, corn syrup, salt, coconut butter and cream are placed in a copper pan on the stove and stirred until dissolved. When the batch begins to boil, the evaporated milk is stirred in. The stirring is continued and the batch is cooked to a medium ball when tested in cold water. The chocolate and flavour are stirred in, and the batch is poured out on a greased slab and rolled out to about 1/8 inch thickness. The 12 pounds of honey nougat are rolled out quite thin and palced on top of the caramel sheet. The batch is folded up, shaped round, and rolled out in long stick on the table. It is then cut into small rolls and packed in bonbon cups on flat caramel trays lined with waxed paper. This amount would yeild approximately 46 pounds of candy.

5. CHOCOLATE HONEY TABLETS

Formulation

Ingredients	Quantity
Sugar	20 lbs.
Corn syrup	5 lbs.
Water	3 qt.
Honey	2 lbs.
Bitter chocolate	2 lbs.
Vanilla powder	1 g.

Process :- The sugar, water, and corn syrup are placed in a copper pan on the stove and stirred until dissolved. When the batch begins to boil, it is covered and allowed to steam for a few minutes. The sides are washed down and a thermometer is placed in the batch, which is cooked to 332° F. The heat is turned off. After the honey, chocolate, and flavour are stirred into the batch, the heat is turned on again, and the batch is stirred and cooked for another minute. Then it is poured out on a greased slab, and the edges are folded together, while the batch is cooling. The kneading is continue until the batch is cool enough. Then it is taken over to the spinning table in front of the batch warmer. It is then passed through a tablet roller machine and allowed to cool on the table. The tablets are broken apart and put through a sieve and packed in tins.

This batch will yield approximately 27 lbs.

6. CHOCOLATE COVERED COCONUT CAR MELS

Ingredients	Quantity
Sagar	12 lbs.
Corn syrup	18 lbs.
Coconut butter	1 lbs.
Water	2 qt.
Macaroon Coconut	16 lbs.
Vanilla flavour	4 tea spoonful

Process :- The sugar, corn syrup, coconut butter, and water are placed in a large copper pan on the sto·e and stirred until dissolved. When the batch begins to boil, the sides are washed down and the batch is cooked to 232° F. The flavour is added and the coconut is then turned out on a greased slab between iron bars and spread out evenly to about 1/2 inch thickness. It is allowed to cool until hard Then it is sized, sliced and cut into small squares. These are coated with a dark vanilla sweet chocolate. After setting the caramels are packed in the usual manner. The batch will yield approximately 75 pounds of chocolates.

7. CHOCOLATED COATING CARAMELS

Formulation

Ingredients	Quantity
Clean chocolate scrap	25 lbs.
Corn syrup	15 lbs.
Fresh light 18 % cream	4 qt.
Evaporated nilk	12 lbs.
Salt	1 table spoonful.
Vanilla flavour	4 tea spoonful

Process :- The chocolate scrap and the cream are placed in a copper pan on the stove over low heat and stirred until all the chocolate scrap is disssolved. The scrap is the strained into another large copper pan, which is placed on the stove over medium heat. The batch is stirred continuously while the corn syrup and the evaporated milk are added. The batch is cooked until if forms a medium ball when tested in cold water. It is then removed from the stove and the salt and flovour are stirred in. The batch is poured out on a greased slab between iron bars and spread out evenly to approximately 3/4 inch thickness. It is allowed to cool overnight. The caramel is then sliced and cut into small squares, which are coated with milk chocolate.

8. SPECIALITY CHOCOLATES

(i) Dietectic Chocolate

This chocolated candy is prepared from the ingredients such as whole powdered milk, skimmed powdered milk, ground cocoa beans, added cocoa butter, sorbitol, flavouring agents especially vanilla, lecithin and a sweetening agent cyclamate or saccharin which provides a milk chocolate composition.

Milk Chocolate has following composition

Ingredients	Quantity
Whole milk powder	15
Skim milk powder	7
Cocoa beans	9
Cocoa butter	38
Sorbitol	31
Saccharin	0.01
Lecithin	0.6
Vanilla	0.01

For preparing dark chocolate, the ingredients such as cocoa beans, cocoa butter, soy flour, sorbitol, synthetic sweetener and lecithin etc. are added. The major constituent should be maintained in approximate amount as in the following formulation.

(ii) Hypoallergenic Chocolate

The hypoallergenic chocolate is prepared from cocoa powder by treating it so as to denature substanitially all of the protein allergens which cause chocolate allergies. The cocoa powder with its denature protein allergen is then mixed with sugar, cocoa butter and desired flavouring additives and further heated to produce the hypoallergenic chocolate.

Formulation

Ingredients	% by weight
Cocoa powder	14
Cocoa butter	33
Sugar	53

These ingredients are mixed and heated for 2 days at 180° F.

This is then centrifuged at 6000 g and analysed. If will be found that most of the chocolate protein has been denatured upto the point where all of the protein allergens are denatured.

This chocolate is helpful to those persons who are allergic to chocolated. This is to be used in chocolate bars and for use as a flavouring ingredient in many food products.

12

PACKAGING FOR BISCUITS

In the eartly days-and in some countries, even today biscuits are packed in bulk in big cartons and tinplate containers. The traditional form of packaging obviously has number of disadvantages. It provides no protection against environmental influences such as humidity, odours and light, resulting in spoilage or reduced shelf-life. The percentage of broken biscuit is relatively high infestation by insects and the manual handling of loose product at the retail outlets may effect the safety of the product.

Today, market demand and consumers preferences have changed or are changing the way biscuit manufacturers package and present their products The obvious winner is the portion packed varieties - from the 250gm family pack to the convenient single-serve packets containing 2-4 biscuits.

PROTECTION PRESENTATION, INFORMATION AND CONVENIENCE

Packaging in general must meet four basic requirements.

Firstly, the right biscuit pack must give mechenical protection to the product. Either by neat portion packs in the classical enfold style, or by an air (gas) cushion as in the case of a pillow pack.,products are prevented from breakage during transport and retail handlig.

Ready-to-sell individually wrapped units eliminates the hygiene factor risks since the biscuits do not come into contact with any external element. The appropriate films and correct sealing prevents any infestation by insects. The result is a product which is fresh and tasty throughout its average shelf-life of 6 months.

The packet must be perfectly heat sealed in wrapping materials with the required barrier properties against light, humidity, gas and external odours.

Secondly, the packaging must appeal to the potential customers and stand out against a host of compeating products on the retail shelves. Beside the brand name, the packets which display the manufacturer's name and logo, also serve as an effefctive advertising medium for the company.

Thirdly, customers are asking for more detailed information on their purchases. In many countries around the world, regulatory body are asking for basic information such as the composition of the product/material used, nutritional values, allow additives, price information and the origin of the product to be clearly printed on the outer wrappings.

Lastly, it has become very important to satisfy consumer's demand for convenience packaging. Manufacturers must be able to provide not only the desired package size (family size or single serve / snack packs), but convenient packet opening facilities as well. These include tear tapes, zig zag or incision cuts on pillow pack fins and tins -tie reclosing possibilities.

THE WRAPPING MATERIALS

The oldest flexible film known is cellophane. Inventd in 1920.It became the most important heat sealable wrapping material untill polyethylene and polypropylene was introduced in the late 1960s. Polyethylene is not used independently biscuits wrapping as appropriate sealing can not be done on the standard machinery available.

Cellophane became less popular when it became too expensive and new synthetic films which offer better properties were introduced.

Today, most biscuits are wrapping in BOPP film (bi-oriented polypropylene), commonly known as OPP. For the less demanding application, an OPP monofilm is sufficient. For higher quality products, Duplex OPP or OPP combinations (pearlised or metalised), such as OPP/PE, OPP/PET, OPP?PUDC, and OPP/Syrlene, in the appropriate thickness and sealing range are most effective. They offer effective barrier against gas, vapour, odour and light.

The wrapping material with the highest barrier properties is aluminium foil of, say 7 micron, which is often used in combination with PET or Syrlene.

A joint consultation between the in-house food technologist, the wrapping material producer and the wrapping machine supplier is essential to ensure that the most effective wrapping film is used.

Principally, only heat sealable films are recommended for the packaging of naked biscuits. They give better sealing results than cold sealing materials and are less problematic in case of, e.g. biscuit dust in the sealing areas.

THE PACKAGING STYLES

There several popular wrapping styles which are applied widely on variety of biscuit of all shapes and sizes.

Biscuits packed using the following two wrapping styles which are applied widely on variety of biscuit of all shapes and sizes.

Biscuits packed using the following two wrapping styles must be of a common size and shape with a certain consistency and rather narrow tolerances in their dimensions. Standard wrapping machine can be used.

Endfold wrapping : This wrapping style is the classic, traditional biscuits wrapper. A portion of biscuits standing on edge is roll - wrapped or fold wrapped into a heat sealable film. The longitudinal packet seal is sealed tightly in a fin seal style. The packet ends are folded neatly and heat sealed. Due to the neat and tight surrounding of the film, this packet give utmost mechanical protection and acceptable barrier properties for hard and semi hard biscuit and many other cracker type. Enfold wrapping considered the most effective in term of presentation by many marketing specialities - not only due to the neat and impeccable shape, but also its ability to clearly distinguish the product amogst the host of pillow pack items on the retail shelves.

Even though this wrapping style is not too common in South East Asia, more manufacturer are looking into this option.

Pillow pack wrapping is the standard wrapping style for smaller biscuit packs (snack packs/single serve packs) containing one or more piles of biscuits.

In addition, pillow pack wrapping is used for bigger packets with products standing on edge (Slug wrapping) as well. In this configuration, it often serves as a primary wrapper, to be over-wrapped by a carton to improve presentation and acceptance.

They main advantage of pillow packs on edge, is its flexibility with regard to the slug length. For instance, it allow the machine to automatically adjust the length during wrapping by mean of tendency controlled check weighers. This feature ensure the highest weight accuracy. Additionally, the pillow pack's typical fin seal style sealing is somewhat tighter than the enfold wrap.

The disadvantage of pillow back slug wrapping is its limited mechanical product protection due to its rather loose packiing. Further, the presentation of products packed using the pillow back style is considered by most to be less attractive than enfold packets.

The odd size biscuits : Beside enfold wrapping and pillow pack wrapping , which by the way cover about 85-90 percent of all biscuit products, there are some specially biscuits with their own unique wrapping needs. These include an assortment of small cocktail crackers filled in bags by vertical FFS, machines and cookies of uneven sizes whose tolerence donot allow a standard wrapping. The latter are automatically or manually losded into decorated trays and subsequently over-wrapped on pillow pack machines. Biscuit assortment such as the famous Danish Butter Cookies, for instance, are automatically loaded into decorated trays and subsequently over-wrapped on pillow back machine Biscuit assortments such as the famous Danish Butter Cookies, for instance , are automatically loaded into decorated tins or stand - up bags.

The product preparation stage

There are two categories of machine feeding options-manual feeding and semi-automatic or fully automatic feeding.

For both categories, the biscuits coming from the cooling conveyer must be channelled into distinct lanes by means of a channelling or dribble board, stacked vertically and positioned upright on their short edge. Stacking may be efffected by a rotary stacker or over a belt edge (as in penny stacks).

Vertical stacking reduces the travel speed of the biscuits and allows easier handling down the line for both automatic or manual feeding.

Manual feeding : For manual feeding, the wrapping machine is positioned 90^0 to the stacking belt, with its in -feed chain strectching across the stacking belt. A team of operators then take the biscuits in the correct portion length for the stacking belt and place them into the partitions of the wrapping machine's in-feed chain.

In cases where potion packes in plies are to be produced, the respective pillow pack machine would be equipped with hoppers above its in-feed chain. These hoppers are mounted on both sides of the stacking belt, allowing the operators to load the stacked biscuits into hoppers. The machine then takes a preset number of biscuts from the hoppers, froms the piles and transfers the configurations into the warpping section.

Semi-automatic feeding : In view of future plans for automation, or to achieve higher wrapping machine speeds, an automatic feeders/portioning machine can be linked to the warping machine. Such fedres can be mounted parallel to the stacking bell or at its end. Feeders for manual loading are equipped with 4-8 channels. These channels are loaded by operators via magazines or preferably, via a so called dead plate at the end of the stacking belt. Two operators can then shift the incoming stacked product rows into the feeding channels using the dead plate.

The feeder automatically measures the required portion length and deposits the ready to-wrap configuration into the in-feed chain of the respective wrapping machine. Depending on the number of channels, usually 4-8 portions are formed and fed simultaneously. This allows wrapping speeds of up to 120-150 packs a minute by only two attendants.

The main advantage of the semi automatic or manually assisted feeding style is its flexibility to accommodate different products produced on the same line. The feeding style is independent from the number of incoming products rows.

Fully-automatic Feeding/wrapping : In environment which require higher oven outputs and multiple shift operations amidst rising labour costs, a fully automatic application becomes necessary.

In such instances, two or more wrapping machines equipped with automatic feeding/portioning machines are connected directly to the processing line. This means that the total number of incoming stacked product rows must match with the total number of available feeder channels. It might then be necessary to reduce or multiply the product rows coming out from the cooling belt. After stacking, the product rows are then diverted into two streams of 8 rows leading to two automatic feeders, each equipped with 8 feed channels. In such cases, the space between the stacker and the feeding machine must be calculated to ensure a buffer area for machine interruptions.

There are two possibilities for the fully automatic wrapping of sandwiches.

For small pillow packs or so-called vend packs containing 2-3 piles of 2 sandwiches, a pillow pack machine is linked-up directly to a 2 row creamer with a combiner at its exit, forming piles of 2 sandwiches. The desired packet configuration of 2x2 or 3x2 sandwiches is then automatically transferred into the wrapper in-feed chain.

In such a set up, the wrapping machine is driving the creamer.

For sandwich slug packs, a special sandwich counting feeder can be connected to a 2 or 4 row creamer. The counting feeder accepts the sandwiches, counts the preset number of products and forms the slug, which is then deposited into the in-feed chain of a wrapping machine.

Pick and place units or robot loading cells: For special products of irregular shapes or big varying tolerances, the above feeding systems are not applicable. Pick and place units are available to automatically load such products into trays.

In case of more demanding applications. e.g.for biscuit assortments, robot loading cells should be used. The robots are equipped with visual recognition feature to distinguish one product from another, and to load them into the cavity of a tray or allotted space in a tin.

13

CEREAL AND LEGUME BASED FOODS-RAW MATERIAL, PREPARATION, PACKAGING

INTRODUCTION:

The rice (81.15MM tonnes) and wheat (65.47 MM tonnes) are the major cereals of the state. Punjab contributes around 54% of its rice production (72.9 lakh tonnes) and 43%of its wheat (58.25 lakh tonnes) production ton the central grain resources pool. Majority of the food grains produced in the country are consumed in the form of traditional foods while only a small amount is processed into convenience foods.

Despite such a large consumption of traditional foods and a great potential for their commercial production and marketing, these products have recieved very little attention form the industry.

- Their high perishability and lack of appropriate technology for large scale mechanised production and marketing of such products.
- Lack of involvement of women in food processing industry.
- Conservative outlook of the consumer towards processed foods.
- High cost of preparation and low purchasing power of consumers.
- Lack of organised marketing channels in rurar areas.

Presently due to increased operations of MNC's, urbanisation, indrustrialisation & women going into jobs, there is an increased demand for shelf stable foods of Indian culinary. This demand is likely to increase in coming years. If low cost technologies for large scale mechanised production along with suitable preservation and packaging methods are devised, this would go a long way to appease the palate of Indian household. The present effort of listing some of the North India traditional foods, their recipes and method of preparation would help industry to consider mechanised production of such products.

WHEAT PRODUCTS :

Wheat is one of the most inportant cereal in India contributing one third to the total food grain basket of the country. In term of area (25.4 million hectares) as well as production (65.47 million tones) India ranks 4th in the world.

Under All India Coordinated Programmes and state/local programmes of the Agricultural Universities a large number of varieties have been identified/recommended for cultivation by farmers and to reach various processors through marketing channels. The important varieties recommended and identified for cultivation in different zones of the country are as follows :

NORTHERN HILL ZONE

i) Irrigated timely sown	HS 240, UP 1109, HD 2380
ii) Rainfed timely sown	VL 421, HS 240, DH 2380, UP 1109, DT 4600
iii) Rainfed timely sown high attitude	HPW 42
iv) Rainfed very early sown	VL 616, HS 277
v) Rainfed late sown	HS 295

NORTHERN WESTERN PLAINS ZONE

i) Irrigated timely sown	HD 2329, HD 2204, HD 2428, WH 542, WH 283, WH 416, CPAN 3004, RAJ 3077, PBW 154, PBW 343, UP 2338, PDW 2159DO, PBW 34 (d), PDW 233 (d, 1), WH 896 (d)
ii) Rainfed timely sown	C 3306, KUNDAN, PBW 65, PBW 175, PBW 299
iii) Irrigated late sown	HD 2285, HD 2270, PBW 226, RAJ 2184, RAJ 3077, WH 2191, UP 2338, RAJ 3765, PBW 373 (I)

iv) Saline soil	KRL 11-4, RAJ 3077

NORTHERN EASTERN PLAINS ZONE

i) Irrigated timely sown	HD 1102, UP 262, HUW 206, K 7410, K 8804, HD 2402, DL 784-3, K 9107, 9DEWAO, HP 1731 (RAJLUXMI)
ii) Rainfed timely sown	C 306, K 8027
iii) Irrigated late sown	HD 2307, HUW 234, HP 1633 (I), PBW 373 (I)
iv) Rainfed late sown	HDR 77, K 8962 (INDRA)
v) Saline soil	KRL 1-4, RAJ 3077

CENTRAL ZONE

i) Irregated timely sown	LOK 1, WH 147, WD 2236, HI 1077, GW 190, RAJ 1555 (D) HI 8381 (D), DL 803-3 (KANCHAN)
ii) Rainfed timely sown	C 306, JU 12 (D), MEGDOOT (D), A 930-1 (D), SUJATA, NARBADA 4, HYB 65, HW 2004 (I)
iii) Irrigated late sown	LOK 1, J 405, SWATI, HD 23227, GW 173, KRL 1-4, RAJ 3077
iv) Saline soil	KRL 1-4, RAJ 3077

PENINSULAR ZONE

i) Irrigated timely sown	HD 2189, DWR 39, HD 4502 (D), HD 2380, DWR 162, MACS 2496, DDK 1001(DIC, I)
ii) Rainfed timely sown	NI 5439, N 59 (D), BIJAGA YELLOW (D), MACS 1967 (D)
iii) Irrigated late sown	HI 977, HD 2501, DWAR 195, ANUIRADHA, D), NIAW 34 (I)

SOUTHERN HILLS ZONE

i) Restricted irrigation	HW 741, HW 971, HUW 318m, NP 200

ii) Rainfed (Dic), NP 200 (Dic)

The coverage of post green-revolution wheat varieties is as follows :

Maximum coverage of major post green revolution wheat varieties :-

>0.5	>0.1	>0.2	>0.4
WG 357 WG 357 RAJ 1555 HP 1102 BW 11 HW 2189 VL 616 HUW 206 LOK 1	HD 2009 HD 2285 HD 2204 WH 147 WH 283 PBW 154 RAJ 3077 WL 1562 LOK 1	WL 711 HUW 234 UP 262	HD 2329

Out of the total production of 62.47 million tonnes, hardly about 9 million tonnes is processed by roller flour milling industry for maida, suji, and resultant atta. Out of this only about 2.8 million tonnes is used by baking industry for bread, biscuits and noodles. Thus around 85% of wheat and a substantial quantity of milled product are consumed in the form of traditional products listed here with.

CHAPATIES (ROTIS) : Wheat is consumed in different form of chapaties like Tandoori, Khamiri(fermented), Missi Roomali etc. Rotis are mostly consumed during lunch and dinner. Medium Strong, elastic dough's are suitable for tawe waali and tandoori roties while a strong and elastic dough is suited for missi(with besan) & Khamiri roti. Chapaties are mostly prepared fresh and highly pliable, soft and had a mild baked aroma. Most of the wheat varieties having medium string characteristics and amber colour have been found to be suitable for chapati baking. Varieties having high molecular weight glutenins and phospholipids have been found to be superior for chapati baking because of simplicity of method of chapati baking and very short shelf life of chapaties, no organised sale of chapaties has taken place though the need for ready to bake or ready to serve chapaties has been felt in cosmopolitan cities and in large industrial canteens. One of the major constraint in the large scale production and marketing of chapaties seems to be the non availability of automatic rolling and baking machines. A semi merchanised leg operated chapati flattening unit and associated baking unit having a production capacity of 400 chapaties per hour with five person has been designed by DFRL, Mysore. CFTRI has also attempted a chapati making system that resembles more with corn tortilla machines available in Mexico.

Chapaties prepared in fully mechanised units crumble during storage in chain stores. They are also susceptible to stalling , ropiness and mold growth. Chapaties within few hours of preparation tends to devolop brittle texture as a result of starch retrogradation and loose aroma and moisture. During subsequent storage, chapaties devolop ropiness followed by fungal growth and fermentative odours. Though it has not been possible to completely arrest the brittleness devolopment, ropiness, fungal growth and bacterial spoilage could be arrested by hurdle technology involving in pack processing, use of antimycotic agents and pH control. Use of stable flavour based on curnene oleorsin and milk powder has been found to considerably reduce the perception of stalling. Process devoloped by arya et at., has been found to keep chapaties in safe condition for more than six month and preserved chapaties are claimed to be liked by troops and members of various mountaineering and rowing expeditions.

PACKAGED CHAPATIES FOR GENERAL MARKETING : Chapaties preserved by the process devoloped by arya et al. (1996) are said to have a shelf life of more htan six months. This much shelf life, though essential for pack rations of armed forces due to logistic reosons, is niether necessary nor desirable for commercial marketing. To attain this much shelf life highly costly moisture proof aluminium foil laminate packaging and in pack processing are necessary which make the process highly costly. Chapaties being a staple food for daily consumption, a shelf life of 5 days should be more than adequate for commercial marketing. In fact a process has been devoloped successfully for the short term preservations of chapaties by using only antimycotic agents in the dough and packing baked chapaties in plastic pouches. This method has also been extensively tried and has been found highly effective.

PUFF AND SERVE CHAPATIES : As already stated earlier, chapaties are mostly prepared fresh and served hot. The consumer highly like fresh puffed chapaties. In order to meet this requirement, DFRL, mysore has devoloped a process for preservation of partially baked chapaties which consumers can puff on an open gas flame or on an open coil heater at the time of consumption. The process enables preservation for 5-7n days and retention of puffing characteristics even after storage. Since puff and serve chapatie's meet consumers expectations in respect of fresh baking and reasonable shelf life for marketing, these are expected to be highly successful in commercial marketing. Howrever, the product has yet to be test marketed.

POORIS : poores are prepared from stiff dough and are deep fried at high temperature using poori aag (full flame). Poories are traditionally prepared during festivities or on sundays by halwa is and consumed for brekfast/brunch/lunch. Pithi wali pooris (with dal stuffing) are also popular.

PARATHAS : Parathas are shallow fried on tawa(hot plate). A simple as well as wallan waala paratha are the breakfast delights in northern india. These are consumed with subzi(vegetable curry) or fried eggs omelette etc. in the morning.

SPICED POTATO PARATHAS : Besides plain chapaties , processes have also been devoloped for the preservation of sliced potato chapaties and parathas. These aer prepared by mixing spices and boiled vegetables in the dough or by giving spices and seasoned vegetables in between two chapaties and subsequently baking them on a hot plate with application of oil/vanaspati on the surface. The spiced parathas can be prepared layers to impart crispness and more uniform baking. Incorporation of vegetables helps in retention of soft texture during storages the moisture content in spiced potato chapaties varied between 30-35% as compared to 28-33% in plain chapaties. Antimycotic agents are required to be incorporated in both flour and vegetable and use of milk solids is not desirable because of tendency of spiced vegetables to brown during storage. The process devoloped by DFRL, Mysore permit a shelf life of one year under ambient conditions. Spiced potato parathas when subjected tol large scale consumer accptence trials involving more than 300 troops were graded highly acceptable in taste, texture and aroma. The type of oil used during baking has been found to considerably influence the keeping quality of spiced potato parathas. While unsaturated vegetables oils like groundnut oil sunflower oil etc., are suitable for fresh chapaties, these tend to impart stored taste and undesirable aroma after few weeks of storage. Considering the high acceptance of stuffed parathas throughout the country and excelent keeping quality of the spiced vegetable chapaties and parathas, these have escelent ptential for marketing. though tortal mechanisation of the product manufacture is yet to be achived, it is possible to atomise some of theunit operations which will keep total investment on machineries and plants within reasonable limits.

FLAT/PITA BREAD : Flat breads with upto 10 days shelf life in polyethylene bags have been produced. The hard wheats like PBW 34, PDW 215, WL 1562, PBW 154 & wg 357 with about 10-12% protein, 64-68% WA, 4 minute dough development time and about 7% Da producedexcellent results in experiments conducted at FST & presented by Bakshi & Nagi.

MAKKI DI ROTI TE SARSON DA SAG : Maize chapaties with mustard leave curry are consumed very frequently in winters in norhtern India especially Punjab. PAU has recently introduced winter maize. The crop is harvested in summers. Maize has a very active lipase enzyme. In summers it finds optimum temperature for its activity. Hence maize atta turns bitter in suumers. In Mexico where maize is consumed the year around, masa (by treating with time) is prepared and converted into chapaties in automatic lines. The machine are shown in slides. A similar machine for chapaties has also been attempted by CFTRI.

MANNS (SWEET ROTI) : Consumed by people baisakhi and at special occasions. Aparalle version Gordita in Mexico is prepared mechanically in automatic lines and is available in chain stores.

DALIA (PORRIDGE) : Wheat as such or after toasting is milted to grits using hands chakkis. The hard wheat or durum wheat are most suited for this product. A oarboiled or lyepeeled wheat product called Bulgar/whirled wheat is popular in the awest. The product is boiled in water, sugar added to taste and served in breakfast as such or with milk.

KARAH (HALWA) : The halwa prepared from either flour or semolina form a part of parsad and ritual servings. It is prepared and served in sacred shrines, gruduwaras, temples and during several religious ceremonies. The consumption of halwa is thus enormous. It is prepared by toasting semolina/flour in ghee to a peculiar browning and aroma to which a thin syrup ofnsugar and water is added and then it is cooked to the required consistency. It may be enriched and garnished with dry fruits. A quick cooking mixture for this can be prepared after dry toasting of semolina to which fat and water may be added at the time of consumption.

INSTANT MIX FOR HALWA : It is prepared by roasting/ cookinig and drying of individual ingredients and blending in suitable proportions. The mixes are generally packed in pollyethylene. pollyethylene of metalised polyrter packs. Because all the ingredients under go heat treatment during cooking.drying operation, infestation during storage is not a serious problem but care should be taken to avoid chances of contamination during packaging. Uniform distribution of ingredients in the manufacture of instant imxes is a major technoogical constraint. Loss of volatile during storage and resulting charger in flavour vis off-flavours resulting from oxidation of lipids is one of the limitinng factor in shelf-life determination. Use of oleoresin and microencapsulatee flours is likely to prove useful in proper blending of flavour and in minimising losses of volatile during storage. Recently somr of microencapsulated cardamom oil has tried in Halwa mix by DFRL. About 80% of the added flavour was retained in microencapsulated flavour incorporated Halwa mix as compared to 50% retantion in powdered cardamom added product.

Degree of sturation and fatty acid composition of oil used during roasting or seasoning mainly determines the stability of the mix. Generally, vanaspati has been found most suitable in imprting longest-shelf life to Halwa, as compared to refined grounnut oil, palmolein and cottonseedoil. Despite very good quality of instant mixes, their market share among processed foods is negligible. However, these are tiems of common Indian dietary and their demand is expected to increase in the coming years.

SHELF STABLE HALWA : Besides instant halwa mixes, processes have also been developed for preservation of Halwa in ready to eat state byusing either Hurdle Technology or thermal processing in retort pouchesby DFRL. Thermally processed Halwa is regularly supplied to Department of Ocean Development for members of America Expeditions. Except slight fading of colour and brown discolouration, no spoilage has been oberved in retort pouched processed Halwa. The know-how for retort pouch processing of Halwa is available from DFRL, Mysore thriugh NDRC. However, due to high cost of cans and retort pouches, thermally processed Halwa is relatively costly in comparion to instant mixes. Ready to eat Halwa has also been preserved by Hurdle Technology using anitmycotic agents and original taste. Because of lower cost on packaging and machiniries, cost of finished products processed by Hurdle Technology is much les as compared to retort pouched processed Halwa.

CHOORMA/PANJIRI : are prepared and consumed in winters. Panjiri is consumed by women in abundance after child birth.

PINNIS : Pinnies are prepared by roasting wheat flour/powdered dals (moong, sabut and mashdhuli) in lots of pure ghee. The taste of pinnies prepared by grand mother still lingers i tounges. These are invereably prepared in winters with lots of desi ghee and dry fruits. Grand mother notion says that these sharpen brain and provides takat (mental strength) to school/college going generation. product is very popular in north.

JOLES (SEVIAN) : were prepared in homes by housewives or by skill artisans. During the last two decades their regular mechanised production has been established along with small and cottage scale sector. Vermicelli are relatively lower priced than instant noodles and and other extrude products. One of the reason for their popularity is their long usage in various forms. Process of manufacture of vemicelli is relatively simple and involves preparation of stiff dough from wheat flour or semolina and extruding the gough through fine orifices, followed by drying under controlled humidity and temperature. In small scale sector, vermicelli are dried in sun which preferred for vermicelli production in our country provided smaller machines are designed for cottage and small scale sector.

ROASTED WHEAT/MAIZE : In winter, consumption of toasted wheat/maize with Jaggery in villages and hostels by students is a common practice.

FRIED PRODUCTS : Fried products form the largest group of snack products in our country prepared either in homes or by small scale confectioner. Frying not only aids in cooking, it helps in destruction of antinutritive factors, aids in moisture evaporation and thereby imparts shelf-stability and above all it imparts most acceptable flavour. Both sweet and salty fried wheat snacks are prepared by frying wheat flour dough after sheeting and cutting into different shapes at oil temperature ranging from 140-1600 C. Inclusion of oil in dough impart crispness and using frying temperature above 1700 C invariably darkens the product causes decisive fragility. The moisture content in fried wheat products ranges from 2-6% equilibrate to 0.20-0.35 water activity. As a result of low was the product does not support microbial activity and have long life if packed in moisture proof packaging. The shelf-life of the products governed by the rate of antioxidation of fat which in turn is determined by the type of oil used during frying. Products fried in unsaturated oils develop rancidify faster than those fried in vanaspati or palm oil.

Despite high popularity of sweet and salty fried wheat snacks, these are mostly marketed by small scale confectioners, their large scale production and marketing has not taken place appreciably shelf-life and packaging. Viewed from different angles it may also be argued that since their preparation is quite simple not requiring any sophisticated processing equipments, consumers find it easier to prepare in their home rather than purchasing from market at a higher price. Whatever may be the reason these products are widely consumed and have considerable market potential. Some of these are as follows :

GOLGAPPAS (PANI PURI) : These are a delicacy and are preferred by ladies and children. Golgappas prepared from atta are large or more crisp, contain less fat and are preferred more. The small golgappas prepared from maida/semolina are less crisp and contain more fat. These are prepared by deep frying. During serving a hole is punched at the top by thumb and the hollow is filled with potato mesal and chilled sweet or salty water. During outings in the evening families guzzle the golgappas with a relish.

MATHIS : Mathis are prepared from stiff dough on mathi aag (slow fire). These are salty snacks which are deep fat fried. Khasta mathis are generally more preferred. Sometimes fenugreek leaves (dry) are also added to the dough. To make them more nutritious soybean flour can also be added.

MATTAR : Mattar are salty snaçk which are cut like pea pods from stiff, salty dough and are keep fat fried to a golden colour and pleasant aroma.

GULABJAMUN/RASGULLAS : are common sweets that contain what flour and are consumed enormously in the north: Instant Gulab jamun mix, Jalebi mix and Rasgulla mix : Such mixes based on chemical leavening are prepared by blending wheat flour, milk flour, milk powder, vegetable oil and leavening agents in suitable proportions and are marketed mostly by packing them in plastic film pouches followed by duplex board cartons. Among these instant Gulab Jamun mix is most popular and has highest sales. Since only one unit operation of dry blending of ingredients is involved, these are no major constraints faced during the manufacture of instant mixes except occasional problem of uneven mixing of chemical leavening. During storage, however, all the mixed lend to develop infestation. Heating of wheat flour and/or low dose (50-100 krads) irrdatiation of packaged mixes have been found to be effective. Control of granularity, moisture land adequate missing are other essential requirements for adequate product acceptability.

CHAAMP, KALEJI, KEEMA : Prepared from wheat gluten are being sold in Paharganj since decades. Sales are enormous.

RICE PRODUCTS :

The predominant varieties of rice recommended for cultivation in Punjab are PR 106, PR 111 (superfine), IR 8 and Jaya (coarase) and Basmati 370, 386 and Pusa Basmati 1 (Basmati). Rice is being consumed in the form of traditional products which are listed as follows :

MARUNDA : is prepared from rice and sugar. A product resembling marunda in mechanised units (Grain slices), prepared a from broken or whole rice is becoming popular in Europe.

PHIRNI : Rice paste is cooked with milk. Chilled and served as sweet dish.

KHEER : is a variation sweet dish. The rice is cooked in milk and served hot or cold after addition of wager (dry fruit).

GUR WAALE CHAWAL : are prepared by mixing cooked rice, jaggery and ghee and are served steaming hot as a sweet dish.

BHELPURI : Contains expanded rice mixed with spices. It is a variation snack in homes or off day outing treat.

CHIRVA : chirva with makhane form part of prasad in many shrines. It is also used to prepare sweet, salty and sour evening snacks.

MURMURA/KHEEL : Puffed and expanded products. Forms

part of rajasthani bhujia or fried salty snacks.

PULAV : Rice pulav with precooked vegetables or meat is called biriani. It is consumed to quite an extent in the north.

KHICHRI : Rice and split channe ki daal is a common easily digestible meal for people with weak stomach. It is also used with curd forms as a part of ritual for people going to attend important job.

PHULWARIAN : are like extruded rice pallets which expand on frying and are consumed as snacks. In India many extruded products are prepared by housewives themselves or by skilled artisans from rice and legumes and served after frying as snacks. With the advent of cooker extruders, a few companies have started marketing extruded pellets (fryums) which need frying before use and ready to eat expanded and spiced snacks in attractive packs. Both these type products are prepared from wheat flour with or without potato or corn flour.

Extruded pellets are prepared from wheat, rice or maize flours or from their blends. After proper conditioning and equilibration, the ingredients are cooked in a primary extruder. The cooked material is then cooled and densified in a secondary extruder. In the secondary stage the temperature of the extrudate is kept below 100 C to eliminate product expansion. Immediately after expansion the moisture content is around 20-25 5 which is brought down to 7-8% by hot air drying in tunnel dryer. The dried pellets are packed in attractive plastic film packs. These pellets equilibrate to 0.45-0.60 a and remain stable for more than six months at room temperature. Before consumption these have to be fried in oil which imparts crispness, softness and about 4-6 times volume expansion. The products have excellent storage stability and impart resistance and can be transported easily. These are also relatively less costly to expanded ready to eat snacks.

EXPANDED EXTRUDED SNACKS : Ready to eat expanded products are prepared by using high pressure cooking and mixing equipments where enough work and heat are applied to the cereal base having appropriate moisture to thoroughly gelatinise or cook all the ingredients. The temperature during extrusion is about 1000 C and as materials are continuously compressed during working, extrudate expands when allowed to pass through die due to sudden fall of pressure and release of steam. The shape and size of the product are dependent on the die design and the cutter speed. The products processed by this method are marely toasted or dried and coated with flavours either by dusting or by spraying with spice-oil mixtures. Advantages of this method are that the products are ready to eat requiring no processing and can be produced from a combination of cereals, pulses and starches. The products are produced and marketed in different shape and sizes and level of fat can be controlled to desired level land those have taste and flavour of roasted and fried products. On the other hand, since the material is expanded and fragile and flavours are applied at the surface, the packing requirements are stringent and shelf-life is relatively shorter than pellets.

Both pellet and expanded extruded products are commercially marketed and are quite popular among children. Mostly these are produced from cereals like wheat, rice and corn and invariably contain low protein. In order to make then nutritionally balanced, processing conditions for manufacturing expanded ready to eat snacks from sorghum plus defatted soy flour and rice plus defatted soy flour have been optimised at DFRL., Mysore. The products are highly crisp and tasty and protein content range from 15-20% thus making then highly useful for school going children.

POPCORNS : Plain salty popcorns are popular among children. No variations of popcorn are available in India, whereas, in western countries popcorn in chocolate, orange, lemon flavours are available. Cheese coated salty products in the country.

WINTER PRODUCTS :

1. MARUNDA : Is a sweet product prepared from puffed rice. Sugar with water is heated to desire consistency and puffed rice rolled into it to a sheet of uniform thickness and cut to pieces of desired sizes and shapes as shown in photograph.

2. GACCHAK : Is a product prepared from jaggery and grounduut. Peanuts are dry roasted and jaggery heated and modified to desired consistency. Both are mixed and moulded into desired sizes and shapes.

3. REORIAN : Is a product prepared by heating sugars till they could be drawn into single thread. Now on they are pulled on or off a wooden speck for quite some time (Process is quite labour inten-

sive). Now it is cut to pieces and at higher temperatures coated with sesame seeds (oilseeds) which get fixed on sugar balls resulting into an attractive candy.

All they above products are consumed to a considerable extent during winters in India. These products have markets worth trillions of rupees. Unfortunately, there exists no quality control & no standards have been laid down for such products. These products are prepared and sold very unhygenically. They have a number of problems of getting soggy, sugar sticking to hand when they absorb moisture. With variation in market batches of rice, sesame and peanuts, quality of these products vary considerably. There are also wide batch to batch variations due to uncontrolled conditions.

Hence work on such products, standardization of recipes, development of machinery and technology would go a long way in encouraging trade between countries. Food processing industry though in infancy in India is expanding at a rapid pace and would welcome international collaboration with foreign companies in production and export of such traditional products.

SUMMER DRINKS :

1. SATTU (BARLEY WATER) : Is a very popular summer drink and is supposed to have a medicinal value and safeguards against sunstroke as per popular belief amongst people. It is prepared by soaking, toasting, grinding barley and preparing drink with sugar or jaggery,. With increase in working couples in India and families going nuclear such products are waning off and are difficult to prepare at home..A raddy beverage thus will have a great scope. It would help integrated use of rice milling machinery that operates seasonally.

2. GANNE KA RAS (CANE JUICE) : People prefer to consume it fresh. On heat sterilization sugars and flavours change character. A cheap product in pouches of 200 ml with freshness and resonable pricing would capture mass markets and would compete with carbonated beverages.

3. KANKI : Is a saltish fermented drink prepared from black carrots and a mix of condiments. It is tasty and highly preferred traditional drink in summers.

Unfortunately, no work by any institution in India on the standardization of these products has been done despite the fact that they are the major consumables of the masses in different weather. It is also evident that there are a large number of grain based convenience foods which are traditionally prepared and marketed either by small scale artisans or by cottage and small scale industry. Many of the products are also prepared in homes or served in food service establishment. The technology of their production has remained more of an art and little emphasis has been laid in infusing in new technological developments in their production and marketing. Though some information has been generated in laboratories and research institutions in scientific evaluation of processing parameters and physicochemical aspects of products, R & D efforts in design of equipments and machineries for up scaling of technologies of their production has not made much headway. Also whatever information has been generated in research institution has not percolated to industries mainly because of poor technological absorption capacity of industries and lack of adequate interaction between research institutions and industries. It is, therefore, suggested that technological needs of this sector be identified and more stress be laid on design/fabrication of indigenous machineries to upgrade the technological base of convenience food industry.

APPENDIX-I

SOME SELECTED RECIPES OF TRADITIONAL FOODS

MATHI

Ingredients :

Maida	:	100 gm
Salt	:	pinch
Ghee (melted)	:	20 gm
Ajwain	:	2-3 gm (1/2 tsp)
Oil	:	for frying

Method :

Mix maida, salt and ajwain throughly. Rub in ghee till grainy even texture is obtained. Use water to make a very stiff dough. Keep covered with wet cloth and leave for 15-20 minutes. Divide into 10 portions. Heat oil in a frying pan and when hot lower the time. Roll each ball thin, then prick with a fork and fry till golden brown.

MATRI

Ingredients :

Flour	:	100 gms
Chillies	:	1/2 tip
Salt	:	to taste
Oil	:	for frying

Method :

1. Knead flour with salt and chilles to make the dough.
2. Make small balls and rolls them into 2 long strips.
3. Deep fry on slow fire till golden brown.

SEVIAN

Ingredients :

Vermicelli	:	1 cup
Sugar	:	1, 1/2 cup
Ghee	:	1 cup
Cashewnut broken	:	25mg
Milk	:	3 cups

Method :

Heat ghee in a pan and fry vermicelli in ghee till golden brown. Then add boiled milk in it and cook it for 15-10 minutes till the vermicelli are done.

SUJI HALWA

Ingredients :

Suji semolina (suji)	:	100 gm
Sugar	:	100 gm
Ghee	:	100 gm
Water	:	300 gm
Almonds	:	optional
Raisins	:	optional
Cardamum (green elaichi)	:	optional

Method :

Heat the ghee, add semolina and stir on a slow fire till the mixture becomes light creamy in colour and the ghee leaves the sides of the pan. Mix sugar in water and make a sugar syrup. And add to the syrup and stir briskly till it is absorbed in the semolina. Mix the crushed cardamon, almonds. Serve hot.

PINNIS :

Ingredients :

Wheat flour/ urad flour	:	1 kg
Ghee	:	750 gms
Powdered sugar	:	850 gms
Dry fruits		

Method :

1. Heat ghee in a large pan
2. Add flour and roast it till golden brown
3. Add dry fruits and roast for 2- 3 minutes.
4. Add sugar, remove from five and mix well

MALL PURA

Ingredient

Wheat flour	:	50 gm
Maida	:	50 gm
Suji	:	50 gm
Powdered Milk	:	25 gm
Powdered sugar	:	10 gm
Sugar	:	100 gm
Baking Powder	:	9 Pinch
Ghee	:	for frying
Water	:	for making syrup

Method :

1. Mix wheat flour, suji, maida together and add powdered milk, powdered sugar and pinch of baking powder in it and make into a thick paste with water.
2. Heat ghee in a deep vessel and add spoon full of mixture and fry till golden brown.
3. Then make a syrup of 2 thread consistency with sugar and water and put the fried malpoora in the syrup for 5-10 min utes and then serve hot.

GULAB JAMUN

Ingredients

Khoya	:	200 gm

Paneer	:	50 gm
Maida	:	60 gm
Soda bicarbonate	:	1/4 tsp
Sugar	:	750 gm
Ghee	:	for frying

Method :

Mix khoya, chenna, maida, soda bicarbonate and knead to a very smooth dough. Make small balls and fry them till golden brown. Ad water to the sugar and make sugar syrup. Add the fried balls to the sugar syrup and keep them for sometime so that sugar syrup penetrates in the balls. Serve hot or cold. It can be garnished with coconut powder.

POORIES

Ingredients :

Wheat flour	:	375 gm
Ghee or oil	:	20 gm
Salt	:	to taste

Method :

1. Prepare a stiff dough with above mentioned ingredients using water and keep it for some time.
2. Divide into small balls and roll out to 3-4 inch diameter puris.
3. Deep fry on both sided in oil or ghee till puffed and brownish in colour.
4. Serve hot.

JALEBI

Ingredients :

Wheat flour	:	1/2 kg
Gram dal flour	:	124 gm
Ghee	:	1, $^{1}/_{4}$kg
Sugar	:	2 kg
Water	:	10 cups

Method :

1. Prepare a batter by mixing and nicely beating wheat flour and gram

dal flour.
2. Make a thick syrup by boiling sugar in about 7-8 cups of water.
3. Remove the pan from fire and keep it on boiling water so that it may not get cooled.
4. Boil ghee in deep karahi.
5. Fill in jalebi mould with batter and let down the better through the hole of the mould into the ghee so as to form circular jalebi with 3 or 5 continuous inner circles.
6. Fry till done on both sides.
7. Remove each jalebi, dip it in the hot syrup for about a minute and drain.
8. Serve hot.

Note : Jalebi mould can be made out of any vessel with a hole in the centre.

SAMOSA

Ingredients :
For covering -

Flour	:	2 cups
Oil or fat	:	3 tsp

For jelling -
Boiled and cooked potatoes along with onions and peas.

Method :

1. Prepare a hard dough with water. Knead well till soft.
2. Divide it into eight portions.
3. Roll each one into a round roti 15 cm in diameter.
4. Cut each into half.
5. Stiff each roti with prepared strffing and shape into samosa.
6. Deep fry in hot oil or medium heat till golden brown.
7. Serve hot.

DALIA (BROKEN WHET PORRIDGE)

Ingredients :

Broken wheat	:	50 gm
Sugar	:	50 gm
Milk	:	500 ml

Method :

Boil the milk and add broken wheat into it and pressure cook it on a slow fire for 5-10 minutes and then remove from the fire and add sugar in it and cook for 2 minutes and serve hot.

PHULVARIAN

Ingredients :

Rice	:	100 gm
Water	:	for boiling rice
Salt	:	to taste
Chillies	:	to taste
Cumin powder	:	to taste

Method :

1. Boil the rice
2. Mash the boiled rice and add the spices
3. Make a cone with hole and pur the mixture to it.
4. Pipe the phylvarian and dry then in sun.
5. Deep fry in oil, serve hot.

RICE KHICHRI

Ingredients :

Rice	:	150 gm
Moong Dal (Washed)	:	30 gm
Vegetable oil	:	1.1/2 tsp.
Salt	:	1 tsp.
Cumin seeds	:	2 gm

Method :

1. Clean and wash the rice and washed moong dal.
2. Add about 3 cups of water and salt.
3. Pressure cook it for 5 minutes.
4. Fry cumin seeds in ghee and add to the khichri.

SWEET RICE

Ingredients :		
Rice	:	240 gm
Jaggery	:	150 gm
Water	:	450 ml
Sauf	:	15 gm
Ghee	:	30 gm

Method :

Wash the rice and soak in water for 1-2 hrs. Make syrup of water and jaggery and strain. Put rice, ghee, sauf in syrup and cook on fire till rice is ready.

SUGARCANE JUICE KHEER

Ingredients :		
Juice	:	200 ml
Rice	:	25 gm
Water	:	60 ml

Method :

1. Clean and wash the rice.
2. Cook in water until half done.
3. Add sugarcane juice and keep on stirring. When the consistency becomes thick, remove it form fire.
4. Serve hot garnished with coconut and dry fruits.

PHIRNI

Ingredients :		
Milk	:	1 lt.
Sugar	:	150 gm
Almonds	:	30 gm
Rice	:	40 gm

Method :

Soak rice of good quality for about an hour and then grind very fine with 4to5 tsp. Full of cold water. Mix the rice paste with the milk, cook on a medium heat and stir till the mixture is of creamy consistency. Remove from fire, add sugar and stir. Simmer till it is fully dissolved and then boil for 1 minutes. Add the shredded branched almond and serve.

PUFFED RICE LADDOO

Ingredients :

Puffed rice	:	100 gm
Jaggery	:	200 gm
Ghee or Oil	:	30 gm

Method :

1. Make syrup of one string consistency with jaggery and one cup of water.
2. Remove from fire.
3. Mix in puffed rice and fat.
4. Form into small balls.
5. For making marunda spread the mixture on a flat greased tray.

MARUNDA

Ingredients :

Puffed rice	:	50 gm
Roasted Bengal Gram	:	25 gm
Roasted Peanut Kernels	:	25 gm
Jaggery	:	25 gm

Method :

1. Make the thread syrup of jaggery
2. Add rice, grams and peanuts.
3. Prepare balls of mixture.

BLACK GRAM : (URAD) PAPPADS

Ingredients :

Powdered dal	:	1 kg
Chillies	:	100 gm
Salt	:	to taste
asafoetida dissolved in water		

Method :

1. Knead the flour with water.
2. Take a little and roll it in dry flour to form thin pappads.
3. Dry them in sun for 1 or 2 days.
4. Deep fry or roast them before serving.

VADIAN

Ingredients :

Green gram dal (split)	:	1 kg
Salt	:	to taste

Black Pepper & cumin, coarsely ground, asafoetida dissolved in water.

Method :

1. Soak dal for 4-5 hours.
2. Remove the husk and grind the dal.
3. Add salt, asafoetida, pepper and cumin and mix well.
4. Keep it over nigh for fermentation.
5. In the morning make small portions from the mixture and dry them in sun for 3-4 days.

BESAN POORA

Ingredients :

Besan	:	50 gm
Onion	:	10 gm
Green chillies	:	5 gm
Salt	:	$^1/_2$ tsp
Coriander leaves	:	5 gm
Water	:	for making batter

Method :

1. Sift the besan and salt.
2. Chop the onion, green chillies and coriander finely. Add the sieved ingredients.
3. Make a batter with water.
4. Spread the batter on a greased tava to form a round of about 12 cm diameter cook for 3 minutes, turn over.

5. Add the melted fat around the edges and little on top. Fry .till crisp.

BESAN LADDOOS

Ingredients :

Besan	:	100 gm
Fat	:	100 gm
Sugar powder	:	100 gm
Cardamum	:	3.5 gm

Method :

1. Roast besan in fat till cream colour.
2. Remove pan from fire. Add powdered sugar and mix well.
3. Add crushed cardamum. Form into even shaped balls with wet hands.

PAKORAS

Ingredients :

Besan	:	
Salt	:	Finely chopped on
Green Chillies	:	granted
Spinach	:	
Carrots	:	
Potatoes	:	
Onion	:	
Oil for frying	:	

Method :

1. Take besan in a bowl and add all spices.
2. Add vegetables.
3. Add water to make thick batter.
4. Heat oil in a deep pan.
5. Fry pakoras.

BHUGA

Ingredients :

Khoa	:	200 gm
Sesame	:	200 gm
Sugar	:	200 gm

Method :

1. Grind sesame and sugar together.
2. Add khoa to it and mix well.
3. Make small balls and serve.

SESAME GACHAK

Ingredients :		
Sesame	:	125 gm
Roasted peanuts	:	50 gm
Cardamon kernels	:	10 gm
Dry coconut powder	:	1/4 cups
Sugar/jaggery	:	250 gm

Method :

1. Roast sesame to light brown colour.
2. Cool and powder together with peanuts.
3. Prepare syrup of 1 strand consistency with one cup of water.
4. Mix all ingredients except coconut and keep stirring till the mixture leaves the sides of pan.
5. Grease a plate of spread mixture on it.

CHIKKI

Ingredients :		
Jaggery	:	100 gm
Peanut kernels	:	30 gm
Water	:	1-2 tsp.

Method :

1. Prepare two strand syrup of jaggery and water.
2. Add peanut kernels.
3. Grease a plate and pour syrup in it.
4. Keep it to eat. Cut into pieces.

GULGULAS

Ingredients :		
Wheat flour	:	100 gm

Jaggery	:	100 gm
Water	:	Pinch
Oil for frying	:	Pinch
Metha Soda	:	Pinch

Method :

1. Make thin syrup of jaggery with water.
2. Add soda to flour and make dough with syrup.
3. Serve it for some time.
4. Make small balls of the dough and deep fry then.

14

MISCELLANEOUS FORMULAES

BISCUIT

CHOCOLATE BROWNIES :

Sugar	:	102.0%	Cream together
Salt	:	1.6%	
Skim milk Powder	:	11.0%	
Cocoa	:	16.0%	
Liquid Glucose	:	12.0%	
Shortening	:	90.0%	
G.M.S.	:	1.0%	
Eggs	:	65.0%	Add in 4 stages and cream in.
Water	:	56.0%	Dissolve baking soda in the water.
Vanilla	:	2.2%	Add alternately with the flour.
Baking Soda	:	0.7%	
Flour	:	100.0%	Sift & add alternately with the
Baking Powder	:	0.7%	Water & vanilla.
Peanuts (Unsalted)	:	50.0%	Add and Blend in to distribute. evenly.

Deposit in squares or Oblong Sheet pans that have been greased well and lined with paper that has been greased. If no paper is used, dust the pan with flour after greasing.

Bake at 365°F. When cool, cakes may be frosted with a chocolate, Fudge icing.

SUNSHINE CAKE :

Sugar	:	96.0%	Blend and then cream together.
Salt	:	1.3%	
Skim milk Powder	:	5.2%	
Flour	:	20.0%	
Glucose	:	4.0%	
Shortening	:	68.0%	Add in 4 stages and cream in.
G.M.S.	:	3.0%	
Whole Eggs	:	80.0%	
Water	:	40.0%	Add alternately with flour.
Vanilla	:	1.0%	
Orange Flavour	:	0.5%	
Corn Starch	:	0.5%	
Flour	:	65.0%	Sift together. Add alternately
Baking Powder	:	3.4%	with water and flavour.

Used for Later Cakes - Loaf Cakes - Shift Cakes.

Cake batter may be stripped with sweet chocolate. Bake at 355°F. Large or thick cakes at lower temperature.

SHORT DOUGH COOKIE :

Sugar	:	50.0%	Mix together to dissolve dry ingredients
Salt	:	1.5%	
Skim milk Powder	:	2.0%	
Eggs	:	12.0%	
Vanilla	:	1.0%	
Lemon Flavour	:	0.5%	
Water	:	10.0%	
Liquid Glucose	:	5.0%	
Shortening	:	65.0%	Add and mix to break up and disperse
G.M.S.	:	2.0%	Shortening.
Flour	:	95.0%	Add mix until a dough is formed.
Corn Starch	:	5.0%	Do not develop.

Refrigerate dough, if possible, before rolling out the dough. It is best to roll dough on a flour dusted cloth. Roll dough 1/8" to 1/4" thickness. The dough top may be brushed with water lightly or egg whites and then sprinkled with chopped nuts and sugar before cutting out the cookies.

STREVESSEL (CRUMB TOPPING) :

Sugar	:	50.0%	Blend well until smooth and soft.
Salt	:	2.0%	
Shortening	:	50.0%	
Cinnamon	:	3.0%	
Vanilla	:	2.0%	
* Flour	:	100.0%	Sift and add. Rub together with palms of the hands until small lumps are formed.

If too moist, add a small amount of flour.
If too dry add some vegetable oil or melted shortening.

* (A blend of 90% bread flour, 10%cake flour may be used)

CHOCOLATE CAKE (CREAMING METHOD) :

Sugar	:	95.0%	Cream together.
Salt	:	1.5%	
Skimmilk Powder	:	10.0%	
Shortening	:	64.0%	
Emulisifier	:	1.5%	
Cocoa	:	14.0%	
Liquid Cornsyrup	:	7.0%	Add in 3 stages and cream in
Water	:	70.0%	Dissolve baking soda in the water.
Baking Soda	:	70.0%	Add Vanilla. Add water alternately
Vanilla	:	3.0%	with the flour.
Cornflour	:	5.0%	
Flour	:	95.0%	100% sift add alternately with the water

Deposit in cup cake pan - Layer pans - Sheet cake pan.
Bake small units at 385°F.
Bake large units at 365°F.

CUP CAKES (YELLOW):

Sugar	:	67.0%	Cream together until soft.
Salt	:	1.4%	
Skimmilk Powder	:	7.0%	

Glucose	:	7.0%	
Margarine	:	25.0%	
Shortening	:	25.0%	
Flour	:	25.0%	
G.M.S.	:	3.0%	
Eggs	:	45.0%	Add in 3 stages and cream in.
Water	:	45.0%	Add alternately with the flour &
Vanilla	:	1.4%	Baking Powder.
Lemon Flavor	:	0.5%	
Flour	:	75.0%	Sift together & add alternately with
Baking Powder	:	4.2%	the water. Mix smooth.

Use this batter for Cup cakes - Layers with Streossel or other topping - Loaf cakes, etc.

Bake at385° - 395°F.

EGG BAGEL :

Teast	:	2.5%
Water	:	15.0%
Sugar	:	6.5%
Salt	:	1.8%
Salad Oil	:	6.5%
Egg Yolk	:	5.0%
Whole Egg	:	4.0%
G.M.S.	:	2.0%
Water	:	30.0%
Flour	:	100.0%

CHEESE BREAD :

Yeast	:	2.5%
Water	:	20.0%
Sugar	:	4.2%
Salt	:	2.0%
Skimmilk Powder	:	2.0%
G.M.S.	:	1.0%
Water	:	40.0%
Flour	:	100.0%
Shortening	:	3.0%

Grated Cheese	:	10.0%

PINEAPPLE FILLING - MADE FROM FRESH PINEAPPLE :

Chopp the pineapple into small pieces - collect and save the juice.

Pineapple juice water	1 qt. or 1 ltr.)	Stir well and bring
Sugar (variable)	900 gms.)	to a boli.
Water	250 gms.	Dissolve the corn starch in
Corn starch (Variable)	165 gms.	the water. Add to above in a slow, steady stream, stirring constantly and bring to a clear boil.
Chopped Pineapple		Add and bring to a boil again
Yellow Coloring	Few drops	

Allow filling to cool before using.

SWEET ROLL DOUGH :

Ingredient		%	Method
Yeast (Variable)	:	7.0%	Disslove and set aside
Water	:	15.0%	
Sugar	:	20.0%	
Salt	:	1.5%	
Skimmilk Powder	:	5.6%	
Margarine	:	20.0%	
Eggs	:	15.0%	Add and blend in
Water	:	35.0%	Add and stir in
Vanilla	:	1.0%	
Lemon Flavor	:	0.5%	
Flour (Bread 80% + Cake 25%)	:	100.0%	Add and stir slightly add yeast and develop dough.
Medium Gluten	:	20.0%	

Dough temp. - 80° - 82°F
Condition : Allow to rise well and take to bench for make up.

Prepare : Cake Crumbs Jelly

Cinnamon Sugar
Egg wash
Melted Margarine
Chopped nuts
Shredded coconuts

Syrup wash - prepare
Simple icing

BAR TYPE COOKIE :

Sugar	:	50.0%	Blend well until soft and smooth.
Salt	:	1.5%	
Skimmilk Powder	:	3.2%	
Liquid Glucose	:	6.5%	
Shortening	:	25.0%	
G.M.S	:	2.5%	
Flour	:	20.0%	
Eggs	:	20.0%	Add ib 3 stages and beld in
Water	:	20.0%	Blend together and add alternately
Vanilla	:	1.5%	with the flour.
Orange Flavor	:	0.5%	
Lemon Flavor	:	0.5%	
Flour	:	80.0%	Sift together and add alternately
Baking Powder	:	3.2%	with the flour. Mix smooth.
Mixed Drtied Fruit	:	25.0%	Add and blend in.

Place on a floured portion of the table.

Scale into units of 250 gms. Roll the units lightly in a little dusting flour to form an even strip about 2" wide and 1/2" thick. Place on a pan that has been greased and dustedwith flour, flatten slightly. Brush lightly with egg washed and sprinkle the top with chopped nuts and sugar. Bake at 400°F. When cool, cut into bars about 1" wide.

BAG OUT JUMBLE COOKIES :

Sugar	:	50.0%
Salt	:	1.0%
N.F.Skim Milk	:	4.0%
Liquid Corn Syrup	:	6.0%
Margarine	:	25.0%
Shortening	:	20.0%
G.M.S.	:	2.0%
Flour	:	15.0%
Eggs	:	32.0%

Water	:	16.0%
Vanilla	:	1.0%
Flour	:	80.0%
Corn Starch	:	5.0%
Baking Powder	:	2.0%

BUTTER CREAM :

Corn Starch	:	3.0%
Powder Sugar	:	100.0%
Water	:	12.0%
Margarine	:	50.0%
Shortening	:	30.0%
G.M.S.	:	3.0%
Vanilla	:	1.0%
Egg Whites	:	5.0%

ONION BREAD :

Flour	:	1Kg.
Salt	:	18 gms.
Dried Yeast	:	65 gms.
Butter	:	50 gms.
Eggs	:	2 Nos.
Milk Powder	:	50 gms.
Oil	:	20 gms.
Onion Slice	:	150 gms.

PALAK BREAD :

Flour	:	1Kg.
Salt	:	18 gms.
Yeast	:	65 gms.
Butter	:	50 gms.
Milk Powder	:	50 gms.
Oil	:	30 gms.
Palak Loaves	:	150 gms.

METHI BREAD :

Flour	:	1Kg.
Salt	:	18 gms.
Dried Yeast	:	65 gms.
Butter	:	20 gms.
Eggs	:	2 Nos.
Milk Powder	:	50 gms.
Oil	:	30 gms.
Methi	:	250 gms.

PLAIN CAKE :

Flour	:	1 Kg.
Sugar Powder	:	1 Kg.
Butter	:	1 Kg.
Eggs	:	29 Nos.
Baking Powder	:	1 Tea Spoon
Temperature	:	170°C

DRY FRUIT CAKE :

Butter	:	1 Kg.
Maida (Flour)	:	1 Kg.
Sugar	:	1 Kg.
Eggs	:	29 Nos.
Dry Fruits	:	200 gms.
Baking Powder	:	1 Tea Spoon
Temperature	:	170°C

EGG BREAD & ROLL DOUGH :

Yeast (Variable)	:	4.0%	Dissolve % setaside.
Water	:		
Sugar	:	5.5%	Blend together well.
Salt	:	2.0%	
Skimmilk Powder	:	4.0%	
Soyaflour (optional defatted)			
Shortening	:	6.0%	
Eggs (Part Yolks)	:	5.5%	
Water	:	32.5%	Add and stir in
Bread Flour	:	100.0%	Add and stir slightly. Add yeast solution and develop dough.

Approximate - dough temp. 80° - 82°F

First Rise - 1-1/2 hrs. (Approx.)

Second Rise - 30 mints.

Divide and round units for Bread and rolls.

Bread Varieties : 3 twist - 4 twist - Snain (Round) shape rolls (Approx. 40 gms.) may be round. Oval, or twisted into various shapes.

RUSKS

RICH RUSK :

Flour	:	1Kg.
Sugar	:	1 Kg.
Oil	:	2 Kg.
Ghee	:	1 Kg.
Yeast	:	200 gms.

MEDIUM TYPE RUSK :

Flour	:	10 Kg.
Sugar	:	1 Kg.
Oil	:	2 Kg.
Yeast	:	200 gms.

15

PROJECT PROFILES

AUTOMATIC BREAD AND BISCUIT UNIT

Capacity — Bread loaves 1200000 + Biscuit 300 Tons

Land & Building
(Land required 500 sq.mt.)

Plant & Machinery
(Flour sifter, Dough Kneader, Divider, Moulding machine, Heating Oven, Bread slicing & sealing machine, Bucket elevater & conveyors hoists, Pumps motors and blowers, Counter scales, Sugar Grinder, Planetary type mixer, Automatic biscuit cutting and punching machine , Electric baking oven, Tanks, Cooling conveyor, Oil Spray unit, Packing equipment)

Fixed Capital
(Land & Building+ Plant & Machinery + Other Fixed Assets) — Rs. 28,50,001.00

Raw Materials
Flour, Sugar, Salt, Dry yeast, Vegetable oil, Miscellaneous, Flour, Fat, Sugar, Milk Powder, Yeast, Salt, Ammonium carbonate, Miscellaneous & Packaging

Total Capital Investment
Total Fixed Capital + Total Working Capital — Rs. 35,71,246.00

Turn Over/Annum
Bread loaves 1200000 + Biscuit 300 Tons — Rs. 1,38,00,000.00

Profit Sales Ratio = Profit / Sales x 100 — 28 50 %
Rate of Return = Operating profit / T.C.I x 100 — 110 12 %
Break Even Point (B.E.P) — 33.29 %

AUTOMATIC BISCUIT UNIT

Capacity 5.00 MT/day

Land & Building
(Land required 800 sqmt.)

Plant & Machinery
Automatic/continuous rotary moulding & cutting machine, Three roll shuter, Oil spraying m/c., Mixing M/c, Planetary mixing m/c. Cooling conveyor, Flour shifter m/c., Sugar grinding m/c., Oven, Multi-colour Flexo-printing M/c., Automatic Biscuit packaging m/c.

Fixed Capital
Land & Building + Plant & Machinery
+ Other Fixed Assets Rs 65,82,200.00

Raw Materials
Wheat Flour, Vanaspati, Sugar, Baking Powder, Fats, Milk, Salt Yeast

Total Capital Investment
Total Fixed Capital + Total Working Capital Rs. 1,68,26,450.00

Turn Over/Annum
By sales of 1500 MT. of various types of biscuits (Sweet,Salty & cream sandwitched)

Profit Sales Ratio = Profit / Sales x 100 19.49 %
Rate of Return = Operating profit / T.C.I x 100 66.02 %
Break Even Point (B.E.P) 39.33 %

BAKERY UNIT (BREAD, BUNS, RUSK, CAKE, TOFFEE)

Capacity 1243.70 KGS/day

Land & Building
(Land Required 500 Kgs.)

Plant & Machinery
Auto Siffter, Dough Kneader, Dough Grinder, State Convet, Dough Rounder & Moulder, Rotary Rock oven, Cooling rack, T Rolly, Automatic Slice, Cream Milk, Dies and Mold, Electrically Heating Kettle, Cooling Chamber, Packing, and sealing M/c., Miscellaneous M/c.

Fixed Capital
Land & Building + Plant & Machinery
+ Other Fixed Assets Rs. 20,54,500.00

Raw Materials
Flour, Shortening, Salt, Sugar, Egg, Milk Solid, Yeast, Butter, Glucose solid.

Total Capital Investment
Total Fixed Capital + Total Working Capital Rs. 40,01,401.75

Turn Over/Annum
By sale of Pastry Products: 120000 Kgs + Paste 30000 Kgs + Bread/Bun/Rusk 99540 kgs
+ Toffee 123570 Kgs Rs. 1,20,15,750.00

Profit Sales Ratio 27.57 %
Rate of Return 82.78 %
Break Even Point (B.E.P) 28.68 %

BREAD PLANT

Capacity		10000.00 LOA/day
Land & Building (Land 1800 sq.mt)		
Plant & Machinery Total Plant and Machinery Cost		
Fixed Capital Land & Building + Plant & Machinery + Other Fixed Assets	Rs.	59,50,000.00
Raw Materials Wheat Flour, Salt, Sugar, Milk Powder, Edible oil, Shortening, Yeast, Wrappers & Other Misc.		
Total Capital Investment Total Fixed Capital + Total Working Capital	Rs.	1,48,06,075.00
Turn Over/Annum 10,000x300 loaves of 800 gms. each & 10000X300 loaves of 400 gm. each	Rs.	4,14,00,000.00
Profit Sales Ratio		4.73 %
Rate of Return		13.23 %
Break Even Point (B.E.P)		71.84 %

CANDY HARD BOILED

Capacity 3500.00 KGS./day

Land & Building
(Land 1000 sq.mts.)

Plant & Machinery
Superplast machine, Extra Rope Sizer 3 stage, Vacuum pan, Copper Coating Pan, Casting cooling plate, Die's,

Total Fixed Capital
Land & Building + Plant & Machinery + Other Fixed Assets Rs. 28,24,420.00

Raw Materials
Sugar, Colour, Essences, Citric Acids, Packaging materials, printed polyethene film

Total Capital Investment
Total Fixed Capital + Total Working Capital Rs. 95,08,486.00

Turn Over/Annum
10,50,000 kg of hard candy (Goli) of different colour and flavour. Rs. 3,67,50,000.00

Profit Sales Ratio 21.56 %
Rate of Return 83.31 %
Break Even Point (B.E.P) 26.03 %

CHOCOLATE

Capacity 500.00 KG./Day

Land & Building
(Land 500 Sq.mts.)

Plant & Machinery
Pulveriser, Mixer, Refiner, Tank (ss), Moulding Tray, Chocolate, Pumps, Pipe fittings valves, Printing and Wrapping M/c.

Fixed Capital
Land & Building + Plant & Machinery + Other Fixed Assets Rs. 20,31,000.00

Raw Materials
Milk Powder, Sugar, Flavours, Essences etc., Cocoa Butter, Cocoa Mass, Packaging material

Total Capital Investment
Total Fixed Capital + Total Working Capital Rs. 41,63,400.00

Turn Over/Annum
30,00,000 Pcs. Chocolate of 50 gms. Weight Rs. 1,12,50,000.00

Profit Sales Ratio 14.36 %
Rate of Return 38.80 %
Break Even Point (B.E.P) 53.86 %

FLOUR MILL (ATTA, MAIDA, SUJI)

Capacity 50.00 MT/day

Land & Building
(Land required 2000 sq.mt)

Plant & Machinery
Reel Machine, Aspirator Separator, Scourer Machine, Washer Whitter Machine, Brush Machine, Carter Disc separator, Spray Damper, Dust cyclone, Elavator system, Warm conveyor, Fabrication Material, Roller Mill, Bran Finisher, Bleacher, Entolator etc.

Fixed Capital
Land & Building + Plant & Machinery + Other Fixed Assets Rs. 54,95,500.00

Raw Materials
Wheat, Chemicals

Total Capital Investment
Total Fixed Capital + Total Working Capital Rs. 1,46,82,220.00

Turn Over/Annum
Maida 9000 MT, Atta 3000 MT, Suji 2250 MT, Wheat Bran 750 MT Rs. 5,42,62,500.00

Profit Sales Ratio 25.48 %
Rate of Return 94.19 %
Break Even Point (B.E.P) 23.25 %

16

Manufacturers & Suppliers of Plant and Machineries

NARANGS CORPORATION

Ph. : 3363547
3368171
Fax. : 011-3734075

Office : P - 25, Connaught Place,
New Delhi - 110 001

Manufacturers of :

COMPLETE RANGE OF :
FOOD/ MEAT PROCESSING EQUIPMENT

Contact Executive :
CAPT. M. N. NARANG
PRAVEEN KALRA

KHARE & ASSOCIATES

Off. : 7045661
Works : 7294414
7892576
Resi. : 7049949

City Office : C-3/14, Sector XI , Rohini, DELHI - 85.
Off & Works : 24/14, Station Road,
Opp. Yadav Nagar,
Samey Pur, DELHI - 110 042

Manufacturer of :

COMPLETE BAKERY PLANT
MACHINERIES AS PER CUSTOMER'S NEEDS
&
Satisfaction

A. G. INDUSTRIES

Ph. : 7103194
Fac. : 7456590
Res. : 2299969
Fax. : 91-11-2113355

A-108, Lok Vihar, Pitam Pura,
New Delhi - 110 034

FACTORY

169. Cross Road, Near Ajanta Builders, Sant Nagar,
Burari Road, New Delhi - 110 009

Engineer - Fabricators & Equipment Manufacturers

Manufacturers of :

BAKERY PLANT & MACHINERY & SPARE PARTS SPARE PARTS, JAAT CHAINS, BAKING MOULDS, MAJOR REPAIR & OVEN NAULING ALSO UNDER TAKEN

Contact Executive : ALOK GUPTA

---

km King Metal Works

Ph. : 5101629
5436897
553685
Fax. : 011-510629
5536851
Mobile. : 9810125762

F - 429, Vikas Puri,
New Delhi - 110 018

Actual Manufacturers of :

ACCURATED BREAD MOULDS
TOTALLY MADE BY DIES & PRESS

Contact Executive :
HARCHARAN SINGH

BAKE WELL ENGINEERING PVT. LTD.

471, JHEEL, DELHI - 110 051
Ph. : 2218236, 2218121, 2218169
Fax : 91-11-2219522

Mfg. of : All Kinds of High Class Automatic Bread Cake Plant & Electrical & Diesel Fire Oven

Contact : Jitender Nagpal

Admir Engineers
Plot No. 1/E-4, Shivaji Nagar,
Govandi,
Mumbai - 400 043
Tel : 556 8446,551 1718
Fax : 91-22-556 8445
(Manufacturer & Exporter of all types of Indl. Diesel Fired Indirect Fully Automatic Travelling Ovens for Biscuit, Bread & Rusk Baking Plant)

A.G.Industries
A-108, Lok Vihar, Pitam Pura,
New Delhi - 110 034
Tel : 710 3194, 229 9969
Fax : 2113 355
Works : 169, Cross Road, Sant Nagar, Burari Road,
New Delhi - 110 009 Tel : 7456590
(Mfg. of Bread Plant Machinery-2000 to 50000 loaves per day, Flour Sifter, Cake Mixer, High Speed Mixer, Dough Bowl Hoist, Divider, Rounder, Moulder Etc.)
Contact : Alok Gupta

Aifso Eneterprises,
B/13, Veena Apartments,
Sewri (W), Mumbai - 400 015
Tel : 4134 568, 4140 292
Fax : 91-22-4137 339
(Mfg. of all types Travelling Ovens for Biscuit & Bread making, Barrel Drying, PVC/ Crown Caps Etc.)

Allied Bakery Machines,
37, Tajpur Village,Baderpur,
New Delhi - 110 044
Tel : 695 31 43
Fax : 694 68 37
(Complete Bread Bakery Plant with sifter, mixer, moulder etc.)

Apple Engineers & Consultants,
16 A, Shreyas Building,
Sleater Road, Grant Road,
Mumbai - 400 007
Tel : 301 2193
Tel Fax : 3073 343
(Rotary Rack Ovens, Kneaders, Bun Divider, Bread Plants, Cake Depositors etc.)

A.R.Micro Edge Engineers,
Nawada Post Office, Uttam Nagar,
New Delhi - 110 059
Tel : 5592 227
(Knives, Moulds)

Aishwarya Consolidates Pvt. Ltd.
Trust Complex, 10 DVG Road,
B'gudi, Bangalore - 04
Tel : 6617576
(Importers of Bakery Machinery)

Associated Furnace Manufacturing Company.,
R. Munverkatappa Building,
Kammagondanahalli,
Jalahalli West Post,
Bangalore - 560 015
Tel : 367 706
(Mfg. of : Oven Bread, Oven Drying, Roaster etc.)

Allied Bakery Machines,
37, Tajpur Village,
Badarpur Border,
New Delhi - 110 044
Tel : 6946 837, 6947 634
(Bread Cake Plants)

Bakery Equipmemts
23, Bhera Enclave, Near Peeragarhi,
New Delhi - 110 087
Tel : 5586 238,5586 150
Fax : 011-5586 150
(Complete Range of Hi-tech Bakery Machines)

Biofoods Private Limited
4-Community Centre,
Lawrence Road Industrial Area,
Delhi - 110 035
Tel : 7183 482/7541/7153 924
Fax : 7193477
(Kwik Lok Plastic Bag Closing Systems for Bread Packaging)

Bishan Das R. Sons
B- 1426, Main Bazar,
Shastri Nagar,
New Delhi - 110 052
Tel :7772 721, 7276 368, 7779 486 (P.P)
Contact: Mr. Harbans Lal Dhiman & Rajender Dhiman
(Manufacturers of : Biscuit, Confectionery machinery and Biscuit Oven Automatic Plants and Specialist in BISCUIT DIES)

Braddy & Morris Engineering Company Limited,
Brady house, 12-14,
Veer Nariman Road,
Fort, Mumbai - 400 023
Tel : 2048 361
(Mfg. of : Bread Making Plants, Biscuit Oven, Bun Divider Etc.)

Brighter International Trade Links.,
P.O. Box No. 5470,
Kathmandu, Nepal
Tel : 977-1-417947
Fax : 977-1-226820
(Mfg. of : Complete Plants for Biscuits, Confectionery Etc.)

B.S. Industries,
Bye Pass, G.T.Road,
Rajpura,Punjab.
Tel : 22791
(Bakery Machines)

Cannon Engineering Industries,
105/106, Reti Wala Indl. Estate,
HA Palov Marg, Bycula -East,
Mumbai - 27
Tel : 022-3727 203/3743
Fax : 022-373 74 13
(Rotary Rack Oven)

Continental Equipment India Private Limited
B-66, Phase - I, Okhla,
New Delhi - 110 020
Tel : 6816 297
Fax : 6815 297, 6813 162
(Oven, Mixers, Dough Kneaders etc.)

Dazzle Engineers,
S-21B, Street No. 12,
Anand Parbat Indl. Area,
New Delhi - 110 005
Tel : 572 6480, 712 8870
Fax : 5815 120
(Semi Automatic High Speed Bread Slicing Machine, All Bread Moulds, Cake Moulds, Corrugated & Taper Bread Moulds & Bakery Equipments)
Contact : Dalip Kapoor

Dhiman Industries,
Dakhni Gate, Nakodar-144040
Distt : Jalandhar (Punjab)
Tel : 0091-1821-20018,20118,22118
Fax : 0091-1821-21118
E-mail : din@jla.vsnl.net.in
Branch :
53/19, Old Rajendar Nagar,
New Delhi - 110 060
Tel : 5783 731, 5842 114
Fax : 5744 865
E-mail : dhiman@del3.vsnl.net.in
(Fully Automatic Bubble Gum Plant, Candy Plant, Toffee Plant)

Doh & Co.
H-2, Anand Niketan,
New Delhi-110 021
Tel : 5766701
(Bakery Machines & Accessories with Flour Elevator, Sifter, Mixer, Rounder, Moulder etc.)

Eastern Trading Company,
Chandra Bhavan, 3rd Floor,
1st Parsiwada Lane, V.P. Road,
Mumbai - 400 004
Tel : 3885 868
(Mfg. of : Bakery & Biscuit Machinery Equipments, Raw Materials, Chemicals etc.)

Elite Engineers,
134, Kundrathur Road, Porur,
Chennai - 600 116
Phone : 4827 567
(Flour Sifter, Kneader, Mixer, Bread Slicer, Oven etc.)

Essco Furnaces Pvt. Ltd,
Manobind, 18/3, Velacherry Road,
Little Mount, Saidpet, Chennai - 15
Tel : 2350 039, 2350 073
(Mfg. of : Oridycts, Industrial Furnaces, Biscuit/Bread Baking Ovens Etc.)

Eurotach Corporation,
69, Mahendra Chambers, 2nd Floor,
134/136, Dr. D.N. Road, Fort,
Mumbai - 400 001
Tel : 022-2871580
(Mfg.of: Bakery Equipments etc.)

Galaxy Industrial Corpn,
92- Marol Co-Op Indl. Estate,
Andheri -East, Mumbai - 400059
Tel : 8505765, 8504104
Fax : 91-22- 8501846
(Semi Automatic Bag Closing Machine)

Grovers Pvt. Ltd,
4-F4, Shankar Dham,
Sundervan Complex,
Off. Lokhandwala Complex Road,
Andheri West, Mumbai - 58
Tel : 6293 092, 6294 574, 6294 079
E-Mail : grovers.gpl@GEMS.vsnl.net.in
Fax : 91-22-6293014
(Diesel Oil fired Baking Ovens)

Grovers Pvt. Ltd,
228, Kaliandas Udyog Bhawan,
Near Century Bazar, Prabhadevi,
Mumbai - 400 025
Tel : 4303 223, 4309 935
Fax : 400 023
(Mfg. of : Bread Baking Ovens)

H.C.S. Enterprises,
Kaushak Road No. 2,
Saroop Nagar, New Delhi - 110 042
Tel : 7290 530, 7291 305
(Automatic Bread , Rusk & Biscuit Plant)

Hari Singh & Sons
3605, Ram Bazar,
Mori Gate ,New Delhi - 110 006
Tel : 231055
(Confectionery & Food Processing Machnines)

Harison Engineers,
B-1673, Main Road,
Shastri Nagar,
New Delhi - 110 052
Tel : 7515146
(Automatic Biscuit Confectionery & Bakery Plants)

Hightemp Furnace Pvt. Ltd.,
No. 14, Meghal Indl. Area,
Devidayal Road, Mulund,
Mumbai - 400 080
Tel : 8322 251, 8329 193, 8329 263
(Mfg.of : Bread Baking Ovens)

Hindustan Engineering Co.,
Aban House, 25-31,
Ropewalk Street,
Opp. K. Dubhash Marg, Fort,
Mumbai - 400 023
Tel : 2433 068
(Mfg. of : Bread/Biscuit Making Machines Etc.)

Industrial Engineering Works.,
Fort house, 38,
Police Court Lane,
Mumbai - 400 001
Tel : 2611 713
(Biscuit Plants, Bread Ovens)

International Space India,
334, Industrial Area,
Phase - I, Chandigarh
Tel : 640 138
(Softy Cone Machines)

Infa Machinery Manufacturers.,
485, MES Road,
Gokula,
Bangalore - 560 054
Tel : 3363754
(Biscuit & Bread Machines)

Jevan Engineer Works,
Gurugobind Singh Nagar,
Gagan Chowk,
Rajpura,Punjab.
(Bread Mixer, Cutter, Bread Packing Machines, Oven etc.)

J.M.B. Engineering Works.,
Shop No. 2, Shed No. 3,
Behind Diamond Restaurant,
Kondivita Road,
Andheri (E),
Mumbai - 400 059
Tel : 8363 113, 8407 241
(Mfg. of : Dough Slicer, Dough Kneader, Cake Mixer, Moulders, Ovens etc.)

Kag Fabricares Pvt. Ltd.
A-26 N, Gali No.4, Anand Parbat
Indl. Area, New Delhi - 110 005
Tel : 5744701
(Bread Bakery Machines & Accessories to manufacture Breads, Buns, Toast, Pao, Khari Cakes, Pasteries, Patties, Biscuits, Cookies

Kay Jay Steel Works.,
No. 33, South End Road,
Bangalore - 560 004
Tel : 3363 754
(Mfg. of : Biscuit & Bread Making Equipments, Ovens Etc.)

Khare & Associates
City Off: C- 3/14, Sector -11,
Rohini, Delhi - 110 085
Works : 24/14, Station Road,
Opp. Yadav Nagar,
Samai Pur,
New Delhi - 110 042
Tel : (O) 7045661 (W) 7294 414,
7892576 (R) 7049949
(Complete Bakery Plant & Machineries as per customer's Need including Oven, Rounder, Mixer etc.)

Khosla Precisions,
644, Sector 16-D,
Chandigarh - 15,
Phone : 0172-548 422
Fax : 0172-770 005
(Pouch making Machines for Biscuits, Bread etc.)

King Metal Works,
F- 429, Vikas Puri,
New Delhi - 110018
Fac : 283/87, Vishnu Garden, Gali No. 3, New Delhi - 110 018
Tel : 5436987, 510 1629, 5536851
Fax : 011- 5101629
(Bread Moulds)

K. S. Engineering Works.,
Factory Area, Near Ranjit Press,
Patiala - 147 001,
Tel : 305535, 60842
Fax : 212022
(Biscuit/Bread Plant)

KSJ Foods & Services Pvt. Ltd.,
7-87, Vishnu Prasad Mahant Raod,
Vile Parle, Mumbai - 400 057
Tel : 573 294
(Biscuit Making Machines, Bakery Equipment)

Mangal Engg. Works
Factory Area, Patiala - 147 001
Phone : 214702, 215180
Fax : 214420
(Biscuit Bread and Confectionery Making Plant & Machinery)

Mangal Agencies.,
12, 5th Cross Road,
Wilson Garden,
Bangalore - 560 027
Tel : 2222771
(Bread & Biscuit Machinery, Ovens Etc.)

Mangal Metal Works.,
Plot No. 237/61-A,
Near Besaveshwar Circle, Go'a
Ves, Khanapur Road,
Belgaum - 590001
Tel : 21877
(Bakery Machines, Indst. Ovens)

Marshal Engineers.,
J-51, Anjanaya Block,
1st Cross Pipe Lane,
Opp. Mahila Vidyalaya,
Seshadipuram,
Bangalore - 560 020
Tel : 364 749, 322 491
(Bread, Biscuit, Confectionery Machines)

Mechtech Designers & Engineers Private Limited,
19-D, Dr. A.K. Paul Road, Behala,
Calcutta - 700 034
Phone : 468 4024
(Production Lines For hard, semi hard, sweet, snacks and cracker biscuits, Bread, Cakes, Pastries and other baked products etc.)

Membrane Filtration Systems (P) Limited.,
265, Phase - I, Udyog Vihar,
Gurgaon - 122 016
Ph.: 342 765, 341 159
Fax : 0124-342 717
(Membrane Cartridge Filter, U.V. Sterlizers, Reverse Osmosis & Nano Filtration Systems, Membrane- Liquid Bag Filters, Membrane Micronic Filters)

Miscab India Pvt. Ltd.
Plot No.43, Sector 34
EHTP, Gurgaon (Haryana)
Tel : 91-371106
(Ovens etc.)

Mittal International Pvt. Ltd.
7, Netaji Subhash Marg,
Daryaganj,
New Delhi - 110 002
Tel : 327 9639

M.M. Fabricators & Engineers.,
246, 2nd Cross Road, 3rd Phase,
Peenya Industrial Area,
Bangalore - 560058
Tel : 8394259
(Bakery Ovens, Cake Mixers, Kneading Machines, Bread Slicers Etc.)

Nagpal Brothers.,
C-127, Phase-II,
Mayapuri Indl. Area,

New Delhi - 110 064
Phone : 5400 407, 540 2631
Fax : 540 3884
(Bread, Fruit Cake, Rusk/Toast, Fruit Buns, Hot Dog/Burgers Plant Suppliers)

Narang Scientific Works
C-255, Mayapuri Indl. Area,
Phase - II, New Delhi - 110 064
Tel : 540 2609
(Ovens, Machines for Baking Bread, Biscuits, Dry Fruits, Roasting)

N.B.E. Foods Systems Pvt. Ltd.
B-97/1,Naraina Indl. Area,
Phase - I,
New Delhi - 110 028
Tel : 579 7764, 579 7765
Fax : 579 7525
(Bread Plant with Know How)

New Bakery Engg.
B-104, Naraina Indl. Area,
Phase - I, New Delhi - 110 028
Tel : 5797 764,5797 765
Fax : 5797 525
E-mail : ricklal@del2.vsnl.net.in.
(Complete Bread Plant, High Speed Mixer Etc.)

New Era Machines Pvt. Ltd.
Campa Cola Lane, Dhandari Kalan, G.T. Road,
Ludhiana - 141 010 (Punjab)
Tel : 91-161-510 777, 510 778
Fax : 91-161- 510776
E-Mail : sales @ neweramachines.com
Website: www.neweramachines.com
(Offers Plc Controlled Complete lines for Cookie & Cracker Production including Batch Dough Mixer, Dough Handling Systems, Forming & Pre Baking Equipment, Equipment for Lamination, Moulding & Cuttilg, Post Baking Equipment, Precision Engraved Biscuit Moulds & Dies Etc.

Om Engineering Works.,
347, Sector 9-D,
Chandigarh - 162 017
Tel : 41513
(Comp 'ete Automatic Plant For Biscuits, Biscuit Baking Ovens, Biscuit Packaging Machines)

Protos Engineering Co. Pvt. Ltd.,
17. , Jamshedji Tata Road,
Churchgate, Mumbai - 400 020
Tel : 240134
(Biscuit Making Machinery)

Rajdhani Engineering Works,
A-50, Ring Road Market, Rajouri Garden, New Delhi - 110 027
Tel : (O) 546 2514, 519 4934
(Fac:) 542 2029, (R) 53 68 60
(Rotogravure Printing Machine, Flexographic Printing Machine, Lamination/Coating Machine, Slitting & Rewinding Machine, Automatic Paper Bag Making Machine, Paper Napkin Making Machine, BOPP Self Adhesive Tape Making Machine, Sheeting/ Waxing/Gumming Machines)

Ratan Equipment.,
69, Lawrence Road, Chennai - 33
Tel : 044-4822 546
(Bread Slicer, Dough Kneading Machines, Bread Baking Ovens, Converised Biscuit Plants Etc.)

Refco & Wassamat Appliances (P) Limited,
248, Okhla Indl. Estate,
New Delhi - 110 020,
Tel : 6830 323, 683 2156, 6832 046
(Ice Cube Making Machine)

R & D Engineers,
A-41, I.D.A.,
Kukatpally,Phase - II,
Road 4, Hyderabad - 37
Tel : 279121
Fax : 040-278668
(Wafer Biscuit & Ice Cream Cone Machines)

Reliance Engineering Works,
4065, Sector - 46 D,
Chandigarh, Tel : 605682
(Soft Cone & Wafer Biscuit Machines)

R.M. Slar Power Systems Private Limited,
Gala No. 3, L.D'Souza Compound,
Mohammadi Jama Masjid Lane,
Kherani Road, Sakinaka,
Mumbai - 400 072
Tel : 5783 484, 5780 743
(Bakery Machinery Plant)

Saggu Engineers Works,
Near Chowdhary Sweets,
Kalka Road,
Rajpura,Punjab.
(Bakery Machine Such as mixer, Cutter, Grinder etc.)

Seghal Engineering Works.,
42, Kartar Park, Alipur Road,
Factory Area, Patiala (Punjab),
Tel : 78842, 212894, 216564
Fax : 212604
(High Class Biscuit Moulding & Rotary Cutting Rollers)

Sheel Industries,
B-23-A, Shivaji Vihar,
Janta Colony, New Delhi - 110027
Tel : 5440 818, 5447 939
Fax : 011- 5429 997
(Bread Moulds, Round Bread Moulds, Bread Crates, Bread Cooling Trollies, Pao Moulds, Rusk Moulds, Cake Moulds, Biscuit Trays)

Sohal Engineers,
C-57, Wazirpur Indl. Area,
New Delhi - 110 052
Tel : 712 19 40, 711 30 34
(Equipments for Tiny , Small & Bakeries)

Sond Brothers,
31/V, Gali No.3,
Anand Parbat Indl. Area,
New Delhi - 110 005
Tel : 5738 392
(Bakery Equipments)

Sun Beam Techno-Logical Services,
5-35/265, Shakti Puram,
Kukatpally, Hyderabad - 39
Tel : 3076 763, 040-3076 631
(Fully Automatic Biscuit , Wafer, Icecream Cone Plants)

Trishul Industries,
B-927, Shastri Nagar,
New Delhi - 110 052
Tel : 354 6052, 3970924,
(R) 397 8867
Fax : 91-11-752 8315
Contact : Jitender Dhiman
(Candy Forming Line, Cooling Conveyors, Candy Wrapping, Toffee Cut and Wrap, Toffee Cut and Pillow, Cooking Vessels, etc.)

United India Electric Works,
A-9, Lawrance Road,
Industrial Area,
New Delhi - 110 035
Tel : 710 1449
(Imported Burners for Ovens & Fumaces)

17

Manufacturers & Suppliers of Raw Materials

BAKING POWDER

Crown Foods Manufacturers & Exporters.,
55/57, Budh Vihar Marg,
Two Tanks, Mumbai - 8
Phone : 3099579, 3078467
Fax : 91-22-3096057

BAKING ENZYMES

Dhampur Invertos Ltd.
24, School Lane,
New Delhi - 110 001
Tel : 3350961, 3350459
Fax : 3352591

Enzyme India Pvt. Ltd.,
7, Briethapet Road,
Vepery, Chennai- 600 007
Tel : 586 463, 580 031
Fax : 044-589 869,587 812
E-mail : amehta@giasmda.vsnl.net.in

Ganpati Adumim Emulsifiers Ltd,
16/2, Mathura Road, Faridabad - 04
Tel : 91-129-262614
Fax : 91-11-4619910

CRATES, BUCKETS, DRUMS, ETC.

Aman Enterprises.,
R-9/55, Rajnagar, Ghaziabad - 02
Phone : 713805
Fax : 91-575-780563, 756334

CAKE GEL

Marvel Foods,
364, KalianDas,Udhyog Bhawan,
Prabha Devi,Mumbai - 25
Tel : 422 5432

Indo Bakel Pvt. Ltd.,
43C, Mittal Tower, Nariman Point,
Mumbai - 400 021
Tel : 2873636, 288 1025
Fax : 2020065

EGG POWDER

Western Foods Ltd.,
Western House, SCO 341-42,
Sector 35-B, Chandigarh - 160 022
Tel : 0172-612943/608403
Fax : 612945/603864

FLAVOURING EMULSION

Ganpati Adumim Emulsifiers Ltd,
16/2, Mathura Road,
Faridabad - 121 004
Tel : 91-129-262 614
Fax : 91-11-4619 910

Indo Bakel Pvt. Ltd.,
43C, Mittal Tower,
Nariman Point,
Mumbai - 400 021
Tel.: 2873 636, 288 1025
Fax : 2020 065

GLUCOSE

Hindustan Starch & Chemicals,
2125, Tilak Bazar,
Khari Baoli,
New Delhi - 110 006
Tel : 2929 329

Punjab Maize Products Ltd.
Uppli Road, Sangroor,
Punjab - 148 001
Tel : 34209 Fax : 30615

Punjab Maize Products Ltd.,
A-8, DLF Indl. Area - 1,
Faridabad - 121 003 (Hr.)
Tel : 2765 50 Fax : 276 884

IMPROVER

Asha Ram & Sons Pvt. Ltd.,
3496, Dariba Pan,Pahar Ganj,
New Delhi - 110 055
Tel : 777 34 77
Fax : 3546 776

Ganpati Adumim Emulsifiers Ltd,
16/2, Mathura Road,
Faridabad - 121 004
Tel : 91-129-262 614
Fax : 91-11-4619 910

Gupta Enterprises,
B-3, Fancy Enclave,
G.T.Road,
Chhaprola,
Ghaziabad. U.P.
Tel : 91-700438

Marvel Foods,
364, KalianDas,
Udhyog Bhawan,
Prabha Devi ,
Mumbai - 25
Tel : 422 5432

P.D. Bros.,
158, Cubbonpet Main Road,
Bangalore - 560 002
Tel : 2273916/2215548
Fax : 080- 2273917

Rita Enterprises,
11B, Vasil Khan Marg,
Mumbai - 400 008
Phone : 3081907, 3710894
Fax : 3717184

LECITHIN

Kancor Flavors & Extracts Ltd.,
Bazar Road,
Mattancherry,
Cochin.
Fax : 0484-225844
Phone : 225 434/3551/3661
E-Mail : kan.cor@gems.vsnl.net.in

Lucas Meyer GmbH.,
Ausschlager elbdeich 62,
20539 Hamburg
Fax : 0049 40 789 8329
Phone : 0049 40 789 550

MILK PRODUCTS

Chamman Lal & Co.,
400, Khari Baoli,
New Delhi - 110 006
Tel : 2528787

Flanders Dairy Products,
C-23, South Extension ,
Part -II, New Delhi - 110 049
Tel : 644 4692

Haryana Dairy,
6153/1, Street No.4,
Dev Nagar,
Karol Bagh.
New Delhi - 110 005
Tel : 5766870

Lactowin Equipment India Pvt. Ltd.
Post Box : 67, Amrit House,
Ambala Cantt - 133 001
Tel : 0171-633092,643092
Fax : 0171- 643092
Mobile : 9812044498
E-Mail : manjeev @nde.vsnl.net.in
Contact : Manjeet Aggarwal

Sterling Agro Industries Ltd.
3rd Floor, 454, Khari Baoli,
New Delhi - 110 006
Tel : 6236868
Fax : 293 5252

Ramratan Kashi Ram Pvt. Ltd.,
406, Katra Medgran,
Khari Baoli,
New Delhi - 110 006
Tel : 251 35 99

SUGAR PASTE

Indo Bakel Pvt. Ltd.,
43C, Mittal Tower, Nariman Point,
Mumbai - 400 021
Tel : 2873636, 288.1025
Fax : 2020065

STARCH

Geeta Trading Company,
2105, Khari Baoli,
New Delhi - 110 006
Tel : 2513852

Punjab Maize Products Ltd.
Uppli Road, Sangroor,
Punjab - 148 001
Tel : 34209
Fax : 30615

Punjab Maize Products Ltd.
A-8, DLF Indl. Area - 1,
Faridabad - 121 003 (Hr.)
Tel : 2765 50
Fax : 2768 84

Hindustan Starch & Chemicals,
2125, Tilak Bazar,
Khari Baoli,
New Delhi - 110 006
Tel : 2929329

YEAST

Asha Ram & Sons Pvt. Ltd.
3496, Dariba Pan,
Pahar Ganj,
New Delhi - 110 055
Tel : 777 34 77
Fax : 3546 776

Bio Foods Pvt. Ltd.
4, Community Centre,
Lawrence Road,
New Delhi - 110035
Tel : 7183482, 7185829, 7187541
Fax : 91-11- 7193477

Gupta Enterprises,
B-3, Fancy Enclave,
G.T.Road,
Chhaprola,
Ghaziabad. (U.P.)
Tel : 91-700438

Saf Yeast Co. Ltd.
C-3, Gane Khadpoli Ind. Area,
Chiplun, Distt. Ratnagiri,
Maharashtra - 415 605
Tel : 237

WHEAT FLOURS

Shivaji Roller Flour Mills Ltd.,
48 Kalwa Ind. Area,
Belapur Road,
Airoli, Dist. Thane,
New Bombay - 400 708
Tel : 7692346, 7692137

WHEAT GLUTEN

Enzyme India Pvt. Ltd.,
7, Briethapet Road,
Vepery, Chennai- 600 007
Tel : 586463, 580031
Fax : 044-589869,587812
E-mail : amehta@giasmda.vsnl.net.in

Jolly Rishi & Associates,
Pearl Palace, Ghumar Mandi,
Ludhiana (Punjab)
Phone : 400194, 426300
Fax : 0161- 475964

WRAPPERS & FLEXIBLE PACKAGING

National Art Press,
6441 Katra Baryan,
New Delhi - 110 006
Tel : 233758, 6914617

Siddhomal Paper Conversion Co.
611 Kailash Building,
26 Kasturba Gandhi Marg,
New Delhi - 110 001
Tel : 3316333, 3315613

Wrappers India.,
4203, Pahari Dhiraj,
Sadar Bazar, Delhi - 110 006
Phone : 519485, 528885, 529686

MISCELLANEOUS BAKERY CHEMICALS

Asha Ram & Sons Pvt. Ltd.
3496, Dariba Pan, Pahar Ganj,
Desh Bandhu Gupta Road,
New Delhi - 110 055
Tel : 352 1515, 354 6777, 777 34 77
(R) 7271561
Fax : 011- 3546776
Contact : Shiv Kumar Gupta

Dhampur Invertos Ltd.
24, School Lane, New Delhi - 01
Tel : 3350961, 3350459
Fax : 3352591

Enzyme India Pvt. Ltd.,
7, Briethapet Road,
Vepery, Chennai - 600 007
Tel : 586 463, 580 031
Fax : 044-589 869,587 812
E-mail: amehta@giasmda.vsnl.net.in

Ganpati Adumim Emulsifiers Ltd,
16/2, Mathura Road,
Faridabad - 121 004
Tel : 91-129-262614
Fax : 91-11-4619910

Gupta Enterprises,
B-3, Fancy Enclave,
G.T. BulandshahrRoad, Chhaprola,
Ghaziabad, U.P.
Tel : 91-700438

High Tech Flavours,
Saraswati Niwas,Vsagashe Road,
Dadar West, Mumbai - 28
Tel : 4372 164
Fax : 4373 701

Kancor Flavors & Extracts Ltd.,
Bazar Road, Mattancherry, Cochin,
Fax : 0484-225844
Phone : 225 434/3551/3661
E-Mail : kan.cor@gems.vsnl.net.in

Lactowin Equipment India Pvt. Ltd.
Post Box : 67, Amrit House,
Ambala Cantt - 133 001
Tel : 0171-633092,643092
Fax : 0171- 643092
Mobile : 9812044498
E-Mail : manjeev @nde.vsnl.net.in
Contact : Manjeet Aggarwal

Lucas Meyer GmbH.,
Ausschlager elbdeich 62,
20539 Hamburg
Fax : 0049 40 789 8329
Phone : 0049 40 789 550

Marvel Foods,
364, KalianDas, Udhyog Bhawan,
Prabha Devi ,Mumbai - 25
Tel : 422 5432

P.D. Bros.,
158, Cubbonpet Main Road,
Bangalore - 560 002
Tel : 2273916/2215548
Fax : 080- 2273917

ROLLING

114 NON-FERROUS FORGING
115. NON-FERROUS FOUNDRY
116. NON PRESSURE
117. INCANDESCENT LAMP
118. NUMBER COMBINATION LOCKS FOR LUGGAGES
119. NUTS & BOLTS
120. PAPER COATED ALUMINIUM AND COPPER WIRE
121. PETROMAX CONTAINER
122. PHOTO ETCHING OF STAINLESS STEEL PLATES
123. PIPE GALVANIZING PLANT
124. PISTON RING-AUTOMOBILE
125: PLANT PROTECTION EQUIPMENTS
126. PLATINUM LABORATORY APPARATUS
127. PRESSURE COOKER & ALUMINIUM UTENSILS
128. PRESSURE DIE CASTING
129. PRINTED ALUMINIUM COLLAPSIBLE TUBES
130. PRINTED TIN CONTAINERS
131. PRINTING PRESS (CYLINDER MACHINE)
132. PUMPS FOR CHEMICAL INDUSTRY (SPECIAL)
133. RAILWAY SLEEPERS (M.S.)
134. RAZOR TWIN BLADE
135. R.C.C SPUN PIPES
136. RE-ROLLING COPPER AND BRASS SHEET AND RODS
137. RE-ROLLING MI LS
138. RESIN COATED SAND
139. RESIN CORED SOFT SOLDER WIRES
140. ROLLER BEARING AND FORGING
141. ROLLING OF STAINLESS STEEL PATTA
142. RUBBER INSULATED PLIERS (HAND TOOLS)
143. RUBBING COMPOUND FOR AUTOMOBILES
144. SCIENTIFIC LABORATORY EQUIPMENTS
145. SECONDARY LEAD EXTRAC -TION BY SCRAP BATTERY PLATES,PIPES & SHEET
146 SEAMLESS M.S. TUBES & PIPES
147. SELF TAPPING STEEL SCREWS
148. SEWING NEEDLES
149. S.G. IRON & ALLOY STEEL CASTING
150. SHEET METAL PRODUCTS, (FERROUS/NON-FERROUS)
151. SHIP/MARINE CONTAINER
152. SHOCK ABSORBER
153. SHOE EYELETS
154. SHOT AND GRITS BY AUTOMIZATION PROCESS
155. SHOVELS
156. SILENCERS (MUFFLERS) EXHAUST & TAIL PIPE FOR ALL TYPES OF VEHICLES
157. SINTERED BEARING
158. SINTERED BUSHES
159. SINTERED METAL PRODUCT
160. SOFT AND HARD FERRITES
161. SPANNERS
162. SPARK PLUGS
163. STEEL PLANT (ELECTRIC ARC FURNACE BASED- EAF)
164. SPHERIODAL GRAPHITE CAST IRON
165. SPRAY DRYER
166. STAINLESS STEEL SHEET ROLLING TO PRODUCE STAINLESS STEEL UTENSIL
167. STAINLESS STEEL UTENSILS
168. STAPLE PINS,PAPER PIN , GEM CLIPS ETC.
169. STEEL CASTING
170. STEEL FOUNDRY
171. STEEL FURNITURES AND ELECTRICAL APPLIANCES
172. STEEL PLANT (MINI)
173. STEEL RODS AND COILS FROM SCRAPS
174. STEEL ROLLING MILL
175. STEEL STRIPS (COLD ROLLED) SILICON WITH GRAIN RIENTED FOR ELECTRIC USE.
176 STEEL TRANSMISSION LINE TOWERS & ROLLING MILL TO PRODUCE STEEL SECTION
177. STEEL FURNITURES AND ELECTRICAL APPLIANCES
178 STEEL WIRE DRAWING AND GALVANIZING
179 SUBMERGED ARC WELDED PIPES
180 SUBMERSIBLE PUMP MANUFACTURING
181. SUPER ENAMELLED COPPER WIRE
182. THREE WHEELERS
183. TIE-ROD ENDS
184. TIN CONTAINERS
185. TRACTOR TRAILERS
186. TRANSMISSION POWER FITTING
187. TUBULAR POLES
188. SUPER ENAMELLED COPPER WIRES
189. TUBULAR POLES FOR ELECTRICAL TRANSMIS- -SION (BY FABRICATION PROCESS)
190. TUBULAR POLES OF M.S. & HIGH TENSILE STEEL
191. VACUUM CLEANERS
192. VACUUM FLASK (STAINLESS STEEL)
193. VALVES FOR REFRIGERA TION AND AIR-CONDITION
194. VEHICLE WELDING & PAINTING
195. VENETION BLIND
196. WASHING MACHINES (AUTOMATIC AND COMPUTERISED)
197. WATER CONTROLLER (AUTOMATIC)
198. WATCH STRAPS/CHAINS/ BRACELETS/BELT BRASS & STAINLESS STEEL
199. WATER COOLERS
200. WELDED WIRE MESH
201. WICK STOVES

WHITE TELEVISION
477. COMPACT DISC
478. COMPACT DISC PLAYER (AUDIO/VIDEO)
479. COMPUTER ASSEMBLY
480. COMPUTER HARDWARE
481. COMPUTER KEYBOARD
482. COMPUTER PERIPHERALS
483. COMPUTER PRINTERS
484. COMPUTER RIBBON
485. COMPUTER RIBBON REINKING OR REFILLING
486. COMPUTER SOFTWARE
487. COMPUTER STATIONERY
488. COMPUTER STATIONERY & IMPORTED HARDWARE PARTS
489. COMPUTER TERMINALS
490. COMPUTERISED WASHING MACHINE (AUTOMATIC)
491. CONDENSER FOR MOTOR USING MPP FILM
492. CONTROL PANEL BOARD
493. COOLING COIL FOR AIR CONDITIONERS
494. COPPER STRIP COIL FROM SCRAP
495. CORDLESS TELEPHONES
496. D.C. MICRO MOTORS
497. D.G.SETS
498. DISH ANTENNA AND CABLE T.V. NETWORK EQUIPMENT
499. DISTRIBUTION TRANS- -FORMERS AND REPAIRS
500. DOMESTIC ELECTRICAL APPLIANCES- ROOM COOLER, WASHING MACHINE, WATER HEATER, ELECTRIC ROOM HEATER
501. ELECTRIC ENERGY METER
502. ELECTRIC FANS
503. ELECTRIC HORN FOR AUTOMOBILE
504. ELECTRIC LAMP/GLS (INCANDESCENT LAMP)
505. ELECTRIC MIXER
506. ELECTRIC MOTORS
507. ELECTRIC MOTOR WINDING (FOR FAN, MIXIES, ETC.)
508.. ELECTRIC STEAM IRON
509. ELECTRICAL APPLIANCES
510. ELECTRICAL FIXTURES
511. ELECTRICAL STAMPING
512. ELECTROLYTIC CAPACITORS
513. ELECTROMAGNETIC RELAY
514. ELECTRONIC BALAST/CHOK
515. ELECTRICAL CHOKE
516. ELECTRONIC DIGITAL WATCHES
517. ELECTRONIC DIGITAL WEIGHING MACHINE
518. ELECTRONIC FIRE ALARM
519. ELECTRONIC GAS STOVE LIGHTERS
520. ELECTRONIC PRESSURE INDICATORS, ELECTRICALS, ELECTRONIC LIQUID LEVEL INDICATORS, ELECTRONIC TEMPERATURE INDICATOR, DIGITAL TACHOMETER
521. ELECTRONIC TELEPHONE INSTRUMENTS
522. ELECTRONIC TOYS
523. ELECTRONIC WATCHES & CLOCKS
524. FAX MACHINES
525. F.H.P MOTORS
526. FLOPPY DISKETTES
527. FLUORESCENT LAMP STARTER
528. FLUORESCENT TUBULAR LAMPS WITH INTRODUC TION TO MERCURY VAPOUR LAMPS
529. GAS DETECTOR (L.P.G)
530. GENERATOR SET & PUMP SETS
531. GENERATOR (BATTERY OPERATED)
532. HARDWARE FITTING FOR TRANSMISSION LINE (OVERHEAD LINE MATERIAL
533. HEADERS FOR TRANSIS- TOR ICS SEMI CONDUCTOR
534. H.T & L.T INSULATORS
535. H.T & M.V INDUSTRIAL CUBICAL SWITCH BOARD
536. INFORMATION MOVING DISPLAY (L.E.D TYPE)
537. JELLY FILLED TELEPHONE CABLES
538. LAP TOP COMPUTERS
539. LEAD ACID BATTERIES
540. LEAD ACID BATTERY PLATES AND ASSEMBLING OF BATTERY
541. LIGHT EMITTING DIODES (L.E.D)
542. LINEAR ICS TRAINER KIT
543. LOUD SPEAKER
544. L.T TRANSFORMER REPAIRING
545. METAL FILM RESISTORS
546. METALLISED POLYPROPYLENE, POLYESTER FILM CAPACITOR
547. MICA BASE ELECTRONIC COMPONENTS
548. MICA PAPER WASTE PAPER FROM MICA WASTE
549. MICRO PROCESSORS TRAINER KITS BASED ON MICRO PROCESSORS
550. MINI COMPUTER (PERSONAL COMPUTER)
551. MINIATURE CIRCUIT BREAKER (M.C.B)
552. MINIATURE WATCH BATTERIES (BUTTON CELL)
553. MIXER/GRINDER (MIXI)
554. MONO CHROME COMPUTER MONITOR
555. MOTOR START ELECTROLYTIC CAPACITOR
556. MULTI LAYER P.C.B
557. MULTIPLE RELAY FOR LOW VOLTAGE
558. NEON INDICATOR
559. NEON SIGN MANUFACTURE
560. OPTICAL FIBRE CABLES
561. OPTO MECHANICAL & ELECTRICAL EQUIPMENTS
562. PHOTO COLOUR LAB
563. PICTURE TUBE (B/W)
564. PLAIN PAPER COPIER
565. PLASTIC FILM CAPACITORS
566. POLYESTER CAPACITORS
567. PORTABLE GENERATOR SET
568. PORTABLE TELEVISION(TV)
569. POWER CAPACITORS
570. POWER INVERTERS
571. POWER PLANT
572. POWER TRANSFORMERS UP TO 600 KVA
573. PRINTED CIRCUIT BOARD PUNCH CARDS
574. PVC WIRES & CABLES
575. RESIN CAST CT & PT (1 KV)
576. SEMI CONDUCTOR DEVICE
577. SEMI CONDUCTORS FOR TRANSISTORS AND DIODES
578. SETTING UP OF A VIDEO STUDIO
579. SMOKE DETECTORS
580. SOLAR CELLS
581. SOLAR MODULES
582. SOLAR PHOTO VOLTAIC SYSTEM
583. SOLDER FLUXES
584. SOLAR WATER HEATING PANELS
585. STEEL FURNITURE AND ELECTRICAL APPLIANCES
586. STEREO AMPLIFIERS
587. STEREO CASSETTE RECORDERS/PLAYERS
588. STREET LIGHT FITTINGS SURGE SUPPRESSOR
589. TANTALUM CAPACITORS

LIME
273. CEMENT TILES (GLAZED)
274. DOUBLE FIRING (HEATING)
275. CHELATED ZINC (ZN EDTA)
276. CHEMICALS FROM PRAWN HEAD
277. CHLORAL HYDRATE

278. CHLORAMPHENICOL
279. CHLORINATED PARAFFIN WAX (C.P.W)
280. CHROMIC ACID
281. CEMENT PAINT & DISTEMPER
282. CITRIC ACID FROM MOLASSES
283. CLEANING OF COOLING SYSTEM AND BOILER
284. COBALT OCTOATE
285. COMPOST FOR MUSHROOM
286. COPPER OXYCHLORIDE
287. DE-NICKELING (ELECTROLYTIC PROCESS)
288. DEXTROSE MONOHYDRATE AND DEXTROSE ANHY DROUS POWDER FROM TAPIOCA STARCH
289. DI CALCIUM PHOSPHATE
290. DI ETHYL OXALATE
291. DI METHYL ORTHOPHTHALATE
292. DIOCTYL PHTHALATE (DOP)
293. DI PHENYL GLYCERINE
294. DI PHENYL OXIDE
295. DINITRO-CHLORO BENZENE
296. DISTILLED WATER
297. DODECYL BENZENE SULPHONATE
298. ELECTROLESS NICKEL PLATING ON PLASTICS
299. ENDOSULFAN
300. ETHYL ACETATE
301. ETHYL ALCOHOL (POTABLE LIQUOR)
302. ETHYL HEXANOL
303. FERRIC ALUM
304. FERRO CHROME LIGNO SULPHONATE
305. FERRO MANGANESE
306. FERRO SILICONE
307. FERRO VANADIUM FROM VANADIUM SLUDGE
308. FERROUS SILICATE
289. FERROUS SULPHATE
310. FLUORESCENT TUBE LIGHT POWDER
311. FORMALDEHYDE
312. FRACTIONAL DISTILLATION OF D.M.O (DEMENTHOLIZED OIL)
313. FRACTIONAL DISTILLATION OF ESSENTIAL OIL & MEDICINAL PLANT EXTRACT
314. FURFURAL FROM RICE HUSK
315. GASKET SHELLAC COMPOUND
316. GIBBERELLIC ACID
317. GLYCERINE
318. GOSSYPOL (POLY PHENOL) FROM COTTON SEED OIL
319. H - ACID
320. HEPTAL DEHYDE
321. HIGH CARBON FERRO CHROME
322. HYDRATED CALCIUM SILICATE BRICK
323. HYDRATED LIME FROM SEA SHELL
324. HYDROCHLORIC ACID
325. HYDRO FLUORIC ACID
326. HYDROGEN PEROXIDE (BY AUTO-OXIDATION PROCESS)
327. INDUSTRIAL ALCOHOL
328. INTEGERATED COMPLEX OF EASTER & ALLIED PRODUCT (D.O.P, D.B.P, ETHYLACETATE WIRE ENAMEL & CABLE JELLY)
329. IRON OXIDE FOR MAKING FERITTES
330. LACTIC ACID FROM WHITE SUGAR BY FERMENTATION PROCESS
331. LEAD EXTRACTION FROM BATTERY SCRAP
332. LEAD OXIDE
(A) LEAD MONOXIDE
(B) LEAD TETRA OXIDE
(C) GREYLEAD OXIDE
333. LIQUID OXYGEN BOTTLING PLANT
334. LIQUID SHOE POLISH
335. LIQUID FLOOR POLISH
336. LUBE OIL VISCOSITY IMPROVED FOR P.P.G/P.E.G.
337. LUBRICANTS ASHLESS 100% COMBUSTION
338. MAGNESIUM CARBONATE AND MAGNESIUM BI-CARMONATE
339. MAGNESIUM HYDROXIDE POWDER
340. MAGNESIUM SILICATE
341. MAGNESIUM SULPHATE
342. MALEIC ANHYDRIDE
343. MANUFACTURING OF CARBON MONO-OXIDE WATER GAS
344. MENTHOL BOLD CRYSTALS FROM FLAKES
345. MENTHOL CRYSTAL AND MENTHA OIL
346. MERCURIC OXIDE
347. METAL PRE-TREATMENT CHEMICALS
348. METHANE GAS BY SODIUM ACETATE & SODA LIME
349. METHYL ACETYL RICINOLATE
350. METOL
351. METOL FROM HYDROQUI -NONE & METHYL AMINE
352. MICANITE
353. MICRO NUTRIENT MIXTURE
354. MINERAL WATER
355. MINI CEMENT PLANT (BY ROTARY KILN PROCESS)
356. MIXED FERTILIZER
357. MONO CHLORO ACETIC ACID
358. MONO CROTOPHOS TECHNICAL
359. MOSQUITO COIL
360. NICKEL SULPHATE
361. NICOTINE FROM TOBACCO WASTE
362. NICOTINE SULPHATE FROM TOBACCO WASTE
363. NITRO BENZENE
364. NITRO CELLULOSE SANDING SEALER/LACQUER
365. NITRO MUSK
366. NITROGEN AND OXYGEN GAS PLANT
367. NON-IONIC SURFACTANT (WETTING AGENT)
368. OCTANOL
369. ORTHO NITRO PHENOL
370. OXALIC ACID FROM MOLASSES
371. OXALIC ACID FROM TREE BARK
372. OXALIC ACID FROM WASTE VEGETABLES
373. OXYGEN GAS PLANT
374. OXYGEN GAS PLANT (AIR SEPERATION METHOD)
375. PARA-AMINO BENZOIC ACID
376. PARA-AMINO PHENOL
377. PECTIN FROM RAW PAPAYA
378. PHENYL
379. PHTHALIC ANHYDRIDE
380. PHOSPHORIC ACID FROM ROCK PHOSPHATE
381. PHOTO EMULSION FOR ROTARY SCREEN PRINTING
382. PHTHALOCYANINE BLUE
383. PLASTER OF PARIS BANDAGES
384. POLY VINYL ACETATE
385. POTASSIUM DICHROMATE/ BICHROMATE
387. POTASSIUM IODATE
388. POTASSIUM NITRATE
389. POTASSIUM PERMAGNATE
380. PTASSIUM PER SULPHATE
381. POTASSIUM PER OXY DI-SULPHIDE
382. POTASSIUM SILICATE

Price Rs. 3000/- for each "Detailed Project Report" Payable in advance through Draft/Cash/M.O. in favour of "SMALL INDUSTRIES DEVELOPMENT INSTITUTE" 4/27, Roop Nagar, Delhi - 110 007 ***OR Ask by V.P.P.***

990. CAPSULE, TABLET & INJECTION WITH MODERN INSTRUMENTS
990A CASHEW FENI
991. CHLOROQUINONE PHOSPHATE (BULK DRUGS)
992. CLINICAL THERMOMETER
993. DENTAL GRADE EUGENOL
994. DEXTROSE MONOHYDRATE LIQUID GLUCOSE
994A DEHYDRATED ONION
995. DEXTROSE POWDER (ANHYDROUS FROM STARCH)
996. DEXTROSE SALINE SOLUTION
996A DISTILLERY (I.M.F.L)
997. DISPOSABLE NEEDLES FOR SYRINGES
998. DISPRIN
999. DISTILLED WATER
1000. EMPTY HARD GELATINE CAPSULES
1001. FILLING & PACKING OF CAPSULES
1002. GLUCOSE - D - POWDER
1003. GLYCERINE
1004. HOMOE & BIO-MEDICINES WITH MOTHER TINCTURE
1005. HOMOEPATHIC MEDICINES
1006. HYPODERMIC NEEDLES
1006A. I.V. FLUIDS
1007. IBUPROFEN
1008. INFUSION & TRANSFUSION SETS (I.V. SET)
1009. INJECTABLE FOR PHARMACEUTICALS
1010. INJECTION AMPOULES PACKAGING BOX
1011. INTEGERATED SURGICAL COTTON
1012. ICE MAKING PLANT
1012A ICE & COLD STORAGE
1013. LACTOSE & BY PRODUCTS PROCESSING FROM MILK
1014. LICHEN (JATAMANSI CHARILA)
1015. LIQUID GLUCOSE AND ITS BY-PRODUCTS
1015A L-LYSINE MONOHYDRO CHLORIDE
1016. LIQUID GLUCOSE FROM POTATOES
1017. MEDICAL COLLEGE
1018. NICOTINE FROM TOBACCO WASTE
1019. PHARMACEUTICAL AND FOOD GRADE GELATINE
1020. PHARMACEUTICAL INDUSTRY (TABLETS, CAPSULES, LIQUID, GEL, OINTMENT POWDER INJECTABLE)
1021. PHARMACEUTICAL UNIT (EOU) WITH FORMULA TIONS, INJECTABLES, ETC. PYRIDINE AND DERIVATIVES
1021A SALT (IODIZED SALT)
1022 SALINE & INJECTION WATER
1023. SALINE WATER & DEXTROSE SOLUTION (I.V.FLUID IN PLASTIC BOTTLES)
1024 SORBITOL
1024A STARCH (MAIZE)
1025 SURGICAL ADHESIVE PLASTER
1027. SURGICAL BANDAGES
1027A SURGICAL GLOVES
1028. SURGICAL COTTON
1029. SURGICAL COTTON AND BANDAGE
1030. SYNTHETIC CAMPHOR POWDER
1031. TABLETS & CAPSULES
1032. TISSUE CULTURE
1033. TINCTURE FROM RECTIFIED SPIRIT
1034 TRIMETHOPIME
1035. VETERENARY MEDICINES (ONLY FORMULATIONS)
1036. VITAMIN 'C', SORBITOL' ANHYDROUS DEXTROSE, STARCH

PULP, PAPER & STATIONERY

1037. AMMONIA PAPER
1038. AUTOMATIC BOOK BINDING
1038A ADHESIVE (FEVICOL TYPE)
1039. ALL PIN & GEM CLIPS
1040. CARBON PAPER
1041. CARD BOARD
1042. CELLPHANE PAPER
1043. COMPUTER FORMS & SECURITY PRINTING PRESS
1044. CORRUGATED BOARD & BOX (PRINTED & LAMINATED)
1045. CORRUGATED BOARD AND BOXES FROM FROM CARD BOARDS
1046. CORRUGATED CARTONS FROM PLAIN PAPERS
1047. CORRUGATRED PACKING AND MATERIAL (BULB AND TUBES PACKING)
1048. DESK TOP PUBLISHING
1049. D.T.P CUM OFFSET PRESS
1050. EGG TRAYS
1051. EXERCISE NOTE BOOK, REGISTER AND PAD
1052. FLEXOGRAPHIC INK
1053. GREETING CARD BY OFFSET PRESS
1054. HAND MADE PAPER
1055. HARD BOARD
1056. INJECTION AMPOULES PACKAGING BOXES
1057. KRAFT PAPER
1058. KRAFT PAPER FROM BAGASSE
1059. LAMINATED PACKAGING PAPER WITH PRINTING
1059A LAMINATION & COATING ON PAPER
1060. M.G. PAPER FROM WASTE PAPER
1061. MILL PAPER FROM WASTE PAPER
1062. MILL BOARD FROM RICE AND WHEAT STRAWS
1063. MILL BOARD FROM WASTE PAPER
1064. MINI PAPER PLANT
1065. MULTI WALL PAPER SACKS
1066 NEWSPAPER FOR CHILDREN
1067. NEWS PRINT PAPER FROM RICE STRAW BAGASSE
1068. NEWS PAPER CHILDRENS (DAILY)
1069. NEWS PRINT PAPER
1070. OFFSET AND TREADLE TYPE PRINTING PRESS
1071. MILL BOARD BASED ON RICE STRAW
1072 PAPER AND BOARD FROM STRAW
1073. PAPER & PAPER PRODUCTS
1074. PAPER BAGS FOR GENERAL USE
1075 PAPER BOARD CARTON
1076. PAPER CONES FOR LOUD SPEAKERS
1077. PAPER FROM AKRA
1078. PAPER FROM BAGASSE WITH CORRUGATED BOARD & BOXES
1079. PAPER FROM BAMBOO
1080. PAPER FROM RICE HUSK AND WHEAT HUSK
1081. PAPER FROM TREE BARK, EUCALYPRUS WOOD
1082 PAPER PRODUCTS
1083. PAPER PLATES, PAPER GLASS
1084. PAPER CUP FOR ICE CREAM
1085. PAPER TUBES SPIRAL WINDING COMPOSIT CONTAINER
1086. PARTICLE BOARD AND BLACK BOARD WITH SAND ING & LAMINATION OF PARTICLE BOARD
1087. PARTICLE BOARD FROM RICE HUSK
1088 POUCH FILLING & MAKING FOR TOMATO SAUCE
1089. POUCH MAKING & GRAVURE PRINTING
1090. PROCESSING OF PAPER FOR FEEDING IN COMPUTER
1091. PULP FROM BAMBOO AND WOOD
1092 SAND PAPER
1093. SANITRY NAPKINS
1094. SILICON COATED PAPER
1095 STENCIL PAPER
1096 STRAW BOARD AND GREY BOARD
1096A STRAW BOARD & MILL BOARD
1097. STRAW BOARD AND PAPER BOARD PLANT
1098. TISSUE PAPER FACIAL
1099. TISSUE MOIST TOILETERY CLEANSING TISSUE AND RELATED PRODUCTS
1100 TISSUE PAPER ROLLS
1101 TOILET PAPER ROLLS
1102 TOILET PAPER & NAPKINS
1103 WET FACE FRESHNER TISSUE
1104 WHITE WRITING & PRINTING

Price Rs. 3000/- for each "Detailed Project Report" Payable in advance through Draft/Cash/M.O. in favour of *"ENGINEERS INDIA RESEARCH INSTITUTE"*. 4449, Nai Sarak, Dehi - 110 006 *OR Ask by V.P.P.*

MIX)
690. INSTANT FOOD (INSTANT FOOD+FAST FOOD PARLOUR)
691. INSTANT NOODLES
692. INSTANT TEA
693. INSTANT TEA FROM BLACK TEA
694. INTEGERATED STARCH BAKING POWDER/YEAST INDUSTRY
695. IODIZED SALT
696. IODIZED SALT (ORDINARY MOISTURE-LESS/FREE FLOWING IN PLASTIC BAGS AND CONTAINERS)
697. JAM, JELLIES, FRUIT JUICE & ALLIED PRODUCTS
698. KATHA AND CUTCH
699. KHANDSARI SUGAR
700. KHANDSARI SUGAR & IMFL
700A. LACTIC ACID FROM WHITE SUGAR BY FERMENTATION PROCESS
701. LACTOSE & BY PRODUCTS PROCESSING FROM MILK
702. LIQUID GLUCOSE AND ITS BYE PRODUCTS
703. MACRONI AND VERMICILLI
704. MALT EXTRACTION FROM BARLEY
705. MANGO PROCESSING (MANGO PULP, JUICE & SLICES)
706. MAYUR BRAND TYPE CHEWING TOBACCO
707. MINERAL WATER
708. MILK PRESERVATION & MARKETING TO WHOLE SELLERS (INPOUCH PACKING BY UHT TECHNOLOGY)
709. MILK PROCESSING AND PACKAGING OF MILK PRODUCTS
710. MILK PRODUCTS (CASEIN, LACTOSE, GHEE & WHEY POWDER)
711. MILK TOFFEE
712. MINI FLOUR MILL
713. MINI SUGAR PLANT
714. MISRI (PEARL SUGAR CANDIES)
715. MODERN RICE MILL
716. MURABBA
717. MUTTON TALLOW
718. NON-BASMATI RICE FROM PADDY
719. OLEORESIN, ESSENTIAL OIL, DYES & POWDER OF SPICES
720. OLEORESIN EXTRACTION FROM DIPTERO-CARPUT TURMINATUS AND PINUS KHASYANA
721. OLEORESIN EXTRACTION FROM CHILLI
722. PAN MASALA AND POUCH MAKING
723 PAN MASALA, TOBACCO, ZARDA & KIMAM
724 PANEER FROM MILK
725 PAPPAD PLANT
726 PAPAIN FROM PAPAYA (PAPAYA LATEX)
727 PECTIN FROM MANGO PEEL PECTIN FROM APPLE POMACE
728. PICKLES AND SAUCES
729. PICKLES MURABBA ETC. (VEG. & NON. VEG.PICKLES)
730. PIGGERY MEAT PROCESS
731. PINE-APPLE JUICE PREPARATION & PACKAGING
732 POTATO POWDER
733. POULTRY FEED
734. PROCESSED FOODS & SPICES (EOU)
735. PROCESSED READYMADE FOOD
736. PROCESSING OF FRUITS AND VEGETABLES
737. RASGULLAS MAKING AND CANNING IN METAL CANS
738. READY TO EAT SNACK FOOD (CRAX, ROLL & BALL TYPE)
739. RICE AND CORN FLAKES
740. ROASTED/SALTED/ MASALACASHEW-NUTS, ALMONDS & PEANUTS
741. ROLLER FLOUR MILL
742. SALT LICKS FOR CATTLE
743. SAUSAGES FOOD CASING
744. SOFT DRINKS
745. SOFT DRINKS ESSENCES
746. SOFT DRINKS (NON CARBONATED) MANGO, LICCHI, PINEAPPLE FLAVOURS- FROOTI TYPE IN TETRAPACK)
747. SOFTY ICE CREAM CONES (FULLY AUTOMATIC)
748. SOYABEAN PRODUCTS
749. SOYA MILK & PANEER
750. STARCH & ALLIED PROPDUCTS FROM BROKEN RICE
751. SUGARCANE JUICE PRESERVATION
752. SUGAR CUBES FROM CANE SUGAR
753. SUGAR PLANT(Rs.30Cr.Proj.)
754. SWEET AROMA BETEL NUT
755. SYNTHETIC TALLOW
756. TAMARIND JUICE POWDER
757. TEA & COFFEE PROCESSING & PACKAGING
758. TOFFEES, GOLIES, CANDY (HARD BOILED)
759. TOMATO PRODUCTS
760. TUITY FRUITY
761. VODKA FROM POTATOES
762 WINE, BRANDY, WHISKY AND CHAMPAGNE
763 YEAST FROM MOLASSES
764. ZARDA, KIMAM NO. 60,90,120,160,240,300 & 400 (TOBACCO)
765. ZARDA-ZAFRANI (BABA-CHHAP TYPE)

GUMS & ADHESIVE

766. ACRYLIC ADHESIVE
767. ADHESIVE (FEVICOL TYPE)
768. ADHESIVE BASED ON POLYURETHANE
769. ADHESIVE FOR BAND AID (JOHNSON & JOHNSON TYPE)
770. ADHESIVE INDUSTRIES (LAMINATED, STICKER,DDL & OTHER TYPES)
771. ADHESIVE FOR GASKET (LIQUID/PASTE)
772. GUAR GUM
773. GUM BOTTLE (PVC)
774. GUM FOR PASTING LABELS
775. OFFICE PASTE
776. RUBBER ADHESIVE
777. SURGICAL ADHESIVE PLASTER

LEATHER & LEATHER PRODUCTS

778. HANDMADE LEATHER
779. LEATHER BOARD FROM LEATHER WASTE
780. LEATHER FOR UPHOLSTRY (SOFA)
781. LEATHER GARMENTS
782. LEATHER GOODS
783. LEATHER SHOES
784. LEATHER SHOE & CHAPPAL
785. LEATHER SUITCASES, BRIEFCASES AND TRAVELLING BAGS
786. LEATHER GOODS AND GARMENTS
787. SHEEP SKIN PICKLING PLANT
788. SHOE UPPER
789. SPORT SHOES (PLASTIC)

MISCELLANEOUS PRODUCTS

790. AGARBATTI (INSENCE STICK)
790A AGARBATTI (Mosquito Repellent)
790B AGARBATI BAMBOO STICK
791. AGARBATTI SYNTHETIC PERFUMERY COMPOUND
792. AIR FRESHNER(ODONIL TYPE)
793. AIR TAXI
794. AMUSEMENT PARK
795. ANODIC ALUMINIUM LABEL
796. AQUACULTURE PRAWN FARMING (100% EOU)
797. AQUA CULTURE SHRIMP FARMING (100% EOU)
798. ARTIFICIAL FLOWERS
799. ARTIFICIAL JEWELLERY

800 ASBESTOS YARN
801. ASH TRAYS FOR MARUTI VEHICLE
801A AIR BUBBLE PACKAGING
802. ASPHALTIC ROOFING SHEET (METAL COMPONENTS)
803. AUTOMATIC BOOK BINDING
803A ALKYD RESIN
803B APPLE JUICE CONCENTRATE
804. BALL POINT PEN FEFILLS (JOTTER TYPE)
805. BANK BRANCH BUILDING
806. BANQUET HALL
807. BIO-COAL BRIQUETTES FROM AGRICULTURAL CELLULOSE WASTE
808. BOOT CREAM/POLISH
809. BUFFING & POLISHING COMPOUND
810. BRASS BADGES BY ETCHING
811. BRIQUETTED FUEL FROM AGRO WASTE
812. BRIQUETTING OF LIGNITE COAL
813. BUFFALO HORN TIP, HOOF
813A BANQUET HALL
814. BUTTON
815. CALCINED PETROLEUM (C.P) COKE
816. CANVAS SHOES
817. CANVAS SHOES, JUNGLE BOOTS
818. CARBON BRUSH, BRUSH HOLDER AND SLIP RING
819. CEMENT SHEETS WITH COIR FIBRE AND OTHER SEGMENTS
820. CERAMIC TILES (GLAZED) BY DOUBLE FIRING/ HEATING
821. CINNAMON
822. COAL BRIQUETTES
823. COLD STORAGE & ICE
824. COLD STORAGE FOR FRUITS AND VEGETABLES
825. COSTUME JEWELLERY/ IMITATION JEWELLERY
826. DECORATIVE LAMINATED SHEET (SUNMICA)
827. DIAMOND CUTTING AND EXPORTING
828. DRINKING STRAW FROM PROPYLENE
829. FASHION TECHNOLOGY INSTITUTE
830. FAST FOOD PARLOUR
831. FAST FOOD (INSTANT FOOD & FAST FOOD PARLOUR)
832. FIRE EXTINGUISHERS (SODA ACID TYPE)
833. FISH NET
834. FLORICULTURE (CUT FLOWER ROSE) WITH GREEN HOUSE
835. FLOOR COVERING SHEET
835A FILM STUDIO (VIDEO)
836. FLUSH DOOR, CHIP BOARD, WOOD WOOL & OTHER INSULATING BOARDS
837. GAS DETECTORS OF L.P.G
837A. GEMS MANUFACTURING
838. GLASS BOTTLE BY SCRAP
839. GOAT & SHEEP FARMING
840. GOLD ELECTROPLATING
841. GOLD JEWELLERY (E.O.U)
842. GOLD PLATED SILVER JEWELLERY & CUTLERY
843. GRANITE SLAB AND TILES
844. GREEN HOUSE
845. HARD CHROMIUM PLATING
846. HEALTH CLUB AND BEAUTY PARLOUR CUM HAIR SALOON WITH SONA BATH
847. HEALTH CLUB CUM BEAUTY PARLOUR TRAINING INSTITUTE
848. HORN TIP,HOOVE BUTTON
849. HOSPITAL
850. HOSPITAL (100 BEDS)
851. HOSPITAL (200 BEDS)
852. ICE MAKING PLANT
853. IMITATION AND COSTUME
854. JEWELLERY (NECKLACE, EARRINGS EAR TOP ETC.)
855. INITMATE SCENT CHEMICAL FROM ALL TYPES OF FLAVOUR
856. INVESTMENT CASTING
857. JUTE, COIR, GLASS ROPE/ SUTLI
858. JUTE TWINE
859. L.P.G BOTTLING PLANT
860. L.P.G REGULATOR (DOMESTIC PURPOSE)
861. LAMINATED PARTICLE BOARD & HARD BOARD
862. LAMINATED SAFETY AND TOUGHENED GLASS
863. LEASING & HIRE PURCHASE
864. LICHEN (CHARILA)
865. MANILA ROPES
865A MEDICAL COLLEGE
866. MATCH UNIT FROM WAXED PAPER
867. MEDIUM DENSITY FIBRE BOARD
868. MELAMINE CROCKERY
869. MINERAL WATER
870. MINI CEMENT PLANT
871. MIRROR SILVER, GOLDEN, PINK, BLACK & SMOKES
872. MODERN ADVERTISING AGENCY WITH DTP & FILM STUDIO
873. MOTEL/SMALL HOTEL
874. MULTI COLOUR PRINTING
875. MULTI STOREY COMMERCIAL COMPLEX ALONGWITH RESIDENTIAL AND DELUX FLATS FOR FOREIGN TOURISTS & REVOLVING RESTAURENT AT THE TOP
876. MULTIPLE LAMINATION INDUSTRY
876A. MUSHROOM GROWING AND PROCESSING (BY DEEP FREEZING METHOD)
877. NEWS PAPER PRINTING
878. NICKEL LINED INDUSTRIAL SCREEN
879. OFFSET COLOUR PRINTING PRESS (SIX COLOUR)
880. OFFSET PRINTING PRESS
881. P.C.C ELECTRIC POLES
882. PHOTOGRAPHIC DEVEL -OPER & FIXER
882A PVC EXTRUSION PROFILE
882B POP- CORN
882C PHOTO ETCHING OF S S
883. PRE STRESSES CEMENT CONCRETE PIPES
884. PILFER PROOF CAPS
885. PILFER PROOF CAPS AND CROWN CAP
886. POUCH MAKING AND GRAVURE PRINTING
887. POULTRY AND FISH FARMING (INTEGERATED UNIT)
888. PRINTING OF TIN SHEETS
889. READYMADE GARMENTS
890. RESTAURANT
891. ROSE PLANTATION AND ROSE OIL EXTRACTION
892. ROTOGRAVURE PRINTING
893. SAFETY BELTS
894. SAFETY MATCHES
895. SHOE LACES
896. SILK COCOON CULTIVATION (GROWING OF SILK COCOON WARM)
897. SILK SCREEN PRINTING FORMULATIONS FOR PLASTIC, PAPER & CLOTH
897A SPIKENARD (JATAMANSI)
898. STENCIL COATING SOLUTION
899. SUGAR CANDY (MISRI)
900. SUGAR CANE PLANTATION
901. SURAT ZARI
902. SYNTHETIC SHOES & SOLES
903. TEA PACKAGING INDUSTRY
904. TENNIS BALLS
905. THREE STAR HOTEL
906. TRAVELLING AGENCY
907. TRAYS, TROLLEYS FOR HOSPITAL WITH SCRATCHLESS COATING
908. WAX EXTRACTS (TANNING POWDER)
909. WIRE ROPE SLINGS
910. WOOD WOOL SLAB
911. WOODEN CANE FURNITURE WITH EXPORT POTENTIAL
912. WOODEN FURNITURE
913. WOODEN PANEL INCLUDING KILN SEASONING
914. WRIST WATCHES
915. ZEDOXY (KACHUR)

OIL FATS & WAXES

916. BEES WAX MANUFACTURE
917. CARDANOL FROM CASHEWNUT SHELL LIQUID
918. CASTOR OIL
919. CASTOR OIL DERIVATIVE OLEORESINS
920. CHILLI OIL

1175. P.V.C COMPOUNDS (FRESH)
1175A P.V.C COMPOUNDS (SCRAP)
1176. P.V.C ELECTRICAL INSULATING TAPE
1177. P.V.C FITTINGS
1178. P.V.C FLEXIBLE FUSIBLE POWDER HEAT FUSIBLE POWDER
1179. P.V.C GRANULES (FOR INSULATION & SHEETS GRADES)
1180. P.V.C GRANULES FROM PVC SCRAPS (WITH POLLUTION CONTROL)
1181. P.V.C HOSES
1182. P.V.C LEATHER CLOTH
1183. P.V.C FLEXIBLE PIPES
1184. P.V.C PIPES AND FITTINGS
1185. POLYTHENE BAGS (PRINTED)
1186. PVC PLASTICS FILM SHEET SOFT/RIGID
1187. PVC RESIN AND COMPOUND
1187A PVC RIGID PIPE
1188. PVC RULAR
1189. PVC STABLIZERS (SINGLE PACK SYSTEM)
1190. PVC WIRE AND CABLES
1191. PAPER BASED PHENOLIC SHEET FOR ELECTRICAL
1192. PHENOL FORMALDEHYDE RESIN
1193. PHENOLIC RESIN
1194. PLASTIC BEADS FROM PLASTIC SCRAPS
1195. PLASTIC BUTTONS
1196. PLASTIC CANS
1197. PLASTIC COLLAPSIBLE TUBE
1198. PLASTIC CORRUGATED SHEET & BOXES
1199. PLASTIC FILM AND SHEETS WITH PRINTING FLEXO & ROTO/LDPE/HDPE/PP/HM/PVC
1200. PLASTIC GRANULES OR POWDER FROM PLASTIC SCRAP
1201. PLASTIC INJECTION MOULDED T.V. CABINETS
1202. PLASTIC ITEMS-MANUFAC TURE FROM POWDER MELAMINE
1203. PLASTIC GOODS
1203A PLASTIC SHEET FROM SCRAP
1204. PLASTIC PLANT (BLOW MOULDING & INJECTION MOULDING)
1205. PLASTIC PRODUCTS (GOLD, SILVER, NICKEL)
1206. PLASTIC TOYS
1207. POLYESTER BEADING
1208. POLYESTER FILM
1209. POLYTHENE BAGS & AUTOMATIC PRINTING
1210. POLYTHENE PRINTED BAGS
1211. POLYURETHANE FOAM AND ITS PRODUCTS
1212. PROPYLENE FILM (PRINTED) & BAG MANUFACTURING
1212A PLASTIC MATS
1213. RAINBOW COLOUR ON PVC FILM & SHEET
1214. RED MUD PVC PIPES AND FITTINGS
1215. RE-RUBBERISED OF SOLID TYPE
1216. RESIN COATED SAND REXINE
1217. REXINE CLOTH & ALLIED PRODUCTS
1218. RUBBER AUTO PARTS
1219. RUBBER BELTING
1220. RUBBER MOULDING UNIT INCLUDING LINING RUBBER SHEETING
1221. RUBBER RECLAIMING
1222. RUBBER ROLLERS FOR TEXTILE MILLS & PAPER INDUSTRIES
1223. RUBBER SHEET AND ALLIED HOSPITAL RUBBER GOODS
1224. RUBBERIZED PVC GASKET
1225. RUBBERISED COIR
1226. SAFETY BELTS
1227. SILVER AND GOLD PLATING ON PVC AND NYLON-6
1228. SPECTACLE FRAMES (PLASTIC)
1229. SPUNGE RUBBER
1230. SURGICAL EXAMINATION GLOVES
1231. SYNTHETIC PEARL COATING ON POLYSTY RENE BEADS
1232. TEFLON MANUFACTURING
1233. TEFLON TAPE
1234. TEFLON TAPES & CABLES
1235. THERMOCOLE SHEET AND MOULDED PRODUCTS EXPANDED POLYESTERENE EXTRUSION PROFILES
1236. THERFORMED PACKAGING (BLISTER PACKAGING AND POUCH PACKAGING)
1237. THERMOPLASTIC POLYURETHANE
1238. TOOTH BRUSHES
1239. TOY BALLOON, DECORA TIVE AND INDUSTRIAL BALLOONS
1240. TREAD RUBBER
1240A TYRE RETREADING (HOT)
1241. TYRE RETREADING BY COLD PROCESS
1242. TYRE TUBES & FLAPS
1243. UNSATURATED POLYESTER FOR REXINE
1244. V-BELT AND FAN BELT
1245. VINYL ASBESTOS AND PVC WALL PAPER
1246. VITON (FLUORO ELASTOMER)

SOAP, COSMETICS & PEFUMES

1247. ACID SLURRY, SYNTHETIC DETERGENT POWDER
1247A ACID SLURRY
1248. AGARBATTI SYNTHETIC, PERFUMERY COMPOUND
1249. AFTER SHAVE LOTION
1250. ANTISEPTIC CREAM
1251. BETA IONONE
1252. BLEACHING POWDER
1253. BLUE DETERGENT POWDER
1254. CLEANING POWDER (VIMTYPE)
1255. COLD CREAM
1256. COLOURED FLAME & PERFUMED CANDLES (RED, BLUE, GREEN FLAME)
1257. COSMETIC INDUSTRY (MODERN)
1258. COSMETIC INDUSTRY-SHAMPO,SPRAY PERFUME, TALCUM POWDER
1259. DETERGENT POWDER (ARIEL TYPE)
1260. DETERGENT POWDER (NIRMA TYPE) FULLY AUTOMATIC PLANT
1261. DETERGENT WASHING POWDER
1262. FISH OIL SOAP
1263. GLYCERINE TRANSPARENT SOAP
1264. HAIR REMOVING CREAM
1265. HERBAL COSMETICS
1266. HERBAL SHAMPO & CREAM
1267. HERBAL/AYURVEDIC COSMETICS UNIT
1268. INCENSE POWDER,INCENSE STICKS & INCENSE CAKE
1269. OPTICAL WHITENERS
1270. ROSE OIL EXTRACTION
1271. SHAMPOOS (COCONUT OIL BASED COLD PROCESS)
1272. SHAVING CREAM
1273. SINDUR (KUMKUM)
1274. SOAP COATED PAPER
1275. SPRAY DRIED DETERGENT POWDER
1276. STAIN REMOVER
1277. TALCUM POWDER (FACE & TOILET POWDER)
1278. TOILET AND HERBAL SOAP
1279. TOOTH PASTE & POWDER
1280. WASHING DETERGENT POWDER AND WASHING SOAP
1281. WASHING POWDER LIQUID DETERGENTS,LOTION & SHAMPOO

TEXTILE INDUSTRIES

1282 ANGORA RABBIT WOOL
1283. CERAMIC THREAD GUIDE
1284. COTTON BUDS/SWABS
1285 COTTON FROM WASTE YARN
1287 COTTON ROLLS
1288. COTTON SPIDERS FOR LOUD SPEAKERS
1289. DENIM CLOTH

Price Rs. 3000/- for each "Detailed Project Report" Payable in advance through Draft/Cash/M.O. in favour of *"ENGINEERS INDIA RESEARCH INSTITUTE"*. 4449, Nai Sarak, Dehi - 110 006*OR Ask by V.P.P.*